GOD'S POWER, JESUS' FAITH, AND

WORLD MISSION

GOD'S POWER, JESUS' FAITH, AND WORLD MISSION

A Study in Romans

STEVE MOSHER

HERALD PRESS
Scottdale, Pennsylvania
Waterloo, Ontario

Library of Congress Cataloging-in-Publication Data
Mosher, Steve, 1947-
    God's power, Jesus' faith, and world mission : a study in Romans /
Steve Mosher.
      p. cm.
    Includes bibliographical references.
    ISBN 0-8362-9031-9 (alk. paper)
    1. Bible. N.T. Romans—Commentaries. I. Title.
BS2665.3.m59 1996
227'.107—dc20   95-48103
                                                     CIP

The paper used in this publication is recycled and meets the minimum requirements of American National Standard for Information Sciences—Permanence of Paper for Printed Library Materials, ANSI Z39.48-1984.

Scripture quotations are basically the author's own translation.

GOD'S POWER, JESUS' FAITH, AND WORLD MISSION
Copyright © 1996 by Herald Press, Scottdale, Pa. 15683
      Published simultaneously in Canada by Herald Press,
      Waterloo, Ont. N2L 6H7. All rights reserved
Library of Congress Catalog Number: 95-48103
International Standard Book Number: 0-8361-9031-9
Printed in the United States of America
Book design and cover by Gwen M. Stamm

05 04 03 02 01 00 99 98 97 96 10 9 8 7 6 5 4 3 2 1

To Sandy, my wife
and partner
in mission

Contents

Foreword

THIS is an extraordinary commentary! It moves beyond the turgid and pedantically repetitive discussions of grammar and syntax sometimes associated with commentaries on the letters of Paul. Mosher's is the first study of which I am aware to give *functional* as opposed to merely *formal* acknowledgment to the significance of this book's missionary author, subject matter, and original readers.

Rather than confining himself to the sometimes intellectually incestuous family of biblical scholarship, Mosher integrates into his commentary the sources and insights of those within the arena of contemporary missionary praxis. He takes seriously the insights and applications of a wide range of collateral sources from around the world who, like Paul himself, are essentially practical persons.

The result is a thoroughly contemporary, delightfully practical, profoundly insightful, and at times troublingly challenging work. This commentary deserves the special attention of missionaries, pastors, Bible students, and academics alike.

—*Jonathan J. Bonk*
  Professor of Global Christian Studies
  Providence College and Seminary
  Otterburne, Manitoba

Preface

MY own interest in Romans first took root in the scholarly world of doctoral dissertations. Such roots inch their way through a lot of academic dirt before they produce much fruit. Paul clearly writes for members and leaders of several house churches in Rome rather than for professional theologians. I also am not writing primarily for theologians or biblical scholars but for the members and leaders of Christian communities around the world. Nevertheless, I am indebted to various scholars.

A main weakness of current scholarship is the specialization that fails to bring together different truths into more of a synthesis or unity. Scholars in biblical studies seldom discuss their findings with scholars in theology or missiology or ethics or church history. Students find it hard to pull together the meaning of all those specialized fields. My study of Romans is designed to provide some synthesis because I think Paul himself had vital truth to share about many of those fields of study.

I take special interest in trying to further the faith and mission of Christians today. Paul's mission included a vision for the whole world, both near and far. Various cities throughout the world are now populated by people from diverse backgrounds and cultures. During most of the 1980s, I was a missionary in the Philippines, living and serving among Filipinos and other Asians studying there. More recently, my neighborhood in Wichita, Kansas, includes Native Americans, African-Americans, Asian-Americans, Hispanics, and European Americans. Each neighborhood Bible study group I have organized has included more than one of those ethnic groups.

As I write, my family is in transition, preparing to move to San Antonio, one of the most multicultural U.S. cities. For over twenty years, my wife, Sandy, and two children, Philip and Leanna, have shared the joys and struggles of all that God's world mission involves. For their support and understanding, I express my thanks.

I also want to acknowledge the affirmation and helpful suggestions of S. David Garber at Herald Press for this book. While I am currently involved with both Baptist and Mennonite churches, my development of the main themes of this thematic commentary especially reflects classical Mennonite emphases.

Most early Anabaptists shared Jesus' and Paul's criticism of wealth and prestige. When I submitted this book to Herald Press, I thought of them as a smaller publisher. They have allowed me to strongly criticize bigger businesses and their influence on mission. We discussed keeping the price of the book as low as possible. However, if they or I make a substantial profit on this book, I will be embarrassed.

Perhaps it would be presumptuous to thank God for special illumination concerning the purpose and message of Romans. Romans remains a difficult book, and I sometimes change my mind about the meaning or application of certain verses. Yet I also think that many Christians have misunderstood too much of Romans. As I add my own special approach, I pray that God will also illumine you, the reader, so that you test and faithfully receive all that is true and right in God's sight. To the extent that I have seen and done the truth found in Romans, I thank God.

—*Steve Mosher*

Introduction to Romans

WHY would a busy missionary like Paul write a long letter like Romans? Did the Roman Christians really need such a heavy dose of Paul's gospel? They already had faith, and the Holy Spirit was at work in them. What more could the apostle of faith want?

Apparently a lot more. Paul's faith was not so simple after all. I think he closely related his faith to a more basic faith—the faith of Jesus. But did Paul know or care that much about Jesus' own belief and special revelation of God? I believe he did. One reason Paul wrote Romans was that he wanted Roman Christians to know and care as much as he did.

Jesus' main message introduced the coming of the kingdom of God. The promised time had come. God's powerful kingship had arrived (Mark 1:15). Both Jesus' life and death showed what faith in God's new work of power really meant. Moreover, Jesus' resurrection from the dead climaxed the beginning of God's dynamic rule.

Several years later, the same God called Paul to share the gospel of Jesus as part of a mission to the whole world. Jesus had taught that his gospel of the kingdom would later be preached throughout the world—to all peoples (Matt. 24:14).

Then the risen Jesus appeared to Paul. Jesus' divine power transformed him into an apostle sent out to the peoples of the world. Just as God sent Jesus on a mission into the world, so Jesus sent Paul—and others—to continue that mission. Everywhere God's power was creating new groups of disciples who shared Jesus' faith and mission.

When Paul wrote Romans, he wanted the Roman Christians to share his vision for world mission and his emphasis on God's ruling power in history—beginning with Jesus. His letter is a mission document.[1] Paul had not yet reached Rome. He was planning to visit soon as he passed through on his way to Spain (15:24; all chapter and verse references are from Romans unless preceded by the abbreviated name of another Bible book). But first Paul wanted to go to Jerusalem with some money he collected, mostly from Gentile Christians for poor Jewish Christians there (15:25-26).

However, Paul faced persecution and possibly death from enemies in Jerusalem (15:30-31; Acts 20:22-25; 21:4, 10-13, 27-33). His mission might soon run into a dead end. Then what would happen? Paul prepared for the worst. If others stopped Paul permanently (or even temporarily), this letter would enable Christians in Rome to continue his mission. That mission included his concern for those in Jerusalem and Spain (15:24). Such harsh realities best explain why Paul wrote the long letter we now know as Romans. Only an in-depth discussion of God's powerful mission in history would be an adequate foundation and challenge for continuing Jesus' and Paul's mission.[2]

Such plans also recognized the importance of Rome. It was the capital of the Roman Empire and the center for travel and communication throughout the empire. There was much truth to the saying "All roads lead to Rome." Those Christians who remained in Rome could influence people who traveled to Rome from all over the empire (1:8; 16:19).

Unfortunately, some of those travelers to and from Rome included certain Jewish leaders like those who often persecuted Paul (see 16:17-20; Acts 14:19; 17:13; 20:18-19, 29-30; 21:27-28). Romans reflects Paul's debates and difficulties with such fellow Jews. Probably earlier conflict in Rome between the Jews and Jewish Christians like Aquila and Priscilla led to the emperor ordering many Jews to leave Rome (Acts 18:2). Paul knew that as the Roman Christians continued the same mission among Jews and Gentiles, they would face similar struggles.

Throughout Romans, Paul uses a diatribe style. He engages in an ongoing conversation with another person, often a fellow Jew. Paul uses that style to teach his Roman readers about Christian faith and mission.[3] Those dialogues also reflect past debates with unbelieving and sometimes hostile Jews or Gentiles. Paul's dangerous and courageous mission often involved arguing and pleading with potential enemies, trying to persuade them about God's powerful kingdom and the Way of Jesus (Acts 18:4; 19:8-10; 28:23). His mission proclamation was not simply a monologue or sermon—and his listeners did not usually sit silently or believe easily.

Paul's debates in the synagogues usually ended abruptly after only a few weeks. His contacts with Jews (and Gentiles) more often came through his teaching in private homes (see Acts 18:7, 11; 20:20-21; 28:23). In Romans, he uses those experiences to prepare his readers for similar mission challenges. By including concrete examples of previous mission conversations, Paul gives his readers a spiritual gift to strengthen their own faith and mission (see 1:11).[4]

This book will emphasize three themes found throughout Romans: *God's power, Jesus' faith,* and *world mission.* They have seldom been the focuses of others who have written on Romans.[5] You are probably more familiar with such themes in Romans as justification by faith or the righteousness of God. I do not deny their importance. But I will show how they relate to the other three themes that are the most significant for understanding Romans—and the Christian life and mission.

Paul wrote primarily as a missionary in whom God's new kingly power continued to extend toward the ends of the earth.[6] Paul's own emphasis on God's power carried on Jesus' emphasis on God's kingdom. Although in his letters Paul does not often use the word *kingdom,* what Jesus meant by that word dominates Paul's theology, ethics, and mission. In fact, Paul's writings do use the phrase "kingdom of God" more often than any other part of the New Testament except the synoptic Gospels: Matthew, Mark, and Luke. Moreover, Acts 19:8; 20:25; 28:23, 31 sum up Paul's message as the kingdom of God.

According to Paul, God's power will spread over all the world and make certain people righteous in the same way that Jesus was righteous. While Jesus was unique—the Son of God who died for the sins of the world—he was also the foundation of a new faith and obedience that could be described in some detail. For Jesus (and Paul), faith meant both believing and receiving. Jesus believed that God's royal power was beginning to invade history in a special way. He received the transforming power of God that enabled a new kind of righteous life and servant mission.

The theme of Jesus' faith has been notably ignored or denied in studies of Paul. But an increasing number of New Testament scholars now prefer to translate 3:22, 26 as the "faith (fulness) of Jesus" rather than "faith in Jesus." Yet most still think that Paul is not that interested in Jesus' earthly life because he emphasizes faith in Jesus, not the faith of Jesus. Many fundamentalist Christians would also claim that Jesus' faith is not relevant for us because it belonged to a different dispensation. The best-selling Bible in the United States this century, the *Scofield Reference Bible*, includes such dispensational notes by C. I. Scofield. He intended for that Bible to be a one-volume reference for missionaries abroad who had few books.

Some have even blamed Paul for creating a new religion, far different from what Jesus taught. Others have insisted that Paul knew little about the Jew Jesus. Paul's own words about independence from Jesus' apostles in Jerusalem have been used to prove that Paul didn't care about the historical Jesus—or about other Jews (Gal. 1:11-12, 15-23).

Yet in Galatians 1:18-19, Paul refers to a fifteen-day stay in Jerusalem with the apostle Cephas (Peter), where he also saw the apostle James, the brother of Jesus. Galatians 1:7-9 makes clear that there is only one gospel. Indeed, Paul later went to Jerusalem again to make sure that his gospel was the same as that of Jesus' apostles (Gal. 2:1-10). Certainly they all agreed that Christ was not to be regarded from the viewpoint of an unbelieving human being (2 Cor. 5:16). But they also agreed that God's new work of power was changing them into the well-known likeness of Jesus' life and mission (2 Cor. 3:5-6, 18).

When Jesus sent his disciples on a mission throughout Israel, they had learned his faith in God's kingship and were ready to pass it on (see Luke 9:1-6; 10:1-12). After Jesus' resurrection, the apostles remained in Jerusalem where they proclaimed God's power in raising Jesus and carried on Jesus' teaching in the early church (Acts 2:14, 24, 32, 36, 42; 3:13, 15; 4:2, 10, 33; 5:20-21, 28, 30, 42; 6:2-4).

Barnabas was an especially important link between the original apostles and Paul. He was first connected with the Jerusalem church and apostles. Then later he helped guide Paul during his early mission years (Acts 4:36-37; 9:27-30; 11:22-30; 12:25; 13:1-7, 43-46; 14:12-14; 15:2). Paul could have learned much of the apostolic teaching about Jesus from Barnabas, his partner in mission. Silas and John Mark also served with Paul after an earlier time in the Jerusalem church.

Although he seldom quotes Jesus, Paul's teaching is full of the new faith that Jesus introduced. Paul's method is simply like that of other epistle writers in the New Testament—and like the early Apostolic Fathers, who seldom quoted Jesus' teachings. Yet there is a freedom frequently to allude to or echo those teachings and to use Christ's example. Such writers could usually assume a foundation of earlier instruction (for Romans, see 6:17; 15:14-15; 16:17).[7]

God's exalted power in Jesus did not lead to what is most associated with human power: domination over others. Jesus was not in the inner circle of organized religious or social powers. Actually, Jesus' strongest opposition came from those in positions of religious, economic, political, and military power. Jewish leaders were zealous for the law of Moses. That law included commands like killing enemies who threatened Israel and rewards like possessing a prosperous land. When Jesus' faith insisted on consistent love of enemies and challenged selfish love of money, the Jewish establishment reacted violently. What kind of Messiah was this lowly Jesus?

While Paul links Christian faith with Jesus' faith, he often contrasts the faith of Jesus with the law of Moses. Most Protestants have failed to see the practical significance of Paul's contrast. The authority of the Bible has meant equally the authority of the Old Testament and New Testament. Paul did use the old covenant of Moses as a witness to Jesus. The Old Testament was God's word. It had authority. Yet obedience to the law or works of the law failed to effect righteousness or salvation. Only the obedience of Jesus' faith revealed righteousness and brought the joy of salvation through God's new kingly power.

Jesus fulfilled the law of Moses to such an extent that it was no longer God's authority for Christian obedience. It remained God's authoritative word on what God had formerly commanded Israel to do. But Jesus' reinterpretation of the law was the authority of knowing God's will in God's newly arrived kingdom. Protestants, however, often give the Old Testament more of a role in knowing God's present will than Jesus or Paul did. Such Protestants have thus missed the newness of Jesus' new covenant. The New Testament—based on Jesus' new faith—must be given priority in the church. By means of the New Testament, Christians should always read the Old Testament through the eyes of Jesus and Paul.

Instead of a verse-by-verse commentary, I have chosen to write a thematic commentary to show how Paul developed three themes in Romans: *God's power, Jesus' faith,* and *world mission.* I have tried to keep my writing style as simple as possible, especially for the sake of those who know English only as a second language. Some readers might want to use this book as a reference for studying, teaching, or preaching on certain sections of Romans. So I have proceeded through Romans section by section. Each section covers about ten to fifteen verses.

Not all three themes will be found in every section. Ordinarily two or three themes will be interwoven in a section. Throughout the book, I will often show how later sections develop the basic thematic message of 1:16-17 and thus confirm my new translation of those verses. Thus part of this book's purpose is to show that the sudden illumination I once received while reading 1:16-17 in Greek was truth from God.

This commentary will not usually discuss various possible

interpretations, but present what I think is the best interpretation. Sometimes, what I think is debatable and I argue on behalf of my own interpretation. If the reader wants a larger choice of interpretations, there are many other commentaries on Romans that give such information.

Finally, I will regularly discuss practical (and impractical) applications of Romans. For eight years I was a missionary teacher of New Testament at a seminary in the Philippines. The concerns, needs, and experiences of Christians and churches in the so-called third world of Asia, Africa, and Latin America are of special interest to me. Over two-thirds of the earth's population lives in the third world, in areas of deep poverty and political repression—and of rich cultural and religious expression.

Most calling themselves Christians are part of the third world. Yet the first world still often ignores or looks down on them as third-class Christians. Privileged Western (Western European and North American) churches sent out well-educated, middle-class missionaries who had trouble relating to the poor and powerless of the third world. The supposed strength of such missionaries—including myself—turned out to be weakness.

Too many of our modern mission institutions, including seminaries and Bible schools, resulted from transferring European and American models of ministry to the third world. Missionaries who serve in those institutions have formal, official roles that add to their already elevated status and power as wealthy white people. Students in professional seminaries and Bible schools prepare to become full-time professional pastors. Most try to please the institutions (churches) they serve so they can advance to bigger institutions. The more educated ministers enjoy higher social status and increased salary. Seminary graduates often think they are superior to Bible school graduates. Bible school graduates consider themselves better than lay leaders. Full-time pastors look down on part-time leaders.

Many church and mission leaders now in power say we can't go back to the first century. Much of the so-called progress of white Western "Christian" civilization is seen as a special gift from God. Most missionaries assume God's past blessings and encourage similar progress and development in "underdeveloped" countries. Even pioneer efforts like church planting usually plan to gather enough converts to support a full-time (well-educated, well-paid) pastor and to build a church structure. Most Western churches and missionaries have been comfortable with power through prosperity—and with those who are most prosperous and powerful. The health-and-wealth gospel has thus had a larger following than most Western Christians think.

Churches lack credibility when they seldom show evidence of God's power as first manifested in Jesus. So in the twentieth century, we have millions of Christians claiming to have a personal relationship with Jesus. But their Jesus no longer requires small groups of obedient disciples who serve sacrificially among the dominated, share generously with the poor, and speak prophetically to the powerful. Jesus becomes merely the frosting on the cake of a privileged life or the friendly counselor who lifts one's spirits in the midst of life's tragedies.

Yet the growth of dedicated small groups, humble house churches, and basic Christian communities among the poor in the third world—and all over the world—shows that some still take seriously Jesus' lowly way. When persons and churches reflect the obedience that comes through the faith of Jesus, they magnify God's power. May God use this book to empower Christians around the world to follow Paul in spreading the faith and mission of Jesus.

Romans 1:1-12

God's Power, God's Son, and World Mission

PAUL begins his letter by emphasizing the world mission that has begun and has continued to spread through God's power. He describes himself as called and set apart by God for a mission of spreading the gospel of God (1:1). God's power has transformed Paul's purpose in life.

Now Paul is a servant of Christ. His commission is to continue the message of Jesus, who began his own mission by preaching the gospel of God. According to Jesus, God's special time to act with kingly power was being fulfilled in him (Mark 1:14-15). The gospel that God promised long ago through the prophets and in the holy writings or Old Testament has now happened (1:2).

The prophecy of Isaiah 52:7 tells of the messenger who would bring good news (gospel) about the peace and salvation of God's ruling power. Jesus fulfilled God's promises through his total submission to God's conclusive work of power. Paul then carries on the faith and message of Jesus as a servant and representative of the risen Christ.

The Old Testament offers an important promise that a descendant of David will rule over a final kingdom of righteousness and peace (2 Sam. 7:12-13; Isa. 9:6-7; 11:1-9). David's kingly descendants were God's sons in a special way. Paul agreed with Jesus that he fulfilled the Davidic promise of the final kingly Son, the Christ or Messiah (1:3; Mark 8:29-30; 14:61-62).

Yet Jesus' sonship was not limited to being the Jewish Messiah. Before Jesus was God's Messiah, he was already God's Son (1:3). Jesus, always God's Son, was finally installed by God as all-powerful ruler through resurrection from a shameful death (1:4).[1]

God's power came to a climax by raising Jesus from the dead.[2] After God's Spirit raised Jesus, the Son of God who had served and suffered was then appointed God's Son in power (1:4; 1 Cor. 15:42-43; Phil. 2:6-11; Acts 2:36). Before his resurrection, Jesus was God's Son and God's Messiah (1:3). But he refused the earthly glory of political power or national prestige. After his resurrection, Jesus was elevated to share God's heavenly glory as Ruler and Lord over all creation. Israel's Messiah became Master of the universe.

When Paul emphasizes God's power, he includes the risen Jesus because he is now Son of God in power, Jesus Christ our Lord. While Paul builds on the rock of Jesus' faith, he also stresses that the risen Jesus, who appeared to him and transformed him, is Lord and God, God's only Son. Jesus' own faith connected the coming of the kingdom (kingship) of God in power with his own rising to power and glory as God's beloved Son. He displayed that ahead of time by his transfiguration (Mark 9:1-10; 14:62). Later, at the very time that Jesus' enemies mocked and beat him, he boldly affirmed his faith that he would soon sit at the right hand of the power of God (Luke 22:63-69).

Through Jesus the Lord, Paul received grace and apostleship (1:5). Paul's apostolic service began through divine grace and continues the same way, through the working of God's power (Eph. 3:7). Jesus is now Lord over the world, and Paul's apostleship includes all the peoples of the world (1:5).[3] Paul is unique as an apostle sent out among the Gentiles. The risen Lord appeared to him and commissioned him to go especially to the Gentiles (1 Cor. 9:1; 15:8-9; Gal. 1:15-17; 2:7-8; Acts 9:15; 22:21; 26:16-17).

Yet Paul knows that he is not God's only apostle or messenger. He writes that "we" received grace and apostleship, apparently recognizing other apostles. Some of them were in Rome. In 16:7 Paul describes the Jews Andronicus and Junia as well-known apostles who were Christians before Paul. Perhaps they were among the seventy sent out on mission by Jesus (Luke 10). If so, they were possibly with the eleven apostles when the risen Jesus appeared to them, commissioned them all as his witnesses, and promised them power from God (Luke 24:33-49; Acts 1:1-8). Apostles were special messengers called by Christ and sent out on mission for him. (The Greek root of the word *apostle* and the Latin root of the word *missionary* both focus on the one sent.)

After God raised Jesus from the dead, the twelve apostles were unique witnesses of Jesus' faith, life, and resurrection (Acts 1:21-22). They thus planted the first churches in Jerusalem and directed the beginning stages of the new communities (Acts 2:14, 42-43; 4:35; 6:2-6), including those in Samaria (Acts 8:14) and Caesarea (Acts 10:24, 39-41; 11:1-18). Yet as the Gentile mission began to take shape, the focus shifted from the twelve to Paul and his co-workers.

While serving the Antioch church, Christ called Barnabas and Paul for a special mission (Acts 13:1-3). As they traveled to various towns forming new groups of disciples, Luke referred to them as apostles (Acts 14:4, 14). Barnabas also had received a call from Christ to plant new churches and care for them during their beginning stages. Like the Jerusalem churches, after a short time the apostles appointed elders to take over the leadership of the new churches (Acts 14:23; 11:30).

In 1 Corinthians 9:1-6 Paul compares the apostolic mission of himself and Barnabas with other apostles. He again mentions those other apostles along with Cephas and the twelve and James, the brother of Jesus (1 Cor. 15:5, 7). In 1 Thessalonians 2:7, Paul describes the behavior of himself, Silvanus (Silas), and Timothy as apostles of Christ when they first went to Thessalonica (see 1 Thess. 1:1, 5; Acts 17:1-15). Thus while Paul and the twelve apostles had special calls from the risen Jesus, later apostles also had commissions from Christ through the Holy Spirit. Those whom Christ later called and sent to proclaim the gospel and plant new churches were just as much apostles as Peter and Paul.[4]

All Christians in Rome have a special calling from Jesus to be instruments of God's world mission (1:6-7). Christ will send some of them on apostolic missions in the future, both near and far. God called both Paul and the Romans to mission. Paul associates his own calling to apostleship (1:1, 5) with the calling of his partners in mission (1:5-7). He is not just trying to get them to support his mission. Paul wants them to have their own apostolic missions. His prayer is that the same powerful grace that converted them into beloved and holy servants will continue to work in all of them as they carry out their mission (1:7).

The purpose of God's enabling grace in faithful apostles is to reproduce that same "obedience of faith" among all the peoples (1:5). God's work is expanding beyond the borders of Israel to include all peoples, both Jews and Gentiles.[5] Paul was an apostle called to the Gentile world, but he continued to minister to Jews also.[6]

Paul's words in 1:4-5 reflected Jesus' great commission in Matthew 28:18-20. The risen Jesus says God has given him all authority in heaven and on earth (Matt. 28:18). In Romans, the apostle Paul says the risen Jesus received authority or power (1:4). Jesus sends apostles among all peoples to teach obedience to his commands and make disciples who follow the way of Jesus' faith (Matt. 28:19-20). The "obedience of faith" is the obedience that Jesus' faith taught and lived. Paul wrote that the living Christ is still sending out apostles among all the peoples to expand the obedience of faith (1:4-5).

The church has often emphasized Jesus' heavenly deity at the expense of his earthly humanity. Jesus as a man became Jesus on the cross, on his way to heaven. Jesus was either a dead Savior or a distant deity. Paul corrects both sides by focusing on both Jesus' present powerful sonship and his former faithful sonship. For Paul, Jesus is both the means by which people become children of God and the model for how such children should live obediently.

Those who emphasize Jesus' divine sonship and prefer "spiritual" matters have also denied that Jesus' life and mission are examples for us. In the Roman Catholic Church, such a distant, dehumanized Christ led to a devotion to other holy people like Mary and the saints. On the other hand, many who prefer Jesus' humanity limit their mission to meeting material needs, thus denying that Jesus' fuller mission is relevant. But Jesus was and is God with us. He was the perfectly obedient Son who called others to turn to God and be transformed into similarly obedient children.[7]

◆ ◆ ◆

Paul's purpose in writing is to help them fulfill their own calling to obedience and world mission through God's powerful grace. The Spirit of holiness (1:4) can produce holiness in all of them (1:7). And whatever is holy is dedicated to God for special service.

For Paul, there are no holy clergy or reverends while the rest are mere lay people with no ministry. All Christians are holy and set apart for mission. To set up one holy leader as the professional who does the main functions of ministry is a retreat into civil religion. Most non-Christian societies also have holy men (seldom women) who perform rituals they think will bring blessing to their families, farms, or villages.

Paul is not writing to just a few leaders in Rome. He wants to encourage all the Christians there to fufill their divinely empowered mission. Most of the Christians are not merely to help a few who do the main work of ministry. God has called them to do a variety of specific ministries like apostolic planting or moving among churches, prophetic teaching of Jesus' faith, or practical help among the poor. No one person will dominate or do most of the "important" ministry, like most priests and pastors throughout church history.[8]

Since the Roman Christians are centrally located in Rome among all the peoples (1:5-6), they can be lights throughout the world. Living in the capital at the center of the well-traveled Roman Empire, they can reach out in all directions. They can also influence those coming to Rome from all directions.

Paul thanks God, who has now been revealed and has come close to him through Jesus Christ (1:8). That same God is responsible for the faith of each reader, and that faith is being spread into all the world. Mission is all-inclusive. In 1:7-8 he refers twice to all the Christians (both Jews and Gentiles) in Rome. And he connects their faith with the spreading of the obedience of faith to all the peoples (1:5), to the whole world (1:8). Paul embraces the Christians in Rome as partners in world mission. God is already using them, and Paul intends to increase their usefulness through this letter.

In 1:9-12, Paul continues to link his own service of God, by the power of his spirit, with the faith and gifts of grace of the Roman Christians. Since Paul writes about "my God" in 1:8, the phrase "my spirit" in 1:9 probably points to the Holy Spirit who enables him to carry out his holy service.[9] As in 1:1, Paul describes himself as a servant, entrusted with the gospel of Jesus and the gospel about Jesus (1:9). Jesus proclaimed the gospel of God (1:1), and Paul is now a servant of that gospel.

God is Paul's witness that he often prayed for the readers and asked God for the chance to visit Rome (1:10). Paul wants to see them in person so the Spirit can use him to give them a spiritual gift (1:11). A special gift of grace from God's Spirit through Paul would enable them to be used like Paul in the service of God's world mission. Paul's faith would encourage them, and their well-known faith (around the world) would encourage Paul (1:8, 12).

✦ ✦ ✦

We look back to Paul as a pioneer missionary who visited many new places. He did not stay in one place for a long time, unlike many more recent missionaries. Yet he also spent time and effort to strengthen new converts so they could fulfill their own mission. He often returned to churches or wrote to churches he planted. Paul wanted to strengthen their faith (fulness) in the midst of opposition to their mission (see Acts 14:21-22; 15:36, 41; 18:23; 20:2). His strengthening their faith led to still others joining the new faith (see Acts 16:5). Paul's purpose in writing Romans was also to strengthen them for their own difficult mission.

Paul's model of training leaders for mission is better than the current academic training of would-be professional leaders in modern seminaries. More recently, some have tried to train local church leaders in more rural areas, especially in the third world. Theological Education by Extension (TEE) has tried to extend seminary training to more remote areas. Yet problems remain with such values of the seminary as abstract information and academic degrees.

Most programmed texts used by TEE have been written by foreign missionaries. As thousands of third world church leaders with little formal education enrolled, TEE leaders (and seminaries with TEE programs) became proud of the vast numbers they had touched. But the touch was very light. The teaching was usually superficial and irrelevant to Jesus' mission. The information was a simpler form of seminary course content. Thus the Western model and content continued to limit TEE's vision. While students could use the materials in their homes or meet monthly in regional gatherings, their local context and participation were not taken seriously. And when the missionaries left, it became too expensive to continue.[10]

Why not make theological education an outgrowth of local churches? Why not let each group of disciples reproduce itself and reach out in mission? Why not let more experienced church leaders in cities and rural areas teach and show Christ's way of obedience and mission to new leaders in a given area? That was Paul's method.

If such mission emphasized a context of house churches, there would be no need for an institutional seal of approval or for training to administer a religious institution. Instead of manufacturing denominational ministers who manage impressive churches, lay people could be trained to make disciples. Through informal apprenticeships, such leaders would come to know a lot about Jesus' faith, teaching, and mission. They would not need to know much about modern theologies, management theories, or ministerial techniques. Those interested in more specialized studies could read relevant books on their own.

Various nonpaid leaders in each group could then do the

core of ministry. To supplement that mission, a few full-time apostles might receive some basic support (not a middle-class salary). They could travel within certain regions, as individuals or teams, to strengthen the mission of local groups. Such theological education would thus be rooted in local groups of Christians. The purpose of theology would be to enable mission at the grassroots level. Paul's purpose in writing Romans—to encourage Jesus' kingdom mission among others—would become the purpose of all theological training.[11]

Churches should not be content to provide prayer and financial support for special missionaries. Such people should be sent out on mission, but those left behind also have their own mission. God calls and empowers each one to spread the faith of Jesus by word and deed. To do that, they do not necessarily need to change jobs or make ministry a full-time job or career. Some might travel long distances and live in different cultures while others might travel next door and continue to live in the local non-Christian culture.

Every nation and every neighborhood is a mission field. The United States, Canada, or any other so-called Christian nation is no exception. There has never been a nation that followed Jesus, and Jesus had no intention of creating Christian nations in the modern political sense. But he did call his followers to form groups of disciples (churches) among all the world's peoples. Thus 1 Peter 2:9 appropriately calls the church "a holy nation."

A return to Jesus' kind of faith in God's power is needed. Paul's mission and the churches founded did not need professional missionaries or pastors. God's mission does reproduce children of God who, like God's Son, serve humbly in the midst of humble circumstances. For them, appropriate worship and service might happen through house churches, basic Christian communities, or home Bible studies.

When the Chinese Communist government took over in 1949, it pressured foreign missionaries to leave. For Chinese Christians, it set up the Three-Self Patriotic Movement (TSPM) to steer churches into being self-governing, self-propagating, and self-supporting. Many missionaries thought Christianity would die. Yet most Chinese Christians refused to compromise with government control of churches through the TSPM. As Chinese lay leaders began to form small underground house churches, the Christian faith came to life as never before.

Two nineteenth-century missionary executives (Henry Venn and Rufus Anderson) had made the three-self vision popular. They wanted to reduce dependence of mission churches on missionaries and foreign funds. Although most missionaries were leaving China, it was not so much the TSPM that fulfilled that vision. It was the house churches, with their lay leaders and traveling apostles. Before then, Western mission churches and schools in China required so much money and so long a training period that Chinese leadership was mostly left out or secondary.

Jesus often taught his disciples in homes (see Mark 7:17; 9:28, 33; 10:10), and humble house churches multiplied because of the early apostolic mission. There were no second-class Christians who simply supported powerful clergy or missionaries. But during those first centuries, certain elite leaders came to hold more power. Churches controlled by such leaders joined with some in the ruling classes of society to "strengthen" religion. That religion eventually became attractive to the top rulers of the Roman Empire.

When the Roman emperor Constantine confessed Christianity as the new state religion, Christendom had arrived, and many believers enjoyed its stay. For around fifteen hundred years, missions were commonly used as an instrument of political leaders to pacify various other peoples. Missionaries arrived side by side with their nation's armies. Professional missionaries served powerful lords who confessed Jesus without following Jesus. Mission meant special agents traveling to remote places. The so-called average church member had no mission.

At the same time, God continually raised up groups of disciples who took Jesus' faith and mission seriously. One such group during the Middle Ages, the Waldensians, became a scattered, persecuted minority throughout Europe. Their founder, Peter Waldo, was once a rich merchant and held powerful positions in his city and church. Then the faith of Jesus challenged him to give up his wealth and power. He became poor. Rather than entering a monastery, a prestigious and respected institution, he chose the lowly path of the apostles. Waldo traveled around, spreading the message of Christ's call to mission. Various people joined him only to have church authorities tell them that they had no authority to preach. They responded by obeying God rather than humans. Eventually they were branded as heretics and faced the terrors of the Inquisition.[12]

In the sixteenth century, Anabaptists complained that the Reformation only went halfway in its reforms. They wanted to return to the life and mission of the early church. Anabaptists also emphasized the apostolate or mission of lay people. There was no longer a distinction between academically trained ministers and the "average" Christian. Anabaptists understood Luther's priesthood of all believers as the mission service of all believers. And all believers included women, who were often more effective than men.[13]

In the midst of a society built around Christendom, Anabaptists were a countercultural community. They began as small groups that met in homes and read Scripture together. When Reformation churches rejected Anabaptist reforms, they formed loose fellowships that spread throughout northern Europe. Their witness was powerful and their message prophetic. Unfortunately, after years of suffering persecution and exile from the established churches, many Anabaptist groups turned into more closed, ethnic communities. Their counterculture, which included a simple lifestyle, turned into a cultural tradition that required a certain kind of simple lifestyle.[14]

By the late seventeenth and eighteenth centuries, pietists in Germany and Methodists in England developed lay movements centered on study of the Bible. They tried to awaken the churches, calling for a regenerate membership and the priesthood of all believers, again understood as personal witness. The result was small circles of devoted lay people engaged in mission.

During the late eighteenth and early nineteenth centuries, Baptists used "farmer preachers" and Methodists used lay ministers and circuit riders as they went westward from the eastern

United States. Such ministers (missionaries) spoke simply among the common people and often worked at a suitable trade to supply their basic needs. As a result, there was less division between "clergy" and laity. Their mission often included strong criticism of eastern elite clergy in wealthy comfortable churches, mocking their ministry as mere "priestcraft."

Many also objected to the mission bureaucracies developed by eastern churches. For example, the American Home Missionary Society (AHMS) claimed to be nondenominational and collected large amounts of money to support preachers and build churches in unchurched areas. The truth was that there were many ministers and churches already in those areas. But they were Baptists and Methodists who preached for little or nothing. The denominations behind the AHMS (Congregationalists, Presbyterians, and Episcopalians) knew that their well-educated, well-paid clergy could not compete in frontier areas without massive support from their mainline denominations.

The mainline missionaries also looked down on more common rural preachers and considered those areas as unchurched. Their own "proper" churches reflected the moneyed machinery of theological schools, denominational conventions, missionary boards, and big buildings. Others accused them of trying to dominate wherever they went. Yet the ordinary rural preachers could also be domineering at times.

Both Baptists and Methodists also used small groups where all the people could participate. Methodists held "class meetings" for prayer and Bible study while Baptists had prayer meetings. Such groups were supportive communities that expressed God's concern for those considered common and marginal. So the "classes" were also mission groups that showed a practical concern for the poor. However, those humble, apostolic groups later educated "respectable" middle-class clergy, constructed impressive church buildings, and organized centralized denominational institutions worth millions of dollars.[15]

After seeing how most missionaries in the Philippines reproduced Western religious institutions, a former Filipina student of mine wondered whether her mission service had much to offer. If mission required material resources, she didn't have the capacity to make much difference. The good news for her, and for most Christians in the third world, is that Jesus was poor. Jesus' mission was good news to his poor, humble followers because its main goal was to produce other disciples like themselves. The mission of a poor, persecuted Jesus best revealed God's power. Humble, obedient followers of Jesus were both the means and the end of God's mission. Obedience to Jesus' faith and mission was the main mark of God's new kingly power. God's kingdom produced messianic mission communities made up of sisters and brothers of the Son of God.

At first Viv Grigg, a New Zealander missionary to the Philippines, worked with middle-class and upper-class Filipinos in Manila. Then God led him to preach good news to the poor. He moved to a slum and lived with the poor to identify with them and share Jesus with them. With the help of a few Filipino Christians, small groups of disciples slowly formed. Bible studies held in outdoor, open spaces led to house churches in homes of the poor. By being a companion to the poor, Grigg received a new extended family, a family that shared Jesus' faith. Those new communities of faith also continued Jesus' mission of showing practical love and help to one another and to neighbors around them.[16]

Such communities are now multiplying among both Protestants and Catholics. Some Catholic basic Christian communities in Latin America have followed Jesus' model. They are basic in the sense of being small cells of poor laypeople who meet to discuss local problems in light of the Bible. They grow at the grassroots level. That is their base. Others have found new life in certain evangelical churches that allow poor laypeople to participate in close-knit Bible study groups and lead them. Pentecostal churches among the poor which promote the participation and mission of lay people have especially increased in the third world. Over the past several decades, house churches have also multiplied in various parts of the world, especially in China, India, Korea, Ethiopia, England, and Scotland.[17]

Such communities should not be confused with small groups in churches where there is little sense of a mission of making disciples among the poor. Some church volunteers might give a little time to help others but don't want to sacrifice too much for those in need. Recovery groups like Alcoholics Anonymous (AA) promise healing to growing numbers of addicted or abused people in the United States. One of the twelve steps of AA is to affirm the need for God's power. Yet they can define God however they want. They can exchange the God of Jesus for a God more "sensitive" to their needs and desires. Close communities of like-minded people, even some poor people, often merely share the values and hopes of their larger society.

Certain African independent churches supply a final example of third world churches heading in the direction of Jesus' and Paul's mission. They separated from traditional mission churches because they rejected the Western values and machinery of the white-man's mission. They have encouraged a widespread voluntary unpaid ministry, including a strong mission of helping the needy, both in the Christian community and in the larger society. Only the few largest independent churches have had paid ministers. Most preferred the fellowship of smaller communities and an apostolic mission.[18]

So Paul's vision for world mission continues to be shared all over the world, especially in the third world. God's power is still at work among those who model the mission of God's Son. Apostolic mission remains mobile. May God's power continue to create new communities and send them next door or to the other side of the world as apostolic sisters and brothers of God's Son.

Romans 1:13-18

God's Saving Power Among All the Peoples

PAUL'S mission has already enjoyed the fruit of faith's obedience among other peoples. Now he wants some more fruit among the Christians in Rome (1:13). So far he has been hindered, at least partly by opposition, from traveling to Rome (1:13; see 15:22). And his plan to visit Jerusalem before going to Rome involves risk and danger from certain Jewish enemies (15:25, 28-31). The fulfillment of Paul's plan to visit Rome is in doubt.

Christians in Rome need to be strengthened and encouraged if they are to bear more fruit in mission service (see 1:11-12). So Paul decides not to wait until his planned visit, which is uncertain anyway, and proceeds to give them spiritual gifts like teaching and encouragement by means of this letter. Whether or not Paul ever reaches Rome, with this letter he will already have strengthened his readers for fruitful service in a fearful world.

Since God called Paul to be an apostle among the Gentiles (1:13), he writes that he is a debtor to Greeks (1:14). Because God gave him that obligation, he wants to spread the gospel message and mission to his readers in Rome, the capital and center of the Greco-Roman world (1:15).

The Greco-Roman world considered its dominant Greek culture to be superior. It despised other cultures as barbarian. Yet Paul's mission doesn't limit itself to only the educated Greeks who see themselves as the "wise" of the world. God also sent Paul to the "barbarians," whom Greeks considered ignorant, the scum of the earth (1:14).

In Acts, Paul often tries to minister to his own Jewish people, who prefer to keep their own Jewish culture and language as much as possible. Paul's obligation includes his commission to all peoples, not just educated people who speak fluent Greek (1:5; Acts 9:15; 26:17-23). He hopes to fulfill his calling even to the outer edges of the "civilized" world, to the supposedly barbarian regions of Jerusalem or Spain (see 15:23-24). And if Paul himself is unable to make those journeys, his present letter will help his readers carry on that commission to all peoples.

Whether a specific culture is civilized or barbarian is a matter of opinion. Most people prefer their own culture and consider other customs strange or funny. A danger in world mission is the desire to spread one's own culture so other peoples might become more "developed" or "civilized." That has been a major problem of Western missions.

For example, many missionaries went to African peoples while thinking of them as primitive savages. Such missionaries had an evolutionary view of culture, including race and religion, which put African peoples and religions at the bottom and their own at the top. Their Enlightenment worldview included ideas about Western superiority. The white man's burden of spreading Western civilization overshadowed a mission of extending the obedience of faith.

That earlier optimism has now turned to pessimism due to increased poverty and pollution throughout the world. Despite heroic and courageous sacrifices by various missionaries, Western mission did not result in the expected victory of progress for most "backward" (barbarian) peoples. The world economy developed by Western nations increased their own wealth and the wealth of a few elite third-world leaders at the expense of most of the world's peoples.

At first, the West thought it could empower the third world without giving up any of its own power. But the power gap became greater, not narrower. Development became just another word for exploitation. Now we see that the enemy was not ignorance or underdevelopment but human power that proudly manipulated other humans (and nature). Third-world peoples and environments cannot tolerate such continued growth of Western wealth and power.[1]

Why doesn't Paul forget the "barbarian" cultures, especially his own people, the Jews? Their leaders have often made life miserable for him. Wouldn't there be more church growth if he concentrates on those more open to his mission? Paul would respond that he is not the one in charge (see 1 Cor. 9:16-17). God entrusted him with a mission to all the peoples.

Paul shares Jesus' faith that God's power is now at work fulfilling the promise of salvation. This has begun with Jesus and his ministry among the Jews. Those so-called barbarian Jews are not merely included in God's fulfillment; they are first in line to receive God's saving power (1:16). Paul switches the order of those divisions of humankind. In 1:14, he describes the divisions from the viewpoint of "cultured" Greeks: Greeks before barbarians, and wise before ignorant. In 1:16, he identifies the peoples of the world from God's viewpoint: to the Jew first and to the Gentile (which included Greeks). Paul's own mission reflects that priority, and his words now call on others to do the same.

Many consider Romans 1:16-17 to be the theme of the letter. They then interpret Romans as the powerful gospel that leads to salvation by faith (1:16) and reveals God's righteousness, which justifies the believer (1:17). But that supposedly powerful gospel is being rejected to such an extent that Paul needs to affirm his lack of shame. Like Jesus, Paul's faith is not in weak human words but in God's power.

I propose a new translation of 1:16 which seems to fit the context better: *"For I am not ashamed of the gospel, for God's power is unto salvation for everyone who is believing, for the Jew first and for the Gentile."*[2] My translation emphasizes God's saving power at work in people, not in the gospel.

In Mark 8:38, Jesus warns about not being ashamed of him and his words due to opposition, and then immediately affirms the nearness of the coming of the kingdom in power (Mark 9:1). Similarly Paul, when faced with frequent rejection of the gospel, immediately affirms the power of God's kingly rule, bringing salvation to those who are believing.

Even if some Jews reject him, threaten him, and drive him out of various synagogues and towns, Paul is still not ashamed (1:16; see Phil. 1:14, 20; 2 Tim. 1:8, 12). For God's power is made perfect and achieves its purpose through the weakness of insults and persecutions. Rather than feelings of shame and sadness, Paul boasts gladly about his weaknesses so Christ's power would remain with him (2 Cor. 12:9-10). The treasure of God's power is even more brilliant when seen in beaten-up clay jars (2 Cor. 4:7-9). All of Paul's hardships are part of a sacrificial service in the power of God (2 Cor. 6:4-7).

After mentioning the gospel, Paul refers to God's power because the gospel is about God's power. In this book, I show that God's power is a main theme in Paul's gospel. In Romans 1:1, Paul refers to the gospel of God, which means the gospel from God and the gospel about God's new saving power. In 1:2-3 he adds that the gospel God promised in the Old Testament has now come to fulfillment in God's Son (see 1:9). Jesus was the Christ, and the Spirit's power raised him from the dead so that he was now Son of God in power (1:3-4). Paul's gospel is especially about God's final work of power in Christ.

In Romans, the gospel itself is not the power of God so much as a message about the power of God bringing the promised salvation in Christ. And God's powerful grace is continuing to have its effect through a mission for the obedience of faith among all the peoples (1:5). When Paul mentions the gospel in 1:16, he can assume that earlier content.[3]

❖ ❖ ❖

Much Protestant theology has used interpretations about the power of the gospel to promote an inspired pulpit proclamation or an inspired written Scripture. While there is a basis for empowered proclamation and inspired Scripture in the New Testament, I don't think that is Paul's point in 1:16.[4] Protestant preoccupation with wise words and orthodox beliefs has missed Paul's emphasis. God's power does not focus on words at the expense of deeds. Yet that has been precisely the problem of the preached word throughout Protestant history.

The church's normal life has seldom lived up to its formal words. Since salvation is not through works, many Protestants decided that believing the gospel message was saving faith. They replaced faith in God's power, as described in the gospel, with faith in the gospel itself. But wherever God's power was not manifested in the lives of the proclaimers, others doubted their gospel.

Paul's preaching and teaching mission did not produce eloquent words behind a privileged pulpit. Even his debates with other Jews did not happen primarily in formal settings like synagogues. After being forced to make a fast exit from many synagogues, Paul carried on his mission in more private contexts like homes. Such contexts included house churches made up of a few people transformed by God's power and experiencing God's salvation as a community of faith.

Paul didn't want to be identified with popular philosophers like the sophists, who were trained and paid well for public speaking that gave them high social status and entertained crowds. Yet more modern pastors and priests often prefer the prestige and pay of preaching in prized pulpits. Instead, Paul embraced a humble status as a Jewish manual laborer who mostly supported himself. He spread the gospel through natural conversations at work and in homes.[5] Paul worked well at his trade of tentmaking (Acts 18:3) but did not count that as his main mission or primary calling, as in some Protestant theology. His humble work was merely a means of meeting basic needs, his own and sometimes those of others. Thus those who shared his faith and mission (and poverty) were not burdened by providing for him (see 1 Thess. 2:5-9; 2 Thess. 3:8; Acts 20:33-35).

Paul's model is a strong contrast to the greed behind much work, including much religious work. Those proclaiming God's power are called to seek a more lowly means of mission that humbly shares and interacts with others. They do not want more powerful positions so they can proudly preach over the heads of others and so they can eagerly receive as much as others can give.

Protestants have often defined the true church as where the Word of God is purely preached and the sacraments of baptism and the Lord's Supper are properly administered. That made most of the people unnecessary. It all depended on a prim and proper pastor. Luther's added thought about a faithful invisible church let the visible churches remain unfaithful. Dynamic words produced detailed doctrines and divided churches. Karl Barth went so far as to say that at each moment and place where the gospel is preached, the church is called into being. But what kind of church is it?[6]

Those who made religious talk and knowledge to be the heart of Christianity fell prey to religious hypocrisy and powerless lives. Intellectual agreement is not the same as the obedience of faith or a fellowship of faith. Neither highly educated nor deeply emotional preaching are central to God's work of power in Jesus. Popular pulpit stars are poor substitutes for God's power. Yet the Protestant focus on the pulpit and the preached word easily led to putting the preacher and his personality in the spotlight. As long as the preacher performed well, the people would applaud and pay accordingly.

Similar things could be said about the written word, including Scripture. Although some advertised it as inspired, inerrant, and infallible, that did not make the words themselves powerful. Many people have read parts of the Bible and have wondered what it all meant, or they interpreted it to serve their own interests. Even Paul's letters are not easily understood or necessarily obeyed. On one hand, Paul wrote as one having authority from God. But only when God's power opens the eyes, minds, and lives of certain readers do the words have their intended effect. The Bible's seeming popularity as a best seller in the United States has not meant that its words had a powerful influence on the nation. God's power is not automatically at work in the words of Scripture (or in any other holy words).

In a recent "word power" fad, some charismatic or Pentecostal leaders claimed that whatever they spoke or commanded would happen. They also connected this "name it and claim it" game to a view of faith that said "believe it and receive it." God supposedly promised to give whatever those leaders wanted. They just had to "believe God," and they would receive the desires of their hearts. Confession of a need would lead to possession.

What did selfish people need most? Televangelists like Pat Robertson, Jim Bakker, Oral Roberts, Kenneth Hagin, and Kenneth Copeland often confessed their need for money, and they came to possess much more than they needed. Many who sent money probably wondered what happened to the health and wealth *they* were promised. Special elite Christians even think they can command events to happen through word power and thus rule the world.[7]

The truth is that no human words will save the world, especially not the fake words of false prophets. Even the true words of Paul's gospel will not bring salvation and righteousness. Only through God's power can God's righteous will be done.

◆ ◆ ◆

In Romans 1:16-18, Paul develops a series of statements about the revelation of God in or upon people. He focuses on three phrases: the power of God (1:16), the righteousness of God (1:17), and the wrath of God (1:18). All three verses have a similar parallel structure. And all three (most obviously 1:18, in standard translations) refer to God's power in, through, or upon people, for better or for worse. That context is even more reason to translate 1:16 as emphasizing God's power poured out on believers rather than merely stressing the gospel message.

If my translation of 1:16 is correct, it also changes the

translation of 1:17 as follows: *"For God's righteousness is being re-vealed in the believing one out of faith unto faith, as it is written, 'The righteous one out of faith will live.' "* Instead of writing that God's righteousness is being revealed in the gospel, Paul echoes 1:16, where God's saving power is being manifested in everyone who is believing.[8]

The connections between 1:16 and 1:17, according to my translation, point to the fulfillment of passages like Psalm 98:1-2. Psalm 98:1 exalts God's saving power (the right hand and the arm symbolizing strength). Then the parallelism of the next verse equates the Lord's making known salvation with the re-vealing of his righteousness among the Gentiles. God's reveal-ing is dynamic, God acting to effect righteousness and salva-tion, not simply enlightenment to the mind.

The Greek translation of Isaiah 51:5 similarly speaks of God's righteousness (deliverance) and salvation going out among the Gentiles by means of his strong arm (compare Isa. 45:8; 46:13; 56:1). Paul quotes from the Psalms and Isaiah more than any other parts of the Old Testament; thus he is familiar with these passages about God's saving power and righteous-ness.[9]

God's power is producing salvation from sin, resulting in righteousness; and salvation from death, resulting in life. The tremendous power of God is so great that God's mighty strength can save those who are believing from the death of sin and create in them a new life of obedience (Eph. 1:19; 2:5, 10).[10] The obedience of faith (1:5) is thus described in 1:17 as God's righteousness reflected in the one having faith.

In 1:17, Paul quotes Habakkuk 2:4, which describes the righteous person. For Paul, the righteous one is the one in whom God's righteousness is being manifested. The righteous person is the one believing in God's power and thereby receiv-ing God's life and reflecting God's righteousness.[11]

One has to receive God's righteous kingship like a child in humble awareness that one's own smallness and weakness make one dependent on someone greater and stronger (Mark 10:15; Matt. 18:1-4). That is why weak sinners like tax collectors and harlots who know they need help will come under God's new kingship and righteousness before so-called righteous ones who already seem strong apart from God's new kingship (Mark 2:17; Matt. 21:31-32). Only the spiritually poor and meek who stand before God as beggars, hungering and thirsting for righteousness, will receive God's kingship and righteousness (Matt. 5:3, 5-6; 6:10, 33; 7:7-11). Righteousness characterizes the new life of God's salvation. Salvation is not just a spiritual experience in the past. God's mighty Spirit of holiness will reproduce that same holiness in people of faith (see 1:4, 6).

In 1:16-17, Paul uses the Greek present tense to emphasize the continual outworking of God's power. The word translated "believing" in 1:16 is present tense, as is the word translated "is being revealed" in 1:17. Both refer to the ongoing process of God's salvation among Jews and Gentiles who keep their faith and remain faithful. For Paul as for Jesus, eternal life (literally: life of the coming age), righteousness, and salvation have now begun in history. They will be fully experienced at the end of this present evil age. God's powerful rule (kingdom) is now proceeding in the midst of present history and will bring history to its final consummation.

I also connect the end of 1:16 ("to the Jew first and to the Gentile") with the phrase "out of faith unto faith" in 1:17. This latter phrase does not mean the ongoing faith of the righteous one. That thought is already present in the continuous "believing" of 1:16 and in the continuous "being revealed" of 1:17. The "out of faith" pointed to some *earlier* faith that was the foundation for present faith. The "unto faith" focuses on the future faith of those who would come to share that same faith. Note the phrase "unto the obedience of faith" in 1:5, which describes the future results of God's world mission.

The mention of "to the Jew first" in 1:16 is a hint about the basis of faith in the "out of faith" phrase in 1:17. For Paul and Jesus, salvation and faith begin with the Jews (see John 4:22; Acts 3:26; 13:46). But 1:16 also refers to believing in God's power now at work bringing salvation, which started with the ministry of Jesus. Jesus was the first Jew to have that faith in God's new saving power. Out of Jesus' faith, others also came to faith.[12] God's final salvation was first found in Jesus. He was the true way to life (John 14:6; Matt. 7:14). He was the first to declare the new day of God's great salvation (Heb. 1:2; 2:3; Luke 19:9-10). He was the pioneer of salvation (Heb. 2:10). The righteous one who shared the faith that was first experienced and defined by Jesus will also share the life of the new age of God's salvation.

Israel looked especially to their king as the one to be given God's righteousness (Ps. 72:1). Jesus, the Son of David, Israel's Messiah (1:3), now fulfills that hope. God's righteous will is to be done on earth by those to whom God's ruling power came (Matt. 6:10). Jesus taught and showed that the purpose of prayer is to open oneself to receiving God's enabling power so that one does God's will (compare Matt. 6:10 and 26:39-42).

The truth and love that Jesus taught and lived can lead others also to be like God in true righteousness and holiness (Eph. 4:15-16, 20-24, 32; 5:1-2, 25). Whoever is in Christ is united with Christ and becomes the righteousness of God (2 Cor. 5:21).[13] To gain Christ and to be in union with him is to have the righteousness from God that comes through "the faith of Christ" and to share that faith (Phil. 3:9, with NRSV note).

Abraham had a certain kind of faith that is foundational for Christians (Gal. 3:6-9). Yet faith in the fullest sense came into history only when Christ came (Gal. 3:23-26). Old Testament examples of faith—like Abel, Enoch, Noah, and Abraham (Heb. 11)—were imperfect compared to Jesus, the pioneer and perfecter of faith (Heb. 11:40—12:2). By a faithfulness that endured even the cross, Jesus pioneered a new covenant and a true obedience. Those under the new covenant follow the faith-life perfected by Jesus.[14]

The phrase "in the believing one" (1:17) does not limit faith to a private inner spiritual experience between the individual soul and God. God's righteousness and salvation are not just emotional experiences of crisis, psychological attitudes of trust, or rational beliefs of sincere souls. The words "out of faith unto faith" show that the faith of "the believing one" is based on and connected with the earlier faith of others, especially that of Jesus.

Jesus' faith manifested God's righteousness, not only through inner attitudes, but also in words and actions that were part of a mission "unto the obedience of faith" of others. Thus the context is about God's ongoing work in a faithful people throughout history, beginning with Jesus. The believing one is not isolated from other believing ones, past, present, and future. People are being united with Jesus' foundational faith and righteousness, and they are affecting others through God's power at work in them. After receiving power from the Holy Spirit, Jesus' disciples were to be witnesses in Jerusalem, in all Judea and Samaria, and to the ends of the earth (Acts 1:8).

Paul writes that God revealed Jesus in him (Paul) so that he might proclaim Jesus among the Gentiles (Gal. 1:16; see Gal. 2:20; 4:6). God's power transformed Paul and reproduced aspects of Jesus' life and mission in and through Paul.[15] The revelation of God's righteousness is incarnational. The messengers are just as important as the message. Jesus as God's Son was the unique incarnation of God, yet God's righteousness will also become incarnate in other children of God.

Jesus sent out his apostles to represent him among the lost sheep of Israel (Matt. 10:5). He also knew that in the future many Gentiles would come under God's kingship while many Jews would not (Matt. 8:5-13). Later, when Paul and his co-workers went throughout Gentile territory, they still made a point of going first to Jewish synagogues. God wanted the new faith to be made known first to the Jews (see Acts 13:5, 14, 46; 14:1; 16:13-14; 17:1-2, 10; 18:4).

There is still a place for world mission to continue the pattern of Jesus and Paul of going to the Jew first. Like Paul, who continually tried to "win Jews" (1 Cor. 9:20) as part of his God-given mission, many now can also make known God's special call to Jewish people. But they must do so with the new life of righteousness that Jesus lived and taught. Apart from a loving community of faithful disciples, their mission will lack credibility.

A main obstacle for Jews, and for others, has been the lack of concrete change among Christians. Where in the world are Jesus' kingdom and righteousness now? Is faith only private feelings or deep thoughts? What kind of righteousness is that? Indeed, the church has even persecuted Jews throughout its history. In doing so, it manifested its own faithless self-interest and violence. Yet sorrow for the terrible abuse of Jews by a corrupt Christendom must not stop the mission begun by Jesus and Paul to their own people.

✦ ✦ ✦

If the emphasis in 1:16-17 is on the present revelation of God's final saving power in the believing person, then 1:18 turns to its opposite: the present revelation of God's final wrath upon ungodly, unrighteous persons. That work of wrath is also expressed as a continuous "being revealed." If God's victory means life for the faithful, it also means death for those who continue to reject God. It is clear in 1:18 that the revelation of God's wrath is not in the gospel but upon people. This is another point in favor of my translation of 1:16-17, due to the close parallel structure of the three verses. Paul is noting God's power for good *and* for "bad" (for punishment) as it is manifested in or upon people (not in the gospel).

Those who reject a relationship of faith in God are ungodly. Instead of receiving God's righteousness, they are unrighteous (immoral) and receive God's wrath. That wrath is a punishment for the suppression of the truth about God. Paul is contrasting an intellectual knowledge of the truth with an experience of God's saving power. Intellectual knowledge means people are not innocent and must experience God's wrath. Even knowledge about the powerful God of Jesus through preaching the gospel often leads to God's wrath since most reject that message.

✦ ✦ ✦

Similarly, modern ideas of faith typically emphasize correct ideas or doctrines about God. One may contrast these ideas with Paul's use of *faith* as the daily experience of receiving God's saving power, which produces righteous living. Evangelism is not a quick exercise in getting people to accept certain facts about sin and salvation. Instead, evangelism means sharing one's life of faith, in word and deed, so God will use that witness to produce new faith in others. For God's righteousness is being manifested in the believing one out of faith unto faith (1:17).

There have been too many nominal Christians in church history who used shortcuts to reach "Christian" status. Religious rituals like baptism, the Lord's Supper, or going forward to accept Christ as Savior for forgiveness of sin are not substitutes for saving faith. Christians are not just sinners who have been forgiven. Such cheap grace, which supposedly justifies the sin but not the sinner, falls far short of transformation by God's power.[16] True Christians do sin sometimes. But their life in general will manifest God's righteousness (see 1 John 1:5-7; 2:29; 3:3, 6-7, 9-10; 4:7). Faithfulness and righteousness are the first-fruits of God's saving power.

Romans 1:19-32

God's Creative Power, an Ungodly World, and God's Wrath

AFTER introducing ungodliness in 1:18, Paul proceeds to portray a world that is rejecting its powerful Creator. That ungodly world, sinking deeper and deeper into idolatry and immorality, seems more powerful than God. But according to Paul's missionary message, sin's strong domination throughout the world is actually the result of God's wrath. By walking away from God the Creator, the world runs right into God the Judge.

Most ungodliness and unrighteousness in world history are not due to rejection of Jesus. Paul connects most evil with a denial of the truth about God, a truth revealed throughout all Creation. Since the beginning of human history, knowledge about the eternal and powerful God was manifested in Creation for all to see (1:19-20). The awesome universe of stars and planets, the vast ranges of mountains and canyons, the frightening storms of lightning and thunder, the billowing waves of oceans and seas, the marvelous beauty of plants and animals, and the amazing abilities of male and female human beings—these all reveal a powerful, invisible deity.

Even less awesome aspects of God's Creation, like birds or plants, witness to God's life-giving power (Matt. 6:26-30; see Acts 14:17; Job 12:7-10; Ps. 104:10-25). Both the tiniest details and the grandest designs of an ordered universe reveal the Creator God. Various Christian songs have celebrated that creative power of God, as does the first verse of "How Great Thou Art."

Those who turn their back on that truth about God have no excuse. There are no innocent "primitive" peoples. So-called primitive peoples are often closer to the beauty and forces of nature, and are more open to seeing spiritual power(s) behind those forces than are so-called civilized peoples.

Most religions of the world believe in a Great Spirit Creator. Mission to such peoples does well to relate Christian faith to those beliefs. One can even use the name of their Creator when referring to the God of the Bible. Yet the God of Jesus is described somewhat differently from the way they speak of their tribal Creator Spirit. As Paul reaches out to non-Jewish peoples, he uses the common Greek term for god (*theos*) when referring to his God. He can then reveal the one true God who created all things as the God who raised Jesus from the dead (see Acts 17:24-31).[1]

◆ ◆ ◆

Most missionaries who translated the Bible used local words for the supreme God. They usually welcomed and received translation assistance from those in the local culture. Such help gave them more sensitivity to the complexity of different beliefs and languages. Then there were other missionary translators who were not so careful.

Like most Africans, the Kikuyu people in Kenya have had a basic conception of one Creator. They use the name *Ngai* for the one who is Creator, Sustainer, and Ruler of all. Another name, *Murungu*, points to the Creator's incomparable greatness and power. When British colonialism and British missionaries took over, they rejected *Ngai*. Some thought the people confused *Ngai* with the spirits. Others said *Ngai* was more distant from daily life, where the spirits were given more importance. As a result, the missionaries were blind to the connection between *Ngai* or *Murungu* and the true Creator God.[2]

When Protestant missionaries first went to the Native American Navajo tribe, they used the English word God so that

Navajos would come to understand the one true God. The problem was that Navajos had a word pronounced almost like *God*—their word for a juniper bush. Even much later, some Navajos viewed the missionaries' religion as worshiping the juniper bush. Other missionaries have since learned that they need to use Navajo language for "the Eternal Spirit" if they are to communicate spiritual truths to the Navajo culture.[3]

People have known about and believed in the existence of a Creator God, but such so-called faith fell short of what God expected. While they feared God's destructive power, people supposed they could persuade God to be nice to them by performing a few rituals. Sometimes more difficult or expensive rituals were thought necessary to get the attention of God or special spiritual forces. Angry spirits needed to be calmed down or cast out, especially when bad things happened. Special secret rites done by those who knew the right prayers, words, gifts, or sacrifices might convince a reluctant spiritual power to act in their favor. God or other spirits would supposedly not give blessings unless they first received gifts and proper respect from those wanting the blessings. Thus religion was sometimes a game of trying to bribe spiritual power to do what people wanted. The goal was the created blessing, not the Creator.

Paul says that the world refuses to worship thankfully the God of power and glory who is known through the wonders of creation (1:21). It has quickly come to value creation more than the Creator. The proper order has been reversed, as suggested by this parable: The letters spelling *god* when reversed turn out to be *dog*, claimed as "man's best friend."

Humankind has chosen to give glory to creation and has made idols of images of mortal humans and animals (1:23). Ancient Egyptian adoration of birds, animals, and reptiles is still around today. Many Hindus consider cows sacred, almost divine. Since they think people are reincarnated as animals (for better or worse), the highest caste, a Brahman, might pray to be reincarnated as a cow. Such a reincarnation would supposedly be another important step on the way to ultimate reality.

Many Roman Catholics have considered Mary the mother of Jesus to be sacred, almost divine. For them, Mary is the "Mother of God" and is sometimes elevated above God in popular devotion. Some use her as a warm motherly mediator who goes before a harsh father God. If they presume that God is the demanding Father and Jesus the dead Son (and the Holy Spirit the impersonal ghost), then they choose Mary to be the sympathetic mother. She shows compassion on God's children and gains favors from the Father.

Mother Nature in the form of Gaia, the Greek goddess of the earth, is now making a comeback. Some who have rightly expressed concern for the pollution of nature have wrongly gone on to connect ecology with Gaia. Their spiritual commitment to nature becomes personalized in the goddess Gaia. That commitment often includes the primacy of nature, or certain animal species, over people.

The Greek and Roman gods and goddesses were all too human. In the midst of a mission to Lystra, a healing miracle caused Gentiles to call Paul and Barnabas gods. Barnabas they called Zeus, and Paul they called Hermes (Acts 14:11-12). Paul's response was to challenge them to turn from idols to the living God, who created the heaven, earth, and sea, and all that is in them (Acts 14:15). Paul's later message to the religious Greeks in Athens (especially Acts 17:22-26, 29) also reflects his instruction to the Roman readers in 1:19-23. Such teaching prepares them to continue his mission.

Paul knows that the Gentiles have made their own powerful heroes or heroines into gods or goddesses. In doing so, they think they will benefit and be the wise ones who know the way to enjoyment of "the good life" (1:22). The "wise Greeks" (1:14) point with pride to the victories of Alexander the Great. Their leaders conquered the populated world and also came to be called gods. Later, the Romans enjoy the security of the Roman Empire due to its imperial forces. The Roman emperors also come to be called gods. Prosperity and peace through strength are the rewards of macho imperial might. They exchange the Creator of heaven and earth for the human creators of power, pride, prosperity, pleasure, and peace. Not too smart!

During the eighteenth century, new scientific knowledge led to a supposed time of Enlightenment. Many people abandoned religious explanations and superstitions and accepted the natural laws of cause and effect as reality. They thought human reasoning by scientific analysis would lead to understanding and to mastery over nature. A religious deism then developed which affirmed that God created the world but then left it to run according to natural laws. Instead of God, human reason and natural law were in charge of the universe.

People reasoned that they had human rights like the right to life, liberty, and the pursuit of happiness. The one to enforce those rights would be the nation-state. Beginning with the French Revolution, the source of "liberty, equality, and brotherhood" was to be the nation-state, a nationally united people—not a king, feudal lord, or God. Progress through human reason and political power would lead to future happiness. People had faith in themselves and in reason. There was no need for a powerful God.

Yet the state often asserted its power by canceling certain rights for the sake of supposed future happiness. The state thus became a god that could not produce everything it promised. Patriotic cries like "Give me liberty or give me death" chose the right of liberty over the right of life. Third-world dictators chose the right of "national security" over most other rights, including the rights of liberty and life. Communist leaders preferred the right of equality over the rights of freedom or religion. Such communists also denied and defied any belief in God or need for God.

Powerful industrialists like the Fords and Rockefellers helped create the American dream of middle-class affluence for many in the United States, but at the expense of the third world. Through domineering businessmen, militaries, and politicians, the United States has come to manipulate much of the world. Moreover, they do it in the name of American gods like freedom, democracy, capitalism, progress, scientific technology, and modernization. Public schools and civil religion honor those gods and their heroes as the foundation of a civilized world. The salvation of success led to accepting those corporate powers as their personal saviors and lords.

How many Christian ministers or missionaries question those gods? How many have been or are their high priests (a combination of religions)? Is not that mixture of gods a form of Western syncretism? How many churches recognize and reject those first world idols? Too few, because they also worship those same false gods.[4]

Many religions, including Christianity, emphasize holy rituals as a means of persuading a powerful God to prosper them. People submit to priestly rites at sacred places and altars for the sake of practical benefits like protection, good health, good crops, social status, or national success. Religious leaders use their special access to God to gain more followers, more influence, and nicer holy places. To date, churches in the United States have spent tens of billions of dollars on buildings. They are honoring a God that Paul described as Creator and Lord over all, who thus does not live in temples built by human hands (Acts 17:24). Wealthy churches love to decorate the "house of God" with new organs, comfortable pews, thick carpet, and air conditioning. Holy sanctuaries!

Those who domesticate the almighty Creator God into their "in-house" God also try to limit that God to their own people. The God over all the world becomes the god of a certain tribe or people or nation. Many Americans think God has given them great prosperity and will bless their side in all their wars. Most Germans agreed with Hitler that God would help them win their wars. Many contemporary Christian churches continue to pray for victory whenever their nation goes to war. The one Creator God has been re-created into many national gods.

As we near the twenty-first century, a modern global civilization continues to emerge. With its center in the first world (especially the United States, Japan, and Germany), this new civilization is crossing boundaries of nations, races, religions, and cultures. Multinational corporations, technologies, and ideals are found everywhere in the world. Democracy is breaking out all over, and capitalism is breaking in. Corporations build massive organizations to promote mass consumption.

Mass media advertise the newest corporate products and

promote the proper corporate ideals. City schools produce mass education through mass information. Likewise, city churches market mass religion through sensitivity to mass feelings and needs. Expert managers in each area including religion make sure that modern mass society remains united, productive, and efficient. They claim they can conquer the created world. Everyone seems to agree and conform.

Happiness is a warm feeling about everyone, especially about oneself. Releasing the human potential of the individual self means freedom from all that is felt to be negative. A warm relationship with Christ and others is supposedly the way to salvation: a happy self. Happy individuals in happy homes, happy stores, happy schools, and happy churches would make a happy world.[5]

So what happened to the world God made? Is God happy with the wonderful world of Disney and Hollywood, McDonald's and Coca-Cola, TV and televangelists? Where does the Creator God fit in the midst of all the human creators and happy consumers? God's creation and human cultures are good until human dominance manipulates other humans and nonhumans into making human creations absolute (and absolutely necessary). God is still being exchanged for a different-sized god to fit human desires and selfishness. In popular thought, the original size never made anybody look that good anyway.

People who want lesser gods for their own glory or happiness still experience God's power as wrath (1:18). That wrath is implied in 1:21, where such thoughts about human glory lead to being given up (by God) to worthless thinking and to receiving darkened minds. Then, in 1:24, 26, 28, Paul emphasizes God's wrath through the phrase: "God gave them up." While the peoples of the world desire the happy days and nights that powerful gods supposedly give, God's wrath lets them dishonor their bodies (1:24). This degradation of their bodies in sexual immorality is part of God's penalty for their idolatry. Because they exchange the truth of God for a lie, they also end up exchanging natural sexual relations for unnatural relations (1:25-27).

Dishonorable desires lead to shameful homosexual actions (1:26-27). Homosexual activity and lust (rather than homosexual orientation) are Paul's focus. Many Greeks and Romans at that time actually preferred such love to that between husband and wife.[6] Currently, various churches approve gay sexual activity, including gay "marriages" officiated by church leaders who themselves might be openly and actively gay. They all worship the God who created them, but the God of Jesus and Paul will not take credit (or blame) for their desires and actions.

Ignoring the true Creator, they also abandon God's natural created order of male and female sexual relationships, in marriage. So God has abandoned them to their idolatrous thinking and improper living (1:28). God's gracious power is withdrawn and they sink to a lower level of sin. In Matthew 10:15 (and 11:23-24), Jesus used Sodom and Gomorrah as special examples of those who would receive God's judgment. While the sins of Sodom were many (Ezek. 16:49-50), its homosexual immorality (see Gen. 19:1-11) was proverbial in later Jewish writings. Jude 7-8 also parallels the immorality of Sodom and Gomorrah (including lust for angelic flesh) with the defiled flesh of certain false teachers involved in sexual immorality, probably including homosexual immorality.[7]

Unfortunately, some have misused such words of disapproval to promote hatred and violence against homosexually inclined people. According to the law of Moses, certain kinds of sexual immorality, including homosexual actions, were to be punished by death (Lev. 20:10-16). But Jesus refused violence against those who sinned in such ways (John 8:3-11). He instead exposed the sinfulness of those who wanted to kill. Paul in Romans 2 confronts judgmental Jews with their own sin. Jesus said it would be more bearable for Sodom and Gomorrah on judgment day than for the Jewish towns that rejected the mission of his disciples (Matt. 10:15). Homosexual activity should not be viewed as the worst of all sins.

Some people accept homosexuality as a natural orientation that can't be changed. They differ from Paul's description of an unnatural sexual lust and activity which is chosen. A significant minority, especially older boys and younger men, have experimented with homosexual activity only to reject it and become happily married heterosexuals. Others develop a strong homosexual orientation that remains with them all their lives. Homosexuality at times grows out of deep roots that go back to childhood abuse. Yet even those roots can sometimes be overcome through God's power.

There may still be an ongoing struggle with homosexual temptations, as with heterosexual temptations for other people, but God's grace can decrease their frequency and strength. The minds of some can be renewed so that their sexual interest becomes more heterosexual, without becoming lustful or immoral. All who by God's power are overcoming the temptations of an ongoing homosexual orientation should be welcomed into the Christian fellowship. They should feel free to share their temptations and be given friendship and encouragement to remain faithful.[8]

In 1:29-31, Paul describes unrighteousness in more detail. He lists such terms as unrighteousness, evil, and bad; included with them is greed or desire for what is not one's own (compare the desires of 1:24, 26). Continually unsatisfied desire for more and more leads to passions that pervert the created order. In Colossians 3:5 and Ephesians 5:5, Paul connects covetousness with idolatry. Jesus also taught the impossibility of serving God and money (Matt. 6:24). God is not happy with a greedy consumer culture. The rest of the list of 1:29-31 includes sins like attitudes of envy and pride that lead to being heartless and ruthless; and actions like murder, strife, deceit, gossip, slander, and boasting.

The poor and oppressed in the third world know all too well about the evil described by Paul. Only a few of their leaders are benefiting from the greed and violence of the first world. Prosperous landlords and powerful militaries keep the many poor in their place, at the bottom. Similarly, second world communist countries require large militaries commanded by elite leaders to enforce their socialist systems. The elites of capitalism and communism look a lot alike. And those elites are consistently ruthless, murdering some who question their leadership and slandering them as traitors. Those who speak out against the greed of the wealthy and the violence of the powerful often experience imprisonment, torture, or death.

Western leaders and third-world friends who slander the poor even boast about being God-fearing persons fighting against godless communists. But their deadly actions show that they themselves are dead, presently abandoned by God.

People knew to some extent that ungodliness (unbelief) and unrighteousness deserved death from God (1:32). If the righteous one out of faith would live (1:17), the unrighteous one out of unbelief would die. God's wrath had left them in such darkness that they not only committed such sins, but encouraged others to do them. Their mission was to multiply sin. Their approval of evil gave evildoers an appearance of respectability.

Paul writes to the Roman Christians about God's wrath to assure them that such evil and opposition to God are not stronger than God. Such overwhelming darkness is rather the result of God's wrath against wickedness. Yet God's power is also transforming certain people all over the world. God is re-creating a righteous people among the peoples of the earth (1:16-17). There must be no compromise with worldly wisdom for the sake of a "successful" world or mission. Paul is preparing the readers of this letter to faithfully follow his message and mission.

Romans 2:1-16

God's Judgment of the World: The Jew First and the Gentile

I N 2:1, Paul begins a conversation with an imaginary individual who is cheering Paul's previous words in 1:19-32. God's wrath against the idolatry and immorality of the Gentile world is right and just. But Paul doesn't welcome that individual with open arms as a partner in world mission. According to Paul, God is working out a process of wrath in history. Yet this other individual acts as though all is said and done. Applauding God's wrath, he pronounces his own final judgment on the Gentiles. He despises Gentiles.

However, Paul has not said that God has completely given up on the Gentiles. The individual's condemnation of the Gentiles sounds a lot like the strife, malice, boasting, arrogance, and deceit described in 1:29-31. His words condemning Gentiles are actually approving the same hateful pride and prejudice found among the Gentiles (see 1:32). He is without excuse because he does the same things (2:1). So Paul challenges him: When you condemn others, you condemn yourself because you do the same things (2:1).

He is deceiving himself and exchanging the truth of God for a lie (see 1:25). Only the powerful Creator has the right to make a final judgment, not the creature (see 1:20). Everyone knows that God's judgment against all evil is according to the truth, the whole truth, and nothing but the truth (2:2). Paul pointedly asks: Will you yourself, a sinful judge of sinners, escape God's final judgment (2:3)?

Just as God's power is unto salvation to everyone who is believing, to the Jew first and to the Gentile (1:16), so God's judgment is according to truth upon everyone who does evil, to the Jew first and to the Gentile (2:2, 9). The reference to Jew and Gentile twice in 2:9-10, where the Jew will be first to receive God's final judgment (2:9) or reward (2:10), shows that Paul is here focusing on the Jew. The individual of 2:1-5 is especially representative of Jews. Most Jews strongly condemn the evil of the Gentile world. After hearing Paul's words in 1:19-32 against such evil, they welcome him as a fellow Jew who speaks the truth. Yet Paul then accuses them of doing the same evil!

The Old Testament prophets denounced the evil of other nations and then surprised Israel by exposing its own evil (for example, Amos 1–2). Jesus contrasted the evil of Sodom and Gomorrah (see 1:26-27) with the worse evil of Jewish towns that rejected the mission of his disciples (Matt. 10:15; compare Ezek. 16:46-52). He especially criticized self-righteous Pharisees who regarded all others as condemned sinners (Luke 18:9-14; John 8:7). God humbles those who exalt themselves (Luke 18:14).[1]

Paul's writing reflects his own previous mission encounters and teaching style. Based on earlier debates, he develops dramatic dialogues as case studies to prepare others to engage in similar discussions. The conversation of 2:1-5 is an example of how Paul's readers can confront certain Jews, and Gentiles, as part of their own mission.

Religious leaders who emphasize one another's positive points have more recently used the word dialogue for such discussions. They might also clarify differences between their religions. Such beginning steps are important in building mutual respect and sensitivity. Willingness to listen to and learn from other religions shows humility and openness to two-way communication. Paul also affirms certain aspects of the Jewish religion and clarifies differences between Judaism and the faith of

Jesus. At the same time, Paul's dialogue with other Jews includes confrontation and challenge. He is certain of the truth and righteousness of Jesus' way. Paul also knows that such dialogue sometimes has led others to condemn and persecute him.

Throughout the world's rebellious history, God continues to show kindness, patience, and long-suffering (2:4). But people must not presume that God will always be so kind. The goal of God's kindness is repentance. Especially the Jew, to whose people God has shown special mercy in the past, should not assume that such mercy will continue in the future. Even in the past, a hardened nation usually rejected continual calls to repentance by Old Testament prophets (see Acts 7:51-53).

Now the climax of God's kindness to Israel has come in the person of Jesus the Messiah. Yet most of Israel rejected Jesus' call to repentance. Such hardness of heart (2:5) is like the darkened heart of those they condemned (1:21). God's present wrath against such evil will come to a climax in a final day of wrath, when God's righteous judgment will be revealed against all unrighteousness (2:5).

Repentance has sometimes come to mean mere sorrow for sin and confession of it. So-called Christians think they are righteous through the penitence of confessing sins or of admitting that they are sinners. As long as they keep confessing (that they have not changed), they think they can be considered righteous due to God's forgiveness. They quote 1 John 1:9 about confessing sins to one who is faithful and just and forgives sin.

But true repentance includes turning from sin and doing right (see Matt. 3:2, 8, 10; 2 Cor. 7:9-11). So repentant children of God can also quote 1 John 1:6 about the lie of those who say they have fellowship with God while walking in the darkness. Those who want to be purified from sin by Jesus' blood must walk in the light (1 John 1:7). All claims to repentance must face the test of walking or living as Jesus did (1 John 2:6). Only the one who has truly repented can have confidence before Christ when he comes again to judge the world (1 John 2:28).

In the end, God will judge everyone according to their works, both Jew and Gentile (2:6; see Matt. 16:27; John 5:28-29; 2 Cor. 5:10). Those who want to increase their own glory and honor by disobeying God's truth and doing evil will end up with trials and troubles (2:8-9; see 1:18, 21-23, 25, 29-30). Judgment against evil will begin with Jews. Their guilt is greater because they disobeyed God's special revelation to them.

On the other hand, all who have patiently suffered trials and troubles because of opposing evil will receive God's reward (2:7). They will find the fullness of what they are seeking: the glory, honor, peace, and immortality of God (see Matt. 6:33). Such steadfastness despite suffering reflects the good work of faith(fulness) before God (see 2 Thess. 1:4). By sharing God's dishonor (1:21) in the present time, they will also share God's final honor and glory. Jesus taught that persecution would result from a world mission of proclaiming God's powerful rule (kingdom). Yet whoever patiently endures to the end will be saved (Matt. 24:9-14).

Certain Jews and Gentiles will finally share in the glorious peace of God's eternal life (2:7, 10). Again, Jews will be first, due to God's special kindness. Their reward will be the result of sharing God's patience and kindness in the midst of a greedy, hard-hearted world. God has no favorites in the sense that only Jews are God's people (2:11; see Acts 10:34-35). God's chosen people, the Jews, cannot condemn all Gentiles. Righteousness is found among some Gentiles, and unrighteousness is found among some Jews. God is not partial (2:11) because everyone, both Jews and Gentiles, will finally be judged according to their works (2:6). God is not prejudiced because all who do good, not just Jews, will be rewarded in the end (2:10). And God is not racist because all who do evil, Jews and also Gentiles, will be punished in the end (2:9).

So why have churches been so racist? White churches which have judged nonwhite peoples as unworthy will be judged according to their works. In the end, God will judge those who judge themselves to be superior to other races. God will not be partial to white people or to so-called Christian nations. For about two centuries, white missionaries have been especially honored in North American churches. White ministers were perhaps next in line as God's supposed favorites. Average church members ended up as third-class citizens in the church.

And nonwhite members and ministers came in last. Special honor went to those with the so-called privileges of white religious leadership. White was right. Brown, get down! Black, stay back!

In contrast to that, Paul portrays his own mission as one of dishonor and disgrace. Apostles or missionaries like Paul are fools for Christ, which means being last, like those condemned to die, weak, poor, persecuted, cursed, and slandered (1 Cor. 4:9-13). Paul thus warns the Corinthians that the world's wisdom which applauds certain Christian leaders at the expense of others is not God's wisdom. Those who now receive rewards like power, popularity, and privilege must be warned like other former false prophets and false apostles (see Luke 6:24-26; 2 Cor. 11:13-20).

If God appears weak by patiently and kindly pursuing a persecuted mission, the final day of wrath will show God's authority to enforce what is right and just. Yet God's power will be seen not only in that final revelation of eternal glory and honor and peace. God's power is also found among those who remain patiently faithful in their life and mission despite the opposition of the world. Such righteous ones will live and gain eternal life (1:17; 2:7; see John 5:29). For God's power leads to salvation, to glory and honor and peace for everyone who believes (and is empowered to work the good), to the Jew first and to the Gentile (1:16; 2:10).

All peoples will finally be judged, whether or not they have the Jewish law. While sinful Gentiles who don't have the law of Moses will perish for their sin, Jews who have the law will also be judged for their sin (2:12). The main issue is not the law, but sin or righteousness.

Those who hear the teaching of the law are not righteous if they continue to break the law (2:13). The law is one of the Jews' privileges that leads to their being the first to receive judgment (2:9). To whom much is given, much is required (Luke 12:48). On the other hand, some Gentiles, who naturally do not have the law of the Jews, practice the most important commands of the law (2:14). Such Gentiles show that the doing of the law is written in their hearts (2:15). Paul is contrasting the law written on stone with the law written in hearts. The former was the law of Moses while the latter refers to a special work of God's power that enables certain Gentiles to do the main work of the law.

Paul has in mind those Gentiles described in 1:16-17 and 2:7, 10. Their faith focuses on God's power, and their righteousness reflects God's righteousness as revealed in the faith of Jesus. Jesus is the ultimate interpreter of the law of Moses and defined the most important requirements of the law. And Jesus fulfilled the promise of Jeremiah that God would make a new covenant and write the law on the hearts of believers (Jer. 31:33; 2 Cor. 3:3).[2]

God's judgment does not depend on the mixed emotions of one's own thoughts or conscience about having done right or wrong, nor does it depend on the judgments of others. Each person will finally be judged according to those secrets that reflect (or reject) God's righteousness (2:16; see 1 John 3:18-20). Only those who do the righteous demands of the law will be judged as righteous (2:13). All other religious behavior or respectable appearance might receive the praise of people. But God will judge according to those secrets written on hearts that lead to manifesting Jesus' kind of righteousness (2:14-16).

Christ Jesus, whom certain "lawless" Jewish leaders condemned to death, will be the one through whom God the Father judges humankind. Jesus himself taught that the faith of certain Gentiles would put to shame the faithlessness of many Jews (see Matt. 8:10). The basis for judgment is not religious words or miraculous works but doing the will of Jesus' heavenly Father (Matt. 7:21; see James 1:22, 25). There will be no reward for those who do good works to be seen and praised by other people (Matt. 6:1-2). Yet those who give alms to the poor secretly will find that their heavenly Father has seen their secrets and will reward them (Matt. 6:3-4).

Through such writing, Paul continues to show how his gospel confronts Jews who are proud of knowing the law of Moses and do certain works of the law so others will think well of them. Similarly, those who claim to be Christians because they know the gospel or do certain good works must be challenged when they fail to obey the gospel. Jesus warns his hearers about the danger of not living according to his teaching (Matt. 7:26). The gospel by itself is not the power of God. God's power is seen when people live righteously as God is righteous (1:16-17).

✦ ✦ ✦

Christian education does not always lead to doing right. Even seminary training is oriented more toward producing successful, professional pastors and teachers, only some of whom may also reflect God's righteousness. Success is often measured by the praise of people, such as increasing popularity and numerical growth.

Many people who claim to be Christians do not reflect the reality of Christ's kind of faith. Too often faith in Christ and belief in Christian doctrines have not included following Christ's teaching and example. Instead, Christianity, Christendom, and the church have often pursued human praise, economic wealth, political power, military might, racial prejudice, and cultural arrogance. But the sin and unrighteousness of the "Christian" world calls for greater judgment, in accord with the principles of 2:9, 12.

Cardinal Jaime Sin, the Cardinal Sin of the Philippines, both worked with and was critical of the former dictator, Ferdinand Marcos. His critical collaboration included jokes about how he rode in a car with Ferdinand and his wife, Imelda, and felt like Jesus on the cross, situated between two thieves. After many years of that conjugal dictatorship, Cardinal Sin finally turned more decisively against the Marcoses. He helped form an anti-Marcos coalition to try to defeat him in an election. He urged a mostly Catholic Filipino nation to vote their conscience. This was another way of saying, Vote for Corazon Aquino.

After Marcos stole the election from Aquino, Sin backed two military leaders who rebelled against Marcos. He called on the people of Manila to protect the officers from the tanks and planes of Marcos. The result was an outpouring of nonviolent people power, including priests and nuns who blocked tanks with their bodies. Marcos was finally forced to flee, seemingly a clear victory of good over evil, of righteousness (Sin) over sin.

Wrong! A nation of a few elites and many poor changed little after Marcos fled. Aquino's and Sin's pious words of hope for the future proved to be empty. They seemed so righteous in condemning the obvious villain, Marcos. Yet it turned out that they were doing the same things. The whole morality play of peaceful people power simply led to control by another politically powerful group with alliances to U.S. and Filipino elites. Their righteous condemnation of Marcos merely masked their own unrighteous greed for greater power and wealth. Cardinal Sin continued to collaborate with the national and international elite, while the many poor continued to suffer.

On another level, the Catholic pope, John Paul II, condemned Cardinal Sin for his involvement in politics and for joining in that power struggle. Yet the reason the pope spoke against Sin was because the pope (like U.S. president Reagan) supported Marcos, an outspoken anticommunist. So the pope himself was deeply involved in politics and in international power struggles.[3]

Liberation theologies of the third world have especially challenged first-world churches and theologians. Western theologies have stressed the authority of the Bible or the pope and most other human authorities or powers that be. Western academic theology has been too abstract and philosophical, too willing to please its own comfortable people. Biblical studies have been too technical and historical to bring much challenge to the status quo.

Liberation theologies call for concrete and practical reflections that relate to the present history of the poor and oppressed. The institutional church has historically sided with the wealthy and powerful and thus been powerless to do right in an unjust world. That church needs a radical conversion to the God of Jesus, who spoke good news to the poor. The church's mission must include a prophetic voice against the high and mighty, and a humble love for the weak and lowly. Sinful social structures and more personal forms of sin must be exposed.

One could also raise questions about liberation theologians. Do they overemphasize national political liberation at the expense of personal (not private) transformation or small-scale acts of love? Are most of them too optimistic about human ability to transform society? Do they often assume that saving grace has already been extended to all people because of Christ's death? Do too many of them accept the priority of Marxist economic theory? Nevertheless, there is a need to continue to listen and dialogue with liberation theologians.[4]

The mission of the church needs to be liberated from many historical ties that bind. The word *mission* only began to be used for the church's extension into nonchurched areas in the late Middle Ages. Established churches in Europe cooperated with political authorities to expand the power of the state and church throughout the rest of the world. So the church's mission involved sending religious specialists (priests or bishops) approved by the state authorities. Such missionaries had the mandate and power to pronounce salvation on those who professed certain truths and to extend the European religious institutions and system.[5]

The close connection between church and state is called Christendom, which tried to build God's kingdom by "civilizing" and "Christianizing" whole societies. Those "inferior" societies were judged as idolatrous and immoral. During much of the Middle Ages, church leaders dominated the state. After that, other rulers in Europe again gained power over the church, yet they still had close contacts with religious leaders and preserved the church's privileges. Professional clergy in state churches enjoyed all the comforts and pleasures of respectable careers. Meanwhile, most of the common people had little to do with their religious "superiors" and their power struggles and alliances with the state.

Later, when countries like the United States officially separated church and state, the idea of a Christian society or nation remained popular. Until more recently, church leaders were also community leaders. Clergy worked with other elite officials to influence the direction of their cities and villages. Although there was not the state church of earlier Christendom, many of Christendom's advantages and disadvantages remained.

The church and clergy remained respectable and reproduced impressive institutions on a national scale. Political leaders continued to use the name of God and the support of churches for their own purposes. Rich businessmen often controlled the pay scale of local pastors, making them religious employees of their society's economic establishment. The problem was that the works of an official Christendom or an unofficial "Christian civilization" were not the works of Jesus. Jesus rejected such pride and privileges and called the religious leaders of his day to repent.[6]

Christendom's churches and schools and hospitals were impressive institutions with large buildings requiring large budgets, professional leaders, and wealthy donors. Wealthy men and nations promoted their civilization around the world. They set out to rescue other peoples, judged as poor, lazy heathens. Third-world mission institutions then became dependent on foreign money and on foreign missionaries to administer the money and institutions.[7]

During colonial domination of Africa, Christian missions that depended on the good will of colonial powers managed most educational institutions. The mission of nation building employed numerous educational workers and had great influence and prestige. When colonialism ended, however, the new independent governments took over many such institutions for the sake of national pride and prestige. African mission employees became government employees. The greater power of the new governments overthrew the considerable power of the missions.[8]

Throughout the long march of Christendom, Christians thought they were making progress, compared to Jesus' way. They were really returning to the Old Testament vision of an awesome temple for worship and a godly nation for service. As in the Old Testament period, God did not remain silent in the midst of such official displays. Because of the proud domination that ignored or oppressed the humble poor, God called new leaders to speak and act. During the later O.T. period, God called prophets like Amos (a shepherd) and Jeremiah (a youth) to confront the country's official leaders. They were lay missionaries, sent by God to call Israel's official priests and princes to repent and return to the primitive rule of life given by God to Moses.[9]

Church leaders knew of Jesus' and Paul's way of small groups composed mostly of poor disciples meeting in homes. But they judged that as being too insignificant for proper worship and service of almighty God. Such house churches were marginal to the surrounding society. Though their impact was felt, they were definitely not mainstream.

Jesus' narrow gate that leads to life was later exchanged for the wide gate that led to Christendom. The active, temporary apostolic mission that shared the gospel for a limited time in various places was exchanged for the long-term, highly specialized careers of Christendom. Jesus' foolishness and failure were traded for the world's wisdom and honor. Only a smaller minority in each generation still chooses Jesus' way. But Jesus will have the final say.

Romans 2:17-29

Lawless Teachers of the Jewish Law

PAUL already named Jews as his main concern in 2:9-10. And in 2:12-15, he repeatedly writes about the Jewish law. In 2:17, he increases the drama of his dialogue with Jews by addressing another Jew directly (as in 2:1-5). Paul begins, You proudly call yourself a Jew and put all your faith in the law of Moses, boasting in God as the provider of those privileges (2:17). Through your law, you know God's will and approve its superior teaching (2:18). You see yourself as a sure guide to the blind and as a light to the Gentiles who wander in the dark (2:19; see Isa. 42:6; 49:6). Your mission is teaching that law to ignorant "heathens" who are like helpless little children (2:20).

Paul's challenge in 2:17-20 fits not only the mission of certain Jews then but also the mission of many Christians in our time. Western Christians have described their mission to the "dark" corners of the third world as representatives of a chosen (Christian) nation. An important part of the task is teaching the Bible (including the law of Moses) to those "pagans." But respect for the authority or inerrancy of the Bible does not necessarily lead to following the faith of Jesus.

A paternalism that treats adults like children causes deep humiliation and anger. Pretending to be civilized, they speak as racists by calling other peoples "lower races" or "dumb creatures." They view other peoples as mission fields but think of their own people as pleasing to God. Thus they repeat the sin of those proud first-century Jews. Every society stumbles around in its own forms of darkness.

Such pride in a mission of teaching Moses' law leads to another challenge from Paul. As in 2:1-5, Paul claims that this Jew does not practice what he preaches (2:21-23). Paul presses his point: You teach others; don't you teach yourself? You preach the law: Do not steal. How about you? Do you steal? You teach: Don't commit adultery. So do you commit adultery? You hate Gentile idols. But do you rob temples? You boast above all in your godly laws. Yet do you dishonor God by disobeying those laws?

Thus his religion is powerless because he fails to follow the law he knows and teaches (2:20-23; 2 Tim. 3:5). Jesus also confronted other Jews because they did not keep the law (John 7:19; Matt. 23:2-3). Instead of being light to the blind, they were blind guides (Matt. 15:14; 23:16, 24). They traveled long distances to win a convert, but made the new convert twice as bad as they themselves (Matt. 23:15).

In 2:21-22, Paul lists three of the Ten Commandments of Moses. Although the Jew's mission taught Gentiles not to steal, commit adultery, or practice idolatry, this Jew was doing those very things. So the one teaching the law was "lawless" (an outlaw). Like the Gentile, the Jew claimed to be wise but became a fool (see 1:22).

The mention of Jewish adultery reflects somewhat the Gentile homosexual activity condemned in 1:26-27. Yet Paul describes a lawlessness that emphasizes the economic exploitation of stealing and robbing temples, with the latter being the counterpart of hating idols. In other letters, Paul also closely connects idolatry with greed or covetousness (see 1 Cor. 5:10-11; Eph. 5:5; and Col. 3:5, all of which also denounce sexual immorality). Such Jews, who despise Gentile idolatry and sexual immorality, are themselves full of idolatrous greed and desires (see 1:23-29). All such desires come out of the same dirty mind (Matt. 15:19).

Jesus likewise warned about the danger of making mammon or money an idol, and trying to serve both it and God (Matt. 6:24). When Jesus upset the business in the temple in a final confrontation, he referred to God's house of prayer as having become a den of robbers (Matt. 21:12-13).[1] The leading priestly families vastly increased their wealth through their exclusive temple business of selling animals for sacrifice. Moreover, the Pharisees and teachers of the law used their religious and legal status to satisfy their love for money through such means as "devouring widows' houses" (Luke 16:13-15; 20:46-47). In the same context, Jesus used the word *adultery* to describe another abuse of women: divorcing one's wife and marrying another woman (Luke 16:18; compare the list of sins in Luke 18:11). Even the lustful desire for another woman was adultery (Matt. 5:27-28).

Paul could also be alluding to a famous scandal in Rome almost forty years earlier. Four Jews who lived in Rome convinced a noble Roman lady to give a large amount of money to the Jerusalem temple. One of the four Jews claimed to be a teacher of Gentiles, and the Roman lady converted to the Jewish faith. The four Jews, however, kept the gift for themselves, thus robbing the Jerusalem temple of the money. When the Roman emperor heard about the scandal, he expelled many resident Jews from Rome. Thus some Gentiles thought of Jews as temple robbers.[2] Acts 19:37 also suggests that some citizens of Ephesus accused missionary Jews like Paul of robbing Gentile temples. In fact, certain Jews did remove gold or silver idols from Gentile temples for the sake of personal profit.[3]

In 2 Corinthians, written just before Romans, Paul warns against Jewish false apostles who are seeking to make money from their mission (2 Cor. 2:17; 4:2; 11:13, 20, 22). In contrast to them, Paul mostly supports himself by working with his hands (1 Cor. 4:12; 1 Thess. 2:9; 2 Thess. 3:8; Acts 20:34). He wants to give the gospel free of charge (1 Cor. 9:18; 2 Cor. 11:7). Paul is willing to endure hard manual labor for low wages so no one can suspect his mission of being done out of greed (2 Cor. 6:3-5, 10). From time to time, Paul does accept certain gifts from churches, but those gifts only help to make up for the need due to his poverty (2 Cor. 11:7-9). His toil and hardship are part of his weakness through which God's power is manifested (2 Cor. 11:27, 29-30; 12:9-10).[4]

According to Paul, those who claim to serve God while seeking their own honor and glory dishonor God (2:23; compare charges against Gentiles in 1:23-25). Paul quotes Isaiah 52:5 to show how the dishonorable Jewish mission to Gentiles leads to the dishonoring and blaspheming of God's name among those Gentiles (2:24). Jesus taught his disciples to pray that God's name be hallowed or honored through the coming of God's kingly power, which would help them do the will of God (Matt. 6:9-10). Obedience through faith in God's power honors God's name and manifests God's righteousness among the Gentiles (see 1:16-17). But the Jewish mission described in 2:17-24 is producing the exact opposite.

Paul knows that the Roman Christians will also have to face competition from such Jewish missionaries if they continue Paul's mission. These Jewish missionaries have been following Paul around, trying to correct Gentile converts. Paul's readers need to know how to deal with such a false mission.

In more recent mission work, greed for money by various Christian leaders has continued to dishonor God. Perhaps the most famous recent scandal was a major news story in 1987 about Jim Bakker, a charismatic televangelist popular around the world. Bakker's evangelistic appeals and stories about God's blessing through miraculous healing and material wealth attracted numerous followers and financial contributions. But then he was forced to admit he had committed adultery with a former church secretary and used hundreds of thousands of contributed dollars differently from what he had promised. The next year, another world-famous and wealthy charismatic televangelist, Jimmy Swaggart, confessed to sexually immoral times spent with prostitutes.

Such infamous characters are only the tip of the iceberg. According to one source, in 1980 over thirty million dollars of church funds around the world were embezzled or stolen. By

1989, the amount had apparently grown to over 762 million dollars![5] The scandal of frequent sexual abuse by religious leaders (clergy and laymen) was also coming to light. Dominating leaders who strongly denounced sexual sin were sexually abusing others in their church, including younger children, sometimes their own children!

Many middle-class Western missionaries have gone to the poor countries of Africa, Asia, and Latin America, and have lived like kings and queens. They transferred their affluence to the third world and became even better off financially than before. Their wealth and wealthy friends led them to think of themselves as masters of the poor more than as servants of the poor.

There is a story about missionaries who brought the Bible to a foreign land. They asked the natives to close their eyes and pray. When they opened their eyes, they discovered they now had the Bible, but the missionaries had the land! Thus the Kikuyu people in Kenya have a proverb: Between the settler and missionary is no difference.[6] Missionaries often settled on the best tribal land, and their farms were the best in the area. They gave special help to other white farmers since they identified more with them and enjoyed their company more.[7]

British and American Protestant missions acquired huge areas of land in East Africa during the late nineteenth and early twentieth centuries. They stressed agriculture to train African converts in Western farming methods so they could become self-supporting missions. So they bought thousands of acres of land on which to raise commercial export crops. British United Methodists procured six thousand acres of land just in the River Tana region.

Sometimes missions paid African chiefs with cloth, beads, etc., to allow them to use their land—temporarily, the chiefs thought. As missions obtained more land, they began to force Africans who wanted to settle on the land to become Christians. Missionaries also required them to do certain farm work as another condition for living on mission land. Those Africans thus became tenant farmers under foreign masters. Missionaries took pride in their Western palaces and church buildings. The

Africans meanwhile suffered, and few willingly became Christians.[8]

For several years, missionaries in South India were called *Dora* and thought it simply meant "missionary." Eventually they discovered *Dora* meant "rich landlord." Like rich landlords, missionaries bought land and then built walled compounds, large houses, schools, churches, and roads for their cars.[9]

The earliest Protestant missions were closely connected with colonial economic adventures. In 1602, the Dutch formed the East India Company, whose goal was to export Dutch commerce and the Christian faith to the East Indies. The company, not the Protestant church, formed contracts with missionaries. As an added incentive, the company paid missionaries for every baptism they performed.[10]

Such an imperial mission worked with the political and economic imperialism of their own national leaders. It produced servants of the foreign powers but not followers of the risen Jesus. Only a few missionaries dared to depart from that mission model. One example was William Knibb, a British missionary who struggled against the harsh slavery in Jamaica. When his mission board heard about the struggle and about the anger of the plantation owners, they wrote to Knibb, advising him not to interfere in civil or political affairs.[11] However, mission must never mean only being polite guests of another country and its leaders, who mostly ignore the cries of the poor and oppressed.

National leaders often promoted a civil religion that took pride in the mission of their so-called godly nation. The political rhetoric emphasized their benevolent aid to poor countries (as in Luke 22:25). But all the talk about developed countries helping undeveloped countries was self-serving. All the development projects over the last several decades primarily developed the wealth and power of the multinational corporations and national leaders of every country involved. The rich got richer, and the poor got poorer. The real scandal was not simply poverty, but poverty in the midst of proud Christians who had plenty. And the gap is getting worse and worse.[12]

In the nineteenth century, Samuel Castle and Amos

Cooke went to Hawaii as Congregationalist missionaries. When their mission board refused any further financial help in 1849, they began their own business. They developed an import supply business, then invested in the new sugar industry. Much later their business took over Dole's Hawaiian pineapple company. In 1963, the company shifted much of its pineapple production to the Philippines, where there was cheaper labor and land. Never mind the unemployed workers left behind in Hawaii or the Filipino farmers forced off their lands to make room for them. In Honolulu they still summarize this in a joke: "Castle and Cooke came to do good. They got out doing very well." By 1986, Castle and Cooke was a multinational corporation with one and a half billion dollars in assets around the world. At the same time, two-thirds of their Filipino banana workers' children were malnourished.[13]

My own experience in the Philippines was that many U.S. missionaries were enjoying the power of the dollar to live more comfortably there than they would have in the United States. Our own family struggled to give up more so we could live more simply and love more generously. During our second term, we moved off the safe mission compound on the edge of a university campus. We transferred to a small barrio on the outskirts of the city. Our duplex was much smaller than our former house, but it was new and sturdy.

We had access to a mission car but mostly used public transportation, jeepneys and buses. No longer did we have a telephone, though we did keep our small Asian-produced refrigerator, stove, and clothes washer. No longer did we have a maid or helper around the house. We even asked our mission board to reduce our large salary, but they refused. So we lived on a small percentage of our salary and gave away a fair amount, though we didn't want to become the local loan bank. During our last few years, we shared mostly through a well-respected, poor Filipina Christian in our barrio. She was an unofficial community social worker, wise in deciding where limited funds could best help.

We are still seeking a simpler lifestyle as we now live in the mission field of our rich and greedy nation. We bought an older, cheaper house and car. No longer are we employed by a mission board or church. I have worked at part-time, low-paying jobs that met some basic needs. This allowed time for different missions like research and writing, teaching Bible studies, listening to and sharing with the needy, and speaking prophetically to political or economic powers through letters or demonstrations. My wife has worked both part-time and full-time as a secretary.

Jesus' advice to his disciples as he sent them out on mission included specific commands to give without pay and to take no money with them (Matt. 10:8-9). Those who welcomed their mission would provide their basic needs of food and shelter (Matt. 10:10-11). That provision would be their wage (Luke 10:7). To receive the same as an American middle-class salary for such mission would have been robbery.

Even now, missionaries willing to live with a local family in a new place could also better identify with that place and its people and bond with them. Such bonding would also mean taking only a few personal possessions and using only local public transportation or walking. Single persons, couples, or families who seek to cross cultural barriers both near and far need to have such humble attitudes and flexibility. They will probably have to give up more than a few of their favorite things. Yet such sacrifice will help build new relationships, learn new languages, and fit into new cultures.[14]

There would still be limits to the degree expatriates could bond with others and to the time they would remain in each place. Yet the main purpose of a bonding process with another people would be to form a new group of disciples in that place. Most might need to work at least part-time so as not to be a burden to their hosts. In learning a new language, such total immersion in a new culture is much better than using a paid tutor. My wife and I had some good tutors in the Philippines. Yet later we discovered that an earlier missionary had become especially fluent by just living with a rural family for several months.

Catholic priests and nuns, including famous missionaries among the poor from St. Francis to Mother Teresa, have generally lived more simply in the third world than Protestant missionaries. In Africa, priests usually lived in mud-and-thatch houses like those of the Africans around them. Seldom was anyone else around who spoke English. In contrast, Protestants typically grouped together in mission compounds or stations, where they lived in nice homes with nice furniture. Each family had a car and hired Africans to help cook, clean, and watch the children. Thus, while priests lived only a little above the Africans, the Protestants lived a great deal higher and enjoyed a far superior social position. But African leaders could never hope to follow the Protestant model of ministry. All the Protestants' words about humility, sacrifice, and servanthood were contradicted by their lifestyles.[15]

In Latin America, however, Catholic priests, along with Spanish or Portuguese soldiers, helped plunder the people and land. By the early nineteenth century, the Catholic Church was the largest landowner in Latin America. Bishops and dictators stood side by side. As long as the upper classes went to mass, gave land and money to the church, and baptized their children, the bishops ignored the slaughter of peasants or even encouraged it.[16]

During the early 1950s, Archbishop Dom Helder Cámara formed the National Conference of Brazilian Bishops (CNBB). This led the way in Latin America for a church of the poor. The bishops declared a preferential option for the poor and supported the growth of Christian base communities among the poor. Despite repressive military dictators and corrupt civilian governments, the bishops constantly called for land reform. Then the CNBB showed its concern was genuine by asking all bishops to turn over their own land to the peasants, and many did. True love for the poor will mean that rich people live more simply and use more money to help the poor. Even then, too much money given away can corrupt those receiving it.

Several decades ago, Wycliffe Bible Translators from the United States celebrated their successful work with Mayan peasant farmers in Chiapas, Mexico. Anticipating later church growth principles, whole communities became Protestant and received Wycliffe translations of the New Testament. Mayan leaders became pastors of the churches, and vices like drunkenness were greatly reduced. Economic and agricultural help also enabled some Mayans to improve their livelihood. North American donors to Wycliffe rejoiced at such news and donated even more.

Yet there was more to the story. What wasn't publicized was that the Mayans still didn't like to read and seldom used their New Testaments. The Mayan pastors were especially interested in increasing their incomes. They were so successful that often they were the richest men in their communities, even to the point of becoming like the local tyrants they helped overthrow. These church leaders wanted to imitate the North Americans and their much greater wealth and power. They thought Christ was the reason North Americans were wealthy. Thus the mass conversion of the Mayan people was based on their decision to side with those richer and stronger. However, most Mayans did not benefit as much as the pastors. They eventually switched to Pentecostal churches, attracted by the seemingly magical rituals of faith healing.[17]

Currently, many professional church leaders in North America expect and receive a middle-class salary. Success in ministry means continuing to advance to a bigger church at each new stage of one's professional career. By doing so, one can neither speak prophetically against the greed of their own society, including the churches, nor demonstrate practically the simpler life and mission of Jesus.

Middle-class white churches which escaped from the hardships of the inner city (including low-income minority groups) became captive to the comforts of suburbia. Their greed enslaved them to their companies or businesses and to the benefits of being faithful to that corporate power. The business of their churches then became that of another organization which could provide religious benefits, comfort, beauty, and status. A prophetic mission in such churches would certainly mean conflict. Many members might leave. Or more likely, the prophet would have to leave. It would not be business as usual. Exactly!

Certain Filipinos doing mission work on large sugar plantations (haciendas) have struggled with the call to speak for the poorly paid laborers. There was a struggle because the *hacienderos* (hacienda owners) were providing financial support for the mission workers. Furthermore, the *hacienderos* had to give their consent to such missions on their land. Many insisted that those leading the mission stay in the *hacienderos'* luxurious homes. They wanted the mission to preach against the poor who stole a few products of their labor. Yet the owners stole from the poor by paying starvation wages. If mission workers decided to speak for fair wages for the laborers, they could lose their financial support, their houses, and their mission. Since many *hacienderos* had armed security guards, there was also a danger of serious injury or death.

In 2:25-29, Paul adds circumcision to the list of privileges for the Jews. The ritual of circumcision is the basis for becoming a member of God's people and for committing oneself to keep the law of Moses. But as with the law in 2:12-24, Paul says circumcision is valuable only if one practices the law. This is a further challenge by Paul to Jews who stress the necessity of circumcision for Gentiles (as in Gal. 5:6-8; 6:12-13). To such Jews, Paul asserts that their disobedience of the law makes them the same as the uncircumcised (2:25).

In 2:26, as in 2:14, Paul then points to certain uncircumcised Gentiles who keep the righteous requirements of the law. While they don't follow the full law of Moses, they do keep the most important demands of the law, as emphasized by Jesus. The righteousness that Jesus lived and taught also required a new level of obedience beyond the law of Moses, both fulfilling and transforming that law. That obedience can be considered a spiritual circumcision. Those obedient Gentiles who are physically uncircumcised will even become witnesses against the Jew who is circumcised and has the law, but is disobedient (2:27).[18]

Paul then gives a new definition of the Jew or circumcision. The real Jew is not the one who has the written law or whose flesh is circumcised. Instead, the true Jew is the one who has the Spirit of God and is circumcised in the heart (2:28-29). The former Jew has the external signs of the Jewish people, but the latter Jew has the "secret" signs of God's people. God's judgment will depend especially on those secret signs (2:16). Those signs will receive God's praise (2:29).

The praise of others (like the Jewish missionaries) focuses on external signs like physical circumcision or the written law (2:29). God's praise is given to those who obey the righteous requirements of the law from the heart through the power of God's Spirit. Paul's use of "circumcision of the heart" and "by the Spirit" suggests the new covenant mentioned by the prophets (Jer. 31:31-33; Ezek. 36:26-27). In 2 Corinthians 2:17—3:6, Paul observes the self-serving ministry of certain Jewish missionaries, whose emphasis on the written law leads to death. He contrasts this with the Spirit-empowered ministry of the new covenant, that leads to life.

Jesus accused certain Jews of searching the Scriptures to find eternal life while also rejecting him who fulfilled the Scriptures and was the source of life (John 5:39-40, 46). They preferred the glory of human praise, which Jesus rejected for the sake of the glory of God's praise (John 5:41, 44; Matt. 23:5-7). Jesus also connected seeking human glory with serving money; the Pharisees loved both (Luke 16:13-15).[19] In contrast, the obedient Gentiles in Romans 2:26-29 are experiencing Jesus' faith in God's glory and power. Like the Gentiles in 2:14-15, they have the work or obedience of the law in their hearts.

Paul's example of mission dialogue with another Jew can relate to mission among some Jews today. Yet there are now more "Christians" than Jews in the world like those self-seekers addressed by Jesus and Paul. So Paul's challenge can apply even more to the hypocrisy of proud Christian missionaries or pastors who educate many converts and raise much money, and then make idols out of that "success." The praise of such lawless teachers of the law comes from churches that support their mission. God's praise, however, is given to those whose hearts and minds have been enabled to be faithful to Jesus' way of mission and obedience.

Romans 3:1-20

Jewish Faithlessness and God's Words of Judgment

PAUL has just finished a strong prophetic challenge to Jewish pride in circumcision and the law of Moses (2:17-29). He argues that those outward privileges are not the sign of a true Jew. Obedience to the righteous requirements of the law is the sign, and some Gentiles have that sign while some Jews do not.

Paul's dialogue partner, another Jew, cannot let Paul get away with such statements. So he responds by asking: Is there any privilege or advantage then in being a circumcised Jew (3:1)?[1] Paul answers that the Jews do have many privileges as God's chosen people. The first advantage given the Jews is the words of God (3:2). God has spoken to the Jews through inspired messengers, whose messages were written in their Scriptures. The Jews of Paul's time are entrusted with God's written words, which include the law of Moses as well as prophetic warnings of judgment for those who disobey that law.

Paul then asks if the faithlessness of some Jews to those words is stronger than God's faithfulness (3:3). Will Jewish unrighteousness become the final proof that their God is also unrighteous (see 2:24)? Paul's Greek grammar in 3:3 implies a negative answer. He responds with a strong denial and expresses his desire that God will ultimately be shown to be true (3:4).

God's words of judgment will show that God is righteous and true even if every person (especially the Jew) prefers lies (see Ps. 96:13). While the Gentiles have exchanged the truth of God for a lie (1:25), the Jews also have failed to judge according to the truth of God's judgment (2:1-3). But God's truth will win in the end. Paul quotes the words of God in Psalm 51:4 to point out that God's power will finally triumph over faithless people (3:4). Psalm 51 is about David's own great sorrow due to his faithlessness. Yet David also saw that his sin led to God's true words of judgment through the prophet Nathan (2 Sam. 12:1-14). Through such words of judgment, God's own righteousness was and will be manifested. Although others have passed judgment against God by being faithless, God's powerful righteousness will have the final word.

Faithless Israel still has the advantage of God's warning through words of judgment, which should lead to sorrow and repentant faithfulness (see 2:4). But Paul knows that Jewish pride will try to avoid such truth. So he raises the question that some Jews might then ask (based on previous discussions with them): Is God unrighteous in showing too much wrath since our sin gives God's righteous judgment (see 2:5) the chance to express itself (3:5)? Paul's Greek grammar again implies a negative answer. He responds to such a question with a strong denial (3:6). Paul asks how God can judge the world (especially the Gentiles) if that is how God should respond to sin. All Jews will agree that God should judge the sin of the Gentile world.

In 3:7, Paul anticipates the next question of his Jewish partner in dialogue: If God's truthfulness increases the glory of God because of the Jew's faithless falsehood, why am "I" (the Jew) judged as a sinner? Then in 3:8, Paul adds a final blasphemous statement that some Jews have claimed Paul said: So if our sin leads to magnifying God's glory, let's do evil so that such good might result. Paul ends such arguments by announcing that the judgment of God against such ones is just and right. They truly deserve their judgment.

Behind all those questions is the Jews' feeling: if Paul is

right that God's righteousness will be manifested through the Jews' sin, then they are no more a sign of God's righteousness than the sinful Gentile world. If God's righteousness is shown only through words of judgment against the sin of all (Jews and Gentiles), the Jew answers that sin seems to be the only way to glorify God. If so, God shouldn't be too angry with such sinners since their sin results in a more powerful display of God's righteous glory. If God's power will win out in the end no matter how great the sin, then what is the big deal about sin? Of course, the Jew asking those questions doesn't really believe that the Jews have been so sinful. He is trying to make Paul's mission message sound foolish.

In 3:9, Paul thus asks if the Jews are really better than the sinful Gentiles. His answer: they are not better. He has already stated (in 1:18—3:8) that both Jews and Gentiles are under the power of sin. Even among God's chosen people, sin's power has prevailed.

As a final way of clinching his argument, in 3:10-18 he quotes several passages from Jewish Scripture that agree with his judgment against the Jews (and Gentiles). Paul quotes mostly from the Psalms to emphasize that there is no one (Jew or Gentile) who is righteous (3:10). Jews may boast that they know God's will (2:17-20). Yet their own Scripture, the words of God, say they really don't know God or seek God (3:11).

All (Jews and Gentiles) have turned away from God (3:12). None are doing kindness, which is a righteous requirement of the law, according to the prophets and Jesus (see Mark 10:18-21). They seem to take God's will seriously, but the reality is different. They are really "snakes" who poison their hearers (3:13; see Matt. 3:7; 23:33).

To those like Paul who challenge their mission, they speak only bitter curses (3:14) and even seek the lives of their opponents (3:15). The result of such ways (3:16) is enmity and division between Jew and Gentile, between Jew and Christian (3:17). Such fearsome Jews have no fear of God or of God's words of warning (3:18).

All of the words of judgment against the Jews in 3:10-18 are taken from their own "law" or Scripture (3:19). So the Jews' advantage of having those words of God (3:2) should lead to the knowledge of their own sin (3:20). Those words are given so every boastful mouth (among the Jews) might be stopped (see 2:23). What Paul quotes in 3:4, 10-18 is only a small sample of God's past words of warning to Israel.

Thus the whole world (Jew as well as Gentile) will be held accountable to God for their sin (3:19; see 3:6). All human flesh has failed. Especially Jews need to admit that their Scripture exposes their continual failure to do the righteous requirements of the law (compare 3:20 and 3:12). While doing various works found in the law of Moses, they do not do the patient and kind good work that is more important than all the rest (see 2:7 in the context of God's own work of patient kindness in 2:4). Although they are doing some works of the law, God will finally judge them to be unrighteous.

When Paul claims that their (circumcised) flesh is faithless and under God's righteous judgment just like Gentile flesh, they curse Paul and seek his death. These particular Jews are not being persecuted by the Gentile world for patient faith and kindness; instead, they are persecuting Paul and other Christians (Jewish and Gentile). So Paul uses their own Scripture, about which they boast, to point out their deep sinfulness. If they have really listened to the words of God given to Israel, they would stop all their boasting and curses. They would humble themselves in the face of Paul's prophetic challenge and pursue God's glory and power instead of their own. Paul writes a description of that challenge (in 2:1—3:20) to help his readers have similar dialogues as part of their own mission.

Similarly, Christians now have the written words of God, including the New Testament. The New Testament includes words of warning and judgment against faithless churches and Christians. As later churches became more powerful, they also became more faithless. They persecuted others who were threats to them, including Jews.

In the heart of twentieth-century Christendom, the vast majority of churches did not denounce the mass murder of millions of Jews. So-called Christians killed those Jews. Most German Christians accepted Adolf Hitler as one sent from God. Hitler's racist mission to restore Aryan supremacy and national glory fit right in with Christendom's mission to rebuild Christian civilization and capture international dominance. The Holocaust was the climax of a long history of Christendom's condemnation of Jews. When put on trial for their atrocities, some Nazis quoted the hero of the Protestant Reformation, Martin Luther, to justify their faithlessness. Only a few faithful critics expressed God's words of judgment against such faithlessness.

Most people in Germany considered themselves to be Christians. They could not accept a Jewish cultural minority who did not fit into their Christendom model. The distinctives of Jesus' faith disappeared in a cloud of nationalistic spirituality and cultural religion. Those who disagreed too loudly disappeared in a storm of religious hatred and persecution.

After World War II, a "God-fearing" Western civilization, especially the United States, embraced a global mission of overcoming godless communists by persuasion, persecution, or death. Prophetic Christians who challenged such evils were easily labeled communists or subversives. Although killing national enemies was ugly, many churches felt called to protect and promote a Christian civilization. Even if the communist danger required war in Korea or the mass murder of Vietnamese civilians, American churches would generally support their generals and troops. After all, these were thought to be holy wars against godless communists.

An anticommunist message has helped a South Korean pastor, Paul Yonggi Cho, build the largest church in the world. He consistently supported his military government and thus became a politically acceptable, increasingly popular leader. More recently known as Dr. Cho Yonggi, the Pentecostal leader is chief executive of the Full Gospel Central Church in Seoul, which has over 500,000 members. Like many authoritarian Pentecostal pastors, he supports dictatorial anticommunist authorities. While developing home cells where lay people provide mutual help in sickness and need, Cho's mostly middle-class church offers a gospel of health, wealth, and success.[2]

In the United States, conservative Christian media celebrities like Pat Robertson have used their influence to support anticommunist armies. During the 1980s, Robertson's Christian Broadcasting Network raised money for the Nicaraguan contras and the armies of El Salvador and Guatemala. In May 1985, he used his *700 Club* TV show to sponsor a telethon for the contras, a rebel army trying to destabilize or overthrow the so-called communist Sandinista government of Nicaragua.[3]

While most Nicaraguans wanted peace, different religious and political powers wanted control. The contra army condemned, tortured, and murdered many Nicaraguan civilians in the name of an anticommunist hysteria found in both Washington (Reagan) and the Vatican (John Paul II). Neither the U.S. government nor the Catholic Church hierarchy approved of the Sandinistas. The left-wing government was a threat to their power over the people and policies of Nicaragua.

Both the Catholic and Protestant churches in Nicaragua were strongly divided over the Sandinistas, and each side condemned the other. The Catholic hierarchy condemned various Sandinista-favoring priests, nuns, and basic Christian communities, who reciprocated by condemning the hierarchy. Conservative evangelical Protestants condemned Sandinista-supporting liberal mainline Protestants, who reciprocated. Perhaps Moravian Church leaders who worked among the Miskito Indians saw most clearly the need to acknowledge evil on both sides of the power struggle. They recognized the importance of helping those suffering and desperate for peace.[4]

Many Christians think that God's judgment will fall mainly on others since they themselves honor God with their words, religious rituals, and avoidance of a few vices. But they have failed to do the most important requirements of Jesus' way of righteousness such as doing kindness to others, including those considered enemies (see Matt. 23:23). When faced with the challenge of such enemies as communists or opponents in the third world, most Christians are all too ready to condemn, go to war, and kill.

Christian prophets have often been called enemies and condemned by certain churches. Earlier prophets like Waldo (twelfth century) or Wycliffe (fourteenth century) or groups like the Anabaptists (sixteenth century) were persecuted for their faithfulness to Jesus' prophetic words against the wealthy, the proud, and the violent. Waldensians opposed the Catholic hierarchy and priesthood. They wanted to purify Catholicism by making it more simple, like the New Testament churches.

John Wycliffe called on popes and bishops to give up their luxury and riches and live a more simple life like most people. He sent out poor priests on missions among the people, sharing the gospel and speaking against the greed and injustice of land-lords. When peasant armies rebelled against landlords, Wycliffe condemned such violent revolts. Yet later leaders, who sympa-thized with many of Wycliffe's teachings, became persecutors of similar prophets. Protestant Reformers (in the sixteenth cen-tury) emphasized the authority of the whole Bible in order to use the Old Testament to justify their persecution of Anabap-tists or their "just" wars against other parts of Christendom.[5]

After Christianity became a powerful state religion in the fourth century, there was wave after wave of persecuted proph-ets throughout the Middle Ages. Their primary "sin" was call-ing for small apostolic groups in contrast to a whole society held together by religion, like the nation of Israel in the Old Testament. The leaders of Christendom's churches, including Protestants like Luther and Calvin, condemned smaller dissi-dent groups as heretics and persecuted them.[6] Faithlessness that deceives itself as being true to God finally leads to God's righteous words of judgment. The mission of Paul and Jesus still calls for courage to speak prophetic words of warning to the faithless who think they are faithful.

When Christian leaders build up the courage to criticize their churches, it's usually for such "sins" as missing worship services or not giving enough money to the church. Churches expect their pastors to scold them about such shortcomings. Likewise, successful churches applaud most of the values of the popular culture to which they belong. In the United States, they rally to preserve the American dream (freedom, prosperity, family, and good clean living) and oppose any enemies of that dream.[7] What if leaders started pointing out real sins, specific sins, big sins—like religious hate, religious pride, greed, racism, or murder?

Violent racism against Native Americans and African-Americans has raged throughout American history. African-Americans experienced the violent zeal of so-called Christian missionaries during their long ordeal under slavery. Some white missionaries preached to them on Sunday and beat on them on Monday. The same men who whipped women until they bled pretended to be ministers of the meek and lowly Jesus. The men who linked purity and marriage also scattered slave families, breaking up husbands and wives, parents and children. Men and women slaves were sold for money to build churches, buy Bibles, and support missionaries to the heathen across the seas.[8]

During the U.S. civil rights struggle in the 1960s, only a few white pastors were brave enough to speak out with their black brothers and sisters. Pastors knew that their churches were not comfortable with such confrontation of the status quo, especially when most members benefited from that status quo. To become prophetic and critical would have resulted in the comfortable church members feeling betrayed. Prophets were quickly labeled radicals, especially by more conservative churches. Middle-class pastors and churches would rather avoid prophetic challenges and angry responses, unless the American dream is endangered.

The forces of darkness remain strong. Meanwhile, most Americans sleep comfortably and enjoy their American dream. For other Americans and for much of the world, that dream has become a nightmare. We think Hitler was insane to murder six million Jews over a period of several years. And we're right. But six million children, mostly in the third world, die every five or six months, due to poverty. That poverty is partly the result of the past and present insane greed of the first world and their few third-world buddies. Forty thousand kids die every day, and we don't call it a holocaust or cry out against it as craziness. We mostly ignore it (like the West did the slaughter of Jews, though some tried to help them escape the Third Reich).

If a white, middle-class American dies tragically, American Christians take it to heart. If each day tens of thousands of malnourished brown or black children die of preventable illnesses like diarrhea or respiratory infections, American Christians prefer not to dwell on such horror. We might lose some sleep—and our American dream. Rich Americans at times use a little money or power to help the third world. But they will not tolerate any words about American money and power being a serious cause of such poverty and death.[9]

One Sunday at a small rural Baptist church, I gave a sermon on using money to help the poor instead of spending it on church luxuries. After the worship service, the richest deacon in the church challenged me. He asked if I thought it was wrong to buy new carpet for the church—something already done before I became pastor there. I replied that I could think of better ways to use that money. He responded by labeling my economics as communist.

A few days later I discovered that he had planned to donate $10,000 that previous Sunday to buy a new church organ. Other church members were upset at this loss but did not blame me to my face. I didn't think we needed a new organ anyway.

A year or so later, the rich deacon died. I then learned that one of his requests was that I not participate in the funeral service. At the wake on the night before the funeral, I talked with one of his sons, another rich deacon, who apologized for that request. I attended the funeral the next day and sat with the other members of the church and community. Yet the deacon's spirit was not really dead. Later, his brother died (in another city) and left our church $10,000! What a coincidence! What do you think the church decided to buy with that money?

A failure of nerve, of courage, to denounce specific sins will lead to God's words of judgment against faithless leadership. Is it better to escape the reactions of sinful churches than to escape the judgment of God? Or is it better to lose members or money or pastoral positions than to lose God's righteousness? The angry words of reactionary churches against prophetic warnings will pass away, but God's words will never pass away.

Romans 3:21-31

God's Righteous Power, Jesus' Faith, and World Mission

PAUL'S mission conversation with another Jew switches from the prophetic challenge against Jewish faithlessness and lawlessness of 2:1—3:20. Before Jesus, God's righteous ways and warnings were made known to Israel in the Jewish law or Scripture (see 3:19-20). Now God's righteousness has been made known in a new way: through the faith of the Jewish Messiah or Christ (3:21-22). The law and the prophets predicted this (3:21; see 1:2-3, 17; Luke 24:44; Acts 28:23). It became a reality with the appearance of Jesus of Nazareth.

The Old Testament promises a future Messiah who will manifest God's righteousness. For example, Psalm 72 speaks of a future Messiah who will rule with righteousness over all the world. His righteous rule will result from a revelation of God's righteousness in the king (Ps. 72:1). Isaiah 9:7 reflects that hope for a descendant of David to rule with righteousness forever through the power of God. In Jesus was seen God's righteous power that overcame sin through a life of perfect faithfulness.

If God's faithfulness and righteousness could be manifested despite Israel's faithlessness, how much more could it be manifested through Jesus' faithfulness, and through those who share his faith (compare 3:3-5 and 3:21-22). God's powerful rule which will finally overthrow all evil was beginning through the faith that Jesus lived and taught. God's power is continuing to effect that same righteousness in all (both Jew and Gentile) who are sharing the faith (belief) of Jesus because of world mission (3:22; see 1:16-17; 1:5).

Most scholars translate 3:22 as faith *in* Jesus Christ. That is a possible translation, but the Greek genitive case is usually translated as a possessive: Jesus' faith (the faith of Jesus, or the faith that Jesus possessed).[1] The King James Version translates 3:22 as "the faith of Jesus," and the New Revised Standard Version now includes a footnote for 3:22 (and 3:26) which says "the faith of Jesus" is an alternate translation. (See also NRSV footnotes for Gal. 2:16, 20; 3:22; Eph. 3:12; Phil. 3:9.) That reflects the increasing number of studies which favor the translation: "the faith of Jesus."[2]

The power of sin (3:9) produced Jewish faithlessness and lawlessness as well as Gentile idolatry and immorality. The whole world (both Jew and Gentile) has sinned (3:23; see 3:9). All are seeking their own glory and honor instead of God's glory. Gentiles refuse to honor God's glory, preferring instead to praise and serve their own created idols (1:21-23, 25). Jews also dishonor God by breaking the law they praise (2:23) and by seeking the praise of others more than the praise of God (2:29). No one is seeking God's glory or reflecting God's righteousness (3:10-11). There is no difference or distinction among sinful humanity in that all have sinned (3:22-23).

But now worldwide sin is being overcome. Something new has come: Christ's faith. Christ's faith, not our faith in Christ, plays the pivotal role. As a result, God's powerful grace is making righteous both Jews and Gentiles who share Jesus' faith (3:24). They reflect God's glorious image by being transformed into Christ's image. No one deserves such grace since all have sinned. God gives it freely.

In Ephesians 2:8, Paul describes the gift of God as being saved by grace. Ephesians 2:1-5 also emphasizes the conversion from death (due to sin) to the new life with Christ (given through grace). For his Roman readers, Paul also describes salvation in terms of new life and righteousness (1:16-17). Thus

God's gift of redemption includes the new life of righteousness (3:24). Titus 3:5-7 similarly links salvation and righteousness with God's grace through the rebirth and renewal of the Holy Spirit that is poured out through Jesus Christ.

Paul's main concern throughout 1:19—3:20 is the grim reality of sin. The primary problem Paul describes is the power of sin, not the guilt of sin (3:9, 23). So the redemption in Jesus Christ is not primarily forgiveness. Above all, God's redemption and grace mean deliverance from slavery to sin and liberation from the power of sin (3:24). Just as the strong arm of the Lord redeemed Israel from their bondage to Egypt, now God's power redeems certain people from their slavery to sin (see Exod. 6:6; Deut. 7:8; 9:26; 15:15; Ps. 77:14-15; 78:42). God's greatest gift is not a righteous status, but a righteous life.

Now one is considered righteous because one actually reflects God's righteousness, as revealed in Jesus. This union with Jesus and his faith—being "in" Christ Jesus—is producing the same faithful and righteous life that Jesus lived. When all were helplessly enslaved to sin, Jesus came to manifest a new freedom from the oppressive power of sin.

Protestant teaching on justification by faith has usually emphasized forgiveness and a righteous status before God. As a reaction to most Catholic teaching, Protestants tended to deny that justification included making one righteous. Theologians like Augustine (early fifth century), Thomas Aquinas (thirteenth century), and Martin Luther (sixteenth century) have shaped the debates on the meaning of justification.

Augustine said that "to justify" meant "to make righteous." God's righteousness was given to people, making them righteous. Justification included a new creation, renewing people according to the image of God. Sin was rooted out, and God's righteous love was planted in its place. God had given believers the power to receive and participate in divine righteousness. In justification, the Holy Spirit renewed them spiritually and ethically. God made the ungodly godly. And justification included an ongoing act of grace throughout the life of the Christian, not just the beginning act of grace in the new Christian.[3]

Augustine's view of justification was basically followed for the next thousand years. Thomas Aquinas, however, added that justification included a basic change (a created grace) in one's soul or mind so that one was then capable of continuing to receive the Holy Spirit. Aquinas also connected justification with the Catholic sacraments of baptism and penance. Justification began in baptism and continued in penance (confession of sin, penance, and absolution).[4]

Near the end of the Middle Ages, some Catholics criticized Aquinas' view of created grace in justification and emphasized the wholly supernatural grace of the Holy Spirit. Then Martin Luther pioneered the Protestant Reformation by teaching that justification involved no new creation at all. The Protestant distinction between justification and regeneration was completely new. For Luther, God's righteousness was revealed only in the cross of Christ. Justification thus meant taking hold of Christ's righteousness, a righteousness that could never be one's own, an alien righteousness mercifully reckoned to one. Justification was an ongoing process, but involved an increasing awareness of sin and the need for Christ's alien righteousness. The Christian remained a sinner but was righteous in God's eyes.[5]

Other reformers, however, disagreed with Luther. Zwingli, a Swiss reformer around the same time as Luther, followed Augustine's view of justification as part of regeneration. Yet Zwingli did not appreciate God's powerful grace in producing regeneration as much as Augustine had.

Many Anabaptists, the so-called radicals of the Reformation, taught that justification depended on regeneration through the Holy Spirit which empowered people to imitate Christ's example. Likewise, several reformers in England, such as William Tyndale, described justification as "making righteous." They emphasized the actual communication of Christ's righteousness to the believer, not just the crediting or imputing of that righteousness.[6]

Protestants have usually preferred to describe the process

of God's making one righteous as sanctification. The practical problem that arose, however, was that salvation was connected with justification (defined as forgiveness and righteous status) rather than sanctification. Many Protestants also said that once one was saved (justified), God would keep the believer secure in that salvation, even if there was not much evidence of sanctification. The result was a Protestant church that thought it had faith in Jesus as Savior, but in fact seldom shared Jesus' faith in God's power to make righteous and liberate from sin's power.

Protestants are correct in saying that Jesus did not define righteousness in terms of participating in the Catholic sacraments. Protestants are wrong in making one's decision to accept Christ as Savior a new sacrament. From the beginning, Paul linked salvation with a faith that believed in and received God's power, which freed one from a life of sin.

The Christian life should be characterized by God's righteousness and life, as lived out and empowered by the risen Jesus. Those who accept Jesus as Savior and Lord but do not reflect his kind of righteousness have not yet been united with Jesus and his faith. A "sanctification" composed merely of attending church, avoiding vices, and being a respectable citizen is hardly the righteousness of Jesus and does not need God's power.

Orlando Costas criticized a Protestant gospel that was content with a one-time inner conversion experience. He responded that it was not enough to say one was converted; one needed to *live* a converted life. Conversion must be more than an initial moment of decision separated from an ethical life. False conversions made no radical changes in one's lifestyle or worldview. In the United States and elsewhere, those undergoing false conversions frequently hoped for a happy, successful American way of life through forgiveness of abstract sins by faith in an abstract Jesus.

On the other hand, true conversions lead to true disciples of Jesus who left behind such deceit, as well as modern idolatry and immorality. They are able to challenge the power of sin that dominates their surrounding religious, economic, and political world.[7]

Some Protestants thought that if justification meant one was made righteous, then salvation would be the result of works instead of faith. They missed the full context of Paul's contrast between works and faith.

For Paul, works in the negative sense are especially Jewish attempts to obey the law of Moses—without God's new kingly power. The main problem is not Jewish legalism or misunderstanding of the law so much as powerlessness to do God's will as revealed in the law. Faith, on the other hand, is believing in and receiving God's new kingship that began with the faith of Jesus. Grace is the power of God's rule which not only forgives sins and reckons one as righteous; above all, grace enables one to live a righteous life.

God's grace and power make one righteous according to the righteousness lived and taught by Jesus (not by Moses). To share Jesus' faith is to do the works he did, through God's power. To try to do the works of Moses' law apart from Jesus' faith will never work. So Paul's contrast is between Jewish works of Moses' law and Jesus' works through faith in God's power. No one who does Jesus' works can boast, because those works are done only through God's righteous power.

In 3:25, Paul refers to Jesus' faithfulness unto death as part of God's revelation of righteousness (see Phil. 2:8).[8] Jesus died because of all the world's previous sins. God's patient kindness toward sinners (compare 2:4) now made Jesus' death a means of release from sin (3:25-26; see Isa. 53:10-11). Through Jesus' blood shed on the cross, God showed a righteousness that was deadly serious about sin and that mercifully redeemed people from sin.

Only at this point is redemption described as including freedom from the guilt and judgment of past sins. Even then, Paul's main concern is not people's sense of guilt, but God's own present righteousness in dealing with sin and in producing righteousness in the one (whether Jew or Gentile) who shares the faith of Jesus (3:26; see 1:17; 3:22, 25). By repeating the phrase "faith of Jesus" in 3:26 (after two references to it in 3:22,

25), Paul shows the importance of Jesus' faith for changing the history of sin into a new beginning of righteousness.[9]

Part of Jesus' own faith was his preaching of God's coming judgment on sin, and declaring that his death would be part of that judgment (Matt. 26:28). Jesus' death was a unique sacrifice for sins. Jesus' faithful sacrifice fulfilled the Jewish Day of Atonement (Lev. 16). Both Jesus' life and death provide the foundation of faith. Sharing Jesus' faith includes agreeing with him that he died for the sins of the world. At the same time, God's righteous judgment against sin is shown by enabling some Jews and Gentiles to live righteously. God made Jesus, who was without sin and thus perfectly righteous, to be the sacrifice for sin so that all those in union with him might come to share the righteousness of God as manifested in Jesus (2 Cor. 5:21). Through his sacrificial death, Jesus represented sinful humanity before God. By his obedient life and death, Jesus represented God's righteousness before humanity.

Given God's righteousness in Jesus, Paul asks his fellow Jew if there is any place left for boasting (3:27). Paul asserts that God now denies any exclusive pride in God (see 2:17). The Jew may boast about having the law of Moses or doing works of the law like teaching the law (2:23). But if one's viewpoint of the law is from (Jesus') faith rather than Jewish works, all such boasting is out of place (3:27).

Jesus didn't boast about Israel's righteousness. As Paul has done in 3:10-19, Jesus used the Old Testament (law) to expose Israel's sin and stop Jewish boasts. Jesus' teaching and fulfillment of the law rejected the proud righteousness of Pharisees and teachers of the law (Matt. 5:17, 20; 23:23). All who interpret the law through the eyes of (Jesus') faith will challenge Jewish pride in works of the law.

Jesus also contrasted Jewish rejection of his fulfilling Scripture with certain Gentiles who were more receptive (Luke 4:17-29). True righteousness that did the most important demands of the law of Moses, as defined by Jesus, resulted from faith in God's present kingly power. Any person throughout the world (Jew or Gentile) who has that same faith will also be made righteous (3:28). Thus God's new mission is to reproduce the obedient faith of Jesus among all peoples (see 1:5).

If righteousness results only from works of Moses' law, it will be limited to Israel, who possesses that law. Then God will only be the national God of the Jews. But Paul asked the proud Jew if God only belongs to Jews (3:29). Is God not also the God of Gentiles? The world does not really have various gods, one for Israel, and others for Gentiles. Israel's law rightly emphasizes that God is one (Deut. 6:4). Jesus' faith, however, went on to emphasize that the one God made righteous both circumcised Jews and uncircumcised Gentiles who shared his faith in the new kingly power of God (3:30). Jesus' international faith focused on God's power and replaced Moses' national law, which depended on human ability.

National laws or faiths still pose problems for the world today. Certain leaders and their followers in various nations consider themselves religiously superior to other nations. While glorying in their own supposed national righteousness, they look down on other nations and their lack of righteousness. Such pride produces evils like racism, classism, and militarism. Well-armed wealthy white nations like the United States take pride in being God-fearing countries. As a result, third-world nations suffer. They are dominated militarily, economically, and racially. So much for the faith of Jesus.

Paul finally asks if faith is against the law of Israel (3:31). Was Jesus' faith a completely new event with no connection to God's words revealed to Israel? Were the Jewish Scriptures of no use? Paul answers with a strong denial and says that he is being true to those Scriptures. The law's basic monotheistic teaching (Deut. 6:4) now means that the one God rules righteously and powerfully among all the world's peoples (3:29-30).

Paul often quotes from Scripture to argue his points. Especially in 3:10-18, Paul quotes a variety of passages from the law or Old Testament (3:19). And that law proves that Israel is not righteous, even though it is quite proud of having the law. Their own Scriptures as well as Jesus have challenged their boasting. Besides that, the Scripture witnesses to a future work of God when God's righteousness will be seen in a Messiah and his people (compare 3:21 and 1:2). Jesus declared that the fulfillment of God's final kingdom was beginning. He added that this didn't mean the destruction of the law and the prophets (Matt. 5:17-18; 4:12-17). It did mean a new righteousness that was resulting from God's kingly power.

Jesus strongly affirmed that not even the smallest detail of the law would pass away until heaven and earth passed away (Matt. 5:18). But then he added another condition right after that: until all things came to pass. Matthew's Gospel emphasized that what the law and prophets had pointed forward to was now coming to pass, being fulfilled (Matt. 5:17; compare the combination of coming to pass and being fulfilled in Matt. 1:22). The law of Moses was finding its fulfillment in the teaching of Jesus, as shown especially by Matthew 5:21-48.

Matthew introduced Jesus' teaching to seek his new righteousness despite strong opposition (Matt. 5:6, 10-12). By doing the good works which Jesus commanded, they would glorify their heavenly Father (Matt. 5:16). Since God's new kingship had now come to pass, and Jesus was fulfilling the law (Matt. 5:17-18), all these commands of the kingdom must be taught and obeyed (Matt. 5:19; see the commission of Matt. 28:20). Those who relaxed even the least of Jesus' commands would be called least in God's kingdom. Those who abandoned Jesus' new righteousness for the traditional righteousness of the scribes and Pharisees, perhaps because of opposition, would lose out completely on God's kingdom (Matt. 5:20). Jesus' disciples could not just teach and follow the law of Moses as it was traditionally understood (Matt. 5:21-48). Jesus' righteousness and obedience fulfilled the law on a new level.

Jesus' obedience unto death fulfilled Old Testament sacrificial rituals and ethical teaching to the extent that he made most of them obsolete. Just as Jesus fulfilled prophetic teachings in an unexpected and new way, he also fulfilled Moses' laws in a more profound way. Jesus' teaching and righteousness fulfilled the law and prophets by transcending them and bringing into reality an even better future than that to which they pointed. Jesus' faith manifested a new righteousness that affirmed and yet transformed the law and the prophets.[10]

Paul's mission message, therefore, is not against the law

when it is rightly understood, with the help of Jesus' faith. The Jewish Scripture or law points to a day when God's righteousness will be a reality in the faith of a newly created people (see 1:17 and the quote of Hab. 2:4). That day has come.

Paul's argument in 3:21-31 is an example for his readers who will also be meeting with Jews as part of their world mission. He is defending not only his gospel about God's righteous power and Jesus' faith, but also his mission to Gentiles as well as Jews. Most Jews think Paul's new gospel and mission are not according to Israel's law or Scriptures. Paul is providing Christians in Rome with a basis for answering such doubts and questions. Jews who are proud of their life under the national law of Moses will also question their gospel and mission.

Paul's teaching can also help Christians today to use the Old Testament properly. Only the Old Testament teachings that Jesus continued or fulfilled are now applicable to Christians. Thus, most Old Testament rules are no longer to be followed. Jesus fulfilled some laws, like the law of limited revenge (only an eye for an eye, Exod. 21:23-24), by taking them a step further so that there is to be no revenge at all, only love for one's enemies (Matt. 5:38-48). There is no longer a chosen nation called to follow the law of Moses. Jesus has now chosen a worldwide people who will follow his way of love. Therefore Christians can and must love even their national enemies instead of killing them through obeying military commands.

In the law of Moses, obedience would prosper both individuals and the nation. Now the obedience of Jesus' faith will lead to giving away wealth and facing opposition and persecution (Matt. 5:10-12; 6:19-20; 19:21; Luke 6:20-26; 12:33). The manifest glory of the (industrialized) first world is far different from God's glory, as revealed in Jesus' lowly disciples scattered all over the world. Christians today must face these serious differences between the righteousness described in the Old Testament and the righteousness defined by Jesus. What "the Bible says" must be seen in the light of what Jesus and the New Testament say. Jesus' kind of righteousness will indeed require the power of God. And Jesus' kind of faith can indeed receive the power of God.

Romans 4:1-12

Father Abraham
and Worldwide Faith
and Righteousness

AT the end of Romans 3, Paul claims that his gospel about
God's righteous power reproducing Jesus' faith throughout the world is not against Jewish law or Scripture. Other Jews
will argue that if uncircumcised Gentiles are righteous through
Jesus' faith, then the law of Moses and Jewish Scripture have
lost their central place. In 4:1-12, Paul uses Abraham as an example that the Scripture of Israel connects righteousness with
faith before the law of Moses is given.

Paul often defends his world mission before skeptical
Jews. As the Roman readers carry on Paul's mission to the Jew
first, and to the Gentile, they will face and debate similar opponents. Paul is preparing them for the same type of arguments
that he and Jesus faced from Jewish leaders. In John 8:39-40, Jesus argues with other Jews that if Abraham were really their father, they would do what Abraham did. But their desire to kill
Jesus shows they are not true children of Abraham. Likewise,
John the Baptist challenged some Pharisees and Sadducees to
repent and not be satisfied with saying Abraham was their father (Matt. 3:9).

Such Jewish leaders can argue that circumcised flesh is required by the law of Moses and even starts with Father Abra-

ham. Thus comes the question in 4:1: What will we (Paul and his dialogue partner, another Jew) say that Abraham, our Jewish forefather, found on the basis of the flesh? If Abraham was righteous through works of the law like circumcision, then he could boast of his accomplishments in the flesh (4:2; compare 3:27).

But Paul denies that Abraham could boast before God, using a quote from Jewish Scripture (4:3). Genesis 15:6, found in the first five books of Scripture known as Torah (law), clearly states that Abraham's righteousness was a result of his belief or faith in God. Because he believed God, his faith was reckoned or considered by God as righteousness.

When Abraham had given up hope for a child of his own, God promised him a son. When Abraham questioned God's impossible promise, God challenged him to step outside (Gen. 15:1-5). They would settle their differences there. So Abraham went outside, where God showed him the stars, a sign of God's power (see 1:20). Abraham stood helpless as God told him to count the stars. The result of God's show of strength was Abraham's renewed faith (Gen. 15:6). Abraham's faith resulted from and related to God's power.

Paul then turns to the Jew who emphasizes Abraham's works of obedience (4:4). If the reward of righteousness is given on the basis of works of the flesh, then it is simply what is owed to the worker. There is no grace involved. Yet for Abraham, righteousness was not connected with works but with continual believing in the gracious, powerful God who makes righteous the ungodly. The Greek word for believing in 4:5 is in the present tense, which means a continuous process of believing (see 1:16).

Abraham started out as an ungodly Gentile (compare 1:18). Through God's grace, Abraham came to believe. His belief was godly, focused on almighty God. Then God counted that faith as righteousness (4:5). God is not a bookkeeper who quietly adds up the good and bad deeds done to decide who is righteous. For Paul, God creates faith and righteousness in those who were formerly ungodly.

Protestants have always strongly opposed salvation or justification by works. Hence, it is ironic that most Protestants, beginning with Martin Luther and John Calvin, also emphasized a Christian's work or vocation as a calling from God. Grace is the key on Sundays, but work seemed to be the key on Mondays. The Protestant work ethic refused to justify those who had little work to do. The good Christian was supposed to work hard at his job.

Missionaries often labeled those in the third world as lazy. In Kenya after World War I, British missionaries supported officials of the British Empire who wanted to require forced labor. Colonial plantations were increasingly in need of cheap labor. Missionaries agreed with the British governor that forced labor was needed for the prosperity of the country and the natives. Such required work would also supposedly stop African idleness and drunkenness. Yet the real reason was to make Africans serve British economic interests. The missionaries, in turn, said that the work of the missions was based on the belief that all natives should work. Such work was a necessary part of Christianity. At the same time, they said nothing about whether it was Christian to force Africans to work for the benefit of the British.

When he heard about these developments in Kenya, Bishop Frank of Zanzibar regretted that he was British. He moaned that he was sick of such Christian institutions, even if one could find Christ riding on such asses.[1]

Another hero of Israel was David. He too spoke in Jewish Scripture about the blessing of God's counting righteousness apart from works (4:6). In Psalm 32:1-2, David wrote about the blessing of one whose sin(s) was forgiven and not counted against him (4:7-8). Earlier, in 3:4, Paul quotes from Psalm 51:4, where David confessed his sin—after asking for forgiveness and cleansing (Ps. 51:1-2). Similarly, ungodly Abraham also received the blessing of righteousness on the basis of his faith, before he was circumcised (4:9-10). The righteousness of Abraham and David was thus not due to any work of the law such as circumcision of the flesh (see 4:1-2).

Circumcision was given later only as a seal or sign of the righteousness that Abraham already had through faith (4:11; see Gen. 17:10-11). God's plan was to make Abraham the father of all uncircumcised Gentiles who later would come to believe (4:11). Such Gentiles would also be reckoned as righteous. Yet Abraham would at the same time be the father of circumcised Jews who were not only circumcised but above all were following in the footsteps of the faith of Abraham (4:12).

So Abraham should not be seen as simply the grand Jewish patriarch or father. The Jewish assumption behind the question of 4:1—that Abraham is only our forefather according to the flesh—is mistaken. He is rather the father of Gentiles and Jews all over the world who walk according to the same faith in God he had. Jews are wrong when they emphasize circumcision as a work of the law necessary to be righteous. The most important part of Jewish Scripture, the Torah (law), shows that they are wrong.

Abraham, as the beginning of a worldwide faith, served to prepare the way for Jesus. Yet Abraham's faith also differed from Jesus' faith, so Paul isn't portraying Abraham as a Christian. Abraham's righteousness was not the righteousness of God's final salvation which began with Jesus. But Abraham's faith and righteousness were a result of God's grace given to an ungodly Gentile. And his believing was a continuing focus on the God who made righteous the ungodly (4:5). Abraham's faith was a daily walk guided by God's hand (power). Exactly how God's righteous power was at work in Abraham is described more fully in 4:17-21.

Perhaps 4:1-8 has been one of the most abused texts in the New Testament. Abraham's faith has been described as simply believing God's promise, and his righteousness as merely being reckoned or counted as righteous due to God's forgiveness. Then Christian faith has been identified as the same faith that Abraham had. The result is a faith that involves only an intellectual belief or inner trust in God's word or gospel. So righteousness supposedly means that while we are still sinners like everybody else, at least we are forgiven. It seems that Christians have been saved from the guilt of sin but are still under the power of sin. That, however, is not what justification of the ungodly (4:5) really means.

The new righteousness that began with Jesus' life and teaching went far beyond Abraham's righteousness. It is wrong simply to equate Abraham's righteousness in 4:1-8 with the righteousness manifested in Jesus and all who share his faith (as in 3:21-31). Jesus did not come to repeat the faith and times of Abraham in terms of a more simple relationship with God apart from the law of Moses.

Both the Protestant and Catholic understandings of justification value human benefits like forgiveness, a righteousness that is formally imputed, credited, or sacramental. They appreciate such benefits more than the divine power that reproduces God's own righteousness. Christ's death for sins, which is part of the basis for justification (3:25), has been stressed to such a degree that Jesus' faith in God's life-giving, resurrection power has been missed. The mission that resulted "converted" large groups of Christians who were not that different from anyone else. Sin's power was still more evident than God's power. It was easy to accept an evangelistic message or to perform certain services or sacraments from time to time. A whole society or nation could come to call itself Christian. But that easy faith was fake, and that so-called justification was fiction.

By defining justification as a new status instead of a new life, Luther continued the Christendom pattern of a state church. Most people in Germany were baptized as infants and became part of the national church, but might seldom or never attend. They were supposedly justified, yet most of them remained ungodly. During Luther's time, Anabaptists challenged the state church and called for voluntary membership in small groups of committed disciples who lived godly and righteous lives. As a result, Catholic and Protestant state authorities suppressed and murdered many Anabaptists.[2] Such authorities showed themselves to be ungodly by suppressing the truth with unrighteousness (see 1:18).

In Germany today, the state church remains. Though other countries have no state church, many still define justification as merely a new righteous status. Why? Because even the churches now established through voluntary membership are usually filled with too much unrighteousness. If justification means a new righteous life, then most church members will have to admit they aren't really justified after all.

During the 1960s, the Latin American Mission under Kenneth Strachan's leadership emphasized mobilizing lay people for Evangelism in Depth. The mass evangelism of men like Billy Graham was not really helping the churches. For example, Graham's 1958 crusade in Barbados resulted in what some said was one-fourth of the island going forward to make a decision for Christ. Yet few who signed decision cards joined churches. In fact, most who attended the crusade were already attending church. They loved the excitement of a famous evangelist and a mass rally. But after it was over, they became bored with their regular churches. Strachan also noticed that growing movements like Pentecostals, Jehovah's Witnesses, and communists made much use of all their members to bring in new members.[3]

So Strachan made the mission of local church members more central than the formerly popular visiting evangelistic teams. Retreats with seminars and Bible studies for interested Christians led to developing visitation programs and witnessing teams in local churches. New Christians then had a direct transition to involvement in a local church. Latin Americans were part of the leadership at all levels, from planning to evaluation, which insured sensitivity to Latin thinking and culture (including the consistent use of Spanish).[4]

However, even Strachan's new strategy had little long-term impact on the churches. Their 1965-1966 campaign in Peru produced 15,000 decisions for Christ, yet no increase in church membership. Moreover, after the campaigns ended, members usually did not continue to be active witnesses. They tended to return to "normal" church life where the powerful pastor preached and the laypeople remained passive. Evangelism in Depth was still too specialized, and the mission focused too much on making lots of converts. In the 1970s, Evangelism in Depth was abandoned, and some of its leaders became outspoken critics of church life.[5]

Orlando Costas was a Latin American missiologist who once worked with Evangelism in Depth. He later challenged North American and Latin American churches to proclaim Jesus' gospel of God's kingdom and to mobilize members to make disciples. Jesus' purpose in gathering a community of obedient disciples was that they would reflect his righteousness and participate in his mission. God empowered each person of faith to join in Jesus' way of mission.[6]

Many Protestants say the gospel message must simply be believed (and perhaps confessed publicly). Many Catholics say the gospel must simply be seen and experienced through celebration of the mass. Many charismatic Christians say the gospel must simply be experienced through miracles like physical healing and speaking in tongues. Such people have not seen Jesus' faith in terms of the kind of obedience God's power produces. Many churches still need to discover the central message of Jesus' and Paul's gospel. Belief or faith will then go beyond an intellectual acceptance, a ritual experience, or a dramatic display. It will focus on God's kingly power which continues to reproduce Jesus' righteousness and mission all over the world.

Costas also pointed out that church growth does not necessarily mean an increase in Jesus' mission. Many churches might simply be getting fat. Perhaps the wide open door at the front through which people flock into the church is matched by one at the back where just as many flow out of the church, often due to disobedience in the church. The mission science of church growth needs to realize that good growth comes from God's power and results in the righteousness of Jesus' faith. There is a basic difference between the growth of God's mission and that of a business. Technicians with church-growth principles like to use the applied science of sound marketing analysis, promotion, and effective controls. The result may be institutional success, but the question remains: Where is the obedience of faith?[7]

The evangelism of many parachurch organizations has

also preferred easy formulas of faith. Bill Bright became the authoritarian father of a worldwide faith through his Campus Crusade for Christ corporation. As a prosperous businessman, he began to advertise and market faith all over the world. By 1984, a global income of $105 million helped support 16,000 staff.

Wealthy business executives liked Bright's product, and contributed accordingly. Bright himself, like his biggest supporters, favored a civil religion which strongly backed U.S. militarism, CIA-sponsored rebels like the Nicaraguan contras, and anticommunist dictators in the third world. But Bright was most famous for his four spiritual laws, an easy plan of salvation that many quickly affirmed—and just as quickly forgot. For some, the formula of God's wonderful plan for their lives was an added spiritual encouragement or assurance as they planned their future success. They dreamed the American dream of Bill Bright.[8]

Some Campus Crusade for Christ staff also developed discipleship groups. The campus where I taught in the Philippines had several dedicated Filipino Campus Crusade staff members. I appreciated their friendship but still felt their ministry depended too much on Bright's plans and on training others to participate in their evangelistic programs. Earlier, while working one summer in California, I visited Campus Crusade's headquarters and heard Bright speak. I was especially struck by the luxury of the buildings and grounds. Bill Bright was clearly the prosperous patriarch of a growing family of faith. The problem was that Bright's faith was a far cry from Jesus' faith.

A misunderstanding of Abraham's faith and righteousness has led to a corruption of Christian faith and righteousness. Paul saw Abraham as one who was faithful to God's promise and walked according to God's power. It was precisely that faith which was fulfilled on a new level—the highest level—by Jesus and his faithful followers. The root of Abraham's faith finally came to fruit in the faith of Jesus. God's promise of a worldwide faith and righteousness was kept by means of a world mission that spread Jesus' faith and righteousness.

Romans 4:13-25

Abraham's Faith and Fatherhood Due to God's Promise and Power

---

PAUL describes Abraham as the father of faith of both Jews and Gentiles who will follow in his steps (4:11-12). Abraham's faith included a belief in God's promise that Abraham and his descendants would inherit the world (4:13). Paul looks beyond God's promise of a special land for Abraham's descendants to God's promise of the world. God's promise had two stages: first, Abraham's descendants would become a great nation; second, all the peoples of the world would be blessed by Abraham and his descendants (Gen. 12:2-3; 17:4-8; 18:18; 22:17-18). Jesus echoed that promise when he taught that the meek would inherit the earth (Matt. 5:5). And Paul's world mission is beginning to fulfill that promise.

As with righteousness (4:9-10), the promise came before Abraham had done any works of the law like circumcision. Before there was any law, Abraham's righteous faith received the promise and believed God (4:13). If only Jews, who have the law of Moses, are to inherit the world, Abraham's faith and God's promise meant nothing (4:14). Then no one would inherit the world because the law only produces God's wrath against sin (4:15).

As Paul stated earlier, the law of Moses leads not to righteousness but to knowledge of sin (3:20). Where there is no law of Moses, transgression or sin against that law is not known or counted against the sinner (4:15; compare 2:12). When the law came, sin against that law was close behind. So the only way God's promise would be fulfilled was through faith (4:16). Not human works of the law but God's powerful grace will insure that the promise is fulfilled for all the children of faith of father Abraham (4:16). When some Jews proud of being the descendants of Abraham approached John the Baptist, he asserted that God was able (powerful) to use even stones to raise up children of Abraham (Matt. 3:9).

Abraham's children include not just certain Jews who have both the law of Moses and the faith of Abraham. He is also the father of· Gentiles who share his faith (compare 4:11-12). Thus Abraham will inherit the world. He will be the father of "us" (both Jews and Gentiles) who follow his way of faith. Jesus' faith is the foundation for the Christian faith of all peoples (both Jews and Gentiles; see 3:22). So also Abraham's earlier faith led to him being the father of faith for all peoples (both Jews and Gentiles).[1] The root of Abraham's faith bore fruit in Jesus' worldwide faith focused on God's new kingly power.

The promise of Genesis 17:5, quoted in 4:17, says God would make Abraham a father of many peoples. For Paul, Abraham's faith in God's promise was also faith in God's power (4:17). Abraham believed the God who makes the dead live and calls into existence what has not existed.

Paul then connects God's promise about descendants (see Gen. 15:5) with Abraham's hope of having his own child. The hope contained in God's promise seemed hopeless (4:18). Abraham and Sarah were "dead" as far as being able to have a child (4:19). Abraham's flesh or body was powerless at that point. His own flesh provided no basis for boasting (see 4:1-2). Jews proud of being physical descendants of Abraham miss the fact that human flesh is too weak to fulfill God's word. Abraham was about a hundred years old at the time of the promise. Yet his faith did not weaken to the point of becoming faithless.

Instead, God's power strengthened Abraham's faith, and he gave glory to God (4:20). He was certain that the God who promised was also powerful enough to do what was promised (4:21). Thus Abraham's faith was both created by God's power and focused on God's power (see Gen. 15:5-6). The God who created the stars could create a child for Abraham. Unlike the Gentiles in general, Abraham was enabled to glorify the powerful God over all creation (contrast 1:20-21). The same God who created the world out of nothing could call into existence a child where none existed (4:17). The God who makes the dead come to life is the God in whom "dead" Abraham believed.

God counted Abraham's faith as righteousness. The repetition in 4:22 of the earlier quotes of Genesis 15:6 in 4:3, 9 shows that Abraham's faith described in 4:17-21 is the same faith Paul introduces in 4:3, 9. That faith is much more than simply an intellectual agreement concerning God's promise. Abraham's faith was impossible if it relied on what he and Sarah could accomplish. Only the God of the impossible made Abraham's faith possible. Abraham's faith thus focused ultimately not on the word of promise so much as on the God who is able and powerful to keep that promise.[2]

That continuous keeping faith in such a God was hinted at in 4:5 (believing on the one who makes the ungodly to be righteous). The God who created faith within an ungodly Abraham continues to enliven his faith despite his hopelessly "dead" body. One might expect that Abraham's difficult situation would have weakened his faith in God's promise. Instead, God enabled Abraham to focus his faith on God's ability and power to make the promise come true. His ongoing faith in that powerful God was counted as righteousness. It was not just a one-time agreement with God's promise that led to God counting his faith as righteousness. It was not just an isolated religious decision. Abraham had a continuing faith in God's power because of God's power at work in him.

While Abraham's faith was not the same as Jesus' faith, there were similarities. Paul says the Jewish Scripture about Abraham was written partly because of "us" (4:23-24). Like the use of "us" in 4:16, Paul seems to be addressing his readers directly. He is leaving his dramatic mission conversation with another Jew to draw out applications that directly affect his readers. Thus far, his comments about Abraham are meant to help his readers talk with Jews about Abraham as a foundation for faith and world mission. Jews who use Abraham as a basis for their privileged physical ancestry, circumcision, or works of the law must be challenged to see Abraham in a different way.

Just as righteousness was the result of Abraham's faith, it is sure to be counted for those believing in the God who raised Jesus our Lord from the dead (4:24). Both Abraham and Christians keep faith with the God who can raise the dead.

Yet the resurrection of Jesus was on a different level. It was the prime time of God's acting in power (see 1:4). Resurrection from the dead is a vital part of God's final kingdom. Jesus' own faith in God's kingly power included the faith that after he was put to death, God would raise him from the dead (Mark 8:31; 9:31; 10:34). Like Abraham, yet on a new and higher level, Jesus kept faith with the God of resurrection power despite the reality of death. Christians who share that faith in the God who raised Jesus will be counted as righteous. Righteousness and salvation will finally prevail through God's power over sin and death.

The salvation of the new age begun by God's resurrection power should not be confused with more recent New Age movements. Resurrection is not reincarnation. Those believing in reincarnation think they have the power to control their future destiny. Even then, the supposed destiny of being reincarnated on a higher or lower level falls far short of resurrection glory.

Likewise, looking to the glory of the stars through astrology will not save anybody. Learning one's fate from the stars rejects the almighty Creator of the stars. Such secret "knowledge" cannot save. God is not hidden in everything or in everyone, as a divine spark, waiting to be discovered. All such ideas are old and wrong. Hollywood or popular culture may celebrate those ideas as the beginning of a new age. But they were already around when Jesus began the true new age. Only the God of Jesus, the God of resurrection power, can create the new age.

In 4:25, Paul ties together Jesus' death and resurrection. On one hand, Jesus was given up by God's wrath for the sake of our sins (compare 1:24 and 3:25). On the other hand, Jesus was raised up by God's power for the sake of our righteousness. God's resurrection power over death was shown in him.

Jesus' final salvation from death was the beginning of our righteousness. As resurrected Lord, he rules righteously in those who share his faith. The salvation and righteousness which will finally be counted to us are already beginning in us.[3] God's power is now leading to salvation for everyone who is keeping faith in that God (1:16). God's righteousness is already being reflected in the believing one (1:17). The power of God which raised Jesus from the dead is creating new life in those who were once dead in sin. To believe in and receive the power of the God of Jesus is to become a part of God's worldwide people and mission.

Abraham's faith, like the faith of other people before Jesus, focused on God's future act of power (see Heb. 11). But Jesus' faith recognized that God's final saving power was at work in his ministry. And that power continues to work in those who share Jesus' faith and mission. Now faith receives God's righteousness and life through God's resurrection power.

While those before Jesus had a certain level of faith, Jesus himself was the true beginning of Christian faith. Paul could merely compare Abraham's faith in God's future work of power with Christian faith in God's future resurrection of the dead. Yet he chooses to connect God's promised power to Abraham and Sarah with God's past and present resurrection power in Jesus. Thus Paul's faith is not so much looking to the future. Instead, it is looking to the recent past of Jesus and to God's ongoing work. Neither Jesus' second coming nor the resurrection of all the dead are at the center of Paul's faith.[4]

The historical past of Jesus makes faith specific. It is not just faith in any God or any religion, or faith in faith itself. Belief is not the key. The key is God's power to do what was already promised. God's power working in Jesus began the final fulfillment of all the promises of God. The fullness of Jesus' historical faith and the presence of God's promised power are the keys.

So faith is not simply believing certain historical facts. Just because people believe in their minds that Jesus' physical body was raised from the dead doesn't necessarily mean God's resurrection power is at work in their lives. The problem is not in the facts but in focusing on only the facts. Early on, fundamentalist faith required five beliefs: the bodily resurrection of Jesus, the second coming of Christ, the substitutionary atonement, the virgin birth, and the verbal inspiration of inerrant Scripture. Whoever believed that all five were factual supposedly had true faith. But such belief fell far short of Jesus' faith. Yet more modernist Christians had trouble believing even most of those facts. The real question was, why limit faith to a few unrepeatable historical events at the expense of the living God who continues to make the story of Jesus' faith and mission come alive?

German New Testament scholar Rudolf Bultmann preferred to call a historical event like Jesus' resurrection a myth. Then other German intellectuals who doubted such miracles could still believe in Jesus. He "mythed" the point by making God's righteousness and resurrection power merely abstract ways of bringing people to decide for a modern spiritualized "Christ." Both fundamentalists and modernists made religious decisions for Jesus the basis of righteousness or salvation. But those decisions were too easy, and the Jesus was either too much like themselves (modernists) or too different from themselves (fundamentalists).

Modernists found some essence of faith that looked too much like their own "civilized" respectability. For example, nice ideas like the fatherhood of God (over every person) and the brotherhood of man (only men?) were supposedly central to Jesus' faith.

On the other hand, fundamentalists found an essence of faith that had too little to do with present faith. The once-for-all past of Jesus' miracles, death, and resurrection was the essence, but those were hard acts to follow. Belief in an inerrant Scripture also looked more to the past since most of Scripture, the Old Testament, was fulfilled (and ended as a national covenant) by Jesus' faith. Belief in an inerrant New Testament might help one discover the fullness of Jesus' faith, but not if one just picks out fundamentals or essences to condemn modernists. The fundamentalist emphasis on Jesus' second coming showed a rejection of any emphasis on God's present kingship or power.

Fundamentalists ignored the power of God in Jesus and in all his faithful followers throughout history. They exchanged that power for the supposed power of believing and confessing some essence of "faith." They substituted the power of the preached word for God's saving power. They substituted the righteousness of good citizenship or good churchmanship for God's righteousness. And they substituted God's blessings of forgiveness and the status of middle-class society for God's transformation of the selfish and satisfied.

Another Abraham, Abraham Lincoln, later became a forefather of U.S. civil faith. As Israel considered Abraham its national patriarch, the United States later made Abraham Lincoln a national hero. Abraham and Sarah received the new life of a child after being as good as dead. Similarly, Abraham Lincoln gained fame by bringing new life to a divided nation. He won a deadly Civil War, but then was assassinated.

Civil religion continues to confuse national heroes or "saviors" with the Savior of the world. In Lincoln's case, the Union he "conceived" and "brought forth" had nothing to do with God's promises to Abraham or Jesus' faith. The sacrifice and martyrdom of Lincoln and others who died in the Civil War led to creating a major holy day, Memorial Day. Every year, towns and cities all over the United States remember the martyred dead and their sacrifice for the nation.

Such Americans also miss the world vision of the God of Abraham and Jesus. National rebirths or resurrections due to martyred men fall short of the glory of God. The wars of nations are the result of human greed and hate, not God's promise. They are fought with male macho might, not God's power. Celebrated warrior martyrs appear to be dead right. They made the ultimate sacrifice, but their righteousness is dead wrong.

I believe a return to the faith of Abraham would be a step in the right direction. If Paul is right, Abraham's faith will lead us to the fullness of Jesus' faith and to God's present resurrection power.

Romans 5:1-11

God's Powerful Love, Jesus' Faithful Death, and Christians' Patient Suffering

I N 5:1-11, Paul continues to draw out the implications of God's resurrection power at work in and through Jesus (see 4:24-25). God's righteous power has made righteous those Roman Christians who share Jesus' faith. Paul now adds to that description of salvation by referring to peace (5:1). Jesus fulfilled the prophecy about a messenger bringing the good news that God had begun to rule in power; he was announcing peace and salvation (Isa. 52:7). Paul encourages Christians in Rome to continue enjoying peace with God on the basis of Jesus' faith. Jesus opened the door for their present access to God's powerful grace (5:2).[1]

Because of God's grace at work in them, the readers can rejoice and boast—not in their own glory, but in the hope of experiencing God's glory (5:2). Paul asks his partners in mission to rejoice and boast even in suffering (5:3) rather than boast in the supposed security of the law (compare 2:23; 3:27; 4:2). The faith of Jesus taught that persecution for the sake of Jesus' righteousness was a blessing and called for rejoicing (Matt. 5:10-12). He warned about persecution in the world but also promised his peace to those united with him (John 16:33). Paul's mission remains faithful to the truth that God's power is made perfect in the weakness of persecution for Christ's sake (2 Cor. 12:9-10).

Celebrating while suffering sounds strange. How could Paul and Silas sing hymns to God right after receiving a terrible whipping in an isolated prison cell (Acts 16:23-25)? Because their suffering resulted from their mission, they could consider it all a joy and a privilege (see Phil. 1:16-18, 29-30; 2:17-18). Some people have thought that if they became Christians, God would ask them to make great sacrifices, become missionaries, and give up some previous pursuits of pleasure. And they were right! Contrary to the call of cheap grace, a true Christian is called to a mission that radically seeks God's glory and rejects human glory.

The surprise is that when one gives up all to unite with Christ, to share Christ's faith and mission, the result is joy! Many can testify that they experience more joy in their sacrificial service with Christ than in any previous self-centered pursuit of happiness. Joy while suffering for Christ is not the sentimental good feeling many people seek from worship leaders, pastoral visits, or congregational gatherings. Such people boast about leaders who inspire them or at least understand them. They also enjoy other church members to the extent that there is good food, clean fun, and close fellowship. Yet the glory that successful leaders or happy members celebrate is their own glory, not God's.

Above all, they want their friendly church to meet their selfish desires and massage their egos. Leaders who busily try to meet such "needs" have successful careers, but little joy from suffering for Jesus. As professional pastoral counselors, they are expected to stand by and bring comfort when crises like sickness, accidents, or war result in suffering or death. Yet as church "chaplains," the suffering they are concerned about, though real, is not necessarily the specific suffering for Christ which Paul mentions here.

Paul is referring to suffering which results from one's faith and mission. Few people who call themselves Christians today face such persecution. The faith of many "Christians" is more of a cultural religion than Jesus' faith. Their mission rarely challenges others or involves real sacrifice for themselves. They seek peace with other people and want nothing to do with confrontations or situations that might cause persecution. Such peace is not true peace with God.

In nineteenth-century Denmark, Søren Kierkegaard strongly challenged the leaders of Christendom. He asserted that those who witnessed to the truth would suffer. Their witness in an evil world would involve poverty, humiliation, even death. Why were the priests enjoying a "peace" consisting of wealth, admiration, and steady promotions in their chosen careers? Kierkegaard answered that they were just playing games with Christianity for their own benefit. They were artists or actors in dramatic costumes performing in artistic buildings. They never offended the civil rulers, they pleased the powerful—and they were paid accordingly. Priests promoted a false Christianity where everyone could easily be called a Christian and cheerfully pay the priests.[2]

Denominational mission societies sometimes boast about the salary and benefits they give. Nondenominational "faith" missions require their missionaries to raise a certain level of support before they go to their "field." Thus the field becomes full of "rice missionaries" making "rice Christians." Not enough money? No missionary.

For example, a well-known U.S. mission agency recently required a couple to raise $46,644 per year as their support level. Their salary would "only" be $18,168. The rest would pay for housing, travel, medical and insurance plans, ministry expenses, cost-of-living increases, and home office administration. In the land where they were going, the average couple earned $3,184, and 38 percent of that was spent on food. As a result, Western missionaries enjoyed the pleasant peace of the world's powerful, affluent people.

Contrast such Western missionaries with the several hundred missionaries of the Indian Evangelical Team serving in North India. Each of them receive close to $20 a month. Other missionaries from the Kachin Baptist Church in Burma served six-year terms without any salary. In the future, more and more of the world's missionaries will be such third-world apostles.

What if Western mission societies drastically reduced their salaries and benefits? How many missionaries would continue? Probably only a few. Yet Western mission would then have real integrity (righteousness) through its faithfulness to the suffering model of Jesus and Paul.[3]

With God's help, they could remain faithful and reflect God's own patience (perseverance) which suffered the evil rejection of the world (5:3; see 2:4, 7). Patient endurance because of mission in an evil world would be evidence that they were to share God's glory (5:4). Proving one's faith by passing the tests of present tribulations would strengthen the hope of future glory. God's grace is powerful enough to turn the obstacle of persecution into a means of strengthening patience and hope.

Special mission strategies based on future special times, like the year 2000, reflect false hopes and often impatient missions. Our hope does not rest on human power, speed, mobility, efficiency, or success. Some Christians who always talk about their future hope show no signs of sharing Jesus' mission of confronting evil and of suffering persecution as a consequence. In fact, their hope includes the belief that they will not have to pass through any great tribulation. In response, we affirm a glorious future hope, but it is meant for those who now join Jesus' patient suffering mission.

Despite all the pain and persecution, the hope of sharing God's glory doesn't disappoint or cause shame (5:5; compare 1:16). They can reflect Jesus' faithful patience in an evil world because God's own love has been poured into their hearts and minds. The world's hate and rejection cannot take away the joyful experience of God's love for them. Since they have been made righteous by God (5:1), God's own love is now being manifested in them (compare 1:17). God's righteous, loving character has been given to the readers so that they are righteous and loving.

That righteousness is not the result of their own abilities, but because the Holy Spirit has been given to them (compare 2:29 and the heart circumcised by the Spirit; also, Ezek. 36:26-27). The power of the Holy Spirit effects such fruit (see Gal. 5:22) as love (5:5), joy (5:2-3), peace (5:1), and patience (5:3).

This is the righteousness and salvation that comes from God, not from people, and that began with Jesus. Paul is writing to strengthen Christians in Rome so their lives and mission will reflect such fruit (1:11, 13).

In the third world, Christians often suffer because of speaking out against the evil practices of wealthy and powerful leaders. A proverb sometimes heard in the Philippines is that those who would shed light must endure burning. When I describe such suffering to American Christians, they often raise the question of whether such suffering is really because of the gospel. My response has been that it depends on one's definition of the gospel.

If the gospel involves showing the love of God poured into our hearts and minds, then persecution due to speaking for the poor and oppressed can indeed be suffering because of the gospel. Not all who work with and for the poor and powerless are doing so because of God's love. Yet for true followers of Jesus' faith, showing concern for the poor and challenging the wealthy are included in the gospel that Jesus preached and practiced. (For a good summary of this common theme in the Gospels, see 1 John 3:16-18.)

When Paul and his readers were still living in their former moral weakness and ungodliness, Christ died for them (5:6). Without Christ, they were helpless, powerless. The old American proverb says that God helps those who help themselves. Some still quote that as if it were Scripture. But the saying emphasizes human power, with God merely providing some extra help when needed.

Jesus' loving faithfulness in dying for sin (see 3:25 and 4:25) was even more amazing since it was for the ungodly. It was even unheard-of to die for a righteous person (5:7). Instead, righteous people sometimes die early due to the hate of an unrighteous world. It is more possible that someone might die for a good person who helped them in some way (5:7).

Yet God's love goes far beyond all human experience. Christ's death for sinners who reject God shows the depth of God's love. Christ's death not only manifests God's righteous judgment (3:24-25); it also shows God's righteous love (5:8).

Jesus' faith(fulness) shows how strong God's love is.[4]

In a similar way, Christians whose mission includes a patient love for their enemies also manifest God's love (5:5). Just as God loved enemies by enabling Jesus to die for them, God continues to love all enemies by empowering Christians to patiently sacrifice themselves for others. God's righteous love is being manifested in the one(s) who shared Jesus' faithfulness (1:17).

Christ's faithful death is the source of present righteousness (5:9; see 5:1; 3:21-22, 24-26). Yet even more than that, Christ will save his followers from the future righteous judgment or wrath of God (5:9). Those who by God's power remain patiently faithful, will share God's glory (5:2-3; compare 2:7). The righteous one(s) out of faith will live (1:17). They already have peace with God and are reconciled to God, no longer enemies, due to the death of God's son (5:10). God's powerful love has transformed former enemies into friends. God's salvation has begun, joining love and faithfulness, righteousness and peace (Ps. 85:9-10).

Since Jesus' death provides righteousness, reconciliation, and peace to believers, then even much more will his risen life lead to their future final salvation (5:10). Jesus' death means reconciliation for God's enemies; likewise, Christ's resurrection certainly means salvation for God's friends. The joy of what God will do in the future is even now enjoyed in part because of the present reconciliation received from God through Jesus' death (5:11).

God's love does not simply tolerate those who differ from the faith Jesus showed. God's love leads to a mission that confronts those who are unfaithful and patiently suffers when they react against such love. Such a mission begins and continues only through God's power. And that mission bears some fruit only because of the power of the Holy Spirit.

The best examples of God's sacrificial love that I know of are third-world Christians who continue to help the poor despite threats, imprisonment, torture, and sometimes death. I have known Filipinos who were aware of the risks involved yet remained faithful to their mission because of God's powerful love at work in them. I have heard a Filipina woman threatened on the radio by a military official because she had called on the military to stop killing innocent farmers suspected of being communist rebels. After she called officials to repentance, she herself was slandered as a communist and threatened publicly. But she did not quit.

The Jesuit priest Rutilio Grande also called to repentance the wealthy landlords and violent military of El Salvador. After years of teaching pastoral theology in the seminary, he was considered for the position of rector of the seminary. Yet when some bishops and landlords heard his sermon about Christian concern for the poor, they stopped their support. After that, in 1972, he returned to his roots by serving in the rural region where he was raised. He sympathized greatly with the land-workers, who were treated like slaves.

After six months, he formed forty local Christian communities that read the Bible and related it to their evil situation of oppression. He usually walked or rode a mule to visit surrounding villagers. He ate and slept with the desperately poor peasants.

Organizing the peasant farmers was what the landlords feared most. As the peasants began to ask for higher wages and lower prices for seeds and fertilizer, the landlords called Grande and other local priests agitators, subversives and communists. A former Jesuit working with those peasants was taken in for questioning. He was beaten and tortured with electric shocks for ten days.

After a Colombian priest was forced to leave the area, Grande preached publicly that if Christ were to come to El Salvador, he would be arrested, accused as a subversive, and crucified again. Grande said the powerful preferred the images of Christ in the popular religion: a heavenly remote figure, the dead Christ of the crucifix, or the wonder-worker. But he followed the faith of Jesus of Nazareth, in whom God's powerful love broke through. In comparison with Jesus, Grande said, all the leaders of El Salvador, the landlords and the politicians, were dwarfs. Not long after that, in 1977, Grande and two peasants were shot down by machine guns. A child who witnessed the deaths said Grande's last words were "I am going where God's love is!"[5]

The hate of Grande's violent enemies was still not satisfied. Two months later, the military attacked Rutilio Grande's community of Aguilares with "Operation Rutilio." Using helicopters, tanks, and machine guns, they killed over three hundred unarmed peasants. Yet God's powerful love also was still not conquered. Catholic leaders responded with words about God's strength helping them to stand and even die for truth, justice, and the suffering way.

Shortly after the massacre, Archbishop Oscar Romero went to Aguilares and encouraged the people. He shared the pain and suffering of those who remained. He affirmed that violence of any kind, especially that of the military, was condemned by their Lord. The priests and peasants had suffered greatly for their patient mission. But they were committed to the crucified Christ. Romero ended his visit by calling for renewed courage. Aguilares could be an example to all the churches in El Salvador.[6]

Various third-world Christians have faced imprisonment, torture, and death because of their call to mission. They remain examples to more comfortable Christians. The climax of God's powerful love is Jesus' faithful death for sinners. Today, the pattern of Jesus' faith continues in those who take up their cross and follow him. Imprisonment or execution of Christians are the marks of evil political and economic powers that violently reject any call to repentance. Every society makes its own marks on those who continue Jesus' mission.

The mark of Jesus is a love that remains patient and faithful despite the worst persecution. It does not use violence or revenge as a last resort. For such believers, the last resort is giving up one's own life, not taking another's life. Even then, that last resort is only the beginning of what one has hoped for all along, the glory of Jesus' resurrection life.

Romans 5:12-21

From Jesus' Obedient Faith to Worldwide Righteousness and Life Through God's Powerful Grace

T HROUGH one man, Adam, sin came into the world, and the result was death for all people (5:12). Adam and all humanity are tied together corporately in sin and death. The power of sin and death has come to dominate the world because of Adam's sin (see 3:9). Adam is the crucial, pivotal figure. Because of him, human history is marked by sin and death (see 3:23).

Some have thought that everyone inherits Adam's original sinful nature (a view called "original sin"). That so-called inheritance is sometimes linked with physical descent and thus with sexual acts (and desires). Thus even babies supposedly inherit Adam's sin. The Catholic Church responded to such ideas by creating the sacrament of infant baptism. Adam's sin within babies was supposed to be overcome by the church's baptism.

Paul, however, is not writing about the evil potential of human nature, but about the evil power of sin that results in actual sins. Infant baptism or any other religious ritual is hardly strong enough to threaten sin's power. Infant baptism can emphasize the truth that God gives grace to those who, like babies, have nothing to offer. Yet it misses the fuller truth that God's grace powerfully transforms sinful people into righteous women and men. A special concern of Paul in Romans is to help his readers understand the depth of the power struggle involved in God's world mission. They need more than mere religion or education or civilization or any other human answer.

In fact, sin often does begin its destructive path during the earliest stages of childhood. Beyond the effects of sinful parents, children also disobey the good rules of parents. The power of sin is present early on and causes children to rebel at times against the good laws of parents or society.

Before the law of Moses was given, some sin was not counted against people because they were ignorant of God's law (5:13; compare 2:12; 4:15). Yet the power of death and thus the power of sin still ruled from the time of Adam to Moses, even though their sin was not disobedience of direct commands of God (5:14). Adam disobeyed God's command, and those who had the law of Moses disobeyed God's commands. But those who lived between Adam and Moses did not sin in that way. Nevertheless, they all died due to sin. The sinful person out of (Adam's) faithlessness shall die (the exact opposite of 1:17).

Jews are wrong who think the giving of the law was the beginning of a new time of obedience. God's covenant with Israel did not result in a new beginning. The old history of Adam's disobedience to God's command(s) merely continued.

But now another person has come to start an even more powerful process: the new age of God's kingdom. There is a second "Adam" who will be foundational for a new humanity and a different way of life. This other Adam introduced God's dynamic gift of grace into the world (see 1:5; 3:24; 5:2). While Adam's sin led to the death of all, God's gift of grace will be much more powerful (5:15). For through another man, Jesus Christ, God's grace overflows into all the world.[1]

Adam's one sin led to a judgment of condemnation. Yet after many sins came God's gift of grace, a new beginning and a new judgment or declaration of righteousness (5:16). All of the evil throughout history is not strong enough to stop God's gracious plan. After Adam's sin, death began to rule like a dictator. People were helpless. But now God's powerful grace has begun to overcome the oppressive tyrant. Jesus proclaimed the beginning of God's kingdom and manifested God's powerful kingship through his life, death, and resurrection. Those who are presently receiving God's generous and gracious gift of righteousness will finally conquer death and thus live and rule forever, all because of the one man Jesus Christ (5:17; see 5:9-10).

Just as Adam's sin led to worldwide sin and condemnation, so Jesus' righteous faithfulness unto death is leading to worldwide righteousness and life (5:18). God's resurrection power in Jesus conquered death (1:4; 4:24) and it will now make alive all those who are receiving God's grace (see 4:17, 25). Although some people will refuse God's gift, everyone (both Jew and Gentile) who receives God's righteousness and life will benefit from Jesus' life of righteousness. Only by associating with Jesus will one receive God's saving power.[2] For the power of God is unto salvation for everyone who is believing and receiving (see 1:16). The righteousness of God is being manifested in the believing one out of (Jesus') faith (1:17; see 3:22, 26). The righteous one out of (Jesus') faith will live (1:17).

Jesus and his followers will be tied together corporately in righteousness and life. Third-world societies more easily understand a corporate solidarity where everyone in an extended family, clan, or tribe is linked together. Western individualism has not made such relationships very important. Yet perhaps Western nationalistic solidarity, as defined by national political leaders, is another example of how a society collectively follows and identifies with a certain leader or leaders. Those leaders, however, usually rely on military power, which causes death and destruction. The power of sin and death dominates the societies and nations of the world as well as individuals. But Christ's people are a worldwide network and have been liberated from evil powers through the grace of God.

Those many believers throughout the world who received and reflected God's righteousness were made righteous by God because of the obedient faith of the one man Jesus (5:19; see 1:17; 3:22, 26). Jesus fulfilled the prophecy about the righteous servant who would make many righteous (Isa. 53:11). Jesus was God's chosen servant who would bring righteousness to all the peoples (Isa. 42:1).

Paul referred to all peoples all over the world to encourage his readers to participate in God's world mission. Unfortunately, some have mistakenly thought that Paul means every person is already saved due to God's grace and Christ's death. If that were true, the result would be either no mission or a mission quite different from that of Paul and Jesus. For Paul, only those whose faith receives God's gift will experience God's grace and Jesus' obedience (5:17).

When the law of Moses came, it did not make sinners righteous. Instead, sin increased (5:20; compare 3:20; 4:15; 5:13). Knowledge of God's law meant that sin was then disobedience of God's demands, an even worse state than before. Even for God's chosen people, Israel, sin was too powerful. The same Israel that treasured its special status in the midst of a sinful world was itself simply a part of Adam's ugly corporate history.

But where sin increased, especially in Israel, grace increased even more, especially in Jesus the Jew (5:20). If evil is a world power (especially among Jews; see 2:9), grace now is a superpower (especially in Jesus the Jew; see 2:10). Human sin is finally no match for God's grace. Beginning with Jesus, God's grace rules. God is the almighty King in a new way. Through the righteousness that began with Jesus, God's grace is increasing its power throughout the world and the result is and will be eternal life (5:21).

Righteousness is spreading throughout the world. Paul and the Christians in Rome are now part of the mission story as they help spread God's righteousness in the world. The result is a worldwide network of humble house churches.

God's superpowerful grace does not mean that the majority of the world will be flocking into the fold. Centuries later, leaders in Christendom claimed God's grace was blessing a whole country or nation or the whole world. They missed both the power of true grace and its effect in producing faithful followers of Jesus. A dominant Christendom forced whole peoples to accept domineering "Christian" leaders. Eventually, religious "corporations" multiplied customers or consumers by advertising grace in the most attractive way possible. Christianity thus became the world's largest religion but did not need God's power or Jesus' faith.

At the same time, throughout the world there were small groups of people who knew that true obedience means sacrifice, conflict, and suffering. Jesus' obedient faith led to rejection from an evil world and finally death on a shameful cross. While God's powerful grace will reproduce that faith throughout the world, the world in general remains evil and prefers civil religion.

During the seventeenth century, Roger Williams was a promising religious and political leader in England and then in New England. Like other Puritans and Separatists, he had been critical of the power and glory of the Church of England. When he sailed to New England, he saw Puritan leaders building a similar model of church and civil power in their Massachusetts Bay colony. After increasing conflict with powerful Puritans, Williams fled to what became Rhode Island.

All along, Williams had struggled with the contrast between Jesus' lowly suffering and the high and mighty leaders of civil religion. He became famous for his call to religious freedom. Yet the deeper basis of his discontent with religious power and force was the difference between such evil and Jesus' apostolic self-denial and suffering. Instead of the false Jesus of religious and political power, Williams wanted to follow the true Jesus of divinely empowered sacrificial obedience. Jesus did not use human power to enforce his mission.[3]

Because of more recent scientific and cultural "advances" in Europe and North America, new missionaries looked to the future optimistically and expected the ongoing victory of progress. Western Christians had confidence that the cooperation of church and state could solve the problems of the world and spread "progress" everywhere. By taking modern culture and the "gospel" to backward countries, "developing" them, and planting Western-style churches, world mission would supposedly produce worldwide righteousness and life.[4] In this program, more faith was placed in human ability and achievements than in God's powerful grace.

The first Adam is still found in those who want to be first. In most large U.S. cities, the biggest churches like to call themselves first: First Baptist, First Methodist, First Presbyterian, etc. Some churches settle for less: Second Baptist or Third Presbyterian. Being first means having the most members, the biggest budget, the largest building, or perhaps simply the longest history.

Mission became multiplication of religious institutions with their own special forms of ministry, doctrine, ritual, and organization. Throughout the past two centuries, different Protestant churches and denominations have reproduced themselves in other countries. Consequently, the churches remained divided all over the world.

New people (mostly men) were trained to administer and officiate over those institutions so they would be faithful to denominational traditions. Mirror images of the mother church kept alive the traditions and divisions of Christendom.[5] Instead of solidarity in the new Adam, Jesus, there were all the divisions and suspicions of the old Adam.

Parachurch organizations flooded parts of the third world with their own special programs that could ignore local churches. This has caused even more divisions. International groups like Youth With A Mission (YWAM) have sent thousands of staff and short-term missionaries all over the world. Young people went everywhere to evangelize as an alternative to summer church camp or a family vacation. YWAM thus operated a hit-and-run ministry, using over two hundred bases around the world. But their mission had indirect effects on other missionaries and churches already there. Backlash sometimes resulted, including some persecution of national Christians.

While YWAM talked about cooperation, they brought their own program and did their own thing. Most decisions for Christ resulting from such programs did not lead to converts becoming church members. YWAM was like a multinational corporation that bypassed local groups and "sold" their own product through their own well-paid staff. Parachurch organizations thus pursued the bottom line of maximum growth by marketing an easy salvation and minimizing demands. Their church-growth experts knew that attracting lots of people meant avoiding difficult social realities.[6]

At the same time, denominations tried to keep their own churches united. They built national headquarters and pushed national agendas. They stressed increased membership and giving in their churches to expand their own national staff members, buildings, and programs. Like their churches, denominational officials spent much of their income on themselves.

Even plans for unity among denominations were more like corporate mergers. United denominations would be more efficient (more centrally organized) and more powerful (more income, staff, and assets). Associations of denominations or churches, like a National Council of Churches or the World Council of Churches, were expected to create more of an impact on the world.

The irony was that those corporate powers often looked to the world for their agenda and mission. As corporate powers, they wanted to persuade and influence other corporate powers like bankers, businessmen, and politicians. They were optimistic that progressive forces could prevail, if only they stood united. Their biblical basis was the frequent Old Testament theme of God lifting the nation of Israel out of poverty or oppression.

The ecumenical movement wanted to unite God's worldwide people and change the world for good. It spoke out on behalf of the poor and oppressed around the world. But strong words by religious leaders with high hopes for humanity have had little impact on the worldwide power of sin. Their faith in people power or in divine liberation of nations was not the faith of Jesus. The deadly evil of many first-world multinational bankers and businessmen, along with their political puppets and "public" armies, continues to manipulate, intimidate, or destroy all optimistic people power.

To all those still belonging to the first Adam, the second Adam (Jesus) says to sell their treasured possessions and give up their measured positions. Human power and wealth are part of the problem, not the solution. By giving generously to the poor and joining Jesus' little group of poor disciples, they will not only end up second: they will end up last. So who wants to be last? What is humanly impossible is divinely possible. All who come under God's kingly power can become last like Jesus. To share in God's powerful grace is also to share in Jesus' obedient faith. And as Jesus promised, the last will be first after all is said and done (Matt. 19:21-30). Only the lowly righteous ones united in Jesus' faith will share God's glory and life.

Romans 6:1-14

From Death to Life with Christ Through God's Resurrection Power

A T the end of chapter 5, Paul argues that when the law of Moses entered history, sin increased (5:20; compare 3:20; 4:15). Such a statement upset other Jews who linked their law with increased righteousness, not increased sin. Some Jews thought their increased righteousness under the law would lead to the final grace of God's kingdom and Messiah.

Paul emphasizes that where the power of sin increased, the power of God's grace increased even more (5:20). So some disbelieving Jews may ask if their increased sin (under the law) is still needed for God's grace to increase (6:1). (Compare the similar debate in 3:7-8, where God's truth and glory abound as a result of Jewish falsehood.) Some probably tried to ridicule Paul's message by asking if he prefers that they continue to sin so that grace may continue to increase.

Paul strongly denies such a deduction from his words in 5:20. Paul's point is that God's powerful grace has already begun in Jesus despite increased sin because of the law (5:21). That present grace is in fact God's kingly power at work overpowering sin and evil.

To help his readers answer a question like that in 6:1, Paul reminds them of their experience with Christ. God's kingdom is already at work in their lives. They have a new righteousness based, not on the law, but on God's powerful grace at work in them. Increased sin is no longer a factor in their lives. Since they have died to sin and its power, how can they still live in it (6:2)? Why would they still want to live under the law if God's kingdom and Messiah have now come? To illustrate, Paul turns to the meaning of their baptism. It was baptism into Christ, which first means baptism into the death of Christ (6:3). They were buried with Christ (6:4).

Jesus was the first to describe his death as a baptism (Mark 10:38; Luke 12:50). The beginning of Christian faith and life is death, with Christ. Jesus' obedience unto death was the turning point in overcoming the power of sin (5:15-21). Now others can die to sin because of Jesus' death. They can reproduce his obedience in their own lives through God's power. Baptism is a sign of both the death of Jesus and believers' present death to sin.

Baptism marks the beginning of a new life of righteousness. Since baptism comes at the beginning of one's Christian life, Paul is not talking about a later growth in righteousness and sanctification. He is referring to the same righteousness as in 1:17; 3:21-30; 4:25—5:1; and 5:9, 16-21. God does not just reckon believers as righteous when they first become a Christian and then produce real righteousness in them later as they grow in faith. Baptism shows that God's power makes one righteous from the very beginning. Sanctification or holiness is the result of becoming a Christian. A Christian is one who has died to sin and received new life from God. One may still sin at times, but one is no longer a sinner whose life is characterized by sin. Believers are expected to grow in understanding of Jesus' faith and in doing right, but they are already made righteous from the beginning.

Paul is more concerned with the reality that baptism symbolizes than with the ritual itself. He assumes that his readers have been baptized. So he interprets the symbolism of their baptism to teach them about matters of life and death. Mere rituals have no power to save. The mission of Christendom to create Christian societies and nations could succeed only through the superficial means of emphasizing the sacraments.

Whole societies became baptized (as infants), participated in holy communion (or the Lord's Supper), and considered themselves Christian. Protestant churches focused on those two sacraments (or ordinances) and the preaching of the gospel (especially Christ's death) as the marks of a true church. Catholic churches added other sacraments but often still emphasized baptism and attending mass. It is striking that Paul did not even mention the Lord's Supper in Romans.

When Anabaptists in the sixteenth century rejected infant baptism, it meant also the rejection of Christendom's mission. At first, Martin Luther favored the ideal of a church made up of "believers" instead of a whole society. Yet Luther soon changed his mind and placed his churches under powerful princes, who protected members and had authority over them. Their dangerous faith did not need to face death.

Anabaptists accused Luther of returning to the Christendom model that dominated the church throughout the Middle Ages. Luther replied that Anabaptists were troublemakers and heretics. Indeed, their dangerous faith did often face death.[1]

However, death is where God's resurrection power is manifested. Christians therefore die with Christ, so as Christ was raised from the dead through the glory or power of his heavenly Father, they also receive new life (6:4).[2] God's resurrection power gave new life to Christ and gives new life to all those who die with him. Faith means death to sin and receiving God's life because it focuses on the God who can raise the dead (1:16; 4:24; see Col. 2:12). That was true first for Jesus and remains true for all who share Jesus' faith.

After World War I, a popular missionary verse was John 10:10, where Jesus explains that he came into the world to give abundant life. But many Western missionaries identified abundant life with the American (or European) way of life. Jesus' new life supposedly meant an abundance of the "good life" such as modern affluence, education, health care, and agriculture. The "higher" level of Western culture would lift up the deprived peoples and nations of the world.

While in the Philippines, I discovered some Filipinos still

used John 10:10 as their main text for a mission of improving the livelihood of poor Filipinos. They interpreted abundant life as abundant physical and material blessings. While their service was often helpful, their mission vision was more cultural than Christian.

God's resurrection power creates an abundant life of righteousness in those who die to sin with Christ. As Jesus said, those who lose their lives for his sake will find true life, eternal life (see Matt. 10:38-39; 16:24-25; John 12:24-25). For "civilized" Western Christians, true life would come from the death of downward mobility for Jesus' sake. But most hold onto middle-class privilege and seek the "blessings" of upward mobility.

Adult baptism was the earliest symbol of that death and new life. By going under the water, the believer witnesses to death with Christ (to sin). By coming out of the deadly water, one proclaims a new and different life of righteousness with Christ. Baptism witnesses to what God's resurrection power has done in that person who now has new life with Christ.

Baptism of infants can never witness to that. Even baptism (or confirmation) of older children seldom witnesses to a death to sin and a new life of righteousness. Jesus' love for children should not be mistaken for God's transformation of sinners. According to Paul, baptism is a sign of the latter, not the former.

Often religious leaders manipulate children into joining their church for the sake of institutional growth. Some children play along to please their parents, join other friends, or become the center of attention at a public ritual. Some churches try to slow down the process, waiting until youth reach some age of accountability, but most usually still baptize children too quickly and easily.

Sometimes children are routinely baptized at ages eleven or twelve, before they enter the teen years, when there would be more doubts, questions, and independence from parents and pastors. Most twelve-year-olds and younger accept their parents' views on religion. Adults may wish to baptize such children out of fear that they might rebel later. Or parents fear that because the children have perhaps reached the age of accountability, they are in danger of God's judgment. But such fears put too much emphasis on an empty ritual. Baptism does not make them more likely to die to sin and to receive a new life in union with Christ. The ritual is not a means of salvation, but a sign that God's power has already transformed their lives.[3]

Certainly children can grow in understanding the truth about God and in love for God. Christian parents can nurture their children so they respect God and want to follow Jesus. While such Christian education is important, it is still connected more with parental power than with divine power. I was reared by Christian parents and was a well-behaved child who attended Sunday school and church services. I was baptized at age nine after a series of evangelistic meetings in our church. Compared to most of my classmates at school, I was a "good" religious kid. Yet I consider my conversion to the faith of Christ through the power of God as beginning when I was seventeen, just after graduation from high school. Of course, God can transform people at a younger age. But I think most churches baptize younger children too quickly without any evidence of new life.

Those united with Christ and his death will also be united with Christ and his resurrection life (6:5). To be crucified with Christ also means that Christ then lives in believers (Gal. 2:19-20; see Phil. 3:10). Their old, sinful humanity has been crucified with Christ (6:6; see Gal. 5:24; 6:14). Their history with the old man, Adam, ended with the death of the new man, Christ (see 5:18-19). No longer are Christians part of the worldwide body of sin under the power of sin (6:6). Paul continues to portray sin as a personal power that rules over a world body of sinners.[4]

The purpose of Christ's death was to end sin's rule so Christians are no longer slaves of that sin. Christians who have died with Christ have been liberated from the kingdom of sin (6:7). For those united to Christ, that old kingdom has passed away, and a new creation has begun (2 Cor. 5:17). A new corporate self (Jesus and his people) has been created in the image of God's righteousness (see 1:17; Eph. 4:22-24). The old, corporate self (Adam and his people) is a separate body made up of those who remain loyal to sin's power.

Dying with Christ includes the faith that we will also live

with him (6:8). That faith focuses on God's power, which raised Christ from the dead (6:9). Due to God's resurrection power, death did not rule over Christ. Christ will never die again. His death was a final one-time death to the power of sin (6:10). The power of sin is associated with the rule of death (compare 5:21). Jesus' obedience unto death was the pivotal time and place where God defeated sin's power. Because of that one death, others can be freed from the power of sin.

Having died to sin's power and realm, Jesus lives to God, that is, in God's power and realm (6:10). God's kingly rule has prevailed in Jesus. What began with the life and death of Jesus came to a climax with the resurrection of Jesus. God's final kingdom, which will overthrow all evil, has begun with Jesus and is continuing with Jesus.

Since that is the case with Jesus, Paul's readers who have died and received new life in union with Jesus should consider themselves dead to sin and alive to God in Christ (6:11). Those who are "in Christ" are part of the worldwide body of Christ that shares his obedient faith and new life by means of his resurrection power. Like Jesus, they now can "live to God," live the life of faith by receiving God's empowerment.

Even if death is still dangerous, the new body (of Christ) should not let sin rule over it again (6:12; see 6:6). Persecution of that mortal body of believers should not drive them back to the kingdom of sin, to obey sin's desires. The members of that body should not present themselves before the "throne" of sin as instruments or weapons of unrighteousness (6:13). Instead, they should continue under the rule of God as those who have come to new life out of death.

Faith means reception of Christ's risen rule and results in faithful service. Their members will then be presented before God's throne as instruments or weapons of righteousness for the sake of God's world mission (6:13).[5] As those made alive by God's power, sin's power will not rule over them (6:14). They are under God's powerful grace, not under Moses' law (which only increases sin; see 5:20). Here the word *grace* (as in 5:20) emphasizes God's power, which overcomes the rule of sin in a way that the law can not do. Thus grace is not forgiveness for those who continue to sin (6:1), but a powerful master that rules through righteousness (5:21). Christians are not perfect like Jesus. Yet in the rule of God's grace, sin is now the exception.

God's grace, Jesus' death, and the church's mission must thus be experienced differently than it is in most churches. Many define God's grace as especially God's mercy which, based on Jesus' death, freely forgives. The mission of the church turns into erasing the inner guilt of invisible souls who in turn seek other individual souls. Or the church generously hands out God's genial grace to natural family units by baptizing their babies or children, marrying their sons or daughters, and burying their grandfathers or grandmothers. In the old saying, the church is where people are hatched, matched, and dispatched.

In contrast, Jesus described God's family as those born into the life of the new age by God's power and joined with Jesus in a holy union, including union with his death (John 3:3, 5–8, 14-16; 12:24-26; 15:4-5, 12-13, 20-21). Paul defines grace as especially God's power which, based on Jesus' death, produces death to the power of sin. Jesus not only died for us. We who are "in Christ" have died with Christ. Both experiences are crucial.

One who has not died to sin with Christ through the power of God has not yet experienced salvation. And not only is the individual soul saved. The believer's whole life and mission are liberated from the power of sin. God unites a new family of transformed faithful ones with Jesus to carry on his mission. By mutual service of one another, they together reflect God's image and righteousness and become instruments of righteousness to others outside the fellowship.

Christ is no longer just a substitute for me. He is also a pattern for us and a power in us. Being a Christian is not a simple exchange where Christ gives sacrificially and I take selfishly. Instead, the Christian life is an interchange where we share in the dying of Christ and follow his pattern of self-emptying love. Those who are truly "in (union with) Christ" are being conformed to Christ's death and are sharing his moral righteousness.[6]

✦ ✦ ✦

The Western church has two major weaknesses which have led to a lack of Christian community. One is individualism, where the church stresses individual salvation, individual morality, individual family units, and individual self-fulfillment. The other is a passion for formal organization. Churches love to organize committees and councils, assemblies and associations, boards and bureaucrats. They tend to be strictly business, organized by leaders who build their own power structures, all the way from powerful pastors to pontiff popes.[7]

In the body of Christ, God's power creates informal communities that die to the sin of the larger official church. Baptism is not joining some nice organization or just expressing one's individual decision for Christ. Baptism expresses freedom from the Western obsession of focusing on the individual or on the nuclear family, even in larger groups organized to satisfy the selfish desires of certain religious leaders. They have died to being slaves, spectators, or consumers of the ministry of one leader.

The church is not a collection of isolated individuals or an association of bored boards. The true church is a more loosely organized group of people who have died to the selfish desires of the individual or family unit and have received a new life of listening to and loving each other. Baptism means membership in a new family. Their community life together is not to become an exclusive club. Like Jesus' group of disciples, they all reach out in mission to others around them, sometimes finding open receptions and more often suffering painful rejections. Yet the small organism lives and doesn't need a large dead shell for protection or security. Death is the way to life.

Paul sees the main danger for his churches as coming from missionaries of Moses' law. That danger sometimes includes persecution or death. Fear of such suffering might tempt some Christians to leave the freedom of righteousness under God and transfer to the slavery of sin under the law. They might decide to hide in the institutional security of the synagogue. Thus the power of death can produce converts to the power of sin. Where the law comes in, sin increases. Yet where the rule of

Christ comes in, suffering increases. An important evidence of being under Christ's glorious rule is a faithful following of the persecuted and crucified Jesus. Dying with Christ continues through such suffering.

In a similar way, those who emphasize obedience to the law of their nation today are choosing the old man (Adam) over Christ. Patriotic devotion to the rulers of one's nation will include becoming weapons serving sin and death. For example, to obey the call to defend one's country or democracy or freedom or whatever will mean wounding and killing other people (who will be slandered as enemies who deserve their fate).

In socialist China, the Three-Self Patriotic Movement (TSPM) has been used as an instrument of the Communist Party's strict control of religion. Christian leaders in the TSPM supervised officially approved religious activities. Designated areas for church services were led by designated clergy. All religious activities outside the control of the state and the TSPM were illegal. House churches with an apostolic mission were violations of state policy. Chinese Christians were also not to have a direct relationship with Christians or churches in other countries. TSPM officials often informed the state of violations by such Christians. Violators could be warned and questioned, or arrested and imprisoned. Thus certain "Christian" leaders in the TSPM chose the security or agenda of their national law and became pawns of unrighteous political leaders and oppression.[8]

At the seminary where I taught in the Philippines, military intelligence used certain students as informants. In the past, some students had joined demonstrations against government evil. So the military marked them and the seminary as a subversive organization. Actually, most students and teachers reacted against such "subversive" activities. Churches that included suspected members or pastors could probably expect some other members to be used as instruments of national security.

Few American missionaries were critical of U.S. domination in the Philippines. Most were defensive when Filipinos (or other Americans) criticized the U.S. military bases, U.S. business interests, or U.S. political manipulation. As a result, they were instruments of American unrighteousness along with trying to be instruments of God's righteousness.

While studying medicine in England, Sheila Cassidy met a young Chilean woman who planned to return to Chile as a doctor. After her internship, Sheila decided to join her and served in several hospitals in Santiago. Later she became director of a clinic for the poor in one of the worst slums in Santiago. A priest asked her to help a wounded leftist revolutionary. She was aware of the danger but agreed to help.

Ten days later, Sheila was arrested and tortured with electrical shocks. Several weeks of diplomatic efforts freed her to return to England. But she never forgot that torture while lying naked with her arms and legs stretched out. She felt like she was present at Jesus' crucifixion, more as a participant than as an observer. Her clear impression was that she herself was there, suffering with Christ.[9] Only by dying with Christ now will we live with Christ, now and forever.

Romans 6:15—7:6

Liberated by God for a Righteous, Servant Mission

PAUL had just asserted that his readers are not under the law of Moses but under the grace of God (6:14). To be under the law is to be under the domination of sin. Then, as in 6:1, Paul interrupts his argument with another question from certain Jews who refuse to connect the law with sin. Paul knows from past mission discussions with other Jews how hard it is for them to accept that message.

Most Jews think they have the power to choose the right way of the law. A few can be expected to disobey the law. But that is their decision. So how can Paul claim that all those under the law are also mere instruments of sin's power? For them, those outside the law are the sinners ("outlaws"). If Christians are not under the law, then isn't Paul making God's grace a partner of sin (6:15)? Since the law doesn't matter, can Christians sin freely? Don't Christians still need to follow the law?

Paul again strongly denies such connections. Grace does not mean freedom to sin. In fact, no one is completely free. Everyone is a slave, either to sin or to obedience. Serving sin leads to death, but serving obedience results in righteousness (6:16). Paul breaks out in thanks to God because the Christians in Rome who earlier were servants of sin have now become obedient from the heart (see 2:29; 5:5). That obedience is not to the law of Moses but to the teaching Paul and others have passed on to them (6:17). Christians are not free to do what they want.

That teaching stresses the obedience of faith founded in Jesus and spreading out to all the peoples (1:5, 16-17; 3:22; 5:19).[1] The life of faith is obedient to God's will as revealed by Jesus, who brought the truth that can set free the slaves of sin (John 8:32, 34, 36). Though his followers were not under the law of Moses, they were not lawless. They were under Christ's law as they carried out their mission (1 Cor. 9:21).

For people to follow Christ, they must be taught about the faith of Jesus. Evangelism must include making disciples, not just making decisions. Religious commitment that is not based on the foundation of Jesus' faith is futile. To accept Jesus as Savior and Lord because of an evangelistic message will not necessarily lead to following the faith of Jesus. To make disciples, one's mission must teach others to do everything that Jesus commanded (Matt. 28:20). Besides Jesus' focus on God's new kingly power, many Christians especially ignore his teaching against storing up treasures on earth (instead, give to the poor) and against using deadly violence (love all enemies).[2]

Paul's emphasis here on teaching and obedience can be abused by religious authorities who become authoritarian and identify God's power with their own power over people. In the Roman Catholic Church, the pope can speak infallibly on certain issues. In most Christian groups, the higher up people go in the leadership structure, the more authority and influence they expect to have. It seems the most powerful leaders have the greatest share of God's power and are closest to God. To obey or follow them is considered to be obedience to God.

Such concentrations of power in religious leaders are not in keeping with Jesus' faith. Jesus' teachings exposed such inflated leaders as hypocrites and called for a humbler style of servant-leader. Teaching the truth about Jesus and his faith is not a one-man show. A team of teachers in each local group can gently point out different aspects of the truth about Jesus. Given the historical faith of Jesus, the New Testament is best seen as the final objective authority.

The best way to teach and learn that truth in a way that does not overpower or dominate others is through small-group Bible studies. In such studies, everyone can participate, raise questions, and speak the truth in love. Some teachers, or even one teacher in particular, may have more truth to share than others, but that does not make that person the master or lord of the group. The final authority is only Jesus and the written record about him in the New Testament.

It's also true that some people take advantage of grass-roots groups and humble teachers by pushing for their own power and authority. Taking away the authority of the elite leader in a church might open a smelly can of worms. People may introduce various religious ideas and practices which appeal to someone's individual conscience or experience. Yet the answer must not be elevating an educated, elite lord. No one individual interpretation, experience, or conscience, clergy or laity, can presume final authority.

Pentecostals give importance to an oral culture of testimonies, miracle stories, spiritual encounters, speaking in tongues, and prophecies. Personal stories of recent experiences rule the day. That culture prevails from small rural churches to an international circle of star performers. Huge settings with loud public address systems add a sense of oratorical power. Tapes, videos, radio, movies, and television also pass on the varieties of Pentecostal experience.[3] Yet true religious authority is found in the specific, concrete New Testament accounts of Jesus' faith and mission. Jesus must remain the authority, and the living Spirit of Jesus can lead all obedient followers in the true and narrow way witnessed to by the New Testament.

Just because new, unofficial religious leaders denounce the authority of professional clergy or pious traditions does not mean they are obedient to the type of teaching Paul passed on in Romans. Just because some leaders say their new movement is based on only the Bible doesn't mean they correctly understand the main truths of the Bible.

Many new groups begin as the result of turning a few minor issues into major issues. Personal power struggles also create new divisions. There must be room to disagree on many issues, but the truths of the New Testament call for careful and prayerful handling. Believers are not free to think whatever they want about God's power and righteousness as first manifested in Jesus' faith and mission.

God is the one whom Paul thanks for his readers' obedience because God is the one who made it happen (6:17). No human being has the power to obey God on the basis of one's own free will. Everyone is under sin's power until God's grace breaks the chains of that slavery. But now they are liberated, set free by God's power from the power of sin and made servants to righteousness (6:18; see 6:7). Like Jesus before them, they can become obedient servants (see Phil. 2:7-8). Paul describes their new freedom as "slavery to righteousness" because of the weakness of their flesh in understanding that grace produces righteousness, not sin (6:19). Freedom from the law does not mean freedom to sin.

Before their liberation, they presented themselves as servants to (Gentile) immorality (see 1:24) or to (Jewish) lawlessness (see 2:23). Some who served lawlessness increased its spread through their (Jewish) mission (6:19; see 2:19-24; Matt. 23:15). But now they have presented their members as servants to righteousness (see 6:13). That righteous service has increased the spread of holiness through their mission (6:19).

When they were servants of sin, they were not serving righteousness (6:20). The result of such shameful service was death (6:21). Yet God has liberated them from sin's power. They now are serving God. The result of that holy service is eternal life (6:22). Though the rule of sin produced shameful fruit, the rule of God produces the fruit of holiness. Death is the final wages for being a slave of sin; in contrast, the free gift of God's grace is the life of the new age that began in and through Christ Jesus our Lord (6:23; see 5:12, 15, 21). The righteous one out of (Jesus') faith will live (1:17).

John Newton was serving as the captain of a slave ship in the eighteenth century. He helped transport millions from their homeland to harsh slavery. Many died on the way, and thousands were fed to sharks. Later he became ashamed of that cruel, sinful system and turned to God's saving grace. He then helped pioneer work against the British slave trade until he died in 1807, the year slavery was abolished there. We know him today for his moving hymn "Amazing Grace."[4]

While most white American churches loved Newton's hymn, they also accepted the slavery of imported Africans. Instead of the obedience of Jesus' faith, southern churches promoted the obedience of black slaves. Early Anglican ministers in southern colonies like Maryland and Virginia preached absolute obedience of slaves to masters as if the masters were God. Such teaching became widespread in the southern United States. Christianity would make them better slaves, more pious and submissive. Liberation from sin's power meant merely liberation from supposed laziness, lust, and lying.[5]

Some of the harshest slavery in the history of humankind happened in the United States, a nation that boasted of being Christian and godly. During the nineteenth century, missions among African-American slaves in the southern United States usually tried to please the slaveholders. They passed on the message that slaves should be obedient to their masters. Missionaries criticized slaves for stealing from the white slaveholders. But the missionaries seldom criticized slaveholders who subjected their slaves to suffocating bondage, kept some slaves' wages, or divided families by selling some family members to even more brutal traders. As a result, the slaves suspected that the preachers and the slaveholders were united against them. White Christianity became a mockery. Its hypocrisy cried out for exposure from courageous prophets. Yet mostly only the slaves themselves saw clearly and spoke truly.[6]

The Catholic church has historically been a powerful institution that often made poor people slaves to its own dominance. During the nineteenth century, the Roman Catholic Church owned about half of Mexico's farmland. Hundreds of thousands of farmers were basically slaves of the church. Meanwhile, the church displayed giant cathedrals, luxurious altars, and awesome ceremonies. Only the few rich enjoyed the expensive services and religious schools. The rest of the people were mere slaves of their master, the church.

Latin American liberation theology has been more correct in pointing to the sin of the oppressors. Modern slave labor demands long hours at low pay in sweat shops under strict supervision. The evil domination by powerful elite leaders and businesses should be challenged before one deals with the evils of those sinned against.

✦ ✦ ✦

Paul clearly expects the Christian life to be one of righteousness and holiness. Yet the obedience of Jesus' faith is the new standard for righteousness, and the power of God is the new source for holiness. Such righteousness is not just a new status due to God's forgiveness or an easy avoidance of a few vices. Jesus' holiness was not primarily holy feelings of ecstasy. True holiness means being delivered from the power of sin so that one's whole life is no longer dominated by sin, though one might still sin sometimes. Moreover, it means challenging oppressive sin that continues to enslave others.

Paul illustrates his earlier statement about not being under the rule of law (6:14). God liberated them from the law as well as from sin. He is still concerned with those knowing the law of Moses (7:1) who might be persuaded to let that law rule over them. Paul describes the law as lording it over people as long as they live (7:1). Similarly, the married woman is bound to keep the law regarding marriage as long as her husband lives. But if the husband dies, she is set free from the law that relates to her husband (7:2). If she has lived with another man while her husband was living, she has broken the law against adultery. But if her husband dies, she will be liberated from the law and will not break the law if she marries another man (7:3).

Paul applies that example to his readers. Through the body of Christ, God has put them to death to the law of Moses (7:4; see 6:6; Gal. 2:19). As in the marriage example, the death of one leads to freedom from the law. Thus the death of Christ leads to the death of the law's rule over them. This suggests that the first husband of Paul's analogy is Jesus, as one born under the law, who faced the power of sin and death (6:9-10; Gal. 4:4).

The bodily death of Christ (the first husband) freed them from the law of Moses (the marriage law). Those united (in "marriage") with the Christ who died can then become united to the risen Christ (the second husband).[7]

It is the "other" earlier Jesus (the first husband in a society under the law) whom Jewish missionaries use to persuade Christians to submit to the law (2 Cor. 11:4; Gal. 1:6-7; 5:1-12). Yet because of Jesus' new faith and faithful death, Christians are no longer tied to the law (Gal. 2:15-16, 19-21; 3:13-14, 21-25). But they still need to watch out for false apostles of Christ who would separate them from their new husband, Christ—to return to the "first" Jesus, the true Hebrew who routinely observed various Jewish customs (2 Cor. 11:2-4, 13, 22).

Baptism symbolizes their death with Christ, death to sin and to the law (see 6:3-4). They now are free to belong to another, to Christ, raised by the power of God from the dead. If Jesus' death liberated them from the law's power, his resurrection provides them with a new power. With Christ as Lord, they will be empowered to fulfill God's purpose for them: bearing fruit for God (7:4; compare the fruit of holiness in 6:22).

Formerly Paul and his Jewish readers were in the (circumcised) flesh and under the law (7:5; see 2:28; 3:20).[8] Sin then worked its desires through that law (see 5:20). Consequently, they were included among the members of Adam's body of sin which bore fruit for death (see 6:6, 21). Their Jewish mission actually led to an increase in lawlessness (7:5; see 6:19). But now they are liberated from the law's rule and are dead to that law which they once served (7:6).

Their servant mission now is the outworking of the new life of the Spirit (7:6; see 2 Cor. 3:6). Because the risen Christ now lives to God, by the power of God, those in union with Christ also receive new life (6:4, 10). The Spirit of holiness which raised Jesus from the dead is giving them the power to bear the fruit of righteousness and holiness (see 1:4; 5:5). The written law possessed by Jewish flesh is ineffective (see 2:29). But God's power has now appeared in and through Jesus instead of the law (see 2 Cor. 3:3; Gal. 3:1-5).

God has made them competent to be ministers of a new

covenant (2 Cor. 3:6). Only a servant mission under that rule of God will produce fruits of righteousness and holiness (compare 6:21-22 and 7:4-6). The fruit of the Spirit will be a righteous, servant mission. God's own righteousness and holiness will be manifested in their mission (see 1:17).

Throughout church history, respect for the Bible has led to different degrees of submission to the law of Moses. Instead of liberation from that law, many have taught that Christians should follow all of God's commandments in the Bible. By making the Old Testament law of Moses of equal importance to the New Testament faith of Jesus, they have misunderstood the latter. Thus people have used the Old Testament to bless their wealth and their wars, all in opposition to the faith of Jesus. Their personal or national missions have led to the poverty or death of others in the world.

Non-Christian cults have also used special interpretations of parts of the law of Moses, or of the Old Testament, as a basis for their distinctive practices. For example, Jehovah's Witnesses have emphasized a supposed Old Testament name for God (Jehovah) and such laws as not drinking blood (interpreted as meaning no blood transfusions). Mormons applied Old Testament words about the Promised Land to their own settlements and finally built a "new Jerusalem" in the wilderness of Utah (Salt Lake City). Such religious movements have multiplied all over the world through their missionary zeal. Yet they still need to be liberated by God from the law, to accept a mission that multiplies the righteousness of Jesus.

Religion, "Christian" and non-Christian, likes to make God a slave of human interests. Instead of becoming servants of the God of Jesus, religious people try to use God as their own powerful servant. Weekly or daily rituals of thanksgiving for God's (material) "blessings" can become a form of insurance so God will continue to be a good provider. Such common games take the name of God in vain. But the name of the game is not personal, institutional, or national success. So why do we play at our worship, worship our work, and work at our play? Jesus' God wants to liberate us from such blasphemy and lead us into a truly righteous, servant mission.

Romans 7:7-25

The Deadly Power of Sin Manifested Through the Good Law

PAUL now raises another question he has heard from other Jews while teaching that sin works through the law (7:5). Is the law of Moses sin (7:7)? Paul's readers will need to be able to answer that question if they are to carry on Paul's mission to the Jew first and to the Gentile (1:16).

Paul strongly denies that Moses' law is sin. However, knowledge of sin came through that law (7:7; compare 3:20; 4:15; 5:13). Sin's desire (see 6:12) or greed was not clearly recognized as wrong until the law said, "Do not covet" (7:7; see Exod. 20:17). Sin received an opportunity through the tenth commandment to produce all kinds of desire in "me" (7:8). Paul has just described the sinful desires that worked through the law when they were in the flesh, and thus not in the Spirit (7:5-6).

In 5:20, Paul also writes about the law's coming in at the time of Moses, and the resulting increase of sin. Paul's use of "me" in 7:8 will make that history more dramatic and personal as he prepares his readers to carry on his mission among the Jews. (See his similar approach in 2:1-5, 17-27, and 1 Cor. 13:1-3, 11-12, where he singles out someone who represents a larger group.) He is not describing his own personal struggle with the law. Before his conversion, he considered his life under the law to be blameless (Phil. 3:6). Only after God transformed Paul did he realize that his former zeal was misguided (Phil. 3:7-9).

Before the law was given, "I" was living, since there was no awareness of sin against God's law (7:9; compare 4:15; 5:13). In 5:14, Paul writes that our old man (6:6), as part of the body or history of Adam (5:12), had a certain period in history (from Adam to Moses) when there was no sin against a command of God. Before the law came in, sin against the law was not counted (5:13). In that sense, the "I" (or corporate body of Adam) was living.

But when the commandment came, sin revived (7:9). This was sin similar to Adam's transgression, disobeying a commandment of God. "I" died. Although the commandment had the purpose of pointing to a life without sinful desire, it led to death (7:10). Sin used the commandment to deceive and to kill (7:11; see 7:5). Just as sin deceived Eve concerning God's commandment (Gen. 3:13), now it deceives those who have the written law of Moses. Sin's persuasive power thus causes disobedience of the commandment, and the result is spiritual death.

By itself, the law was holy, and the command was holy and right and good (7:12). Yet because of the comments in 7:8-11, certain Jews asked if the good commandment caused death in "me" (7:13). Paul strongly denies this and again focuses on sin as the cause of death. He adds that God's purpose in giving the law to those under the power of sin is that sin might be exposed. Sin is producing death in "me" through the good commandment so sin might become extremely sinful or be shown as just that (7:13; compare 5:20; 7:8). Thus, disobedience of the good commandment is supposed to manifest the awful power of sin. Sin can use even a good thing like the law for its evil purposes.

Sin likes to manipulate good laws. It finds ways to get around them, even creating its own new laws. For example, a capitalist free-market economy makes covetousness a basic law promoting materialistic growth and prosperity. A communist socialist economy makes covetousness a basic law that promotes materialistic growth and equality.

Moses' law against covetousness might be useful as a private value in certain contexts, as in protecting private property or preventing stealing. But many suppose that it must be reversed in the public world of producing and consuming goods. The more one works, the more one produces; the more one produces, the more one consumes; the more one consumes, the more the economy grows. Then people are caught up in a circular rat race of working and consuming. Even those who win the rat race are still rats.

In 7:14, Paul says they all (especially Jews) agree that the law is spiritual rather than sinful. Yet "I" (the Jew) am not spiritual. Instead of being controlled by God's Spirit, "I" am under the control of sin. "I" am a part of the flesh (compare 7:5) of the old man (6:6). As a part of the body or history of Adam (5:19-20), "I" (the Jew) am also ruled by sin (5:21). "I" am like a slave sold to sin, my master (7:14; compare 6:6, 14, 16-17, 19-20). Given the strong contrast in 6:16-23 between slavery to sin and slavery to God, 7:14 is not a description of those under God's powerful lordship. If some today can describe themselves as both "sold under sin" and as Christians, they seriously misunderstand the meaning of being a Christian.[1]

At that point, Paul begins a dramatic "speech" by another Jew who describes his present struggle with sin.[2] This is the "I" (introduced in 7:8-11, 13) who now speaks (from 7:14b-25). (Again, 1 Cor. 13:1-3, 11-12 shows how Paul can use "I" to give more general instruction rather than a personal confession.)[3] Paul's purpose is to show in more detail how the deadly power of sin is being manifested in the Jew through the law. Paul's portrayal can help his readers in their mission discussions with Jews who elevated the law while downplaying the power of sin.

The Jewish dilemma centered on doing evil while desiring to obey God's commandment. He didn't want to disobey but ended up doing the sin that he hated (7:15; compare 2:1, 3). In his mind he agrees that the law is good (7:16; compare 2:17-20). But in actual practice, he disobeys that same law (7:16; compare 2:21-23). So it is not really he who produces this but sin which dwells in him (7:17, 20; compare 7:8).

Most wealthy Christians have tried to excuse their wealth by using the Stoic argument that their attitude toward wealth is what really matters. As long as they detach their minds from wealth, there supposedly is no covetousness. Sin thus deceives them with the comfort that spirituality is especially what is inside their minds. Nevertheless, the private, inner devotion to purity can not erase the bodily deeds of greed. They keep so much wealth for themselves or their family when there are so many others in desperate need. Such selfish action exposes the truth. According to Paul, God's goodness means serious sharing of wealth with a goal of more equality (see 2 Cor. 8:13-15).

Good does not dwell in devoted Jewish flesh because although he wants to do good, he is not able to do it (7:18-19). That continuing experience shows that, with respect to the law, whoever wants to do good will discover the terrible reality of evil (7:21). He even delights in the law of God in his inner being or mind. But another law, the law under the power of sin, is at war with the law in his godly mind. Sin's strength, using the law, takes him captive as a slave so that the other members or parts of his body do evil (7:22-23; compare 7:14).

The losing struggle between his mind and the rest of his body makes him miserable. He desperately pleads for someone to deliver him from that body dominated by sin's deadly power (7:24). The only solution is God's power, which has begun to manifest its fullest strength through Jesus Christ our Lord (7:25; compare 6:6-14, 18-22; 7:4).

Without God's power, he himself, through his own power, can "serve" the law of God with his mind. Yet he is not able to serve it with his flesh or body, where sin's power over the law wins out (7:25). Only God's power can effect salvation from the power of sin (1:16).

In the United States, Norman Vincent Peale promoted positive thinking as the key to successful living. Television personalities, like Robert Schuller and numerous other pastors, now emphasize positive mental attitudes and motivations as a means of achieving personal goals. Usually the individual's goals are desires like peace of mind, happiness, health, and wealth (such as Schuller's 18-million-dollar Crystal Cathedral).

These leaders say that people can do anything they want if they just try hard enough. Possibility-thinking which pictures or visualizes desires as already fulfilled will help bring them to fulfillment. As Americans become more "successful," they need such help to reduce the emotional stress and anxiety that go with upward mobility. A religious mind-cure method is easy and fast with instant results.

Possibility-thinkers assume that negative thinking or attitudes cause negative experiences like poverty or suffering. People think they can save themselves through the power of positive thinking, with a little help from God. As the old saying goes, God helps those who help themselves. Meanwhile, they ignore God's power and God's goals, or identify them with their own willpower and selfish goals. For them, faith in God is really faith in oneself.

God's salvation can hardly be identified with self-help, self-esteem, self-love, self-worth, self-fulfillment, self-awareness, self-actualization, or self-realization. The faith of Jesus and Paul repeatedly points out that people can not save themselves. Salvation cannot be defined as positive mental attitudes or upward mobility. Such desires are simply covetousness.

Modern psychology is too optimistic about the hidden potential of the human mind. The therapy of many individual counselors or recovery groups is shallow and short-lived. Clients become consumers who keep coming back. Human healers can sometimes be helpful. Expert counselors, however, are too "helpful" when they cause their clients to become dependent on them.

In-depth psychotherapy can clarify past problems and current feelings, but its future solutions often cause new problems. The inner depths of the individual's mind and feelings are not the answer to the power of sin. Whenever one's world revolves around oneself, the self gets dizzy.

Paul emphasizes that human thought or willpower cannot solve the problem of sin. Free will does not include freedom to do what one wills. Any mission to those who depend on their own obedience to the Old Testament law, or any other law, must emphasize Paul's diagnosis and solution for the power struggle with sin.

The Enlightenment worldview emphasizes that individuals should be free and independent. An Arminian type of theology stresses the ability of humans to make right choices and to do right. People only need to know what the choices are, and then out of their own free will, most will make the right decisions. Most people are reasonable and will act rationally. But Paul says that even the best people, those who choose to do God's will, face a losing struggle to carry out God's will.

An earlier theologian, Pelagius, also thought that people had the power to accomplish every good thing. If people just tried hard enough, they could produce true justice and peace. Whatever they set their mind to do, they could do. Where there was a will, there was a way. Yet the world's injustice rolled on like a mighty river. As they ran themselves ragged, they became increasingly frustrated.

Full-time, highly trained Christian leaders often are frustrated at how little they can accomplish. Coming fresh from colleges or seminaries, they are full of great ideas that they think can change the world, or at least their church. They have a lot to offer, and they expect to be paid well for their efforts. That idealism later turns to despair. Sometimes it turns into self-promotion, coveting more powerful positions or more prosperous careers.

In the third world, there are few such positions or careers for Christian leaders. Most churches are small and unable to pay for full-time ministers. That was also the case for churches in the first few centuries after Christ. Those early churches did not have formally educated, well-paid ministers. Deacons or bishops could use part of church offerings for certain basic needs. But those needs always varied. There was no set salary. Most church elders supported themselves as much as possible. Even by the fourth century, Basil said most clergy in Cappadocian Caesarea worked at making crafts to earn their daily bread.[4]

Using teaching from Jesus and Paul (Luke 10:7; 1 Tim. 5:18), early church leaders relied on informal hospitality and almsgiving. Church members brought food for a common meal. Leaders were only a small part of those who needed such help. Others included widows and orphans, the elderly, the imprisoned for their faith, visiting Christians, and those with sudden emergencies. A third-century writing said the bishops could take what they needed from the offerings. Yet they were to take only what was needed for essentials like food and clothing. They were not to take all or even most of the offering. Echoing Paul's quote of Deuteronomy 25:4 (1 Cor. 9:9; 1 Tim. 5:18), this writing said the ox should not be muzzled as it worked in the grain field. It could eat as it worked. But it was not to eat everything![5]

So there was no fixed salary as the early churches made do with freewill offerings. When the idea of clergy salaries was introduced later, many Christians were appalled. They considered such preaching as done for the sake of greed and gluttony. Yet more and more clergy became attracted by such offers of better pay. Thus throughout the first five centuries, there was an increasing movement for more regular support of clergy. This movement was also encouraged by the growing wealth of the church after it became the official state church in the fourth century.[6]

Many churches today spend most of their offerings on pastoral salaries. The United Presbyterian Church in the United States is typical. In the late 1970s, a Presbyterian missionary estimated the denomination spent around $300 million of its annual income on support for U.S. pastors. It gave only $7 million of that income for mission and service around the world.

The missionary also said some pastors in the third world seemed to expect more help than was given to more-needy church members. For example, after the Guatemala earthquake in 1976, a group of leading pastors and a few laymen in Guatemala City formed a Presbyterian emergency committee (CESEP). Two missionaries also informed home churches about pastors who lost homes. A year later, CESEP reported giving $24,165 to 310 laypeople whose homes were destroyed or damaged—and $38,300 to six leading pastors who had not lost any property. And most of the six were members of CESEP! At a time of extreme need, six pastors greedily improved their own lot. All the while, U.S. missionaries helped raise the money and cooperated with and approved CESEP.[7]

When we were in the Philippines, a Filipino denominational executive made urgent calls for help to the United States whenever a typhoon caused extensive damage. When funds arrived, most were used for those in need, but some disappeared. Later, the executive became a regional ecumenical leader in Southeast Asia. He eventually built a nice new house and became infamous for grabbing more than his fair share of relief funds (and women). As our mission's representative to related Filipino church institutions, my wife had to confront him at various times. She also warned others about him. Some listened and some didn't.

Throughout church history, males have dominated and often linked the individual physical body, including sexuality, with the lower nature. Many then blamed women for the covetous desires or sensuality connected with the body. Reflecting a Greek philosophy that separates the soul and the body, many church leaders taught that the soul was imprisoned in the body. The spiritual realm of the soul was constantly at war with the evil flesh.

Such philosophers denied Paul's portrayal of the deadly power of sin winning over the weakness of the good law and the willing mind. Instead, they accepted the power of the evil body winning over the weakness of the good soul. Paul's solution of God's power producing righteous actions, in mind and body, was changed to saving invisible souls for a heavenly spiritual existence.

Such ones who only looked at the evil deeds of the body confused the symptoms with the real problem: the power of sin that has dominated the history of the corporate body of Adam. The pursuit of inner, private spirituality missed the new arrival of God's power in the concrete history of the corporate body of Christ. According to Paul's gospel, the individual's physical body is not evil in itself. It is simply an instrument for good (by

God's power) or for evil (by sin's power).

The church has usually been uncomfortable with, and suspicious of, the human body and sexuality. When sex was mentioned, the dangers of sexual passion and activity were emotionally denounced. The goodness and joy of sexuality within marriage were seldom mentioned. Yet the strong rules against sexual covetousness were no match for the power of sin.

There is now growing evidence that conservative religious fathers are among the most likely to sexually abuse women and children. Men can be dangerous when they misunderstand headship in the family as power over submissive wives and children. Fathers and husbands who think God gave them control over their wives and children, sometimes decide they can do whatever they want to them. If exposed, they might try to turn over a new leaf. But the old leaf and forbidden fruit remain dangerously delicious. Granting forgiveness apart from demanding changed behavior simply condones past abuse and encourages future abuse. Both abusers and abused will need ever-new touches from God's healing hand, and from divinely gifted human healers, before true repentance, restitution, forgiveness, and reconciliation can occur.[8]

Christ's teaching or law will also produce a frustrated struggle if separated from Jesus' faith in God's power. The gospel message itself is not the power of God since it, like Moses' law, cannot be obeyed apart from God's might. The supposed power of the word is not really so powerful after all. Many human attempts to change others are based on a faith in words. They think people just need to know what is good for them. If people don't change, or merely change for a short time, they think they just need to try harder to persuade them. At that point, they try such tactics as threats or charm, shouting louder or speaking more eloquently, enticing or seducing. The result is usually that the one seeking to change others through dynamic words ends up being manipulated by the one resisting change.

Christian education cannot create Christians. Nor can Christian homes or parents create Christian children. A mission that emphasizes the influence and teaching of other Christians as the main means of making disciples is wrong. Others might

agree with and affirm the law of Christ, but they will not be able to do it until the power of the risen Christ transforms them.

On the one hand, this means that one must be realistic about the limits of what mission can accomplish. One should not get too excited if many express agreement with the message. Agreement and even confession are not yet obedience. To become excited because another or hundreds of others accept one's message is to presume that everything depends on human activity. On the other hand, this means that one must also be realistic about the transformation which God can accomplish. One should not get too discouraged if most of those who agree with their message eventually disobey that message. Even if most fall short, conversion, transformation, and obedience will continue to happen because they depend above all on God's power. Thanks be to God through Jesus Christ our Lord! (7:25).

Romans 8:1-16

The Life-giving Power of God's Spirit and the Righteousness of God's Son

I N 7:7-25 Paul portrays and dramatizes the deadly power of sin. In 8:1-16 he provides the answer, the only answer: the life-giving power of God's Spirit. Sin and death dominate even those who love the law of Moses, and the result is condemnation (5:16, 18; 7:7-25). That was the root problem until the time when God's kingly power was manifested in a new way through Jesus Christ. But because of God's new work, there is now no condemnation for those who are united with Christ (8:1; see 3:21-22; 5:9, 18). Christ by faith believed in and lived out that new power of God in history; now that same Christ is ruling with God. The risen Christ can enable those united with him to share his faith (fulness) and life.

Moses' law is not the key to life and righteousness (see Gal. 3:21). Instead, the key is the law (under the power) of the Spirit of life as fulfilled and transformed by Jesus' faith (compare the law of faith in 3:27). The Spirit can liberate one from the law (under the power) of sin and death (8:2; see 7:6, 23). The real power struggle is between God's Spirit and sin. Moses' law was merely under the dominance of sin (7:5, 8-11, 13, 22-23). Now, however, since the time of Jesus Christ in the flesh, those in Christ, united with Christ, are liberated from sin, death, and the law of Moses (compare 3:24; 6:22-23; 7:4, 6). Moses' law is powerless compared to the power of sin which rules through the flesh (8:3; compare 7:14).

However, the good news is that God's own Son was sent on a mission into the world of sinful human flesh (8:3; see Phil. 2:7). Through his faithfulness unto death (see Phil. 2:8), Jesus confronted and condemned the power of sin even while sharing human, Jewish flesh (compare 1:3; 3:25; 6:6, 10). As a result, the righteous demand (singular) of the law of Moses, as defined by Jesus, can now be fulfilled in those who walk according to the Spirit (8:4; compare 2:26, 29).

Here Paul reflects Jesus' teaching about the great commandment that fulfills the law of Moses (see Matt. 22:36-40; Gal. 5:14). Jesus filled that demand with radical new meaning. He did not understand love from just the Old Testament context. His demand(s) for living under God's rule transformed the law of Moses. Yet Jesus' greatest demand can be fulfilled in all who walk and live by the power of God's Spirit (compare Gal. 5:16, 25; Eph. 3:16-19). The Holy Spirit will pour out God's love into their hearts and lives (5:5). As in 1:17, the righteousness of God will be manifested in the one keeping faith in the same way that Jesus was faithful (see 3:22, 26; 5:18). The source of that righteousness is the power of God's Spirit (see 1:16).

Jews must be persuaded of the weakness of the way of Moses. Those visited by Jewish missionaries must be able to explain why Jesus' way is better. Roman Christians who carry on Paul's mission will now be better prepared to face such situations. The mission of the new covenant, a ministry of righteousness and life through the power of the Spirit, has replaced the mission of Moses' law, a ministry of condemnation and death due to the weakness of that written word (2 Cor. 3:6-9). If the law of Moses became more important than the power of God as manifested in Jesus' faith, then a Jewish ethnic mission would replace God's world mission (to Jews and Gentiles).

✦ ✦ ✦

As Christians work out the details of their life and mission, there is always a danger of leaving behind the law of Jesus' life-giving Spirit. Even when Western Christians commit themselves to obeying Christ's great commission (Matt. 28:19-20), many do so by means of the flesh. Their minds are full of zeal for God, but the deadly flesh of human superiority and domination exploits such zeal. Instead of limiting their mission to the law of Jesus' faith and allowing the Spirit to give life, some godly missionaries have played god. New Christians and churches had to learn and submit to the heavy traditions of Western doctrines and denominations. Mission headquarters and mission stations stayed in control. They remained the spiritual centers and directed the lives of third-world converts and churches.[1]

Modern apostles led by the life-giving Spirit will limit their mission to the New Testament focus on Jesus' faith and fellowship. They will not have to spend a long time to build and maintain Western institutions of the flesh. Jesus' servant mission will build up other servants in each place and let them continue that mission through the Spirit's power. Only the Spirit can create and sustain new life. Only the Spirit can unite diverse groups of servants into a visible fellowship and witness.

The concerns of the flesh differ from the concerns of God's Spirit (8:5). The flesh depends on its own power and privileges to please God. For example, the flesh boasts that its religion or race or culture or good works make it spiritually superior to others. Such spiritual flesh is only skin-deep. In Romans thus far, Paul has emphasized the problem of pride in Jewish flesh (2:17-20; 3:27; 4:1-2). Jewish concern for circumcised flesh (2:25-28; 4:9-12) or for their own special law (2:17-20; 3:20, 27; 7:1-5), is not the concern of God's Spirit as revealed in Jesus. Seeking to please God in the flesh only means death (8:6; compare 7:5, 24).

On the other hand, the Spirit brings life and peace with God (8:6; see 8:2). To reject the Spirit and to favor the flesh is to become an enemy of God (8:7). Although Jewish flesh loved and taught the law of God given to Moses, it did not submit to the law in actual practice (8:7; compare 2:21-23; 7:8-11, 13-25). Human flesh is simply not able to submit in that way (8:7; see

7:18). Those focusing on the flesh do not have the power to please God (8:8).

The human mind is thus clearly part of the flesh. The mind may agree with God's law, but only God's power can enable one to practice the law. Currently, New Age spirituality contrasts the mind with the flesh. In fact, the Universal Mind is made to be God, following certain Eastern religions. Or perhaps mindless ecstasy is the means of unity with God. Rituals like transcendental meditation (and its mantras) become one of many means to reach a higher spiritual state. The spirit behind such spirituality is simply part of what Paul calls the flesh. It is still trying to use human abilities to gain access to false gods. It is not able to please the true God, the God of Jesus. The Spirit of God is not a divine spark in every person that merely has to be discovered. Human souls or spirits must not be confused with God's Spirit.

Paul quickly mentions his confidence that his readers are not in the flesh but in the Spirit (8:9). Being in the Spirit means that God's Spirit is dwelling in them (8:9). Thus they are in the sphere or realm of the Spirit whose power enables them to please God. Certain people are transformed so they can please God, but this happens only by the power of God's Spirit, which comes from outside the human flesh of soul, mind, or body.

Whoever doesn't have the Spirit of Christ doesn't belong to Christ (8:9). God's Spirit, which is the same as the divine Christ's Spirit, enables one to be in Christ, to be united with Christ, to share the faith of Christ (compare 8:2, 4). Likewise, to be in Christ means that Christ is dwelling in them (8:10). They are in the sphere or realm of Christ, whose power enables them to please God. The risen Lord again lives his obedient faith through his Spirit at work in them.[2]

Some have tried to divide history into different periods where different divine persons were in charge. A popular division is that God the Father ruled during Old Testament times. Then came God the Son during his brief time on earth (or perhaps for a longer period during part of church history). Finally

God the Holy Spirit took charge after Christ. Dispensationalism also divided history into several dispensations and separated the time of Jesus from the time of the church (where Paul became more the authority). Similarly, charismatics or Pentecostals can put present gifts of the Spirit, including new prophecies of spiritual truth, on a higher level than the faith of Jesus described in the New Testament.

In Mexico, a certain Father Elias declared himself the incarnation of the Holy Spirit. He supposedly was the beginning of the last Age of the Spirit. God was speaking directly, face-to-face, through mediums like Father Elias. God gave him twenty-two commandments against such things as alcohol and family instability. Those accepting his form of Spiritualism performed regular rituals of healing the sick. Individuals, especially the sick, were told to listen to communications from spiritual power.[3] Yet Paul's faith and the Holy Spirit cannot be separated so easily from Jesus' faith. The Age of the Spirit cannot be separated from the Age of the Son. According to Paul, the Holy Spirit empowers certain people to please God the Father by enabling them to share the obedience of God the Son. Jesus remains the historical key for how future disciples will live through the Spirit's power.

Those who belong to Christ have crucified the flesh and its sinful desires (Gal. 5:24). The real test of having God's Spirit is sharing the life and faith of Jesus. Other so-called tests like religious enthusiasm, speaking in tongues, or physical healing can manifest a lot of human spirit. Yet if they lack Jesus' sacrificial obedient love, they fail the real test of having God's Spirit (see 8:3-4; 1 Cor. 13:1-3).

Paul does not promote the Spirit's power in terms of miracles or speaking in tongues or being slain by the Spirit. The power of the Spirit is not a means of pleasing human desires for release from suffering or boredom, or for acquiring new status or domination. While today the Spirit's power can still produce miracles or speaking in tongues, those should not be glorified at the expense of Jesus' obedient faith. Spiritual power, according to Paul, is found above all in release from sin and in the obedience of Jesus' faith.

Jesus' own victory over sin was due to the presence of God's Spirit. After the Spirit descended upon him at his baptism, the Spirit led him into the wilderness to be confronted by the power of sin (Mark 1:10, 12). According to Luke 4:14, Jesus returned to Galilee in the power of the Spirit and began his mission as the Servant-Messiah, anointed by the Spirit of the Lord (Luke 4:18). As Jesus liberated those oppressed by the power of sin, such as those possessed by demons, he proclaimed the good news that God's powerful kingship was at work through the Spirit of God (Luke 4:18; Matt. 12:28).[4]

If that same Jesus is now present in their lives, although the body will still die due to sin's continuing power, the Spirit will give life because of God's righteous power (8:10). If Christ dwells in them, the Spirit of Christ can produce life because of God's righteousness. That righteousness was first manifested in Jesus, who condemned sin and died to sin (see 1:17). The new life produced by Christ's Spirit will reflect Jesus' own life of righteousness. The righteous one out of faith will live (1:17).

Furthermore, if the Spirit which raised Jesus from the dead (see 1:4) dwells in them, the same indwelling Spirit will give life to their mortal bodies (8:11). Certainly that will be true for the final resurrection. Yet it is also true for the new life experienced now in the Spirit (compare 6:4-5, 13).

Since they are now alive, they are debtors to God's Spirit, not to human flesh (8:12; see 1:14). Those who have been influenced or helped by Jewish flesh might have pressure to pay back what they owe to that flesh. But as brothers and sisters in Christ, they owe nothing to the flesh since it is too weak to please God (see 8:7-8). They can leave behind the ways of the flesh. Otherwise, they will surely die a hopeless death (8:13). They will live only if by the power of God's Spirit they continually put to death the sinful works of the body or flesh (8:13).

Sometimes nominal Christians who confess Christ and then live as they want are called carnal (flesh) Christians. Paul does describe carnal Christians in 1 Corinthians 3, but they are not uncommitted nominal Christians. Instead, they are over-committed to one Christian leader, Paul, Apollos, or Cephas, at the expense of other good leaders. They are clothed with Christ, but their boasting, jealousy, and quarreling over certain leaders exposes their flesh. Still, they are clearly not just nominal Christians who care little about the new life of the Spirit.

Because evangelists, revivalists, pastors, and priests have made becoming a Christian so easy, others have felt the need for a second blessing, a baptism of the Holy Spirit. This two-stage model of the Christian life tries to bring in the transforming power of the Spirit at a later stage of the Christian life.

John Wesley used such a model with his teaching about Christian perfection. Donald McGavran, the pioneer of the science of church growth, has described a later perfecting phase after an initial discipling phase of getting people to join a church. Nineteenth-century revivalists like Charles Finney and D. L. Moody saw the need for a baptism of the Spirit after conversion. That was their solution to the lack of change among their converts. The Holy Spirit could deliver ordinary Christians from their shallow faith and transfer them into the deeper waters of the Spirit, the victorious Christian life. At the beginning of the twentieth century, Pentecostalism used similar teaching but connected the baptism of the Spirit with special gifts of the Spirit.[5]

The two-stage theory tends to see Paul as an example of the frustrated carnal Christian in 7:7-25, who is later delivered from the flesh by the Spirit (8:1-16). Yet 7:7-25 is not about Christians at all, and 6:4 connects the new life of victory over sin with baptism and the beginning of Christian faith. Thus the life-giving Spirit of 8:1-16 is not a second blessing, but the basis for being a true Christian in the first place. The problem with the two-stage theory is that the first stage of carnal or fleshly Christianity is not true faith. It is just the flesh with a spiritual tattoo. True faith can also feel the deadly pull of the flesh, but it generally remains true to the fruit of the Spirit. God's righteous love is the norm.

Only those constantly led by God's Spirit are children of God (8:14). The new life of the Spirit is not a second or third blessing. It is the ongoing blessing of being part of God's family from beginning to end. The Spirit they receive has made them children who are obedient and at peace with their heavenly Father (8:15; compare 5:1-2, 5, 9-11). Certain Jews want to make some of them afraid so that they become slaves of the law again; such fearmongers are not led by God's Spirit (8:15; see Gal. 2:12; 4:3-10).

The Spirit of God's Son will lead Roman Christians to cry out to God in the same way as Jesus did. Just as Jesus in the garden of Gethsemane addressed God as *Abba* (Mark 14:36), so those who receive Jesus' Spirit will cry out to God in the same way. *Abba* is the word for father or dad in Jesus' own Jewish dialect (Aramaic).

The situation Jesus faced in Gethsemane was tense. Because he had not become a slave of the law as interpreted by certain Jewish leaders, Jesus faced death at their hands. Yet he still cried out to his Father as an obedient Son, who was willing to suffer and die according to God's will.[6] Calling God *Abba* expressed both intimacy with Almighty God and the submission of an obedient child as a result of a faith which received God's power and righteousness.[7] Jesus did not teach a vague, sentimental fatherhood of God and brotherhood of man. The God of Jesus did create a worldwide family of obedient children. But most people were not part of that family.

That faith(fulness) of Jesus is now shared by those Christians who can also cry out as obedient sons or daughters in the midst of similar fearful situations. Jesus' Spirit is the same Spirit now at work in them, giving them assurance that they are children of God (8:16). Despite the attacks of those who deny they are children of God, the Spirit witnesses to the truth by crying out to *Abba*.

Like Jesus, God's children will cry out in their own languages. There will be unity in the Spirit because they share the same heavenly father. Different races, languages, and nations, when focused on human flesh, lead to competition, suspicion, and division. Only when God's powerful Spirit creates new life and peace is there unity in truth and righteousness among the world's diversity.

Romans 8:17-30

Sharing Jesus' Faithful Suffering and Final Glory

H UMAN flesh is too weak to do God's will. Only the power of God's Spirit can produce faithful children of God who reflect the righteousness of God's Son (8:1-16). Yet some Jewish leaders or missionaries who are proud of their own flesh and emphasize circumcision and their special law, try to stop the new movement begun by Jesus. The result of that opposition is suffering and new questions about God's present and future purposes concerning salvation.[1]

So Paul emphasizes that since they are children of God, the inheritance promised to God's family is also theirs (8:17). That includes the promise God gave to Abraham and those who shared his faith: they will all inherit the world (4:13). Christ's followers will share that future inheritance with Christ (8:17).

They are suffering with Christ now so that in the future they will be glorified with him (8:17). Jesus combined his faith in God's final victory with his faithfulness in the face of persecution. Tribulations at the hands of powerful enemies can even strengthen hope in God's power (see 5:3-4). In the midst of such troubles and trials, one can still have peace with God, have access to God's grace, and boast in the hope of sharing God's glory (5:2). All of that is possible through the faith(fulness) of Jesus Christ our Lord (5:1-2). Jesus taught that such persecution would lead to a great reward from God (Matt. 5:12). As one shared his mission and suffered with him, so one will share God's glory with him (see Matt. 10:16-42; 16:24-27; John 12:23-26).

That suffering must be clearly understood as suffering for the faith of Jesus. It does not refer to troubles unrelated to Jesus' mission such as most sickness or poverty in the world. Suffering with Christ means suffering at the hands of enemies of Jesus' faith and mission. If one has simply gone along with the law of Moses, or any other exalted law, as the final law of God, that particular suffering is avoided. If one has not challenged the faith of others as part of God's mission, such suffering will not happen. If one does not question the comfortable cult of civil religion, including its professional profiteers, one will not suffer for Christ's costly truth. But where there is no sharing in Christ's sufferings, there also is no sharing in his glory.

The present suffering of God's children is not so awesome when compared to their coming glory (8:18; see Luke 22:28-30). That future glory will include a marvelous new world, a new heavens and a new earth (compare 8:17 and 4:13; Rev. 21:1). Even now, the hope of the created subpersonal world is based on that future manifestation of glory to God's children (8:19). Present suffering seems to deny their status in God's family, but in the end they will be revealed as the true children of God. The nonhuman creation of earth, sky, and sea eagerly awaits that final revelation.

Ever since Adam's sin, the earth has been subjected by God to share the punishment of futility, decay, and death (8:20; compare 5:12; Gen. 3:17-19). While the ground cursed by God produces weeds which make the farmer's work more difficult, people have also increasingly exploited, poisoned, and polluted the earth, sky, and sea.

Most, especially in the first world, are unlike many in the third world who deeply respect the natural world around them. In the history of North America, Native Americans thought the Great Spirit had loaned them the land and other natural resources. They were in solidarity with all the rest of creation and could groan with suffering creatures. They even asked forgiveness when they killed an animal for food. While they might have over-spiritualized the natural order, Europeans who came to North America exploited the land mercilessly. They thought that everything, the land and the living creatures, was theirs to buy or to take. Even Native Americans were exploited and killed. So who were the real savages, disguised as Christians?

Even missionary agricultural development has contributed to poisoning the earth by using toxic pesticides. Modernizing farming by developing such crops as miracle rice was supposed to create a green revolution. Filipino farmers discovered that they could indeed have bigger harvests if they used the new miracle rice. But the new seed required more expensive imported fertilizers and pesticides. That added expense often canceled the added income from the bigger harvest.

Some farmers began to wonder whether Western fertilizer and pesticide companies had funded the research that produced miracle rice. Because of the heavier input required, many farm workers began to get sick and some died from the dangerous chemicals. The pesticides also killed other animal life like fish and snails in the wet rice fields. Rains also carried some of those chemicals to the same streams where people drank, bathed, and washed clothes.

Western progress means more pollution from large industries and automobile exhausts as well as agriculture. As the first world made laws to decrease and clean up some industrial pollution, corporations simply moved to the third world. Now every major city in the world is a center for pollution and smog. The old joke about people in Pittsburgh waking up in the morning to the coughing of birds now applies to people and birds all over the world.

Virgin forests are being destroyed on a large scale along with some original plant and animal species. Nitrogen fertilizers have filtered through the world's soil and become noxious nitrate in rivers, lakes, and water supplies. Cancer-causing rural pesticides are now found in the milk of mothers everywhere. Radiation from previous nuclear explosions and disasters like

Chernobyl as well as radioactive waste have spread every-where. Future explosions or wars can destroy large sections of the earth.[2]

Especially since World War II, first-world corporations have expanded and exported deadly technologies in industry, agriculture, energy, and transportation. Attempts to control or prevent that capitalistic process and its pollution have usually failed so far. Short-term profits and corporate political power have been too great, but the long-term costs will be even great-er.[3]

The created world which manifested God's divine power (1:20) is increasingly being overshadowed and plagued by the creations of human power and wealth. The future looks bleak. Who will deliver creation from corporation boards and billion-aire executives?

God's promises of a new world can still give hope that cre-ation will be liberated by God's power from its bondage. That liberation will lead to sharing the freedom of the future glory of God's children (8:21). In that new creation, there will no longer be any slavery to death and decay. God's new earth might not include your dear dead dog, but it could include various ani-mals. The humorist Woody Allen once remarked that in the fu-ture, the wolf might lie down with the lamb, but the lamb wouldn't get much sleep. God's future glory will not be like the common idea of sitting on clouds and playing harps. Those who completely spiritualize heaven have missed the full glory of a new heavens and a new earth.

Due to its present slavery, all creation suffers and groans together (8:22; see Isa. 24:4-5; Jer. 12:4). Even God's children, who have the firstfruits of the Spirit's work in them, are groan-ing as they wait for the glory of that future manifestation (8:23; see 8:15; 2 Cor. 5:2, 4). They are also now suffering at the hands of enemies who consider them enemies of God. Yet in the end it will be clear they are the true children of God. It will be re-vealed for all to see (8:23; compare 8:19). And it will lead to the final redemption or salvation of the persecuted body of Christ (8:23). The power of the risen Jesus will transform the body of their humiliation so that it will be conformed to the body of his glory (Phil 3:21). Future hope focuses on a resurrected body, not on an immortal soul or spirit.

God's power has already saved them from the domination of sin. That salvation also has a future fulfillment for which the child of God must wait with confident hope (8:24). The final salvation of freedom from suffering and physical death is not yet seen (8:24). It must remain only a future hope for which one waits with patience (8:25). Although all seems hopeless, God will empower the child of Abraham to be fully confident that the One who promised is also able (powerful) to do what was promised (see 4:20-21).

God's Spirit also helps the suffering children of God to pray rightly in the midst of their weakness (8:26). If left alone, God's children will cry out to God for immediate salvation from such suffering and persecution (like Paul in 2 Cor. 12:8-10). Perhaps they will let go with a "war cry" to God against their enemies. While such requests to God are understandable and natural under the circumstances, they are not correct. Only the Spirit can lead God's children to pray according to the will of God (8:27). God's Spirit can quiet the natural cries of God's children and substitute a groaning that focuses on the will of God (compare the groaning in 8:23). Such prayer confesses one's own powerlessness. At the same time, it turns to God and begins to experience divine power to do God's will, as defined and lived by Jesus. As a result, the Spirit helps the saints or righteous ones of God to face suffering courageously and patiently.

Western Christians, who suffer little and are comfortable and secure, turn prayer into praise for the abundant blessings of a good God. Such tokens of gratitude do not need God's strength since those who are giving thanks are pretty much in control of their privileged life. Jesus rejected such a life and chose to become poor, partly in order to call the rich and powerful to repentance. He then suffered at their hands because he was disturbing their pious prayers and prosperous peace. Prayerful groaning results from faithful suffering and expresses the cries of weak, desperate people who are near the end of their rope—like Jesus in Gethsemane.

Jesus faced persecution and death by crying out to *Abba* in the garden of Gethsemane (compare 8:15). Jesus was aware of the difference between his natural fear and *Abba*'s own will (Mark 14:36). He knew God's will was that he be obedient even unto death when he suffered rejection from the Jewish and Roman leaders (Mark 8:31; 9:31; 10:33-34).

Because one shares Jesus' faith, one also knows that God can work in all circumstances to bring about good (8:28). For those who love God more than their own lives, God's power is at work even in their suffering, indeed, especially in their suffering (8:28; see 5:3-5; 8:18). There is no need to be ashamed, for God's power is unto salvation to everyone who is believing or keeping faith (1:16). God's power can make even bad things serve a good purpose.

✦ ✦ ✦

Most missionaries who went to India the past few centuries seldom challenged the evils of colonialism. But in the middle of the nineteenth century, a group of missionaries came to sympathize with the harsh conditions of workers at indigo plantations in Bengal. European planters and Indian landlords joined to rent out large estates to Indian peasants for growing indigo. Although they gave the farmers loans, the loan agreements required the farmers to grow so much indigo that they had little land left for growing food for themselves. While the cost of growing indigo gradually increased over time, the selling price of indigo remained fixed. The farmers and their families became virtual slaves and were at the point of starving. If they protested, they were kidnapped, imprisoned, and beaten by the security forces of the landlords.

At the same time, European landlords helped missionaries who wanted to preach to the peasant farmers. After awhile, some missionaries realized that as long as they received favors and privileges from the oppressive landlords, the farmers would not accept their message. One missionary took the first step at a conference of Bengal missionaries by reading a paper on the cruelty of the plantation system. After some initial controversy and resistance, most missionaries agreed to appeal to the government for a change in the system of forced labor. The landlords responded by accusing the missionaries of interfering in political issues when they were supposed to stick to religious matters. The government agreed with the landlords and refused the appeal.

Then a certain missionary, James Long, decided to translate, publish, and distribute a Bengali satire about the plantation system and its oppression of the farmers. As a result, a libel case was brought against Long, and he was put in prison. Yet his willingness to expose and challenge the cruel plantation system made a favorable impact on most in India who heard about it. Here was a missionary who turned against the racial arrogance of other Europeans. He also witnessed to his faith with his joyful acceptance of suffering for righteousness' sake and his lack of bitterness toward his persecutors. Long's attitude and stand promoted his faith more than any earlier preaching. Now the people listened to his message and considered him a true Christian missionary. God's power had worked through all the suffering to bring about a good purpose.[4]

God's purposes call for sharing the suffering connected with the faith and mission of Jesus. From the beginning God planned to transform certain people into the image of Jesus, the obedient Son (8:29). Those people are known in a special way by God and destined by God to fulfill God's purposes before they are even born (8:29). God's powerful grace will fulfill those purposes of transformation and salvation.

Jesus learned obedience through suffering and is now the pioneer of salvation for all who follow in his steps (Heb. 2:10; 5:8-9; 1 Pet. 2:19-23). Jesus is the image of God in a special way (Col. 1:15; 2 Cor. 4:4), yet his followers are also being renewed by God according to the image of God (2 Cor. 3:18; Col. 3:9-10). Being conformed to the image of God as incarnated in Jesus involves a process of identification and union with the faith of Jesus. The righteousness of God is being manifested in the believing one out of Jesus' faith (1:17).

Because they share the faith(fulness) of Jesus in the midst of persecution, they will also be conformed to Jesus' resurrection existence (compare 8:17; Phil 3:10-11). That has all been planned by God. Jesus is to be the firstborn of many brothers and sisters (8:29). All who share his obedient image are the true children of God. To all who receive him, he gives power to become children of God (John 1:12). Whoever does the will of Jesus' father is his brother and sister (Matt. 12:50). And God, the heavenly *Abba*, is responsible for producing such children (8:15).

Those God has predestined, God also calls (8:30). God's powerful calling produces the righteousness of obedient children (8:30). Despite the present pain of persecution, such children will be glorified by God. Although their enemies consider them ungodly and unrighteous, God has chosen and predestined them to be conformed to Jesus' righteousness and glory. The fearful power of the enemies of their mission will not overcome the power of God at work in history. God's children must suffer, but God's power will prevail, producing a patient faithfulness and a final glory.

Paul's description of predestination focuses on God's plan and power to produce faith in certain people. He does not use predestination to mean God predestined everything in world history. Paul isn't concerned here with God's providence and lordship over all events and persons. His reference to predestination is rather a tribute to God's sovereign power that has fulfilled and will fulfill the eternal plan to produce a faithful and finally glorified people. All who are faithful have looked back at their experiences of faith and concluded that it all resulted from God's will and power.

Romans 8:31-39

Secure in God's Love Through God's Power

PAUL now asks what is to be concluded from the truths of
8:17-30. Since God's power is at work even in the sister
and brother of Christ who suffer for Jesus' faith, what is the
right response to their enemies?

If God is for them—and God is—there is no need to be especially anxious about those against them (8:31). Such suffering should not raise doubts about the future fulfillment of God's plans and purposes. Even God's own special Son was not spared from such suffering, but was given up to death for all of them (8:32). Because of that great gift, no one should worry that God's grace might fail to give them everything they have been promised (8:32). As they suffer with Jesus now, they will be glorified with him in the end (see 8:17).

It is quite another matter for religious people who carry out an imperialistic mission of hatred and violence to claim that God is for them. Religious wars have been fought with each side claiming that God is on their side. Each prayed for God's help to conquer their enemies (by killing them). The problem for such people, who confidently claim God's favor, is that their faith is not the faith of Jesus. Thus the god in which they find security is not the God of love who empowers Jesus and his followers to love even their enemies.

The context of 8:31-32 is assurance of God's blessing in the midst of suffering for the faith of Jesus. We miss Paul's point if in response we voice our assurance of being blessed because of material prosperity and financial security. Paul describes a security that is not obvious in the eyes of the world.

So why have most Western missionaries preferred the comfort and security of wealth and power? Why have mission agencies spent so much money and energy just to make sure their missionaries did not suffer in any way? It seems a main goal of the modern missionary enterprise has been to avoid personal want or suffering at all costs. While sacrificing certain relationships and pleasures to travel abroad, missionaries usually become better off in terms of status, affluence, and influence. But their influence was often that of showing off or advertising Western goods and "superiority." They lived in luxury and built walls for security. Instead of being secure in God's love through God's power, they were secure in gold's luxury through gold's power.[1]

Paul reminds his readers that God chose them and made them righteous (8:33). So the main question is whether the God who has empowered, and declared, the elect to be righteous will then bring an accusation against them. No way! Moreover, in the face of false condemnation, they should focus on Jesus, who died because of similar condemnation (8:34). Jesus was condemned to death but now rules with God and intercedes for them, as their defense attorney. Would that Jesus then condemn them? Never!

Above all, they should focus on the fact that the condemned Jesus was raised according to the powerful purposes of God (8:34). Hope is not a fantasy, but trust in the power of God to transform what appears to be hopelessly lost. The same Jesus who was condemned, put to death, raised again, and enthroned as powerful Son of God, is now their chief witness and advocate before God (8:34; see Heb. 2:18; 4:14-16). Jesus himself said he would acknowledge before his heavenly Father all whose faith overcomes fear and acknowledges him before others (Matt. 10:31-32).

Jesus' faith led him to die for them, and his love for them continued to help them as they faced suffering and death. Who or what is powerful enough to separate them from that love (8:35)? What about persecution from the enemies of Jesus' faith (8:35)? Can that separate them? How about a rejection of their mission that leads to a lack of food and clothing (8:35; see 1 Cor. 4:11)? Will that separate them? Indeed, not even the most dangerous threats (see 2 Cor. 11:26) or the use of the sword can separate them from the love of the powerful, ruling Jesus, who was put to death and raised again (8:35).

Such problems are part of God's plan. God spoke about that before in Psalm 44:22, which says that because of God, they are in danger of death all the time (8:36). Their enemies see them as mere sheep to be slaughtered (8:36). The same violence shown against the nonhuman creation (see 8:22-23) is now attacking the newly created people of God. Those whom God now rules are like sheep among wolves.

Jesus described mission in exactly that way (Matt. 10:16). He said that danger called for being as careful and shrewd as snakes while remaining as harmless and innocent (of evil) as doves. He warned against wolves in local Jewish synagogues and in higher Roman governmental positions (Matt. 10: 17-18). Even family members might turn into wolves (Matt. 10:21, 34-37). That was the bad news. The good news was that all sheep which lost their lives for Jesus' sake would find the life of the new age (Matt. 10:39).

In 1982, the Guatemalan military entered the town of Santa Cruz. In front of the villagers, the military accused five Catholic leaders of being subversives. Those leaders were teaching the people how to read and write, study the Bible, and form cooperatives. The army said all five must die that very night at the hands of their own relatives or they would bomb Santa Cruz and other villages in the area. Those were not empty threats because General Ríos Montt had just taken over the presidency and had begun a scorched-earth policy. He liked to think of himself as a born-again emissary of God, called to a holy war against communism. That war included intense bombing of suspect towns and villages, and machine-gunning men, women, and children. During his one and a half years in power, over 15,000 Guatemalans were murdered and massacred by bombing. Dozens of villages were erased from the map.

So the villagers of Santa Cruz took the army's threats very seriously. Yet they loved the five accused and decided they could never kill them. But the five insisted that it was better for them to die than for thousands of others to die. One said, "We're going to die, but don't worry, we're going to be with God. If we're not killed, our children, our wives, our relatives, and our whole population of these villages will die." They willingly gave up their lives for the sake of the others. Such people of faith did not fear death, only faithlessness to the way of Jesus, the way of the cross.[2]

✦ ✦ ✦

Instead of a denial of God's love, persecution for Christ's sake is a sign of being part of God's elect or chosen ones. In all those things, those trials and troubles, they were the big winners (compare 8:28) because of the faithful love of the Son of God (8:37). Jesus' loving faith led him to die and even now is helping believers as they follow him in that difficult way (compare 8:34-35). The powers of sin and death are not strong enough to win out over the powerful love of God manifested in Christ Jesus our Lord (8:38-39).

Whoever unites with Christ and shares his faith can be sure and secure, knowing that God's power has no equal. Not even the most violent and fearful powers on earth can separate believers from God's love. The strongest hate is no match for God's love. Neither the troubles of life nor the threat of death will hinder God's loving plans for them. Neither the designs of demons nor the rule of evil spiritual forces can conquer God's purposes for them. Neither present persecution nor future fears can cause God's chosen ones to abandon Jesus' faithful love. Neither the highest forces of evil nor the lowest depths of demonic desires can draw God's elect into their sphere of evil. No powers in all creation have the strength to separate them from the Creator's love (8:38-39). The same God whose power creat-ed all things (1:20) will finally overpower every evil in creation.

Jesus' death defeated the ultimate weapon of the powers —death—and thus disarmed them (Col. 2:15). Although most North Americans and Europeans don't take evil spiritual pow-ers seriously, much of the rest of the world does. In the Philip-pines, mysterious unfortunate events are often blamed on evil spirits. Despite the high degree of superstition, such people are closer to the truth than those who deny such forces. Traditional African religion has tried to balance various life-forces, includ-ing the power of dead ancestors. Yet such traditions prepare them to appreciate the biblical God of power, of new life and ac-tion, more than the religion and education of Western missions.

Throughout Paul's world, people feared the demonic realm and often used magical practices to protect themselves. As Christians faced persecution, they also saw demonic opposi-tion as empowering their opponents (see 1 Thess. 2:14-18). Likewise, false apostles who deceived others showed they were servants of Satan, the master of deceit, who liked to pose as an angel of light (2 Cor. 11:13-15). But fearful Christians have ac-cess to divine power. There is no need to manipulate demons or call on angels or dead saints (including Mary the mother of Jesus). God's power may still allow demonic opposition, but it will keep believers secure in God's love as shown in Christ.

Jesus and his disciples confronted the power of demons and their prince, Satan (Mark 3:11-12, 15, 22-23). Satan tested Jesus by suggesting that if Jesus was really the Son of God, he would not go hungry (Matt. 4:3). If Jesus was royalty, the Son of God, then Satan claimed God would not allow Jesus to suffer or die a cruel death (Matt. 4:5-6). True princes, Satan said, ruled in glory after conquering grand human kingdoms (Matt. 4:8-9). The prince of the power of the air (see Eph. 2:2) offered Jesus all the political and military power of the world. Yet Jesus re-jected the powers of this world and remained faithful to God's mission of sacrificial service and obedient sonship. Later Jesus recognized Satan's influence when Peter refused to accept a suffering and dying Messiah and wanted to fight to the end (Matt. 16:16-23; John 18:10-11).

Martin Luther's courageous fight against Catholic powers was also full of danger. They condemned him as a heretic. They hunted him like a criminal. The powers of Christendom wanted him dead. For Luther, those powers were the forces of darkness. Satan and his devils wanted to devour him. He had challenged the power of the pope, and he was ready to die rather than admit that the pope was the final authority over the church. All the pope's moneymaking pardons (indulgences) were worldly. Most of the Roman traditions, including the selling of church offices or sacraments, were mere human traditions. Rome's dominance not only endangered Luther; it was choking all Germany.

But then Luther called upon German princes to destroy the pope's power in Germany. He knew that the clergy could not reform the church or nation. So Luther persuaded kings and princes to overcome the evil Roman principalities and powers. Luther told princes not to worry about excommunication from the church. The result was a new power in Germany: Protestant princes and magistrates. Luther ended up preferring a powerful majority to a persecuted minority.[3]

A generation later, John Calvin said that Protestant church authorities should have more power than political authorities. He tried to restore the power of clergy in the city of Geneva, Switzerland. And he was somewhat successful as the clergy, especially himself, shared domination of the city with city magistrates. While pastors and magistrates often protected the elderly, orphans, widows, children, and the sick, they also ruled over a long list of religious traditions. Whenever church authorities delivered a sinner to the civil power, the civil power was supposed to punish him.

Calvin saw sin everywhere. He became upset when some citizens held a dance in a private home, and he tried to punish them accordingly. Calvin wanted the punishment of harlots to be severe, but the city council never agreed to it. In 1553, Geneva burned Servetus to death because of false beliefs about the Trinity. Calvin had worked for the execution, though he wanted a death more merciful than burning. Thus Calvin dominated the city of Geneva for decades. He was not popular there. The people feared his power more than anything else.[4]

Throughout church history, evil powers tempted Christians with devotion to social structures like family, school, city, race, class, and nation as well as cultural and religious traditions. Most people have highly valued such social structures. They took pride in distinctive traditions like third-world respect for ancestors and the family or first-world dedication to democracy. Yet evil powers used such structures to hold people in bondage and take the place of God's rule in Christ. Satan and his forces even used the Old Testament or law of Moses to persuade people to follow a different way than the faith of Jesus. Remember that the leaders of Jewish society were the main opponents of Jesus and Paul. Jesus, however, can liberate his faithful followers from slavery to such powers.[5]

The powers of sin and death thus work through the world's dominant institutions and structures. Multinational or global corporations seek to dominate national economies and promote materialistic consumerism to satisfy their greed for profit. Science and technology create systems of destruction by which one race can oppress another race (sometimes within the same nation). Militaristic ministers of defense multiply arms and armies for the sake of violent domination. They can even use Jesus' sacrifice for others as a basis to call on citizens to make the supreme sacrifice of dying for their country. Churches then call on God and their members to support war efforts for the sake of invisible religions like national success and corporate power. Such powers become religions because they end up as the chief goals for which people live and die. Yet they are invisible religions because the most powerful individuals and spiritual forces remain hidden.

Who trained all those third-world dictators to threaten, torture, and murder so many of their own people? And whose idea was it to train and manipulate such gangsters in the first place? Could it be as simple as ABCD (American Bankers or Businessmen, CIA, and Defense Department)? The power brokers of national or international success and corporate power work their magic behind a veil of secrecy and bureaucracy. The more visible authorities are mere public-relations manipulators for the invisible powers and vested interests. Positive public images of progress lead many to give glory and honor to the power of successful business, government, education, and religion. Throughout all those hierarchies, elite men grab power, at the expense of others, especially women and children.[6]

When a wealthy Southern Baptist Sunday school teacher, Jimmy Carter, became president of the United States in 1976, a new moral tone echoed across the world. He would respect human rights and punish violators. Carter promised to withhold aid from countries that consistently violated human rights. Later, some legislators called for U.S. representatives to the World Bank to vote against loans to countries that consistently tortured and imprisoned people without trial. But Carter sent a personal letter to all congressmen urging them to defeat that amendment.[7]

The Carter administration also worked with the International Monetary Fund to force various third-world countries into cruel economic measures that led to deeper poverty and wider unrest. Yet it helped countries like Argentina and Nicaragua to receive millions of dollars in loans while they were bombing and murdering their own people. Clearly, economic interests won out over human interests.[8]

Even Carter's definition of human rights masked the larger violation of the rights of the poor. The Carter administration focused on human-rights violations against isolated individuals who were tortured or murdered by death squads. As a result, the villains turned out to be certain evil military leaders, with little said about the local elites or American businesses the military was trying to protect. In fact, international capitalism, which provided luxurious lifestyles for a few and miserable poverty for most, liked to describe itself as a development model. But who was being developed?[9]

One hidden development was the wealth of Western churches. In 1980, the Catholic Church owned around $25 billion in real estate, stocks, and bonds. In addition, religious communities, like the Society of Jesus, had assets of around $250 million. Most mainline Protestant churches had corporate executives on their national boards and depended on the biggest U.S. firms to help them invest church funds in corporations like Gulf Oil. The United Church of Christ's (UCC) Board for World Ministries once even loaned $250,000 to the International Basic Economy Corporation owned by the Rockefellers. The UCC had bought 1,000 shares of the corporation and claimed they wanted to help developing nations. Yet the UCC also expected to make a handsome profit from their loan. So corporate wealth did help develop churches, but at the expense of the poor.[10]

Protestants and Catholics have recently become suspicious about church ties to corporate wealth. Churches talk more about responsible investment and corporate accountability. Religious lobbies try to use their own wealth (stock) and power to pressure corporation boards not to invest in repressive countries. While such protests expose certain unethical practices, they have little effect on corporate policies. The U.S. National Council of Churches (NCC) once organized churches with a total of 200,000 shares of IBM stock to persuade IBM not to sell computers to Chile's government. The dictator there, Pinochet, was using them for military intelligence, which led to arrests and murders. The NCC was not successful.[11]

One apparently successful challenge of such powers had to do with the Nestlé corporation. During the 1970s Nestlé found itself under a worldwide boycott because of its sales of infant formula in the third world. As Nestlé pushed its expensive formula in poor nations, it used employees dressed as milk nurses to give free samples of formula to nursing mothers. This decreased breast-feeding and increased diarrhea, since the formula was often mixed with unclean water. And diarrhea can be a killer in the third world. After several years of the boycott, Nestlé officially agreed to most of the demanded changes.[12]

Yet there is more to the story. While in the Philippines during the early 1980s, I was asked to accompany our highest denominational executive from the United States on a tour of some local hospitals. The executive was part of a fact-finding committee chosen and funded by Nestlé to show that they had reformed. After visiting some nicer hospitals in Iloilo City, it seemed Nestlé was no longer giving away samples of infant formula. Then a nurse at the government's Provincial Hospital answered yes when I asked her if Nestlé was still giving samples there. Most of the poorer people went to that hospital. It had halls full of patients.

As we were walking out of the hospital, I asked the executive if he noticed her admission. He replied that she probably just misunderstood my question. I responded that we could go back and ask her again to make sure. He refused, saying there was no need. I felt then that his investigation was not really serious. He was merely going through the motions to justify his free trip to the Philippines at Nestlé's expense. He was on the side of a powerful global corporation and thus opposed to those who might still find fault.

Despite all such attractions or opposition this evil age could manage, God's power will still keep the chosen ones faithful to the one who loved them. In the face of overwhelming manipulation and power, they will be more than conquerors (8:37). As with Jesus, prophetic mission that seriously challenges the evil of the world will meet resistance. As Roman Christians continue that mission to Jews, and to Gentiles, they will meet similar resistance.

Humble, persecuted house churches and other faithful groups should reject any vision of becoming power structures that make their societies more Christian. Religions that become part of the pillars of society have merely joined the evil structures which will compromise Jesus' love and faith. Jesus' mission vision is not to gather enough followers with enough power to change, influence, or bless a whole society. Power over power structures is the gift of Satan, not Jesus.

When Paul writes Romans, he is planning to go soon to Jerusalem, the center of Jewish power. He knows that persecution, perhaps even death, awaits him there (see 15:25, 30-31; Acts 20:22-25). The purpose of Paul in writing Romans is to encourage the house churches in Rome to carry on his mission and message, even if Paul can't, and even as they face similar suffering.

Romans 9:1-13

God's Consistent Mission of Election and Rejection Within Israel

I N 8:17-39 Paul discusses suffering and persecution for Christ's sake. These have resulted primarily from certain Jewish leaders and missionaries. Most Jews have rejected his mission. Some may think Paul is angry and disgusted with most Jews.

Paul thus strongly emphasizes that the truth (9:1) is that he feels grief and sorrow for the many Jewish people who reject Christ (9:2). In fact, like Moses (see Exod. 32:32), Paul has even considered the possibility of choosing to be rejected by God for the sake of God's people. Paul is willing to be separated from Christ if it leads his Jewish brothers and sisters to turn to the God of Jesus (9:3).

For the God of Jesus is the same God who called them to be Israelites (9:4; see Gen. 32:28; Isa. 48:1) and spoke to them about being children of God (see Deut. 14:1-2). Israel's privileges also included God's glory (as in Exod. 24:16-17); various covenants, including the giving of the law (Gen. 17:1-21; Exod. 24:7-8); the worship (service) of God; and many promises of future blessing (9:4). Israel descended from the great forefathers, beginning with Abraham, Isaac, and Jacob, and will produce the Jewish Messiah or Christ (9:5; see 1:3). Yet the Messiah turned out to be much more than a Jewish leader (according to the flesh). Jesus the Jew now rules in power over all creation (including the Jews). He is thus worthy of praise and worship as God (9:5; see 1:4; Phil. 2:6, 9-11; Col. 1:15-20; 2:9-10).[1]

Thus Paul doesn't hate other Jews, even those who pursue him constantly and persecute him cruelly. Paul knows that any mission to Jewish people which results in rejection and antagonism might lead to anti-Semitism. He also knows that his readers' future mission encounters with Jews will need to avoid such prejudice. Anti-Judaism, the strong disagreement with the religion of many Jews, should never become anti-Semitism, the prejudice against Jews as a race or ethnic people.

Since the time of Paul, countless Christians have been guilty of anti-Semitism. The hero of the Protestant Reformation, Martin Luther, became a violent enemy of Jews after years of failing to convince them of the truth of the gospel. The older Luther once remarked that if a Jew asked for baptism, he would take him to a bridge, tie a stone around his neck, and throw him into the river. No, Luther had not become a Baptist. He had, however, become anti-Semitic. Another time, he demanded that all the Jews' cash, jewels, silver, and gold be taken away, their synagogues and schools be set on fire, and their homes be destroyed.[2]

Paul, however, appreciates the ways God has worked in Israel in the past. But his Jewish opponents can then raise the question, and have raised it: If most of Israel now reject God's Messiah (as you claim, Paul), doesn't that mean that God's revelation to Israel has failed?

Paul replies that the present rejection of Christ by many Jews doesn't mean that God's former word to Israel has failed (9:6). For the truth is that God's word included God's call of only certain Israelites. Not everyone who belongs to Israel has been chosen to fulfill God's word. Just because some are the physical seed of Abraham doesn't mean they are true children of Abraham (9:7). God's mission of choosing only certain ones within Israel is consistent with God's word.

The first choice God made was between Abraham's sons: Isaac and Ishmael (9:7; see Gen. 21:12). All Jews agree that they are descendants of Isaac, not Ishmael. God's call of only part of Abraham's children, leads Paul to conclude that the children of God do not include all the physical descendants of Abraham (9:8). All that descend from Abraham are children of his flesh, but only some become children of God. For Abraham's flesh was not the main factor in fulfilling God's righteousness (see 4:1-3). Only those children of Abraham who are also called according to God's promise are to be considered the true (spiritual) seed of Abraham (9:8; see Gal. 4:22-23). The word of promise to Abraham was that at the right time, God would come in power, and elderly Sarah would have a son (9:9; see 4:19-21; Gen. 18:10-14). God's power fulfilled that word and produced the chosen child (see Gen. 21:1-2).

That process didn't happen only once. With the Jewish forefather Isaac and his wife Rebecca, there was another choice (9:10). This time it was between two sons born at the same time from the same mother. God's choice between the two twins showed even more clearly that election depends only on God's purpose (9:11). (Concerning Isaac and Ishmael, some Jews might answer that since Sarah was Abraham's wife, while the Egyptian Hagar was only Sarah's handmaid, Isaac would naturally have been God's choice. They can add that God's promise about Isaac was after Ishmael's birth, so God saw the evil Ishmael would do.) Paul uses Jacob and Esau to emphasize that God's election has nothing to do with what either twin (or their mother) has done, whether good or evil. Everything depends on God's choice before either twin was born. And like Sarah, Rebecca had been barren and only conceived because of God's power (Gen. 25:21).

God likes to choose those who are weak, lowly, and despised by the world so that no one can boast (see 1 Cor. 1:27-29). As childless wives most of their lives, Sarah and Rebecca met such criteria for God's election. Much later, when the church often followed the way of the world, women supposedly had lesser roles to play in the church's mission. Especially single women called by God faced rejection from male mission leaders. Through much of the nineteenth century, women could be missionary wives or stay home and raise money and pray. They could not be missionaries in their own right.

Only after women formed their own mission agencies and showed great dedication and success in mission service, did denominational churchmen begin to change. They slowly allowed single women to serve in their mission societies. Most men decided that the apostle Paul would not mind if women taught foreign or local natives as long as they didn't preach in local white churches. Impressed by the women's mission work, they made ways to fit them into their own mission plans. The men still made and make most decisions about mission strategies and goals.[3]

For Paul, God's predestined purposes and promises are all part of the powerful calling of God. They have nothing to do with the works or deeds of supposedly superior people (9:12; see 4:1-2, 17; 8:28, 30). In the case of Jacob and Esau, God's word was that the older—the firstborn, with the natural advantage—would serve the younger (9:12; see Gen. 25:23). Before they were born, God chose and loved Jacob and rejected or hated Esau (9:13; see Mal. 1:2-3).

The contexts of Genesis 25:23 and Malachi 1:2-3 relate the election of Jacob and rejection of Esau to two nations, their historical descendants (Israel and Edom). The context of Romans 9:3, 6-9, however, relates God's election and rejection to two groups within Israel: those in Israel presently rejected, and those who are God's elect. Consequently, the Old Testament context must not be used to escape the clear thrust of Paul's argument in 9:1-13. God chose from within the same people, Israel. Thus 9:10-13 shows that God intervened in the lives of Jacob and Esau to fulfill the ongoing mission of election and rejection among Abraham's descendants. God's choice was not based on foreknowledge of their future behavior so that God's purpose of predestination and election might predominate (9:11).

Again, all Jews agree they are descendants of Jacob, not Esau. And again, Paul's point is that from the very beginning, God's call has to do with the selection of only certain descendants of Abraham. God displayed a consistent pattern that remains true for God's future mission within Israel. Thus by the time of Paul's mission, the rejection by most Jews of their Messiah doesn't mean that God's word to Israel has failed (9:6). It does mean that most Jews at that time (who reject Christ) are the spiritual descendants of the rejected Ishmael and Esau, not Isaac and Jacob!

Besides Paul's Jewish listeners, many Christians have trouble with this teaching. It seems there is no need for human choice or free will. Some who emphasize this teaching also deny the need for human mission activity since everything depends on God. For example, when young William Carey presented his plan to start a missionary society, ministerial authorities told him to sit down. When God chose to convert the heathen, God would do it without Carey's help. Yet Paul is not denying the need for human choices or mission activity. Paul himself is an active missionary and expresses his own struggles with the feelings and choices that result from mission (for example, 9:1-3; see 1:9-13). He does not just wait for fate. The electing grace of God makes Paul what he is: an apostle who works harder than all the others (1 Cor. 15:9-10).

Yet it is not up to missionaries to make the crucial choice about who are children of God. They are not able to produce such children. It is not even up to the children themselves. As long as Jews continue to reject Paul's mission, they are not God's chosen children (even if they assume they are). Other Jews or Gentiles, who choose to come to faith and continue in Jesus' faith, show they are God's elect children, chosen and called by God. Their human choices are possible because God's power enables them to do so. Yet the choices are real and often involve real struggle. While God elects before anyone does good or evil, God will finally judge all according to their actual deeds of good or evil (2:6).

The fact that God's mission and election result in children of God should be an encouragement to Christian mission activity. No matter how often others may reject Christian mission, one can know that God is still at work in the world. God will produce children by means of such mission. How often that happens is up to God. But God will at least use some mission activity of some missionaries to fulfill the promise of producing children.[4]

As for the idea of free will, Paul does not consider people to be in a neutral situation. On one hand, people are free to some extent to make various decisions based on personal tastes and cultural preferences. They are not robots or puppets. God accepts whatever choices they make about many aspects of life. On the other hand, each person is not free to simply choose their own destiny. Ever since Adam, sin and death have dominated people (see 3:9; 5:12, 17, 21; 6:6, 16; 7:14). They are not free to do God's will. They may freely will to do good, but they still eventually do wrong (7:15-25). So they will remain slaves of sin unless a greater power liberates them. That greater power is precisely the election and calling of God described in 9:11-12 (compare 5:17, 21; 6:7, 18, 20, 22; 8:2, 30). Only God has the free will to decide and act against sin's power.

Because God's power is the source of salvation, our mission depends on God's mission. Churches or Christians must be careful, however, not to connect God's sovereign power with their own ruling power. John Calvin became famous for his teaching about God's predestination. He was also infamous for his ruling through human domination.

Once in Geneva, Jerome Bolsec challenged a pastor who taught that faith was a gift determined from eternity for the elect. Bolsec argued that such a God was a tyrant. While he spoke, Calvin secretly entered the meeting and listened. Calvin's response was to send Bolsec to prison. I would assume that Bolsec then thought that Calvin was a tyrant, a more correct conclusion than his earlier arguments against a God who predestined. The Geneva city council banished Bolsec from the city.[5] Calvin got his way, but who elected Calvin to act with such power? Not the God of Jesus. Jesus rejected domination over others and asked his followers not to lord it over others like Gentile rulers (Luke 22:25-26).

Lordly human leaders, who use the Bible while rejecting Jesus' divine lordship (see 9:5), have also dominated certain non-Christian cults. The founder of the Jehovah's Witnesses, Charles Taze Russell, especially disliked doctrines like predestination. He didn't think it was logical or sensible. So he started his own religion that would simply focus on the Jehovah God of the Old Testament. He also considered his own books to be more important than the Bible. His wife, Maria, eventually separated from him and later sued for divorce, on the grounds of his "conceit, egotism, domination, and improper conduct in relation to other women."[6]

Another fast-growing worldwide cult with an authoritarian leadership is the Church of Jesus Christ of Latter-day Saints (Mormons). A hierarchy of General Authorities, with the Prophet and his Counselors at the top, oversees the male-dominated organization and its huge missionary program. The founder, Joseph Smith, claimed he began the only true religion. All who obeyed the righteousness revealed to Joseph Smith and later Prophet leaders, would rule with Christ. For Joseph's visions revealed that men could become gods like Jesus, if they totally obeyed Joseph. Those who even criticized church leaders could be thrown out of the church. Mormon church leaders have increasingly claimed absolute authority. In fact, Joseph taught that God the Father was once a human ruler. Joseph's faith was indeed far from Jesus' faith.

Joseph also said that Mormon elders could marry more than one wife. Such marriages were supposed to be eternal since such patriarchs and their submissive wives would rule over eternal kingdoms when they achieved godhood in the heavens. After polygyny (multiple wives) was later officially rejected, the family remained a key to ruling in the future Celestial Kingdom. In the Celestial Kingdom, men would progress to be like God. Such men would then inherit all the blessings of Abraham and Jacob, including polygyny. The God-Kings would thus have their own queens and their own planets to rule. The purpose of marriage, both now and eternally, was to have children so that preexisting spirits might enter the mortal bodies of those children.[7]

By the early 1980s, Mormons were a worldwide empire with around 30,000 missionaries all over the world. It was the fastest growing church in the United States and especially successful in Latin America. They have become one of the wealthiest and most secretive churches in the world. Their missionaries are easily recognized: two young men in white shirts and ties going door-to-door. Yet for Mormons, the United States remained God's chosen land. Ever since the second Prophet, Brigham Young, led his followers to Utah, the world headquarters was Salt Lake City. It was a nation within a nation, the true Israel within a country that from its early days saw itself as God's chosen people. According to Mormons, God rejected the rest. They are just apostate Gentiles, and some day the true descendants of Abraham (Mormons) would rule over that larger nation.[8]

An international Mormon church outside the United States has increasingly developed in many countries. Yet the center of power and wealth remains centralized in Salt Lake City. American Mormons abroad continue to rule over the international church. The model of the successful Mormon in other countries is the middle-class American missionary. Especially young Mormons want to look American, wearing the white shirt and tie, and want to go to Utah and study at Brigham Young University. Then they can assume the power of middle-class church leaders themselves.[9]

Despite all the privileged power and world mission of such people presuming to be the true Israel, God knows the real descendants of Abraham, Isaac, and Jacob. And they aren't Mormons. God's mission continues to consistently call and create certain faithful Jews. Though most Jews sadly remain rejected, God's power is not defeated. God's mission of election and rejection within Israel remains consistent.

Romans 9:14-29

God's Absolute, Righteous Power Shown in Mercy— and in Wrath

IF God's consistent mission involves choosing some descendants of Abraham while rejecting others (9:6-13), what will some Jews conclude? They will ask whether Paul's God is unrighteous (9:14) since racial descent and/or human effort are not used in deciding who will be elected or rejected (see 9:6-8, 11). But Paul strongly denies that there is any unrighteousness with God.

The question raised in 9:14 is similar to the earlier question in 3:5, where Paul is also debating with another Jew. Paul again focuses on former mission conversations. Those are questions and answers that Roman Christians need to be prepared for if they are to continue Paul's mission.

Paul defends God's righteousness before other Jews with a quote from Jewish Scripture (Exod. 33:19). Moses was told that God would be the one to show mercy on whomever God chose (9:15). The context of Exodus 33:18-19, 22 relates God's mercy to God's goodness and glory, and to manifesting God's name. God's goodness (righteousness) and glory are connected with giving mercy (or wrath, in Exod. 34:7) to whomever God pleased, no matter who they were or what they did. Thus Paul uses Exodus 33:19 to argue that God's merciful election of Jacob (and rejection of Esau), before they were born (9:11-13), was righteous. God acted on behalf of a divine glory and goodness that included the sovereign freedom to give (or not give) mercy.[1]

Becoming children of God, therefore, depends on what God chooses to do (9:16; see John 1:12-13). No one has a claim on the divine mercy that elects and produces children of God. Mercy does not depend on human righteousness or reward. God can show mercy whenever God chooses and still be righteous.

Those God calls, receive mercy. As for the others, what did God say to Pharaoh in Jewish Scripture? God elevated Pharaoh to his powerful position so that God's greater power could be shown through him (9:17; see Exod. 9:16). Pharaoh's stubbornness in refusing to free the children of Israel led to more and more acts of power by God (Exod. 7:3-4; 9:14, 17-18; 10:1-2; 11:9; 14:4, 17, 31). And the news about the God who did those mighty deeds would be spread across the whole earth (compare Exod. 7:5; 14:4, 18; 15:12-16; Josh. 2:9-11; 9:9; 1 Sam. 4:8).

That example from Exodus shows that God has mercy on persons or even hardens their hearts, at God's own discretion (9:18; for God's hardening, see Exod. 4:21; 7:3; 9:12; 10:1, 20, 27; 11:10; 14:4, 8, 17). So the key is what God wants and does, not what people want and do. Just as God's mercy (love) does not depend on what people do (9:15-18), so God's hardening (hate) is independent of what people have done (9:17-18; see 9:11-13). From the beginning, God's purpose was to harden Pharaoh (Exod. 4:21). Pharaoh hardened his heart because God had first hardened it (compare Exod. 7:3-4 with 7:13).[2]

Paul's Jewish dialogue partner will not be so likely to question God's choice to harden Pharaoh. That is not a problem as much as God's rejection of some Israelites (as stated in 9:6-13). Yet that partner knows Paul uses Jewish Scripture to confirm God's right to choose all those (including Jews) who will receive mercy (salvation in being God's children; 9:8) or wrath (condemnation). Paul is arguing that God's righteousness can freely elect or reject (harden), based only on God's purposes to

display divine power and to proclaim the divine name throughout the world (9:17; see 9:11).

Paul's opponent(s) will then raise another question: What
about the responsibility of the one rejected or hardened? Paul
uses God's hardening of Pharaoh as an answer to objections
(9:14) about God's rejection of part of Israel (9:6-13). If rejection and hardening were God's doing, why was the one hardened still being blamed (9:19; compare 3:7)? That question
shows that Paul has referred to God's hardening before one has
done anything bad. If history is only the working out of God's
ultimate purposes, who has ever resisted God's will or purpose
for them (9:19)? No one has resisted or can resist. It is one thing
to blame a lawless Pharaoh (as God does in Exod. 7:16 and
10:3). But how can God blame Jews who are trying to keep
God's law?

Such questions and conclusions are attempts to stand up
for those Jews who have rejected the faith of Jesus (9:2-3).
Those unbelieving Jews suggest that if Paul is right, then God
must take the blame. The Jewish questioner in 9:19 is close to
blasphemy against God (compare 3:8). Yet since he doesn't
agree with Paul anyway, his conclusions are only hypothetical.
If Paul is right, God must be blamed for the rejection of Jesus'
faith by most of Israel. For the unbelieving Jew, however, Paul
is wrong, and God is not to blame.

Jesus was the first to face such opposition to God's new,
powerful kingship. He explained it in terms of God's election
and rejection (or hardening). Near the end of Jesus' ministry,
he prayed for the disciples God had given him out of the evil
world (John 17:2, 6, 14, 16, 25). He did not pray for the world
which hated him, but for those God had given him (John 17:9,
14). Jesus sent those disciples into the world to continue his
mission (17:18).

In his prayer, Jesus also said he had guarded his disciples,
and none were lost except the one destined to perish, Judas
(John 17:12). As for others who refused to believe "in him" (literally, into him, union with him), Jesus quoted Isaiah 6:9-10 to
show that they were not able to believe. God had blinded their
eyes and hardened their hearts (John 12:37, 39-40). Paul later

quotes Isaiah 6:9-10 when Jews from Rome reject his mission message about God's powerful kingship as revealed in the teaching (faith) of Jesus (Acts 28:24-27, 31).

Now, on behalf of his Roman readers, Paul continues his case study of mission conversation by directly addressing another Jew. Paul asks if a mere human being has the right to raise such blasphemous questions about God (9:20; see 9:14, 19). Does anyone have the right to judge God? Paul asks if the clay pot can challenge the potter concerning why the potter made it as he did (9:20; see Isa. 29:16; 45:9). In the Greek, Paul's question assumes a negative answer.

Then Paul asks if the potter doesn't have the right (the authority or power) to use the same lump of clay to make some vessels that will receive honor and others that will receive dishonor (9:21). After all, it is the potter's lump of clay. And the honor or dishonor does not depend on different kinds of clay but on the potter's own purposes and designs for the one lump. (The two sons from the same parents in 9:10-13 are in contrast with the two sons of Abraham from different mothers in 9:7-9).

As the divine potter of human vessels, God is patiently working out several purposes: to manifest wrath, to show power (9:22), and to make known the riches of divine glory (9:23; see 9:17). To accomplish those purposes, God bears with great patience the vessels of wrath. The divine potter has prepared or made such vessels for destruction, to manifest God's final wrath (see 2:5, 8-9). God also patiently puts up with a disobedient Israel and hardened Gentiles like Pharaoh so that God's future glory can be shown upon the vessels of mercy (9:23; see 9:15-17). On one hand, God's patience pointed the way to repentance by giving commands (to Pharaoh and to Israel) to do right (see 2:4). On the other hand, God's final purposes prevented Pharaoh and many in Israel from obeying those commands (9:17, 22-23). The patience described in 9:22 focuses on God's final purposes rather than on repentance (as in 2:4).

God uses the vessels of wrath to fulfill a higher purpose for the vessels of mercy. Those vessels of mercy are prepared beforehand to receive the final riches of God's power and glory (compare 2:7, 10; 8:18, 29-30). Moreover, the vessels of mercy will include not only some Jews but also some Gentiles (9:24). That show of mercy is the ultimate purpose of God's powerful calling in the present time (compare 8:30; 9:12).

Paul goes on to use other prophets as witnesses. He will continue to argue his previous points about the rejection of many Jews, and especially about showing mercy on some Gentiles as well as Jews. Hosea 2:23 says that in the future those people who are presently not God's people will be called the people of God (9:25; see 1 Pet. 2:10). For Paul, that refers to some Gentiles who are now part of the people of God. God's call and love are now shown to those Gentile vessels of mercy, who are now among the children of God. So it is possible that those formerly living like vessels of wrath will later become vessels of mercy.

Mission outreach should never give up hope that some who presently seem to be clearly rejected by God might in the future be transformed by God's power. Since no one now knows the final outcome of God's predestination, and since God continues to transform even the most ungodly people, human mission must humbly and patiently reach out to all (not just to those who are more appealing).

Hosea 1:10 also prophesies that in the place where Gentiles are said not to be God's people, there they will be called children of the living God (9:26). Paul uses Hosea to show that God's children now include some Gentiles as well as some Jews (though not all Jews; see 9:6-8). Both of those claims are upsetting to Paul's Jewish conversation partner(s). But both are crucial in defending Paul's gospel and mission.

As for Israel, Isaiah cried out in the midst of judgment against Israel (and Assyria), saying that although the children of Israel are as numerous as the sand of the sea, only a remnant will be saved (9:27; Isa. 10:22). God kept the promise to childless Abraham that his descendants would be as many as the sand of the sea (Gen. 22:17). Yet that did not mean all of them would enjoy God's salvation. God's power will save only a few, a remnant. For God's righteous word of judgment against most of Israel will be carried out fully upon the earth (9:28; see Isa. 10:23).

Isaiah 1:9 also predicts that if the powerful Lord of the heavenly hosts had not left a small seed (a remnant) in Israel, Israel would have been totally destroyed, like Sodom and Gomorrah (9:29). Thus the Jewish prophet Isaiah spoke the most strongly about a time when a small remnant in Israel would be the true children of God. So Jews should not be surprised if the people of God's final kingly rule, which began with Jesus, includes only a few Jews and more than a few Gentiles (see Matt. 7:14; 8:5, 10-12). All of that is consistent with the message and predictions of Jewish prophets like Isaiah and Hosea. It is not against the Jewish Scriptures or Jewish people. The word of God to Israel has not failed (9:6). It is all part of God's consistent, righteous purposes to make known divine wrath and, above all, to manifest God's powerful mercy upon the chosen ones.

As with 9:6-13, a mission message like 9:14-29 which includes God's purpose to reject, harden, and make known wrath still remains repugnant to many. Even many Christians, who don't consider themselves rejected by God, dislike such teaching. It seems that if God is all-powerful in that way, then God is not at the same time good. And it appears that those rejected or hardened are not to blame. Such reasoning, however, exalts humankind and its values, and does not let God be God.

Paul strongly denies that God is to blame. God has the authority as Creator over all to decide what is good and what is bad. Earlier, in 3:1-8, Paul argues that God's righteousness can be manifested through wrath against sin. If God chooses to achieve that purpose through rejecting and hardening some people, who are we to define that as bad? It is only bad when judged by some human standards of fairness, equality, or free will. But God is not human and does not say that everyone must be treated equally or left alone to use their own free will. The kingdom of God is not a democracy with a bill of rights. People do have freedom to make most daily decisions, but only God decides who will become children of God.

Those who prefer a different God than the God of Paul and Jesus will reject the exalted Creator in order to serve a fallen creation (see 1:22-23, 25). Some may feel sorry for the rejected and call God to the witness stand to give an accounting to human judges. The truth, however, is that those rejected by God are to blame for their human decisions to pursue idolatry and immorality (see 1:20, 27, 32). While 1:18—3:20 shows how everyone, both Jew and Gentile, is responsible for their sin, 9:14-29 shows how God is righteous in hardening and punishing sinners, both Jews and Gentiles. The final judgment of God will rightly fall on those who do such things (2:2, 5). Otherwise, how can God judge the world (3:5-6)? God's judgment will consider the special circumstances of each person, such as their amount of knowledge about God (2:12). God's absolute power is always used righteously.

Why wouldn't God always want to show mercy? Why would God also want to show wrath? Part of Paul's answer is that God's wrath against sin is essential to God's character, and God wants to display that character to humankind. Also, Paul explains that God's wrath promotes a higher purpose, the purpose of showing mercy. God raised up and hardened Pharaoh so that God's power might be manifested. The message about that powerful God can then be proclaimed throughout the world (9:17). Similarly, when God's Messiah finally came, God's righteous wrath against humankind was poured out on him (by using Judas and others) as a means of making many righteous, both Jews and Gentiles (see 3:25-26, 29-30).

The present persecution against Christians by those God has rejected and hardened will turn out for the good of those who are called according to God's purpose (8:28). God's present show of wrath against some will lead to others being conformed to the image of Jesus, including final glorification with him (8:17-18, 29-30). By means of the vessels of wrath, God will make known the full riches of divine glory for the vessels of mercy (9:22-23). God's show of wrath is the basis for a more impressive showing of God's glory and mercy than if wrath had never been shown. Such truths should lead one to praise the powerful, righteous mission of the one true God rather than to doubt the possibility of reconciling God's rejection with human responsibility.

God's thoughts and ways are higher than ours (Isa. 55:8-

9). Our limited human minds cannot understand how God's powerful kingship can rule over a history of good and evil while those who do evil are still accountable. Yet God has affirmed both as true. So we must be content to hold together two apparently contradictory truths. Jesus taught both truths, even in the same verse.

In Luke 22:22, Jesus says he is going to die just as it was determined or destined (by God). But woe to the one who will betray him. God predicted (see Acts 1:16-20) and determined (John 17:12) that Judas would betray Jesus, yet Judas was still punished for his actions. While it might seem that God should ultimately be responsible, that was not the teaching of Jesus. If we share the faith of Jesus and Paul, we will confess that God rules righteously as mighty king over even evil events, and that God judges righteously all who do evil.[3]

Romans 9:30—10:10

God's Righteousness, Christ's Faith, and a Mission of Confession

---

PAUL now begins to draw some conclusions from his previous conversation with another Jew. Paul has tried to answer questions about God's right to show mercy on only certain Jews rather than on all Israel (9:6-23). And Paul has added that the chosen vessels of mercy include not only certain Jews but also some Gentiles (9:24-26). Those particular Gentiles have not previously been in the race for the prize of God's righteousness (9:30).

Because of Gentile idolatry, God has generally abandoned them to a history of immorality (1:18-32; see Acts 14:16). Yet now God's powerful love has overtaken some of them (9:25). Thus some Gentiles also possess the prize of righteousness on the basis of (Jesus') faith (9:30; compare 1:16-17; 3:22, 30).[1] On the other hand, Israel in general has been running after righteousness by focusing intently on the law of Moses, but they do not attain it (9:31; see 2:17-29).

Most Jews fail because they think the basis for righteousness is works of the law, not the new faith of Jesus (9:32). They are running as if they are on the road to righteousness. But they have stumbled over the rock, Jesus (and his faith), the rock which can end their quest (9:32). Jesus used Psalm 118:22 to describe himself as a stone which the Jewish leaders rejected. Yet he was the most important stone of all (Luke 20:17; see Eph. 2:20; 1 Pet. 2:7).

The stone that was a scandal to most Jews turns out to be put in Israel by God (9:33; see Isa. 28:16; Ps. 118:23; 1 Pet. 2:4, 6). God sent Jesus to Israel, and he manifested a new kind of faith, the final, definitive faith focused on the powerful kingship of God. Jesus' faith is the foundation stone for all who will submit to God's power and righteousness (see 1 Cor. 3:11). Whoever is believing upon and honoring Jesus will not be put to shame, despite the strong opposition of those who reject Jesus (9:33). Those Jews who have stopped running after righteousness and rested on the stone, Jesus and his faith, have reached the goal of the race: sharing God's righteousness. Note that Paul has just mentioned both Jesus' faith (9:30, 32) and faith in Jesus (9:33).

But the historical fact is that Israel in general stumbled over the scandal of Jesus and his faith. As a result, Paul writes that his heartfelt prayer to God for Israel is their salvation (10:1; see 9:2-3). Paul prays to God about that because it is up to God to give salvation. Only God can produce children of God (see 9:8, 10, 29).

Paul can witness to the zeal Israel has for God, but it lacks a true understanding of God. For Paul has often experienced the strong opposition of Jewish zealots who persecute those following the way of Jesus. Even Paul himself was once such a zealot with the brutal mission of persecuting the disciples of "the Way" of Jesus (Gal. 1:13-14; Phil. 3:6; Acts 9:1-2; 22:3-4). Such violent Jews are willfully ignorant of God's righteousness as manifested in Jesus, their fellow Jew. They will not submit to Jesus' way of righteousness but insist on seeking their own way of righteousness (10:3; see 9:31-32).

Instead of receiving God's righteousness based on Jesus' faith, the Jewish zealots insist on trying to attain their own righteousness by means of their own faithfulness. They pursue righteousness through human rather than divine action. By seeking to follow the law, they hope finally to stand tall as God's righteous people. More recently, various nations (in addition to

Israel) have claimed to stand on higher moral ground. In fact, they likewise stumble over the faith that humbly loves enemies rather than proudly killing them.

Christ has brought an end to such claims and hopes for righteousness (10:4). Jesus' faith says to seek first God's kingdom and righteousness (Matt. 6:33). God's righteousness results from the powerful kingship of God now at work since the life, death, and resurrection of Jesus. Jesus called on other Jews to share his faith in that powerful new work of God. Jesus didn't try to persuade Israel to try harder to keep the law of Moses. Because the promised kingship of God has now come to pass, Jesus' kingdom commands have fulfilled the law and the prophets, and his righteousness is much greater than the traditional righteousness of the law (Matt. 5:17-20). Someone greater than Moses has arrived!

Everyone (especially the Jew but also the Gentile) who keeps faith with Christ can give up the pursuit of Moses' law and submit to God's saving righteousness (10:4; see 6:13-14; 7:4-6). Faith in God's new powerful rule will lead to keeping those righteous requirements of Moses' law that Jesus emphasized (see 2:26; 8:4). Jesus' faith fulfilled and replaced most of Moses' law. Only through that faith will God's righteousness be reflected in a righteous people (1:17; 3:22). Those Jews who have left behind their national law are now part of a worldwide faith that includes Gentiles as well as Jews.

Concerning the righteousness based on works of the Jewish law, Moses wrote that the one who did the things in the law would live by them (10:5; see Lev. 18:5). Yet Paul has just argued that those trying to achieve their own righteousness through Moses' law have failed to receive God's righteousness through Christ's faith (9:31-32; 10:3-4).

So how will the righteousness based on (Jesus') faith respond to what Moses wrote (in Lev. 18:5)? First, the righteousness based on faith asserts that one's heart should not say: Who will ascend into heaven? (10:6; see Deut. 30:12). According to Paul, that question refers to those who try to bring Christ (Messiah) down from heaven (10:6). Some Jews think that if all Israel will obey the law for only one day, the Messiah will come.

Paul replies that they don't need to try because it is impossible for them. Besides, the Christ (Messiah) has already come down from heaven in the person of Jesus.

The righteousness based on faith will also assert that one shouldn't say, Who will descend into the abyss? (10:7; see Deut. 30:13). According to Paul, that means those who try to bring Christ up from the dead. Again, the reasons no one should try are that it is humanly impossible and it has already happened through God's power. Christ has risen!

Paul then adds that the righteousness based on faith does say that the word is already near, that is, it is in the mouth and heart of the believing one (10:8; see Deut. 30:14). Paul explains that the word of the believing one is the word of faith being proclaimed and taught as part of their ongoing mission (10:8). The Christ has already come and has revealed the righteousness of faith, and that faith is being passed on through the words of those who share that faith. The righteousness of God is being manifested now in the believing one out of Jesus' faith unto the faith of others who will come to believe through their mission (1:17).

God's final salvation has begun in those who confess with their mouths (see 10:8) that Jesus the Jew is not only the human Messiah of Israel but also the divine Lord over all peoples (10:9; see 1:3-4; 9:5). Jesus' faith has also proclaimed that he is much more than the Messiah of Israel (for example, see Matt. 25:31-32; 28:18-20; Mark 12:36-37; 14:61-62; John 10:30; 12:20, 32). The mission of that same Jesus calls for an ongoing confession by those who continue to share his faith (10:10).[2]

Jesus sent the twelve disciples throughout Israel to preach (confess) without pay about God's new kingship (Matt. 10:7-8). While they could receive food and shelter, they were not professional prophets or priests (Matt. 10:9-11). Their unpatriotic mission message about God's kingship would be a threat to national leaders, including nationalistic religious leaders (Matt. 10:17-18). The faith of Jesus was not the same as the national law of Moses. The rule of their heavenly Father would even divide earthly families (Matt. 10:20-21, 34-37). Despite all that, if their mission of confession endured to the end, they would be saved (Matt. 10:22). If they courageously continued to confess Jesus, he would finally confess them before his heavenly Father (Matt. 10:32).

◆ ◆ ◆

Before and during World War II, certain Christians in Germany were called the Confessing Church. They refused to go along with the popular civil religion that Hitler was using to gather support from most churches. Their mission was to confess that only Jesus was Lord (not Hitler), in the midst of strong political and religious opposition.

More recently, courageous Christians in the third world have spoken out against repressive political, military, and religious leaders. They rejected an imaginary national righteousness or salvation because of their faith that God's righteousness comes only through confessing Jesus as Lord. The word of faith in their hearts and mouths spoke of divine power and refused human power.

For many years, the Filipino president, Ferdinand Marcos, portrayed himself as the savior of the nation. He told lies about his military heroism (in World War II), political plans, and religious devotion. Most Filipinos either believed the lies or refused to pay the price for exposing them. Some Filipinos angrily denounced Marcos or violently rebelled because of their own political ambitions. And a few Filipinos boldly spoke the truth about Marcos because they also openly confessed that only Jesus was Lord. Indeed, leaders (lords) of every nation still exalt themselves at the expense of many of their people (Luke 22:25).

The power-hungry political lords of every nation who claim to be public servants must also be confessed as impostors. They need to confess that they are not servants in the same way Jesus was (see Luke 22:26-27). Jesus was an outspoken prophet whom the political and religious leaders wanted to kill, and finally did. Jesus confessed the kingship of God. That was good news to those poor disciples who followed him but bad news to those wealthy "masters" who wanted to live like kings themselves (Luke 6:20-25).

Today, the popular leaders of Christendom (and its mission) also live like kings and confess their loyalty to national lords. The official biography of Billy Graham, the most popular religious leader of American presidents and American society, has the title: *A Prophet with Honor.*[3] Even foreign dictators like Ferdinand Marcos have honored Graham. When he held a crusade in Manila in 1977, Ferdinand and Imelda Marcos greeted Graham at the airport. Graham responded by asserting that no one in the Philippines was in prison for their faith. At that time, however, there were around two thousand prisoners of conscience detained throughout the country. Some of those prisoners were there because their faith demanded that they confront the evil of their leaders, including the Marcos dynasty.

Some Filipino Christians wrote to Billy Graham before he arrived, questioning his preparations, such as a school of evangelism in Imelda's immaculate International Convention Center. Graham and his staff were planning to stay in one of the best hotels, and the Marcoses would give them the reception of a visiting king. The Filipinos challenged Graham not to be isolated from the people he sought to lead to salvation. The vast majority would be desperately poor and needed to see the love of God in concrete ways. Yet Graham's crusade would be more of a symbol of the church's unholy alliance with American influence and affluence. The Filipinos concluded their letter by saying that Graham's style of evangelism was something they could not afford.[4]

Billy Graham has continually emphasized the need to make a public confession of faith. He expects that declaration to include a confession of sins, a prayer to accept Jesus' death as the means of forgiveness and salvation, and a one-time public stand for Christ as a response to an evangelistic invitation. Such a religious ritual can be a valid first step for a few Christians. Usually it has been an isolated step divorced from an ongoing mission of confessing Jesus' faith and reflecting Jesus' powerful lordship in one's life. Someone once commented that many sing "Just As I Am," go forward just as they are, and go out the door just as they were.

Perhaps the greatest weakness of Graham has been his popularity and lack of conflict with American values like national pride, prosperity, and power. He made friends too easily with political leaders and presidents, with business and church leaders, with so-called important people. His crusades applauded and paraded national and local celebrities as examples of godly Americans. By means of a reduced gospel and a massive number of decisions for Christ, Graham hoped to revive the churches and the nation. He represented American righteousness while confessing Christ's sacrificial death. Yet Christ represented God's righteousness while confessing God's kingly power which would create that righteousness. God's righteousness results from God's re-creation, not from a revival or reform of Christendom.

Many in the world today who confess Jesus as Lord do not reflect God's righteousness as revealed in Jesus' faith (see Matt. 7:21). So despite their sincere confessions, Jesus will finally confess on the day of judgment that he never knew them (Matt. 7:23). For Jesus, disciples were more important than decisions. Evangelists have persuaded numerous people to accept Christ as their personal Savior, to ask Jesus into their heart, or to invite Christ into their life. As a result, millions of Christians think they are saved because they prayed such a prayer or walked down an aisle. But most of them are not yet saved from the power of sin through the powerful grace of God. False disciples join because of what they can get out of it: a better conscience, spiritual peace, a respectable reputation, or even better business, wealth, or health.

The quick fix of an intellectual or emotional decision for a heavenly Christ often simply adds Jesus to one's collection of gods. Hindus who accept Christ can easily add him to their thirty million other gods. Mormons can confess Christ as Lord while hoping to become lords themselves of another planet in the future. Most Americans willingly accept Jesus into their civil religion of God and country—or more correctly, country and god. Instead of costly confessions which come from living Christ's faith, they have substituted cheap religious rituals that make a show of confessing Christ. While honoring Christ with their lips, they seek to honor themselves or their extended selves (family, church, nation) with their lives.

On the other hand, there are servants like Christiana Grinado from the Philippines. She lives in Manila on "Smoky Mountain," a huge pile of garbage that is the city dump. That mountain of trash is home for thousands of squatters who try to support themselves by salvaging items from the garbage. Christiana has chosen to live there with them so that she can be Christ's living presence among the people. Her consistent confession of Christ on that mountain is more authentic than most contented confessions in the church.

Another servant is Christine Tan, who works with Filipinos threatened, imprisoned, and/or tortured by an abusive military giant. In order to serve her Lord, she has chosen to confront those who lord it over the poor and powerless. As a result, she has been labeled a subversive by her military, political, and religious leaders. Still, she is not afraid of the power of death because she confesses a Lord who was treated the same way.

For Paul, true confession comes from those who are believing in their hearts (see 10:8) the missionary word that God has raised the suffering servant Jesus from death (10:9). Their reputations and lives may be destroyed, but those who believe and confess will be saved (10:9-10). Their confessions will be in a context of denying themselves, taking up their cross, and losing the life which temporarily is more comfortable and secure. By following Jesus and confessing Jesus' gospel now, they receive salvation and eternal life in the end (Mark 8:34-38).

The secret house churches in China that have multiplied since the 1950s have emphasized confessing or testifying to Jesus. Located mainly in rural areas, they continue to meet and testify despite the dangers and risks. Many have faced persecution, prison, or death at the hands of suspicious government and religious authorities. Their testimonies in the house churches praise God's power for strength in the midst of suffering. By sharing and confessing their present lives of righteousness and suffering, such Chinese Christians express and extend that reality to others around them.[5]

God's salvation and righteousness belong to those who also believe in the power of God which raised Jesus (compare 1:4, 16-17; 4:24-25; 5:10; 6:4-5, 8-11; 8:11). After his resurrection, Jesus ruled as Lord with his heavenly father. Belief in God begins in the heart, the center of thinking and willing and feeling. Then it becomes manifested in a mission message that confesses the rule of Jesus and his heavenly Father (10:9-10). The reason confession comes before belief in 10:9, but not in 10:10, is because of the use of Deuteronomy 30:14 in Romans 10:8, where the mouth is referred to before the heart.

The righteous ones through faith will not ask who can ascend into heaven to bring Christ down, but will confess that the Christ has already come in the person of Jesus of Nazareth (see 10:6, 9). They will not ask who can descend into the abyss to raise Christ from the dead, but will confess that he has already risen (see 10:7, 9). Such people believe and confess the mission word about God's power which raised Jesus from a humiliating death to heavenly lordship. In doing so, they will also share in God's righteousness and salvation (10:9-10).

In Romans, the gospel is above all the good news about God's saving power, seen first in Jesus, and about the risen Jesus, who rules with God as Lord. Although Paul meets strong opposition because of that gospel, he is not ashamed—for the power of God is unto salvation to everyone who believes (1:16; 9:33-10:2; 10:9-10). Only the righteous one on the basis of Jesus' faith will live (1:17), not the one who merely tries to follow the laws of Moses (10:4-5).

Romans 10:11-21

World Mission and the Word of Christal

CHRIST'S past faith and present lordship can be experienced by everyone (Jew or Gentile) who shares that faith and confesses that lordship (9:30—10:10). In 10:11-21, Paul points out the importance of world mission in order to spread the good word of Christ. Christ continues to speak through the word of faith being proclaimed to all peoples (see 10:8).

Paul begins by using Isaiah 28:16 again (see 9:33). This time he adds the word *everyone* at the beginning of the quote (10:11). His purpose now is to emphasize that everyone (both Jew and Gentile) who believes on and honors the risen Jesus, who now rules as divine Lord, will not be put to shame in the end (10:11; see 10:9). Since the Jewish law is not the basis for God's final salvation, there is no distinction between Jew and Gentile. Jesus is the one Lord over all peoples (10:12).

As Lord over the world mission, Jesus gives the riches of God's righteousness and salvation to all who call upon him, to all who ask him (10:12). All those who call upon him will become vessels of God's rich mercy (see 9:23). Their calling out in faith to Jesus will show that God has called them, even if earlier they were ungodly and immoral Gentiles (see 9:24-26). As Joel 2:32 says, "Everyone who calls on the name of the Lord shall be saved" (10:13). In 10:11-13, Paul uses the word *all* or *everyone* four times (see also the use of *everyone* in 10:4). He continues to challenge his readers and partners in mission to share his world vision for all peoples.

While Joel refers originally to the God of Israel, Paul applies the same verse and title (Lord) to Jesus (see 10:9). The same Jesus who first believed in the final powerful kingship of God, now rules as Lord at the right hand of God. God is now known to include both the God of Jesus and Jesus himself. To believe and call upon the God of Jesus is also to believe and pray to Jesus, who is also God or Lord. Paul again combines the faith of Jesus and faith in Jesus.

Paul then raises a series of questions to show the relationship between a focus on Jesus as Lord and world mission. He begins by asking how people can call upon the name of the Lord (see 10:12-13) unless they have first believed into him and thus been united with him (10:14; see 10:9-11). Only those who come to rest on the rock of Jesus and his faith will call on him as the Lord who gives salvation (compare 9:33 and 10:11-13).

Next, he asks how they can believe into a Christ whom they have not heard.[1] And how can they hear Christ apart from people who proclaim or confess the word of faith (10:14; see 10:8- 10)? Finally, how can people spread the word of Christ unless they are called and sent by Christ as his apostles or ambassadors (10:15; see 1:1, 5-7)? Thus Paul ties together the causes and effects of world mission mentioned in 10:8-13.

Part of the word of Christ includes the words of the risen Christ about going to all the peoples. Jesus' followers are to make disciples by teaching them to obey all his former commands or words (Matt. 28:19-20). Jesus now is Lord with authority over all the earth (10:9, 12; Matt. 28:18). So his mission is a world mission, which will lead to the obedience of faith among all the world's peoples (see 1:4-5).

Paul then turns to several Old Testament passages to show how Christ's world mission is now fulfilling those earlier words. In 10:15, he quotes Isaiah 52:7: "How beautiful are the feet of those bringing good news." When Jesus walked the dusty trails, his dirty feet were beautiful because they brought the good news of God. Just think how many Gospel stories would never have happened if Jesus had been driving around in a car and preaching only in a synagogue.[2]

In the sixteenth century, Anabaptists walked from town to town calling the established Protestant or Catholic churches to repentance. German church leaders ridiculed them as *Läufer*, runners or messengers. Such supposed heretics went out two by two, dressed simply, roaming about and preaching Jesus' good news. When Christendom thought the only mission was authorized pastors preaching in their own designated parishes, the lay *Läufer* considered everyone within walking distance a mission field.[3]

More recently, an older missionary in Guatemala walked for several weeks at a time through the mountains to visit Indian congregations in the villages. Even after a new road was built, he continued to walk because the people he wanted to reach were not used to seeing someone drive up in a car. As he walked, he found he could share the good news more easily with those who walked down the same road with him.[4]

In some South American countries like Ecuador, poor farmers walked long distances to encourage others to form basic Christian communities. Such apostles were dedicated members of their own small groups, where they were often part of a team of coordinators. Yet they went out with no social prestige, no ordained ministry, and little money. They did not build new structures in new places or try to organize whole villages. They simply tried to encourage other people to form their own small Christian communities.[5]

I knew an older Filipino circuit pastor whose churches were in the remote mountains. There were no roads, and he had no car anyway. In fact, he usually didn't wear shoes. His feet were wrinkled, rough, and rugged. After hearing about his mission in the mountains, I thought his feet looked beautiful. Wherever Jesus calls us to walk, whether in mountains or villages or cities, let us be up and about, going out to those who need good news.

Such apostles might not work as fast or efficiently as most Western missionaries. Yet they are also not as alone and isolated as those depending more on modern technology. Western missionaries commonly plan their strategies by assuming technologies like cars, airplanes, and four-wheel-drive vehicles. The problem is that their modern, fast-paced, individualistic busy work increases the distance between them and the people they seek to serve. They prefer time-saving mobility to time-consuming relationships. More jobs are done at the expense of fewer friendships and personal contacts.

Too much time is spent buying, using, and maintaining technology. Even those using computers to plan new strategies, like identifying unreached people groups, are seldom able to identify with the people behind the numbers. Instead, poor third-world apostles are more likely to embody Christ and walk among the poor. All the charts, graphs, books (including this one), and programs are no substitute for incarnation among the poor. Western missionaries need to remember that most people in the world still walk.[6]

Thousands of Asian missionaries have now traveled all over Asia and far beyond. Local churches, not denominational or other mission agencies, sent out most of those apostles. Most also served in grassroots projects of evangelism and church planting. They didn't have the resources of Western missions which built big churches, hospitals, and schools. Yet they were then better prepared to identify with the economic, social, and cultural situations of the people to whom they went. The churches they planted did not depend on support from a larger denominational body. They could thus develop theologies more appropriate to their situations.[7]

During our first term of four years in the Philippines, we lived on a university campus in somewhat of a mission compound. We had a car like the other missionary families. But for our second term, we moved off campus to a barrio on the edge of the city. We also gave up our car and used jeepneys like most Filipinos. We discovered that we were less isolated and formed new friendships with people who appreciated our more simple lifestyle. As we walked or waited for jeepneys, we had more opportunities to talk with those around us.

Likewise, in the United States I meet more people when I walk. The American love for the automobile has meant each driver riding alone in a world of their own. When I want to talk to my neighbors about important matters, I don't just call them on the phone. I walk to their homes. If I plan to form a neighborhood Bible study, I walk around and invite neighbors, some near and some farther away. The less I use technology like cars and telephones, the more God's message becomes incarnate in the feet, hands, eyes, and ears of the messenger. A beautiful voice behind a pulpit, on television, or on a telephone cannot replace beautiful feet on a dirt path, on a city sidewalk, in a front yard, or in a living room.

A traveling preacher in China knew from the beginning that his work would be quite tiring, but he began by dedicating his feet to God. He also depended on God's power to give him faith and confidence in the midst of danger and persecution. Wherever he went, brothers and sisters in Christ welcomed him warmly and suggested what area to go to next. Other Chinese brothers and sisters who joined in such apostolic missions also had large areas to cover. Yet wherever they went, dozens of people would follow behind. At day or night, they would all sing as they walked along the mountain paths. Whenever they came to a family, the host would receive the apostle as a servant of God. The beauty of the mountains was even more profound by the sight of the feet of those bringing good tidings of God's power.[8]

The context surrounding the beautiful feet of Isaiah 52:7 introduces the good news as a message about salvation, with an announcement, "Your God reigns." That was the same good news which Jesus proclaimed (for example, Mark 1:15). Although Christ's word about the powerful kingship of God is being passed on, it nevertheless meets much resistance (see Matt. 13:3-7, 19-22). Paul also confirms that not all have obeyed the gospel (10:16). That too was prophesied by Isaiah. Shortly after the passage about the beautiful feet, Isaiah 53:1 raises a question: Who has believed our message? The good news is going out into the world, but most don't obediently share Christ's faith.

Paul also uses Isaiah 53:1 (in 10:16) to show the connection between faith and the missionary message. In 10:17, he answers the questions raised in 10:14-15 by concluding that faith comes from hearing the mission message, and the message comes through the word of Christ. Christ continues to speak through his commissioned messengers. Those sent out on apostolic mission confess with their mouths the word that Jesus the Jew is now Lord over all the peoples (see 10:9-10). Their mission of confession passes on Jesus' faith in the saving power of God, revealed above all in raising Jesus from the dead (10:9). The word of Christ is the word of faith (see 10:8).

Consequently, while God's powerful mercy produces faith in those who are predestined (compare 8:29; 9:23), God also uses the missionary message in that process. God's sovereign power in forming faith doesn't mean people can forget world mission. For the same power that forms faith also sends out those faithful few with the message of Christ. Paul writes Romans to strengthen the faith of his readers so their faith will continue to spread around Rome and around the world (see 1:5-8, 11).

Paul now asks if that world mission is not already going on. Have the peoples not yet heard (10:18)? In the Greek, the implied and stated answer is that they have indeed heard. Paul quotes Psalm 19:4 and applies it to the missionary message: their words have gone out into all the earth, even unto the ends of the inhabited world (compare 1:8). Even if many (especially most Jews) have not obeyed the message, the word of Christ is spreading to the ends of the earth.

Paul asks next if Israel has not known about the gospel for all peoples (10:19). Again, the implied and stated answer is that they have known. He then proves that from both the law of Moses (Deut. 32:21) and the prophets (Isa. 65:1-2). Deuteronomy 32:21 points to a mission where those not a chosen people like Israel (compare 9:25-26) will make Israel jealous (10:19). A foolish people, Gentiles (see 1:21), will challenge Israel by receiving the gospel, and make Israel angry as a result.

During Paul's first visit to Antioch of Pisidia, he spoke in the synagogue about Jesus. On the next Sabbath day, the whole city came to the Jewish synagogue to hear the good news (Acts 13:44). But after seeing all those Gentiles so interested in Paul's words, the Jews became jealous and began to argue with him and denounce him (Acts 13:45). After that meeting, they persuaded the leaders of the city to drive Paul out (Acts 13:50).

Apostolic mission in the footsteps of Jesus takes the more narrow and dangerous path. Hector Gallego was born in the hills of Colombia to a poor farmer. He had always wanted to be a priest, but a special kind of priest. He wanted to remain poor and have no special privileges. After becoming a priest, Gallego left the security of being a parish priest in Colombia for a mission in the rain forests of Panama in 1967. He became known for his self-sacrifice, living on the same level as the poorest peasants. He walked long distances through mountainous jungles to visit neighboring hamlets.

To break the cycle of poverty and dependence, Gallego suggested agricultural cooperatives. But the better-off townspeople didn't like the idea. They said he should stick to his priestly duties in town and not wander all over the mountains talking to peasants. Rejected by those in town, Gallego turned to the peasants. They loved his simple, humble way.

After two years of walking through mountains and jungles, Gallego had formed thirty Christian communities. Their lay leaders he called "responsibles," since he stressed communal responsibility. They formed cooperatives that helped free them from a long dependence on townspeople. The townspeople then became more angry with Gallego. Because the peasants were reading the Bible and cooperating in new ways, some said the New Testament was a communist book which Gallego brought from Colombia.

Anger led to threats, and later police arrested Gallego. As he talked with the communities, Gallego had often quoted Jesus' warnings about the world's hatred, and the need to respond with love, not violence. In 1971, Gallego was kidnapped at night by two armed men and was never seen again. Nevertheless, the cooperatives and Christian communities continued. A peasant later said that Gallego was still with them because he left them an ideal of Christ. He added that Gallego was a true apostle of God.[9]

Those who seem least likely to respond to the gospel sometimes later receive God's word through God's power. In 10:20-21, Paul uses Isaiah 65:1-2 to contrast the different ways Gentiles and Jews have received the gospel. Isaiah 65:1 points to Gentiles who have not been seeking God (see 9:30) yet who found God through God's revelation (10:20). Those words are about Gentiles who were converted because of God's revelation to them and in them. They echo the words of the second half of Isaiah 53:1: And to whom has the arm of the Lord been revealed? (In 10:16 Paul quotes the first half of Isaiah 53:1, concerning those who reject the gospel.) God's arm or power is now being manifested to and in those Gentiles whom God has chosen and who have responded to the gospel message (compare 1:16-17; 10:12). It is a bold prediction by Isaiah since it will generate strong anger among the Jews (10:20).

On the other hand, concerning Israel, Isaiah 65:2 tells how God has continually reached out to them, but they have remained disobedient (10:21; compare 10:16). Paul is referring to the results of taking the gospel to the Jews. Yet that should be no surprise since Isaiah foretold such disobedience (compare 10:21 and 9:27-29; 10:16). The word of God has not failed (9:6).

Romans 11:1-12

God's Ongoing Mission of Election and Rejection Within Israel

PAUL has just described the general disobedience of Israel as far as the gospel is concerned (10:16, 21). Israel has rejected Christ's world mission which has spread the word of Christ through Paul and others. That raises a new question: Has God therefore rejected Israel (11:1)? Did the God who previously loved or chose Jacob, while hating or rejecting Esau (9:13), now choose Gentiles and reject Israel completely? In Greek, the question implies a negative answer, and Paul answers by strongly denying such a conclusion.

The first reason God has not completely rejected Israel is Paul himself. He is an Israelite (see 9:4), a physical descendant of Abraham (see 9:5, 7), through the tribe of Benjamin. Paul is living proof that God has not given up on Israel.

A second reason God has not rejected Israel is that they are a special people whom God foreknew (11:2). God's purpose from the beginning was to know Israel as an elect, chosen people. Even if most Jews end up disobeying God's word, they remain a special people. Because of God's gifts to them (3:1-2; 9:4-5), the gospel is to be preached first to them (see 1:16).

Paul then points to the example of Elijah, who faced the similar situation of a disobedient Israel. Due to his suffering,

Elijah prayed to God by complaining against Israel (11:2). According to Elijah, Israel had killed God's prophets, destroyed God's altars, and he alone was left. They were even seeking his life (11:3). Elijah saw himself as part of a suffering remnant, and felt he was the only one who had survived (1 Kings 19:10, 14).

Yet God solemnly assured Elijah that there were still seven thousand people who had not worshiped or served the idol Baal (11:4; 1 Kings 19:18). When everything seems lost, God's gracious power continues to keep a remnant faithful for the sake of God's own purposes (compare 9:29). Thus Paul concludes that even as he writes, the same grace of God continues to elect from within Israel a remnant (Paul and other Jewish Christians) (11:5). Furthermore, if election depends on God's powerful grace, then it is clearly not based on mere human works (11:6; see 9:12, 16).

While God's grace is at work in a Jewish remnant, Israel in general has failed to reach the goal it seeks (11:7). Israel is seeking to be righteous by obeying its law, but Israel has failed (9:31). It will not submit to God's righteousness as manifested in Jesus (10:3-4). Only the elect, the chosen remnant, receive God's righteousness (compare 11:5 and 11:7). The rest are hardened by God, like Pharaoh was hardened (compare 11:7 and 9:17-18). God's mission of election and rejection within Israel began with Abraham's children and grandchildren (9:6-13), continued throughout Israel's history (9:27-29; 11:2-4), and remains consistent during Paul's time (11:1, 5-7).

To compare hardened Israel with Pharaoh is quite upsetting to Jews. So Paul turns to Jewish Scripture again to show that God hardened Israel. First, he uses words from the prophets (Isa. 29:10) and the law (Deut. 29:4) which refer to God's hardening Israel (11:8). Just like before, God has put Israel into a sleep so that their eyes cannot see (Isa. 29:10). Their ears cannot hear until that very day (Deut. 29:4). That hardening process continued up to Paul's own time. Israel remains a disobedient people (see 10:21, quoting Isa. 65:2).

Second, Paul points to David and Psalm 69:22-23, where the psalmist calls on God to curse his enemies (11:9-10). Paul uses the suffering righteous one of Psalm 69 because of the suffering remnant of his own time. In both cases, the main source of the suffering is certain other Jews (see Ps. 69:8). Like Elijah (11:3), Isaiah (Rom. 10:16), and Jesus, Paul's own suffering as part of the remnant in Israel comes especially from hardened Jewish leaders and missionaries (see 10:2-3). In a similar situation, David called for God to turn their table of triumph into a trap or stumbling block. He also called on God to darken the eyes and continually to bend the backs of those who looked proudly at the suffering they caused. Thus David spoke of God's ongoing mission of rejecting and hardening within Israel.

Paul, therefore, is saying that God hardened a disobedient Israel, which persecuted a Jewish remnant. Those Jews like Paul who continue Jesus' message and mission are facing the same suffering that Jesus did. Yet despite such violent power against them, God continues to elect and enable a suffering Jewish remnant to be instruments of God's ongoing mission. However, unlike David, they do not cry out to God to curse their enemies. Instead, Paul has considered asking God to curse him if it means blessing for his hardened fellow Jews (9:3). Paul's prayers are for Israel's salvation, not condemnation (10:1).

In 11:11, Paul raises another question about the possible implications of what he has just written. If Christ and his followers turn out to be the major stumbling blocks (9:33 and 11:9), has Israel now stumbled and fallen from God's grace? In Greek, the question implies a negative answer, and Paul responds with a strong denial. For Paul, God's hardening of Israel has a positive purpose: their sinful stumbling leads not to their final fall but to salvation going out to the Gentiles (see 9:22-26).

Acts 13:46-47 portrays Paul as saying salvation went out to Gentiles all over the world because the Jews rejected his mission (compare Acts 18:5-6). In Acts 28:23, Paul later talks with interested Jews in Rome about the powerful kingship of God and the faithful way of Jesus. But that led to disagreement among the Jews, and they departed (Acts 28:25). Consequently, Paul quotes Isaiah 6:9-10 concerning their inability to hear and see the truth (Acts 28:26-27; see Jesus' use of Isa. 6:9-10 in Matt. 13:14-15 and John 12:40). Paul thus concludes that the salvation of God has been sent to Gentiles who will listen (Acts 28:29).

Nevertheless, God's purposes are not yet complete when salvation goes out to the Gentiles. Another part of God's plan is that the Gentiles' reception of salvation will make the Jews jealous (11:11; compare 10:19). Furthermore, in 11:12, Paul suggests that Israel's present sinful stumbling and failure to follow Christ will change in the future. Now, their disobedience has meant the riches of salvation for the world, for the Gentiles (9:23; 10:12). Though only a small suffering Jewish remnant is receiving salvation now, that has led to a world mission to the Gentiles. Then Paul adds, Just think how much more will happen when the rest of Israel (the full number) receives salvation (11:12). If God uses their defeat through being hardened to bring salvation to the world, what will happen when God's power leads them to submit to salvation through Jesus' faith?

Jesus compares God's powerful kingship to planting the smallest seed (the mustard seed) which finally turns out to be the largest shrub (Matt. 13:31-32). The tiny Jewish remnant composed of Jesus and his followers seemed insignificant, and their opponents seemed to overpower them. As the mission later spread among Gentiles as well as Jews, the body of believers in each place remains a tiny remnant, compared to the larger society around them. Each body continues to seem insignificant, easy targets for those who oppose their mission.

Yet from Paul's day until the present, God's ongoing mission has preferred to work in and through the weakness of a small remnant of believers. There is no time during church history when God does not elect a faithful remnant. Every century and every decade since Jesus, small groups of faithful followers and certain more isolated individuals have continued Jesus' mission in many places. The total number of believers in the world has never been that limited. Yet the number in each place remains small compared to the majority of Jews and Gentiles who still are hardened. So the mustard seed remains the best picture of how God's powerful kingship works.

Consequently, the growth of modern Christendom and many local Christian churches today is not the large shrub predicted by Jesus. The large shrub will be the final fellowship of the full number of elect Jews and Gentiles in the new heavens and new earth. If church growth recruits members that reflect the values of their own society more than the righteousness of God, it is producing more weeds than mustard seeds (compare Matt. 13:24-30).

Certain missionaries, like Donald McGavran, have promoted people movements as the way quickly to grow churches. Sometimes God has indeed chosen to elect several within a family or group all at once. Indeed, many third-world cultures emphasize the community more than the individual. But I'm suspicious of Western missionaries who use communal values to make their work go faster and seem more successful. If a chief chooses Christianity and the village goes along, is the resulting church a faithful remnant or an established community with a few added beliefs and rituals?

A remnant is a communal group, not isolated individuals. Yet it's a smaller group within a larger cultural group, clan, tribe, or people. The God of Jesus does not get so excited about people movements where a large group supposedly becomes Christian all together. The thousands who repented in Acts 2:41 (and 4:4) included both Jews and other peoples, especially proselytes or converts to Judaism. They represented languages from all around the world, having come to Jerusalem for the feast of Pentecost (Acts 2:1, 5-11). When many of them later returned to their homes, they were the beginning of faithful remnants in those places.

U.S. churches have especially promoted a church growth that glorifies large numbers and successful statistics. Big churches with big budgets and many members have more influence or power and are proud of God's obvious blessing. But the mystery of God's kingdom is not so obvious. Jesus' mission did not try to cater to large crowds or Christianize a whole society or culture. He spoke unpopular truth to crowds and humbly served God's ongoing mission of election and rejection. His God would choose a small remnant to manifest God's righteousness in a particular place or among a particular people.

Thus, even in so-called Christian nations, God's kingship is found only among a small, insignificant remnant. Indeed, even in the churches of those nations, God's righteousness as manifested in Jesus' faith is found in only a remnant. The main leaders or the core supporters of a church program and budget might think of themselves as a faithful remnant. Yet their faith is often more geared to their church's former or future glory and success.

Jesus' remnant, however, continues to call others to turn from the pursuit of proud status, material wealth, and dominating power. New churches or sects often begin because of disagreement with established churches. As churches or denominations become successful, wealthy, and respectable, a few feel they must leave to be faithful to Jesus' mustard-seed faith. A more poor, outcast minority leaves behind those churches that have become comfortable with the world around them. Yet when new groups later become more successful, the cycle begins again.[1]

New grassroots movements have often made a fatal choice at certain moments. They chose to use economic and/or political power to serve the church. That was true for Luther, Calvin, Anabaptists, Methodists, Baptists, and more recently for Pentecostals. All are examples of movements that came to prefer upward mobility and institutional power. The newly successful and respectable churches then forgot the simplicity of their early witness and the lower classes from which they came.

Currently, in Brazil, Protestants who were once outsiders in a Catholic society are now gaining popularity and power among government officials, to whom they give great support. Meanwhile, prophets in the Catholic Church are becoming outcasts because of their criticism of the state's oppressive policies. As they return to a church of the poor, they also challenge their own Catholic institutions that are among the most wealthy, centralized, and traditional institutions in the world.[2]

Changes in European or North American churches often were repeated in their mission churches elsewhere. For example, the beginning of Methodists among the poor in England included John Wesley's teaching that slavery was the greatest of all evils. Then, as Methodists spread to America and became the largest American denomination, they said less and less about slavery. When given the choice of either growing into a popular, nationwide church or rejecting the evil of slavery, Methodists preferred growth and prosperity.[3]

That change was repeated in the middle of the nineteenth century when Methodists began a mission to Brazil. More than any other mission group, they worked among the poor and outcasts, including slaves. As time went on, Methodists became more involved in mission to the higher classes. Such mission then changed from humble meetings among the working class to education through prestigious secondary schools and universities. Today, there are many such Methodist schools in Brazil. As Methodists gained power and respectability, and spent large sums on institutions of higher education, they lost their original grassroots mission and spiritual strength.[4]

In Washington, D.C., a powerful, prosperous, and proud church also happened to have a remnant elected by God. National Presbyterian Church worships in a "cathedral" and celebrates centuries of tradition. Then during the 1970s, a small group of people became concerned about world hunger. Wanting to do more than give a little money, they developed a Hunger Covenant. From a congregation of eighteen hundred, about two hundred participated and began to sacrifice something to simplify their lifestyle. The money saved went partly to a village in India and partly to the hungry in Washington. Most sacrifices were small, but it was a first step.

The same group next developed an Urban Ministry Team. Most of them had never been in the slums, and Washington has more than its share of slums. They began to cooperate with African-American leaders involved in helping the poor. After they saw the plight of the poor and worked with them to repair buildings, they had additional questions about the roots of poverty. Other committed Christians working among the poor and living simply, like the Sojourners Fellowship and the Church of the Savior, came and shared with the group. As a result, a few have now made significant changes. One couple moved from an expensive suburban neighborhood to a smaller city apartment so they would be close to their area of mission. Some other families moved to an inner-city neighborhood to begin a community ministry.[5]

Jesus told his little flock that seeking God first means humble service among the poor (Luke 12:30-34) and prophetic suffering among the majority, especially from the more wealthy and powerful among the majority (Matt. 10:16-42). God will always be selecting a remnant, no matter how great the opposition. God's mission today still elects a remnant within Israel and among the Gentiles.

Romans 11:13-24

God's Family Tree of Faithful Jews and Gentiles

W HEN Paul writes Romans, there are more Gentile
Christians than Jewish Christians in the churches he
has started. Although the Jews have a long history of receiving
privileges and promises from God, most have rejected the faith
of Jesus. Consequently, some Gentile Christians are tempted to
boast that they have attained salvation while the Jews in general
have failed. It appears to them that the Jews have completely
fallen out of God's favor.

Paul responds to that attitude by directly addressing his
Gentile-Christian readers (11:13). He begins by describing
himself as an apostle to the Gentiles (see Gal. 1:16; 2:7-9). He
glorifies that mission service, even among those Jews who hate
Gentiles. Paul is not ashamed of his servant mission to Gentiles
because God's power is transforming even them (see 1:16). He
continues to speak boldly about his Gentile mission in the presence of other Jews (his own flesh and blood). He wants to make
them jealous of God's new work among the Gentiles (11:14; see
10:19; 11:11). Paul hopes that the good news about God's new
worldwide family of various Gentiles and a few Jews will lead
other Jews to receive God's salvation.

Shortly after writing Romans, Paul went to Jerusalem, the

Jewish center and challenged Jews with the fruit of his Gentile mission. Several Gentiles went with him to represent that mission (Acts 19:21; 20:3-5). Because of Paul's glorying in those Gentile Christians, some Jews became jealous and accused him of taking Gentiles into the temple (Acts 21:28-29).

When a Jewish mob tried to kill him, a Roman military officer and soldiers rescued him (Acts 21:30-36). Yet Paul still asked to speak to the angry crowd, who listened to Paul's experiences as a persecutor of Christians and as an apostle of Christ. But when Paul mentioned his mission to the Gentiles, the people cried out against him again (Acts 22:21-23). Even in the face of death, Paul elevated his Gentile mission in Jerusalem to lead some other Jews to embrace his new worldwide faith.

Paul is not willing to forget the Jews. Even as apostle to the Gentiles, Paul's mission still gives special importance to the Jews (see 1:16). If the Roman Christians are to continue his mission, some will need to change their attitudes about mission to the Jews. As Paul writes this letter, he knows that his trip to Jerusalem will be dangerous and that the Roman Christians might need to carry on his mission without him. So Paul emphasizes that God is not through with Israel. The risen Lord is still giving grace to empower apostolic mission among all the peoples, both Jews and Gentiles (see 1:5).

Presently, God has rejected most of Israel (see 9:13, 18; 11:7-9). God's purpose is to pour out the riches of reconciliation and salvation among all other peoples (11:15; see 11:11-12). So if Israel's rejection leads to such reconciliation, what will be the result of their future acceptance? It will lead to the final fulfillment of God's kingly power through resurrection from the dead (11:15; see 11:12). Israel will not remain hardened forever. In the final days of this present age, Israel in general will be reconciled to God. Then God's power will bring the history of salvation to a climax by raising the dead.

The conversion of much of Israel at the end should not be confused with political developments in the present nation of Israel. God can convert most Jews to the faith of Jesus the Jew whether or not the nation of Israel survives. Certain wealthy and powerful leaders dominate that nation, like every other nation. Those leaders have given violent treatment to Palestinians living in and around Israel. The Jews are still God's special people. Yet those who continue to do such evil will be among the first to receive God's judgment. God's power will also be unto wrath to the Jew first (2:9). If we share the faith of Jesus, we must speak prophetically against the evil of such Jewish leaders and their followers (see Matt. 23:37-38; Rom. 2:17-24).

God's future work among Jews will relate to God's first work of foreknowing or setting apart Israel as a special chosen people (see 11:2). If the firstfruits of the dough (see Num. 15:20) are holy or set apart, so will the final lump of dough be holy (11:16). Likewise, if the root is holy, so also are the branches. That is, if Israel's founding fathers are chosen and set apart by God (see 9:7-13), in a similar way Israel in general will finally be God's holy redeemed people (see Isa. 51:1-6; 62:11-12). For the sake of Abraham, Isaac, and Jacob, God will not forget Israel. God will bring to fulfillment what has been started with Abraham, the father of Israel (see 4:1).

Paul then develops in more detail his picture of a Jewish root growing into a tree with many branches. He uses a cultivated olive tree as a symbol of God's special mission in Israel (see Jer. 11:16). The tree stands for God's chosen family, beginning with Abraham. But now God has broken off some Jewish branches (11:17; see 11:15). Certain Gentiles, who were originally part of a wild olive tree, are taking their place. God has now grafted them into the Jewish olive tree. Those Gentile Christians now share the rich, fat root of the Jewish olive tree. That is, they merely share with Jewish Christians the root that is Jewish. Such Gentiles now are children of Abraham and share his faith in God's power (11:17; compare 4:11, 17-21). Like Abraham, Isaac, and Jacob, they are part of God's family, chosen and called to receive God's mercy (see 9:7-16).

Because Gentile Christians now are part of God's family, they should stop despising the many Jewish branches God has broken off (11:18). Those who boast because of Jewish hardening need to remember it is the Jewish root that supports them. There should be no Christian anti-Semitism since Abraham, the forefather of the Jews, is also the forefather and root of the faith of Jesus. Just as Abraham believed that God's power would fulfill God's promise, so Jesus believed that God's power was now beginning to fulfill God's final promise of salvation, righteousness, and life (compare 1:16-17; 4:17-25).

Similar to earlier portrayals of dialogue with another Jew (for example, 2:1-5, 17-27), Paul creates a conversation with a Gentile Christian. The Gentile objects to Paul's reason for not boasting by arguing that Jewish branches have been broken off so that he or she can be grafted in (11:19). Paul agrees, but adds that they have been broken off because of unbelief (11:20). God's judgment of breaking them off is a response to their unbelief. They are responsible for rejecting the faith of Jesus and the faith of Abraham (the root).

Similarly, the Gentile brother or sister stands fast through faith in the gracious power of God as manifested in Jesus and Abraham (11:20). So the Gentile shouldn't think highly of himself as if he were naturally better than Jews. (Such boasting is also a sin of certain Jews; see 2:17-20, 23.) Mission debates between Gentiles and Jews can become racist attacks. Yet such proud boasting is against the new law of Jesus' faith (see 3:27).

Paul reminds the Gentile Christians that the reason they stand strong in the faith of Jesus is that they have received God's power through that faith. They should not try to stand up to Jewish pride by means of their own pride. Instead, any boasting should be in the hope of sharing the glory of God (5:2). Gentile Christians should humbly retain a faithful fear of God or reverence for the God whose power is the cause of their salvation and righteousness (11:20). If they leave behind such faith and emphasize pride in themselves, God can also break them off the olive tree (11:21). So they also need to fear God's judgment against them.

God's sharp severity is seen in those who have fallen away from God (11:22; compare 1:18; 11:20). For those who boast about themselves instead of about God, there is reason to fear. What they need to do is focus on God's kindness to and upon the Gentile Christian (11:22). To have faith means to receive and reflect God's kindness. However, Gentile Christians who do not remain focused on God's kindness will also be cut off God's family tree (11:22). Not everyone who begins in the way of Jesus' faith continues to the end. Christians who have a present assurance of sharing Christ's faith must still remain faithful to the end. Only those who continue in the faith to the end are those who truly share in Christ (see Matt. 24:14; Col. 1:23; Heb. 3:12-14). True faith remains faithful.

Paul's image of an olive tree being grafted again and again points more to the marvelous working of God than to a natural process of growth. Jesus' image of the mustard seed has often been used to suggest a natural, constant growth of the church. But Jesus used that image to show the contrast between God's power in small groups of disciples and God's power in the glorious consummation of salvation at the end of history.

A good image for the movement of God in church history is the banana plant. After growing fairly fast to maturity and beginning to die, new shoots arise at the base as the beginning of a new plant. Thus God's new movements do not mostly develop as fruit from the top of the church plant but begin more as outgrowths from the bottom of the plant. Grassroots groups that give importance to the faith and mission of a few humble laypeople and possibly a few clergy can generate new life, as God gives the growth. God's power continually creates humble new shoots of small groups of faithful disciples when the proud older plants have become humanly impressive structures.[1]

God's powerful mercy (see 9:15-16) has grafted the Gentile Christian onto the Jewish olive tree. That fact alone should keep the Gentile from looking down on the many Jews who have been broken off and from being unmerciful to them. Jesus said that only the merciful, only those who receive and manifest God's kindness now, will receive God's mercy on the final day of judgment (see Matt. 5:7). Gentile Christians should be showing God's patient kindness as they call Jewish people to repentance and faith (see 2:4).

Jesus used a similar picture of a vine and its branches. He warned his disciples that if they became branches which bore no fruit, they would be taken away (John 15:2). And they would bear fruit only if they remained united to Jesus, the true vine (John 15:1, 4-5). Every branch that did not abide in Jesus or remain united to him would be thrown away and burned (John 15:6). To remain united to Jesus means to share his faith. His true disciples or friends would keep his words or commands about love (John 15:7-10, 14-15, 17). Jesus' kind of love would not proudly boast about being Gentile branches when they saw Jewish branches being broken.

Paul adds yet another reason not to despise unbelieving Jews: God also has the power to graft such Jews back into the family tree (11:23). To look down on broken-off branches is to look down on the power of God to graft them back again. It is possible that some hardened Jews will come to share the faith of Jesus. Paul himself is a good example of that possibility (compare 11:1). He was once an unbelieving Jew who persecuted God's family. As Paul's readers face such Jews in their future mission, they may prefer to avoid them rather than confront them. So they should remember God's power to graft back in even those violent Jews.

✦ ✦ ✦

So what kind of faith led churches in Germany to approve or tolerate the mass murder of six million Jews during World War II? How could one of the most educated, "civilized," and Christianized countries in the world condone such a Holocaust? Neither Jesus nor Paul would have remained silent when so many other Jews were herded like cattle into train boxcars and transported to slaughterhouses like those in Auschwitz. Could a committed Nazi share the faith of Jesus? No way! All of the Christian words or confessions, all of the higher education of supposed higher civilizations—none of this can make up for the crude, cruel, and crass treatment of other human beings. The Jewish people will never forget the Holocaust, and Gentile Christians do well to remember it when they approach Jews with the gospel.

Can neo-Nazis today speak for the God of Jesus? God forbid! American Nazis and the Ku Klux Klan claim white supremacy. They are just an extreme expression of what many white Americans have always believed: those who are not white are lower or lesser beings. Early Americans used such racism to justify the slave trade and the slaughter of Indians. How could citizens of a so-called Christian nation buy and sell human beings unless they created the lie that African-Americans were not as human as the rest? A Christian can not work another Christian brother or sister to death for profit.

Even after the Civil War, the new freedom for slaves led to simply a new kind of slavery. Freed African-Americans became sharecroppers, and thousands were tortured, imprisoned, and murdered. Contrary to popular American mythology, the nation was not a melting pot. Many churches followed the racist culture around them. White Christians in white shirts went to white buildings to worship a white Jesus.

However, Jesus was not white. Jesus was a Jew, and the Greco-Roman culture of Jesus' world was prejudiced against Jews. Nevertheless, Jesus rejected racist attempts that stepped on others to elevate themselves. Jesus believed God would form a family which included persons from every race. Paul's house churches included both Jews and Gentiles. Those who share that same faith today will seek and welcome sisters and brothers from any and every race.

Paul concludes his portrayal of the olive tree by contrasting the wild branches (Gentiles) with the natural branches (Jews). Still speaking to the proud Gentile Christian, Paul says it is more likely that natural branches will be grafted back into their own tree than that wild branches would be grafted in (11:24). The Gentile Christian who is tempted to look down on unbelieving Jews should realize that those broken-off branches have more of a natural right than Gentiles to be on the family tree in the future. A mission to Jews should humbly remember the history and future of God's family.

Beyond all supposed natural advantages stands the truth of God's power. The tree belongs to God. It was planted, cultivated, and grafted according to God's will. It is God's family, formed by God's power. If one must boast, then boast in the glorious power of God. Only then will one's mission glorify God. For the power of God is unto salvation to everyone who is believing, to the Jew first and also to the Gentile (1:16).

Romans 11:25-36

The Revealed Mystery of World History: God's Power over Jews and Gentiles

B EGINNING with 11:13, Paul directly addresses his Gentile sisters and brothers in Christ. That is still true in 11:25 as he introduces a mystery which God has now revealed. Paul emphasizes that mystery so those Gentile Christians will not feel superior to Jews who have now fallen out of favor with God (see 11:18, 20).

While God has hardened most of Israel, not all of Israel is hardened (11:25; see 11:5, 7, 17). Moreover, such hardening will continue only until God has grafted the full number of Gentiles into the olive tree of faithful Jews (11:25; see 11:17). In 11:11-12, 15, Paul connects Jewish hardening or stumbling with a consequent world mission to the Gentiles (compare 9:17-18, 22-24). God's hardening will serve to advance God's mercy! Now he adds the mystery that when the world mission has been completed, God will remember the descendants of Abraham, Isaac, and Jacob (11:26).

Above all, Gentile Christians should not look down on Israel because of God's future plans for Israel. After the full number of Gentiles chosen by God have come into God's kingdom, then all Israel will be saved (11:25-26). At the end of history as we know it, God's power will save the vast majority of Jews.

That is the main point of God's revealed mystery. Paul now makes clear what he means by the Jews' future fullness (11:12) and their future reception by God (11:15).

Paul then uses some quotes from Isaiah (59:20-21; 27:9) to prove the truth of the revealed mystery. Isaiah 59:20 speaks of a deliverer who will come to Zion or Jacob (Israel) to turn it from ungodliness. Similarly, Psalm 14:7 asks who will bring the salvation of Israel out of Zion (Jerusalem), and answers that the Lord will deliver his captive people. Only God's power can overcome their evil and godlessness (compare Ps. 14:1-3 and Rom. 3:10-12).

In 11:27 Paul continues to show how Scripture speaks of the mystery of Israel's future salvation by using Isaiah 59:21 and 27:9. God will make a new covenant with Israel (Isa. 59:21), and it will involve taking away their sins (Isa. 27:9). Jeremiah has also prophesied about a future new covenant with Israel that will include God's forgiving their sin (Jer. 31:33-34). That future covenant does not require a rebirth of Israel as a nation. Those who religiously support the modern nation of Israel have confused the old covenant with the consummation of God's gracious new covenant through Jesus.

Since God has such great plans for Israel, Gentile Christians should not think they have taken Israel's place as God's chosen people. The mystery of Israel's future salvation means that the Jews are still of special concern to God, and thus they should also be of special concern to Gentile Christians. But that is easier said than done if some Jews are still persecuting certain Gentile Christians. Paul alludes to this in 11:28, where he refers to unbelieving Jews as enemies of the gospel.

On one hand, most Jews are enemies of the gospel of God proclaimed by Jesus and his followers. Yet since the result of God's hardening is a world mission to the Gentiles, Jewish enmity is due to God's saving purposes for the Gentiles (compare 11:28 with 11:11, 12, 15). On the other hand, the Jews are still loved as God's elect, chosen people on account of their forefathers (see 9:5; 11:16). If so, who do Gentile Christians think they are if they hate the Jews or avoid them because they are enemies of the gospel?

God's grace promises many gifts to the descendants of Abraham (for example, see 4:13; 9:4-5). Those promises and God's calling of Abraham's descendants still have their fulfillment (11:29; see 9:7, 12). God's word has not failed (9:6). In the future, God will make righteous an elect Israel that so far has mostly rejected Jesus, God's Messiah (11:26-27).

Gentile Christians need to remember that before Jesus, Gentiles in general were disobedient to God. But now, with the coming of God's kingly power in Jesus, many Gentiles have received God's saving mercy due to Jewish disobedience (11:30; see 11:11-12, 15,28). God's powerful mercy and grace have now made Gentile Christians obedient and righteous (see 5:17-21; 9:23). The Jews, however, are now disobedient to God's mercy being poured out on the Gentiles. But that mercy will lead to the Jews finally receiving God's mercy also (11:31). As a result, all Jews living at the end of the world mission to Gentiles will come to receive God's salvation (see 11:26).

Paul concludes his description of God's mysterious movement through world history in 11:32. Gentiles were once disobedient to God, and Jews are now disobedient to God (11:30-31). That situation shows that God has made all (Jews and Gentiles) prisoners to disobedience at one time or another (11:32). Earlier, God's wrath gave up the Gentiles to all kinds of disobedience (see 1:18-32). Now, since the time of Jesus, God's wrath has hardened the Jews so that they are disobedient to the gospel (compare 10:21; 11:7-9).

More important, God's purpose is that all (Jews and Gentiles) will come to receive God's mercy (compare 9:22-23). When Gentiles were disobedient, it led to many Jews receiving God's mercy (9:6-16). Now that the Jews are disobedient, it has led to a world mission where many Gentiles are receiving God's mercy (compare 11:11-12, 15). God's purpose in making all (Jews and Gentiles) disobedient, at one time or another, is to show merciful saving power on all (Jews and Gentiles), at one time or another.

The key to receiving salvation does not depend on Gentile or Jewish superiority, but on God's sovereign choice and powerful mercy. God's power is so awesome that it can use disobedient opposition as a means of showing mercy (11:32). Paul's Gentile readers should give glory to God alone, and not glory in themselves over against Jews (see 11:25). Consequently, Paul praises the depth of God's rich mercy, wisdom, and understanding (11:33).

God's judgments and ways in governing world history are beyond human understanding (11:33). The history and mystery of God's saving power and wrath do not depend on Jewish or Gentile wisdom, but on God's sovereign purposes. Using Isaiah 40:13 in 11:34, Paul asks who can claim to be equal to God in understanding. Who will presume to be God's counselor? That challenge to Gentile (or Jewish) pride continues in 11:35 with a quote from Job 41:11. Who has given a gift to God so that God is indebted to them? Of course, the answer to those questions is that no human being can boast that God has favored their superior knowledge or special sacrifices.

The history of salvation is not God's reaction to human capabilities. Instead, Paul affirms that all depends on God (11:36). Everyone who does right must boast only about God's foreknowing, God's predestining, God's calling, God's making righteous, and God's glorifying (see 8:29-30). There is nothing special about Jews or Gentiles that leads to God's mercy. For both groups have known the prison of disobedience, and both groups have experienced the liberation of God's mercy (see 11:32). So it all depends on God. To that sovereign, powerful God, Paul gives all the glory and will always continue to do so (11:36).

❖ ❖ ❖

God's purposes and strategies can be mysterious to practical, problem-solving Western mission leaders. Optimistic Americans supposed they could make right a disobedient world. American money, knowledge, and energy would lift up a lazy, ignorant, poor world. American superiority could overcome the most hardened peoples. It sounded easy, but the mission failed. An evil world was harder than expected. Indeed, the evil world had penetrated the mission itself.

Since the mission failed, some American churches, colleges, and mission agencies concluded that they needed an even better plan. How about a more powerful, all-encompassing plan that would send out even more North Americans and would raise even more money to support them? Billy Graham's famous world evangelism conference in Lausanne in 1974 resulted in a call to increase fourfold the number of North American missionaries by the year 2000. In the same quarter century, more and more foretellers were predicting the end of the world by 2000.

At another famous missions conference (at Mt. Hermon in 1886), A. T. Pierson challenged college students to evangelize the world in their generation. He believed Christ would return after such a mission, and that the mission could be completed by the year 1900. The Lausanne Congress was likewise hoping to bring in the fullness of the Gentiles by the turn of the century. But why use North American missionaries when national Christians and churches all around the world were better equipped to reach others around them?

At Lausanne, Ralph Winter, soon to become head of the U.S. Center for World Mission, came up with the basis for the new strategy: hidden peoples. According to Winter, there were still 16,750 unreached people groups in the world. Those cultural groups supposedly could not be reached by normal church growth or evangelism. Only a special cross-cultural evangelism could break through the distrust and racism of the local social system. Thus tens of thousands of missionaries from North America were needed now more than ever.

If mission agencies concentrated on reaching those hidden peoples, the great commission could be fulfilled in the final era of world evangelism (Matt. 28:18-20). Many agencies did cooperate and used the hidden-peoples rationale to recruit new missionaries and to raise more money. Many churches loved the new yet old emphasis on pioneer mission among unreached tribes.

The grandiose plans for world mission led to sales pitches for multinational mission agencies. It seemed only the multinationals could supply the needed products: cross-cultural missionaries. National Christians and churches around the world could just sit back and watch. Some of the national churches responded to North American wisdom by wondering if the parachurch agencies were just inventing reasons to build up their corporations and to bypass national churches.

Another question was how one defined hidden peoples. Winter's huge number included not only tropical tribes or castes in India, but also such groupings as Chinese restaurant workers in France. The idea of unreached people groups later became so flexible that some considered nurses in St. Louis as another such group. The numbers and definitions of hidden peoples became so mysterious that they could justify new missionaries going almost anywhere.[1]

Some U.S. evangelicals thought they had revealed the newest mystery of world history: American multinational mission power over unreached hidden peoples. Yet it turned out to be the same old Western way of doing mission. The biggest mystery was how mission agencies expected North American missionaries, full of cultural feelings of superiority and ambitious for personal success and upward mobility, to do all the cross-cultural evangelism in pioneer areas. How could the sending of so many Western young people, and the spending of so many millions of dollars to support them, witness to God's power as first seen in Jesus?

Another mystery was that while Western missionaries became hardened in their plans and methods, God continued to show mercy through poor, unrecognized apostles throughout the world. Traditional missionaries called those apostles native evangelists. Because they had little education or financial support, Western missionaries didn't consider them proper missionaries.

Mission, according to the world's wisdom, proceeds from powerful centers of wealth and education to those who are poorly paid and uneducated. But the mission of Jesus and Paul, according to God's wisdom, proceeds from the more powerless periphery of poverty and oppression. Precisely there, God's power continues to raise up missionaries in the image of Jesus, those who with integrity bring good news to the poor.[2]

God still cares about all the peoples of the world. God also still uses hidden apostles to reach out to supposed hidden peoples. Even those apostles sometimes need to be careful about feelings of superiority over those to whom they go. The more they appreciate God's power, God's mission, and God's mysteries, the less they boast of their own strengths and strategies. God's foolishness is wiser than all human wisdom, and God's weakness is stronger than all human power (1 Cor. 1:25).

Romans 12:1-8

God's Powerful Mercies and a Faithful Mission of Mercy

PAUL has just concluded an awesome and humbling description of God's sovereign power over world history (11:25-36). He has emphasized God's widespread mercy toward both Jews and Gentiles throughout human history. Now he begins to describe how God's powerful mercy leads to a world mission of merciful actions.

In 12:1, Paul directly appeals to his Christian sisters and brothers in Rome. He exhorts them to present their bodies as a sacrifice that is alive, holy, and acceptable to God. The priesthood of all believers involves sacrificing themselves. And the source of power which enables such sacrifice is the mercies of God. God's mercies here are not mainly forgiveness, but God's power to produce an obedient people (see 11:30-32; 9:15-16, 18, 23; 11:22). They will be obedient through God's present powerful mercies. Obedience is not just a human response to God's previous mercies. Without God's power, would-be sacrifices will slowly crawl off the altar.

Sacrificial service is the reasonable, appropriate, and consistent outworking of God's love as seen in Jesus' sacrifice (12:1; see 5:5-6; 8:32, 35-36). In 1:9, Paul refers to his apostolic mission as a service of worship (see Phil 2:17). He is also preparing to sacrifice his mortal body by going to Jerusalem, the headquarters of deadly opposition against him, with his collection for poor Jewish Christians (15:25, 31; Acts 21:4, 11-13). Romans is Paul's means of preparing others to continue such sacrifices, even if he himself is detained or killed in Jerusalem.

Special times of worship in churches have too often been worthless due to the absence of a daily worship which consists of a sacrificial mission of mercy. Daily actions of mercy and love have not usually been considered worship. The priesthood of all believers has become the priesthood of a few leaders who are mostly male. Such holy men performing holy rituals on holy days and saying holy words in holy places tend to limit holiness to themselves (and in a lesser sense, to those who watch them perform). Jesus agrees with the prophet Hosea that God desires mercy (steadfast love) and not sacrifice (like the burnt offerings in the temple) from a disobedient people (Matt. 12:7; see Hos. 6:6). The worshipful noise of solemn assemblies, or ecstatic assemblies, is not acceptable when divorced from daily merciful service.[1]

Holy, acceptable worship or service means one must not be conformed to the present evil age (12:2). Paul thus appeals to his readers that they be continually transformed by God's power, which renews the commitment of the mind and will to the new age. The renewed mind and will leads to approving and demonstrating the will of God, defined as what is good, acceptable (to God; see 12:1), and perfect (12:2). God is working for good despite all the evil of this age (8:28) so that believers are able to please God.

God's goodness and righteousness will be manifested in the renewed believing one (1:17), who is perfect (righteous) as God is perfect (Matt. 5:48). One context of Jesus' teaching about perfection is that of loving all without exception, especially one's enemies (Matt. 5:43-48). In Luke's version of that teaching (Luke 6:27-35), the summary statement speaks of being merciful as God is merciful (Luke 6:36). God's powerful mercy will result in showing merciful love toward one's enemies.

Again, the main enemies of the Gentile Christians, on whom Paul is now focusing (see 11:13, 25), are Jewish leaders and missionaries. It would be more natural for Paul's readers to conform to the racism that exists between Jew and Gentile. But if they are to continue the faithful mission of Jesus and Paul, they must think differently and act sacrificially for the sake of their worst enemies, the disobedient Jews (see 11:28).

God's grace leads Paul to speak on behalf of such love (12:3). God's gracious love calls all Christians in Rome (both Gentile and Jew) to humble themselves and not think more highly of themselves than they should (see 11:20, 25). God has given each of them one standard or measure of faith: the faith of Jesus (12:3).[2] The mind of Christ led him to humble himself and become obedient, even unto a lowly death on a Roman cross (Phil. 2:5-8).

Instead of comparing their faith to those they consider weaker in faith (or without faith at all), they should humbly consider how their faith compares to that of Jesus. He is the one and only standard of Christian faith. They will share the mind of Christ if they give up selfish ambition or conceit and concentrate on what is best for others (Phil. 2:1-4). Paul thus appeals to his Roman sisters and brothers to approve and demonstrate the will of God as found in Jesus' faith (12:1-3).

In 12:4-5, Paul again uses a corporate image to describe the unity of Jewish and Gentile followers of Jesus (compare the olive tree in 11:17-24). Like the human body, the body of Christ is a unified whole, though it has many members with different functions. Although they are many and include both Jews and Gentiles, they are one body in Christ (12:4).

Divided denominations do not manifest Christ's united body. Too often mission has multiplied denominational traditions all over the world at the expense of Jesus' one true faith. Religious cultural and social traditions have produced pride and competition among different churches. Such division points more to Adam's worldwide body of sin than to the body of Christ. While everyone is different in Christ's body, differences due to various forms of service should not become divisive.

As those united by the faith and new life of the living Jesus, they have different gifts to express that faithful service.

Those abilities are God-given, the result of God's powerful mercy. They are gifts of grace (12:6), divinely empowered actions, not natural abilities or hidden talents. God has not secretly given the gifts earlier as if people just needed to discover what gifts they already have. Gifts of grace are acts of God's powerful grace which enable certain kinds of mission activity. In 12:3, Paul refers to the grace God gave him so that he can write to them about right attitudes and God's standard of (Jesus') faith. The many functions are to be true to the one faith and to build up the one body.

Paul's first grace-gift is prophecy, which is to be expressed in agreement with the faith of Jesus (12:6). Earlier, Paul has already affirmed his own gift or ministry of apostleship (1:1; 11:13) and has included apostolic mission among the gifts belonging to his readers (1:5; 10:15). In Romans, as in the rest of the New Testament, the work of apostles relates more to mission outside the body of Christ.

For a mission of building up the body of Christ, prophecy is an important gift. As members of Christ's body, some or even most will be empowered at times to prophesy as Christ has done (see 1 Cor. 12:27-29; 14:1, 3-6, 24, 29-32). Prophetic speaking is not restricted to some privileged theologians or professional clergy. An impressive style of preaching or an academic study of Scripture is not the test of good prophecy. Claims of new Spirit-filled prophecy are not necessarily acceptable. Prophetic visions or dreams may just be false prophecies. Paul instead calls for a content that is consistent with the faith (of Jesus). Prophecy is the mutual sharing of gifted members of small, intimate groups.

The Greek grammar of 12:6-8 suggests that prophecy and service are two general gifts that Paul then describes in more detail by the other gifts listed after them.[3] Prophecy thus includes both teaching and exhortation (see 1 Cor. 14:3-4, 18-19, 31); service in this context includes giving money, giving help, and acting mercifully (12:6-8; see 15:25, 31; 16:1-2; 2 Cor. 8:4; 9:1, 12-13).

The English word *charismatic* comes from the Greek word for gifts of grace, *charismata* (12:6). Yet the gifts listed in 12:6-8 do not include the more spectacular gifts often associated with so-called charismatic Christians. When Paul does refer to gifts like speaking in tongues or healing, he also tries to decrease the attention given to them. Then there will be more room to use more important gifts like prophecy and teaching, to build up the body of Christ (see 1 Cor. 12:28—14:40). Since every Christian has one or more gifts of grace, every Christian is charismatic. The word *charismatic* should not just describe certain enthusiastic Christians or spirited leaders.

Paul has already expressed his prophetic gift through the teaching of this letter (see 6:17) and through exhortations like 12:1-3. His hope is that his readers will then be prepared and encouraged to continue that prophetic world mission. Paul is strengthening them now so that they in turn can strengthen others as part of their future mission (see 1:11-12).

Most think of theological education today as done exclusively in professional seminaries or Bible colleges. When modern seminaries started in the early nineteenth century, theology came to be considered as something only for professional ministers. But what if theology has to do with the living reality of God's power at work among those sharing Jesus' faith and mission? What if teaching is a grace-gift given to several people in each Christian community? And what if they use that gift to strengthen the faith and mission of the others in that community? Then teaching and theology has to do not with elite sciences but with the truth of Jesus' faith and his ongoing mission. Such teaching will best take place in smaller informal settings rather than in formal classrooms.[4]

The best place for training leaders is thus not in the power structures of reputable seminaries. That is even more true in the third world. There, missionary teachers and administrators, like myself earlier in the Philippines, have passed on the formal Western model of training and ordaining full-time clergy. Rural third-world seminarians in the city for education faced a different culture. Especially different was the formal seminary training that tried to fit them all into a Western mold.

In Bolivia and Peru, twenty-four years of training by U.S. Maryknoll missionaries for eight hundred Aymara Indian seminarians produced fourteen priests. Even those priests no longer fitted in with their local culture when they returned.[5] That model also required continued funding from mission executives whose power over funding decisions kept seminaries and Bible schools dependent on them.

A radical conversion is needed to transfer theological education to local bodies of Christ. The goal of leadership development can become helping leaders in each group to share the faith of Jesus: to be like Jesus, to know how God's power worked in Jesus, and to act out a similar faith(fulness). A context of shared ministry is required for disciples to become part of Christ's body by serving sacrificially, teaching faithfully, and showing mercy to those in need.

Suppose theological education was to return to a local informal church context. By becoming more independent of divisive Western institutions, local churches could then better express their unity as the larger body of Christ.[6]

Then lay people would not just have minor responsibilities in a clergy-dominated church. So-called nonministerial laypeople would instead be directly involved with the main roles of ministry: interpreting, applying, and proclaiming the faith of Jesus. All would be ministers, with several in each group especially gifted for prophetic or teaching service. Several others would be gifted for practical acts of love on behalf of the poor and needy.

There would still be specialized ministry, but every member would have one or more such ministries. More-experienced teachers could informally train less-experienced teachers. Yet everyone could at times share a prophetic word or do a compassionate deed. All the various offices and titles mentioned throughout the New Testament would not be as important to restore as the specific functions shared by various special leaders. Everyone would be a servant leader in certain areas, and no one would be counted as the one true full-time master leader.[7]

Even in more informal groups like house churches, certain individuals sometimes still want to dominate (see 3 John 9-

10). Paul faced that problem in Corinth where those favoring religious ecstasy, in the form of speaking in tongues, wanted to be first. Small groups where there is freedom for everyone to participate can become out of order or taken over by out-of-control individuals.

Paul's response to Corinth was that human love for religious ecstasy is different from Christ's love, which builds up the rest of the body, especially through gifts like prophecy, teaching, and exhortation (1 Cor. 14:1-28). Even prophets need to take their turn and be willing to listen to other prophets, so that there is peace instead of disorder (1 Cor. 14:29-33, 37-40). While certain women can prophesy, other women who always want to ask questions should remain silent and ask their husbands at home (1 Cor. 11:5; 14:34-35).

Besides encouraging ministry within Christ's body, much of Paul's teaching in Romans has also tried to help Christians interact with nonbelievers, especially Jews. Paul's exhortation has likewise included appeals to sacrificial mission which even reaches out to enemies. By following Paul in such a mission, they also follow Jesus. All prophecy, teaching, and exhortation should be according to the faith of Jesus.

Service through merciful acts of sharing reflects God's own gracious mercy (see 12:1). Four of the seven grace-gifts in 12:6-8 have to do with showing mercy through concrete assistance to the poor and needy. Some Jewish missionaries blaspheme God's name by stealing and robbing temples, contrary to what they teach (2:21-24). But Christian missionaries who serve by multiplying mercy will honor God. They not only teach "Do not covet." They also practice generous and joyful sharing of possessions (12:8).

Emmanuel Baptist Church in the city of San Salvador has practiced a similar diversity of grace-gifts. It called itself a people's church and practiced its faith in a variety of ways. Its institute for theological training was a church-based model for theological education. It also ministered through a food cooperative, a women's center, an orphanage, and as part of an ecumenical program to distribute medicine, food, and clothing. As part of a missionary outreach, that church cooperated with over fifty congregations, from Pentecostal to Roman Catholic.[8]

During the middle 1980s, I was in Mexico City for a few weeks and heard the witness of some former members of Emmanuel Baptist Church. They were in exile due to threats from the military. In El Salvador, the military has not been merciful and has not appreciated merciful acts. People were suspected as subversives if they began to change the status quo by showing mercy.

Jesus once defined perfect (see 12:2) as selling one's possessions, giving to the poor, and following him (Matt. 19:21). The law of Moses says God will prosper those who are faithful (for example, Deut. 7:12-14). The faith of Jesus says God will make generous those who are faithful to the new age. Jesus agreed with those Jewish prophets who emphasized God's concern for the poor and criticized the peoples' greed for more (Isa. 1:23; 3:14-15; Amos 4:1; 5:11-12; 8:4-6; Matt. 6:19-20; Luke 12:29-33; 16:13-15, 19-31). So why do the prayers of richer Christians often simply thank God for their many material blessings? They have misinterpreted Jesus' teaching about abundant life (John 10:10) or God's providing some basic needs (Matt. 6:33). All this they take to mean an American middle-class life. Holy greed!

The test of one's generosity is not the quantity of help given but the amount of sacrifice involved. Jesus contrasted the generosity of the poor widow who gave her only two coins with the rich who gave much while keeping much more for themselves (Mark 12:41-44). The question that continually needs to be asked is not how much someone gives but how much they keep for themselves. Rich Zacchaeus gave half his goods to the poor and promised to pay back four times as much as what he had stolen through tax fraud (Luke 19:2, 8). Such sacrifice shows that Zacchaeus received God's saving power (Luke 19:9).

At the end of this letter, Paul informs his readers of a special collection of money he is gathering for poor Jewish Christians in Jerusalem (15:25-26). Especially the churches in Macedonia that contributed to the collection are an example for others. The Macedonian Christians manifest God's merciful grace through their generous and joyful sacrificial giving (2 Cor. 8:1-2).[9] Now Paul asks his Roman readers to contribute generously, eagerly, and joyfully to the poor (12:8).

How important are such grace-gifts in churches today? What percentage of money given to the church is used to help the poor and needy? Or is most of the donated money used to pay middle-class salaries of staff and the costs of constructing, furnishing, and using church buildings? Jesus said to sell and give to the poor; pastors and priests say to save and give to the church. Only a small percentage of church offerings are used for mission outside the church.

There are many mission projects in the third world funded by the wealthy first world, like hospitals, schools, and church buildings. But they serve mostly the elite middle and upper classes, which can afford to use them, administer them, and maintain them. Instead of spending so much on doctors and hospitals, many more (poor) people would be helped by preventative primary health care.

Basic necessities like safe drinking water can save hundreds of lives at the same cost as saving a few lives in a hospital. Eighty percent of the causes of illness and death in the third world are preventable. People who have little or no formal education can learn how to prevent many sicknesses by using primary health care. Some medical missionaries have started to share some of their medical knowledge with local churches and communities. In order to make available simple basic health care for more of the poor, they are promoting community-based health care.

Churches use community developers to gather people so they can discuss together their health problems. The people then choose from among themselves health committees and/or a health promoter to receive training about simple treatments. As a result, trusted leaders use inexpensive solutions to prevent deathly illnesses like dehydration from diarrhea. Their homes become health clinics, bases from which they diagnose, treat, and teach others in their communities.[10]

Thus third-world Christians would do better to depend primarily on small, local Christian communities led by spiritually gifted local people who understand local needs and use mainly local resources. Then mission in poor rural and urban areas would no longer depend so much on foreign money or missionaries, or even on local ordained ministers. Moreover, the mission of the poor would not depend on deceit or manipulation of rich donors. Instead, those most in need in grassroots churches can work and plan together with only occasional help from the larger international body of Christ.[11]

Wealthy Western organizations like World Vision sometimes lack appreciation for local needs and groups, including churches. World Vision first became famous for its promotion of child sponsorship. By giving ten or twenty dollars a month, wealthy givers could support poor third-world children. By 1985, World Vision helped 360,000 such children.

While such projects are popular and raise a lot of money, there are also many problems. What about the other children in the family who don't receive help? What about jealous neighbors who don't receive help? What about the child at an older age? Would relief money for certain children be better spent on developing whole villages? Such questions led World Vision to turn more to community development.

Because they raised more money than they had good ways to spend it, World Vision multiplied development programs, sometimes recklessly. In 1985, they were a mammoth multinational corporation with an income of $232 million. They wanted to help the poor in appropriate ways and choose leaders with simple lifestyles. But they also needed to make use of the money entrusted to them, as soon as possible.

In Latin America, World Vision at times chose to give a few evangelical leaders or pastors large amounts of money for development projects. Those privileged individuals then became new elites who sometimes kept more than their fair share. By giving so much money to special individuals or projects, World Vision could create pockets of privilege in the midst of massive poverty. Those privileges, in turn, tended to corrupt the lucky individuals (often pastors) and divided churches.[12]

Many rich Christians in an age of hunger avoid a sacrificial mission of mercy among the poor. Thus they merely show that they have missed God's powerful mercies which enable such mission. On the other hand, poor Christians often show more sympathy and mercy toward other poor people who need help. Both their faith and their poverty enable them to sympathize with and sacrifice for others in desperate need. If rich Christians and their leaders would have simpler and healthier lifestyles and meet in homes instead of extravagant church buildings, this would free them to be more available for helping those in need.[13] Jesus looked at his poor, humble disciples and blessed them (Luke 6:20; Matt. 5:3) because they were the ones receiving God's merciful kingship and showing mercy to others (Matt. 5:7).

Romans 12:9-21

Jesus' Love
for Persecutors
and Persecuted

GOD'S powerful mercies produce merciful actions among members of the body of Christ (12:1-8). Practical acts of mercy prove that Jesus' kind of love practices what it preaches. Such love is without hypocrisy. So Paul encourages his readers to reflect Jesus' genuine love (12:9). They must hold on to the good of the new age begun by Jesus and reject or hate the evil of the old age (12:9; compare 12:2).

Sisters and brothers in Christ are to love and serve one another (12:10; compare 12:5-8). Instead of feeling superior to certain other family members, they will take the lead in honoring others (12:10; compare 12:3). God's Spirit empowers them to serve eagerly with love (12:11; see 12:8; 5:5). They will be on fire because of the Spirit. That does not mean religious emotion or excitement so much as divine energy for humble, obedient service of the Lord Jesus. For as they help even the least of Christ's followers, they serve the Lord himself (12:11; see Matt. 25:34-40).

In the midst of trouble and rejection, they can rejoice in the hope of sharing God's glory (12:12; see 5:2-3; 8:17-18, 24). That hope helps them remain patient and faithful despite opposition and persecution (12:12). Jesus warned that those who continued his mission would be hated wherever they went, but whoever endured to the end would be saved (Matt. 10:16, 22). Such trials can be endured as long as they continue to call on God for encouragement and empowerment (12:12).

So wherever in the world there are saints (sisters and brothers in Christ) in need, Christ's love will share generously to help meet that need (12:13; see 12:8). Christ's practical love will be shown even to those far away or strangers passing through (12:13; see Heb. 13:2; 3 John 5- 8). Jesus' worldwide church is one, and all are members of Christ's body, called to serve one another. For those whose mission means traveling from place to place, they are to receive the material help needed to continue their mission (see Matt. 10:8-14).

Before missionaries had to leave China, churches from different regions identified with the denominations of their missionaries. After the communists rose to power and the house churches went underground, such denominational divisions mostly disappeared. Although some regional distinctives remained, most house churches saw themselves as simply Christians (not Lutherans or Presbyterians). Their newfound unity as Christ's body also began to manifest itself in mutual aid. They often gave offerings to Christians in other areas, especially those most needy.[1]

Direct involvement in mission by local churches is better than giving money to professional missionary or development agencies. Instead of delegating their love to leaders of larger institutions, laypeople can become partners in ministry with other churches, both near and far. While professional theologians, denominations, and preachers debate and divide over whether evangelism or social concern is central to mission, local churches with gifts for both can carry out a balanced ministry.

A local group of disciples can begin a partnership of mutual mission with other groups. For example, a mostly white group in the United States could link with a mostly black group nearby. Those two churches could link with a third-world church. They could share gifts of teaching and encouraging about Jesus' faith, and gifts of serving and showing mercy in practical ways.[2]

Merciful Christians do not limit their love to Christians who are poor and persecuted. A certain U.S. Christian was once walking through the streets of Calcutta, and the poverty made him so angry he wanted to scream at God. Why would God allow such miserable suffering? Suddenly he realized that, through such suffering of the poor, God was screaming at him. He began to ask why those people were poor and hungry. Why did American churches seem not to care what caused the suffering?[3]

He discovered the dark truth that American corporate, military, and governmental policies have hurt the poor all over the world. Moreover, American churches often reject such truth, refuse to see justice (righteousness) as essential to the gospel, and renounce those who speak such truth as un-American and non-Christian. But the faith of Jesus emphasizes a risky mission of mercy, risky because it strikes at the root causes of poverty: oppression by the religious, idolatrous rich.[4]

Dom Helder Camara, former archbishop in Brazil, once stated: "When I give food to the poor, they call me a saint; when I ask why the poor have no food, they call me a communist." In the Philippines, Bishop Antonio Fortich grew up in a wealthy sugar-growing family. Later, after seeing the terrible poverty and repression of sugar workers, he urged the landowners to share their wealth and supported the workers in their organizing. Fortich strongly supported land reform so that workers could own their own land. As a result, huge signs were hung on the streets near Fortich's house, denouncing communist priests and sisters.[5]

As Paul's readers continue Jesus' mission, they will be persecuted. Prayerful patience in the midst of such opposition must bless opponents, not curse them (12:14; see 12:12). The faith of Jesus calls for blessing and praying for one's enemies (Luke 6:28; see Matt. 5:44). Paul clearly uses the teaching of Jesus about loving one's enemies.[6] The way of Jesus' faith is to love and do good even to persecutors. Whenever Paul faces cursing, persecution, and slander because of his apostolic mission, he responds with blessing, endurance, and kindness (1 Cor. 4:9-13).

Persecuted followers of Jesus also need to remain united. Members of the one worldwide body of Christ must be sensitive to the different situations of one another. When some are rejoicing in a certain experience, even in suffering, the rest should also rejoice (12:15; see 5:2-3; 12:12; Phil. 2:17-18; Col. 1:24; Matt. 5:12; Acts 5:41; 1 Pet. 4:13). When some are mourning, the others should sympathize with their sorrow (12:15; see 1 Cor. 12:26; Matt. 5:4; Luke 6:21; John 16:20-22; James 5:13). If the persecuted are to stand firm, they need the strength that comes from struggling side by side for the faith of Jesus (see Phil. 1:27).

Unity despite persecution requires having the same attitude toward one another (12:16). All must share the mind of Christ in such situations (see Phil. 2:2, 5). The poor, persecuted Christians should not be looked down on by other Christians (12:16). Instead, the humiliated ones should be honored more highly (compare 12:10; Phil. 2:3). The faith of Jesus led him to humble himself and become an obedient servant, even unto a shameful death on a cross (Phil. 2:7-8). If Paul's readers are to share that same faith, they must neither avoid nor despise those who are suffering as Jesus suffered (12:16).[7]

Such suffering ones might seem to be the least of God's favorites. The truth is that receiving God's final favor depends on how one treats them. When Jesus sent disciples out on mission assignments filled with hardship, he said that those who did not receive them or give them practical support would be judged (Matt. 10:14-15). On the other hand, everyone who received such disciples or apostolic missionaries also received Jesus, the one who sent them (Matt. 10:40). Even giving a mere cup of water to thirsty missionaries would show support for them and their mission (Matt. 10:42). There was both solidarity between Jesus and his disciples and between the disciples and those who received them. By doing God's will, as defined by Jesus, they were part of Jesus' family, his brothers and sisters (see Matt. 12:48-50).

At the end of the age, when all peoples would be judged,

the basis would be their treatment of Jesus' brothers and sisters (Matt. 25:40). Those brothers or sisters were least in the world's eyes, due to mission hardships like hunger, thirst, strange places, lack of clothing, sickness, and imprisonment. Yet they were in fact Jesus' own contact with the world's peoples (Matt. 25:32-40). Those who united with them and welcomed them with food, drink, clothing, and companionship would be judged as true sheep of Jesus' flock (like the jailer in Acts 16:30-34). But those who refused them would be judged as goats who never really knew Jesus (Matt. 25:41-46).[8]

Paul knows how important the support of others is during difficult times. He knows the disappointment of being dishonored and abandoned by others during his imprisonments (see Phil. 1:17; 2 Tim. 1:15; 4:10-16). Thus, followers of Jesus should seek out such suffering ones in order to show love (12:16; see 12:13).

Jesus' parable in Matthew 25:31-46 taught that those who continued the apostolic work of proclaiming Jesus' faith would also follow Jesus' example of experiencing poverty and suffering. In that context, those representing Jesus were called not so much to help the poor as to become poor and outcast themselves as part of their world mission.[9]

The training of pastors in urban theological seminaries does not prepare their graduates for such hardship. After graduating, some pastors are willing to go to a low-paying rural church, but most see it as a temporary first step up the ladder of professional promotions. The seminary in the Philippines where I taught was located on a university campus. It was a step up in the world for poor Filipino students to go to a university in a large city.

By the time the seminarians graduated and found a rural church to pastor, most were willing to go, but often could not stay more than a year or two. It was reverse culture shock. They missed the more exciting and promising life of the city. For the best students, the highest hope was to continue to study abroad, especially in the United States. Yet again, after finishing further education, many did not want to return to the Philippines. They preferred the better life in the United States to the hardships of serving in a third-world country.

In 12:17, Paul returns to the issue of how persecuted Christians should respond to their persecutors. Blessing one's enemies (12:14) means not repaying their evil with one's own evil actions against them. It also means a concern for doing what is good in the sight of everyone, including one's enemies (12:17). Jesus defined love for enemies as including good deeds toward them (Luke 6:27). That rules out the later distinction between an inner attitude of love at the same time one kills the body of an opponent in war! Greek dualism between soul and body was especially responsible for such limited views of love. In contrast, Jesus said the greatest love was shown in laying down one's own life (John 15:13). Love is seen especially in concrete actions of the body, not through inner feelings of the soul.

Instead of continuing the spiral of violence and hatred, Jesus' followers are to decrease the level of conflict by being peacemakers (12:18). Jesus taught that nonviolent peacemakers would be revealed as the true children of God (Matt. 5:9). Of course, the violence would not always stop completely. Paul is realistic and only refers to what is possible in certain situations. Yet the Christian is to pursue peace always with all people, including their worst enemies. There is no one the Christian should hate or seriously injure or kill. Like Jesus, they would rather die for the sake of their enemies (see 5:6-8, 10).

Taking up one's cross was the point of Jesus' often misunderstood sayings about nonresistance in Matthew 5:39-41. Jesus was not being impractical when he talked about turning the other cheek, giving away one's cloak (and being naked!), or walking a second mile for Roman soldiers who forced one to help them. After Jesus was arrested, both Jewish leaders and Roman soldiers struck him in the face because of his claims and challenges (Matt. 26:67; 27:30; John 18:22). As those Roman soldiers led Jesus away to be crucified, they made him carry his own cross toward Golgotha (John 19:16-17). Later, they forced Simon from Cyrene to carry the cross the final distance (Matt. 27:31-32).

When Jesus was on the cross, the soldiers cast lots to see

who got Jesus' undergarment—leaving Jesus naked on the cross (Matt. 27:35; John 19:23-24; see Matt. 27:28, 31). Thus Jesus' teaching in Matthew 5:39-41 was pointing forward to his final suffering and shame. He was calling his disciples to take up their cross and follow him. Jesus' way was to be willing to suffer and die, but not to inflict such suffering or death on others.

The way of the world is to get revenge if one has been shamed or injured. The way of Jesus refuses revenge (Matt. 5:39) and gives way to God's wrath on evil (12:19; see 1 Pet. 2:23). Followers of Jesus are not to be instruments of God's wrath. Like Jesus, they are to be patient in doing good. To add support, Paul quotes Deuteronomy 32:35, which affirms that vengeance belongs to God alone. Until that final day of judgment, God calls the Christian to give food and drink to any enemies in need (12:20).

Jesus taught about giving to everyone who begs for help or asks to borrow something. The context of that teaching is that of loving one's enemies (Matt. 5:42; Luke 6:30, 34-36, 38; see Matt. 5:38-48; Luke 6:27-29, 32-33). Jesus used the word *every-one* to emphasize the inclusion of even enemies or persecutors who need help. Christians should help all enemies who lack basic needs like food or drink. Quoting Proverbs 25:21-22, Paul says that such good deeds will pile up hot coals on the enemy's head. In other words, practical acts of love toward enemies will cause them to be ashamed of their earlier evil deeds and might lead them to repent.

Whenever a Christian gives in to the rage for revenge or violence, the power of evil has won a victory. In the struggle with hatred and opposition in the world, Paul calls on his readers not to be conquered by evil. They can overcome the power of evil through the power of good actions (12:21). In short, don't be conformed to this evil age of hatred, violence, and revenge (see 12:2). Rather, be transformed by God's power so that one might do God's good will (12:2).

In a world where people are quick to use violence to defend themselves, family, friends, or nation, Jesus still calls for a new and different way. The world would limit one's love to only certain people and defend them by hating any enemies (see Matt. 5:43). Jesus, however, defined the neighbor as including one's enemy (Matt. 5:44). That was the point of the parable about the good Samaritan (Luke 10:25-37). Jesus told the parable as a response to the question: "Who is my neighbor?" The one who asked the question was a Jewish teacher of the law who thought he had kept the law. But Jews hated Samaritans, and Jesus' parable made the Samaritan a hero. When Jesus concluded by asking who in the parable showed neighborly love, the teacher couldn't say the hated word *Samaritan*. He could only blurt out, "The one who showed mercy."

Natural enemies of one's friendly neighbors are too easily hated. Under the law of Moses, the Israelites approved revenge or retaliation against Gentiles, and they fought holy wars against national enemies (see Deut. 19:21; 20:1). For Muslims, a holy war or jihad is acceptable against certain enemies. But according to the faith of Jesus, such violence is not the will of God in the new age which began with Jesus (Matt. 5:20, 38-39). Jesus is now the only commander-in-chief of his disciples, and Jesus only wages peace.[10]

After World War II, the worst enemy of many Western nations was the communist. So-called Christian peoples went to war in the name of God against so-called atheist peoples or foreign aggressors. Many conservative church members have supported and joined with dictators in fighting left-wing rebels. On the other side, some (not all) Latin American liberation theologians expressed the need for revolution, including violent armed struggle, to overthrow repressive dictators. Neither side could be consistent with Jesus' way of loving enemies.

During the 1980s, many poor Christians in El Salvador and Guatemala fled to the United States because of persecution from anticommunist militaries. Supported by the U.S. Reagan administration, death squads machine-gunned churches and murdered priests, nuns, and other Christians who denounced the violence and challenged the rich and powerful oppressors. Rather than joining the armed rebellion and fighting violence with violence, many went into exile. Those who escaped to the

United States then faced further persecution, especially from the Immigration and Naturalization Service (INS), which claimed the refugees were merely looking for work. Yet by deporting them, they endangered their lives even more due to the violent governments awaiting them on their return.

As a result, a few U.S. Christians began a Sanctuary movement to try to keep those persecuted sisters and brothers from being deported. They kept numerous Salvadoran refugees in their homes and helped others cross the border into the United States. Such illegal actions led to threats by the INS of arrest and prison for U.S. Sanctuary workers. But the refugees would face death if deported, so those U.S. believers accepted the lesser risk of working with them. Thus former law-abiding citizens risked jail for the sake of Central American refugees. They did so because Christian love required such a mission. They needed to obey God rather than human authority (Acts 5:29). Obedience to God sometimes means civil disobedience.

Sanctuary workers began to experience government harassment similar to what the refugees had faced, such as infiltration of spies, break-ins, intimidation, and death threats. Several were formally charged and faced court trials, and a few landed in jail. Nevertheless, they remained faithful to their mission of love. While speaking against evil, they did not seek revenge or adopt the same tactics as the INS or FBI or police. Some left behind their comfortable middle-class existence because of their new commitment to the persecuted poor among the worldwide people of faith.[11]

While in the Philippines, a seminary student asked me to visit his brother who was detained in the stockade because of organizing poor dock workers. It was risky to visit there, though less so for me and my wife than for Filipinos. At the stockade we met others who were detained and tortured because of their concern for the poor and their words against the wealthy and powerful. They were labeled subversives.

They had challenged the deadly status quo in a way that most people in the churches were afraid to do. By speaking out, they had made enemies with the most powerful and brutal leaders in the Philippines. Military might and private armies protected elite leaders from their underpaid workers, who made up the majority of Filipinos. To tell the truth about the evil of that oppression was a supposed threat to national security. In truth, it was only a threat to the security of the few elite who profited from the status quo.

When the trial of our friends began, they asked us to attend. It soon became clear that the military was manipulating the justice system. The whole process was polluted by delayed hearings and witnesses who were puppets of military officials sitting on the front row. Then one day an acquaintance who was connected with the military intelligence saw my wife at the trial and later warned us that we could be deported for attending the trial. A friend who knew the acquaintance thought the threat was mainly just to intimidate us, so we did not back down.

A few months later, when I made a regular visit at the stockade, I discovered the so-called subversives had escaped about a week earlier during a typhoon. Then I remembered that the morning after the typhoon, a jeep of heavily armed military men came to our house. They asked about some dangerous criminals who supposedly had been near our house the night before. At the time, we had no idea what criminals they were talking about.

Unfortunately, those who escaped joined the armed rebellion in the mountains. But after several years, the brother of my former student left the mountains and returned to civilian life. The need to confront evil and oppression remains. When one begins to do that, the added challenge then is to love the enemies that result from speaking the truth and helping the poor. Yet following that good way of Jesus is still possible for those who share his faith in the new kingly power of God. The way of the cross is possible for those who, like Jesus, receive God's powerful mercies and so present their bodies as a sacrifice (12:1).

Alicia Domon left her French worker family in 1967 to go to Argentina and serve God by evangelizing children. In 1969 she turned to the people in the slums whom the church had ignored. She was the first church worker to move into a slum in Buenos Aires. After five years, Alicia decided the rural people needed her even more. So she moved to a small village and stayed with a large and poor family, working in the fields for her room and board. She worked with Christian rural organizations and joined strikers to get higher prices for their products from the large landowners who exploited them. Other leaders of those organizations were imprisoned and tortured.

In 1977 she returned to Buenos Aires to help a young country girl who had been kidnapped, tortured, and imprisoned. Alicia visited various girls and women in prison and heard their screams in the torture chamber. She began to work with the families who had been persecuted for their Christian principles, especially the mothers of political prisoners. On December 8, 1977, after a meeting with the mothers of "disappeared" children, Alicia was arrested. Reliable witnesses said she was murdered several weeks later at the Buenos Aires naval school.[12]

Jesus' love for the persecuted often leads to more persecution. Because the power of evil is so great, others who optimistically think they can transform society will be disappointed. Sometimes, prophetic words and actions lead to positive change in a certain segment of society. Even if they don't, it is still important to speak and act in solidarity with the poor and oppressed. Loving one's needy neighbors sometimes means speaking the truth in love to their wealthy and powerful enemies. But the powers of evil will usually resist fundamental changes or manipulate the changes for their own purposes. That is why the good way of Jesus is a narrow way involving suffering and sacrifice, and only a few go that way.

Both conservative and liberal segments of Christendom have often underestimated the power of evil in the world. Whether they approved the status-quo or tried to reform society, they failed to realize the extent to which evil can use or exploit any human system. All the proud accomplishments and lofty ideals of humankind, even religious humankind, fall far short of the glory of God. The righteousness and power of God is reflected clearly only in Jesus' mission of practical love for the persecuted and for their persecutors.

Romans 13:1-14

God's Ministers
of Wrath and
Jesus' Mission of Love

P AUL has just encouraged his readers to respond to persecution by loving their persecutors (12:14,17-21). They are not to seek revenge, but to do good to their enemies. Both Jesus and Paul have practiced such love.

Although God's new kingly power is now shown through Jesus' mission of love, God can also show wrath, but by means of other chosen instruments. Paul describes those other ministers in 13:1. God has not left Jesus' followers completely defenseless. Everyone who acts violently against another person is to be subject to the ruling authorities (13:1). The all-inclusive word *everyone* includes Christians, but here it especially refers to those who are persecuting Christians. Paul has just used the word *everyone* twice for non-Christians in the preceding verses, 12:17-18.

Christians should try to make peace with everyone who persecutes them (12:18). They are not to become instruments of God's wrath (12:19-21). Instead, everyone who persecutes them is to be subject to the wrath of the governing authorities, not to the revenge of those persecuted. The context is subjection to those with authority to punish (see 8:20), not obedience to all authority.[1]

Throughout Paul's mission service, Roman authorities have often come to his rescue. When Jewish leaders or others persecute him, the governing authorities usually put a stop to that violence. (Examples of such rescues before Paul writes Romans: Acts 16:35-39; 18:12-16; 19:35-41. Rescues after writing Romans: Acts 21:31-40; 22:23-30; 23:10, 17-35; 24:22-23; 25:9-21; 26:30-32; 28:16-19, 30-31.) Paul never takes the law into his own hands. As Paul's readers continue his mission of love, the only defense they are to rely on is God's wrath (12:19) and the expression of that wrath through the governing authorities (13:4). Everyone who persecutes them is to be subject to the punishment of such rulers.

Several years earlier, around A.D. 49, the Roman Emperor Claudius threw Jewish Christians out of Rome, along with the rest of the Jews (Acts 18:2). Apparently there was unrest due to the witness of Jewish Christians like Aquila and Priscilla. Now that some of those Jews and Jewish Christians have returned to Rome (see 16:3), there might be unrest again. Yet Paul's message here applies to persecuted Christians everywhere, not just to those in Rome.

Unfortunately, 13:1 has often been used to persuade people to be totally obedient to all rulers. Too often missionaries used such persuasion on other peoples oppressed by the national authorities of the missionaries. Missionaries who entered other countries along with soldiers and merchants commonly sided with those colonial exploiters. Catholic and Protestant missions were mostly part of the larger wave of expanding Western power. Western military, political, economic, cultural, and religious power all worked together for the good of Western civilization. Thus most missionaries worked from a position of strength, not weakness.

Paul's mission was just the opposite. He worked from a position of weakness. As a Jewish-Christian missionary persecuted mostly by Jewish leaders, he called on Roman authorities when he was most desperate. Paul did not use friendly authorities to increase his influence or power. He only appealed to formal authorities in order to survive.

Later, the Roman Empire used Christianity to form the political religion of Christendom. They fought bloody wars in the name of Christ against other political religions like Islam or Judaism. The few Christians who challenged Christendom's crusades were quickly silenced. Those persecuted individuals or groups were often misunderstood as being totally against the government. Actually, they were totally against the church assisting or dictating government violence. They knew that Jesus' faith was not to be enforced by political power.

American Christians have usually viewed the Pilgrims and Puritans as the beginning of a new Christian nation. The Pilgrims and Puritans themselves thought they were God's chosen people with a mission to be the moral and political example for the world. Their new nation would be God's special agent, and they would be in control. That control included condemning outsiders, especially Native Americans, whom they regarded as quite barbaric and uncivilized. The Puritans used 13:1 to approve deadly violence against Native Americans. Our so-called Christian America continually resorted to violence, slaughtered countless Native Americans, and violated or broke over three hundred treaties.

The Puritans were thus like other cruel invaders such as Columbus in that they all gave religious reasons for victories that resulted in conquest, slavery, and mass murder. Only certain Christians like Bartolomé de Las Casas, a sixteenth-century Spanish priest, dared to oppose early Spanish cruelty. Las Casas constantly traveled, spoke, and wrote on behalf of Native Americans and against the evil which Columbus brought to the Americas.[2]

Sadly, Las Casas at first agreed to replacing Native Americans slaves with black slaves from Africa. The blacks' long history of cruel slavery was affirmed or excused by most white religious and government leaders. But later, Las Casas learned that the conquests of parts of Africa and the consequent plight of black slaves were similar to the oppression suffered by Native Americans. As a result, he was sorry for the ignorance behind his earlier agreement and denounced black slavery as well. Despite his false hope that a reformed Christendom could accomplish Christ's mission, he constantly spoke truth to power and sharply criticized church and crown for their terrible atrocities.[3]

There have also been American missionaries who lived with Native Americans and stood up for them against oppressive laws and presidents. For many years, the state of Georgia wanted the Cherokees to give up their land and make room for more white people. That desire became more urgent in 1829 when whites discovered gold in north Georgia and when Andrew Jackson became president. Georgians knew Jackson would support their greed for gold and land at the expense of the Native Americans.

Jackson quickly pushed through Congress the Indian Removal Law. He commented that perhaps later the "Indians" would also become a civilized, Christian community. In 1830, Georgia also passed a law requiring all white people to get out of Cherokee country. Several white missionaries stayed and spoke for their Cherokee friends, but they were arrested. The missionaries were beaten, chained, and found guilty by a jury. The sentence was appealed to the Supreme Court, which decided to free them, but Jackson refused to enforce the Court's decision.[4]

During the past three centuries, most missionaries were sent from powerful, wealthy nations which were also expanding their imperial designs through conquest and colonialism. During the high time of colonial expansion, British missionaries went to British colonies, French missionaries to French colonies, and German missionaries to German colonies. Almost all of those missionaries thought the colonial rule of their own country would be better than anyone else. They considered their nations as Christian, founded upon Christian principles.

More recently, missionaries from the United States have flocked to third-world colonies or allies like the Philippines. U.S. churches which sent them have consistently valued U.S. rule and influence in such "uncivilized" places. Many U.S. churches still display both Christian and American flags. That could be quite a surprise to Christians visiting from other countries where the American flag can be a symbol of American military aggression.

Conservative American Christians have connected evangelism with a revivalism that would call the nation back to its supposed Christian roots. Currently, leaders of the "religious right" like Pat Robertson and Jerry Falwell hope to restore the political power of "true" Christians. They want to save America and the other nations of the world for God.[5]

Their basic assumption is wrong. The United States has never been a Christian society, as defined by Jesus' faith. The United States has viewed itself as a new Israel with a manifest destiny from God. They thought God had manifestly destined Americans to take both Christianity and democracy to the whole North American continent, to the whole world. But that view was an illusion. The faith of the founding fathers was not the faith of Jesus. They instead pursued Enlightenment goals like the equality and happiness of all "men" at the expense of Native Americans, African-Americans, and female Americans. Even later national heroes (Saviors), like Abraham Lincoln, who often spoke of God, had little to say about Christ and mostly ignored churches.[6]

From the beginning, the United States gave religious reasons for its imperial designs in the Philippines. President McKinley told some Methodist pastors he prayed for several nights before receiving God's answer on what to do with the Philippines. God supposedly told him it was America's moral duty to educate, civilize, and Christianize Filipinos. Filipinos soon learned that "civilized, Christian" U.S. soldiers would massacre hundreds of thousands of the "little brown brothers" who rejected their rule. U.S. churches and missionaries overwhelmingly supported the use of U.S. military force. The U.S. government therefore favored the work of Protestant missions since they tried to reconcile Filipinos to their "God-given" fate.[7] As a Filipino recently remarked, reconciliation then means: I'm in power, and you need to get reconciled to it.

✦ ✦ ✦

All ruling authorities exist by means of God's own authority (13:1; compare John 19:11; Dan. 2:21; 4:17, 25, 31-32; 5:20-
21). Yet they serve only limited functions in God's management
of the world. Those not subject to certain God-given functions
of the authorities are resisting what God has ordered (13:2).
Paul is now focusing on the functions of punishing evil and
protecting the innocent. He concludes that those who resist will
receive judgment from rulers. The rulers are not a threat to
those who do good but are a threat to those who do evil (13:3).

The good and evil that Paul has in mind here can be seen
in 12:17-21. He uses the word *evil* in that context for the persecution of the mission begun by Jesus and Paul. Revenge against
the persecutors is also evil. Loving one's enemies, however, and
doing good to one's persecutors are the good work which rulers will not punish, Paul says.

Yet history shows that governing authorities have often
punished those who do good. In many third-world countries
today, to speak and act in solidarity with the poor is to be labeled a communist or a subversive by the government. It can
lead to imprisonment, torture, or death. Even an archbishop
like Oscar Romero in El Salvador, who spoke courageously
against violations of the rights of the poor for several years, was
murdered by Salvadoran troops as he spoke at a mass. He was
demanding that the military stop the violence.

However, Paul's use of good and evil in 12:17, 21 is in a
context of persecution of the Christian mission by enemies that
are not governing authorities. Acts of love toward those particular enemies will not lead to punishment by the authorities.
Acts of revenge would. So if one wants to be free from worry
about such judgment, doing good to one's persecutors is required (13:3). Indeed, such patient good work in the midst of
dishonor and danger will finally lead to sharing God's own
honor and glory (see 2:7).

Because of those limited functions given to rulers by God,
they are God's ministers or servants on behalf of persecuted
Christians (13:4). As ministers of defense, they are to stop the
evil of violence against certain individuals or groups. Yet if
Christians choose the evil of revenge, they also need to fear

punishment from the authorities. The rulers are quite willing and able to bear the sword and use force against all such evil. They will be the ones to enact revenge (compare 13:4 and 12:19). Their punishment will express God's own wrath against such evil. The rulers are God's ministers of wrath in the present time. Even in the past, God used a ruler like Nebuchadnezzar, king of Babylon, to be such a servant. He expressed God's wrath by punishing others with the sword, including Israel (Jer. 25:8-9, 15-16, 27-31, 38).

Note the clear difference between the function of the governing ministers of defense and the function of those called to share Jesus' mission of love. To combine God and country in a patriotic, nationalistic way is to miss Paul's point. Paul is not making a distinction between a Christian's private and public service. He is contrasting consistent Christian nonviolence with the use of violence by non-Christian government authorities. Jesus made a similar point when he contrasted the lowly servanthood of his disciples with the dominance of political authorities (Luke 22:25-26).

Most Protestant churches have wrongly followed Martin Luther, who followed Augustine, by allowing Christians to use deadly violence when in government service like the military or police. They denounce such violence in personal relationships but approve it in public office. They think Christian soldiers can have God in their hearts and a gun in their hands.

Yet the Reformers were only carrying on the unholy alliance of church and state begun with Roman emperors like Constantine. They looked to ruling princes to protect their Protestant privilege and power. Various Reformers like Melanchthon, Zwingli, and Calvin believed that mission work was the responsibility of the governing authorities. It was thus only natural that Protestant mission work began through the political and economic expansion of certain Protestant countries like Holland, England, and Denmark.[8]

In Christendom, including modern unofficial Christendom, the institutional church is the source of salvation through an elite clergy who administer the necessary rituals or practices. Political leaders protect the church's privileged status and are blessed by the church. Business leaders support the church's budget and programs and are blessed by the church. Military leaders protect the comfortable church from outside threats and are blessed by the church and its chaplains. The church's clergy and symbols (the Bible and prayer) are often found in public ceremonies. The society is thus an extension of the church.[9]

Missionaries could usually be added to that list of unholy alliances. In the sixteenth and seventeenth centuries, European colonizers recruited and supported missionaries. Even by the eighteenth century, only the Moravians began missionary work that was the responsibility of the church instead of a business corporation or government. Their mission was also noteworthy for supporting themselves by manual labor. In one place, Saint Thomas, they even became slaves to minister to other slaves.

The "father of modern missions," William Carey, spent his first several years in India as an administrator of an indigo plantation due to limits imposed by the English East India Company. After five years there, he was finally able to move to Serampore with some new missionaries, all of whom then supported their basic needs by manual labor.[10]

The famous missionary David Livingstone explored vast areas of Africa to pioneer the way for English commerce as well as Christianity. He hoped his explorations could open trade routes for businesses that would replace the slave trade. But for awhile, he opened areas more to slave traffic than to anything else.

After earlier missionary work with the London Missionary Society, Livingstone returned to Africa in 1858 as the British Consul in East Africa. He planned to develop African trade and British civilization. If successful, he hoped to create an English colony in East Africa. Such an imperial mission could not distinguish between British civilization and Christian faith. But by the time the British fought in two world wars in the twentieth century, Africans began to wonder who was really civilized. How could the British churches preach a gospel of love and still approve the massive violence of those wars?[11]

American churches cheered loudly to inspire war cries during World War I. It was supposed to be the good guys against the bad guys, God's American civilization and democracy against Satan's German militarism and dictatorship. World War II was somewhat of a repeat performance, with Hitler now an even worse evil. God's holy warriors responded by bombing German and Japanese civilians mercilessly, climaxed by the nuclear bombs dropped on Hiroshima and Nagasaki in Japan.

The next evil threat, Russian communism, led to an ongoing Cold War for several decades. Since World War II, over twenty-five million people have died in that Cold War, mostly in the third world. Truman and Eisenhower used civil religion (democracy and religious values) in the struggle against atheistic communism.

Billy Graham emerged as an enthusiastic admirer of supposedly God-fearing presidents and their crusades against godless communism. Graham said the Vietnam War was necessary to stop communism. When Senator Mark Hatfield called for national repentance (as if that were possible), Graham said Hatfield should rather be promoting a national unity that backed President Nixon. The United States was the world's policeman, but the rest of the world kept crying "police brutality." It seemed that the policeman primarily was protecting capitalism.[12]

The capitalist vision of progress and profit has founded schools that promoted personal honesty, a good work ethic, respect for civil authorities, and avoidance of vices and worldly pleasures. Mission schools became especially popular during the "civilizing" missions of the nineteenth century. In 1819, the U.S. Congress passed a bill that set up a "civilization fund" to finance educating Native Americans in reading, writing, arithmetic, religion, and farming. Churches used the fund to send missionaries to teach Native Americans how to become good Christian citizens.

Native Americans who had been hunters were to become mechanics and farmers. They were to live in villages where schools and churches would promote good work habits and good clean living. Cleanliness was rated next to godliness. So school children were to cut their hair, use combs, wear neat trousers and dresses, wash with soap and water, and eat with proper utensils. The result would be productive citizens who fit into white culture and supported the national welfare.[13]

The wealthy and powerful have often used such teaching to keep the poor and oppressed, the common laborers, in their "proper" place for the sake of greater profit and power. Missionaries easily concluded that if they spoke out against oppressive government policies, they would be forced to stop their mission or leave a foreign country. Then they could no longer witness to Christ there. They did not seem to remember that Jesus was forced to leave many places, including his hometown of Nazareth. During Paul's mission travels, he was often asked to leave a place or was simply run out of town. Yet the shorter witness that led to such persecution was worth more than all the long-term witnesses that watered down Jesus' message.

◆ ◆ ◆

Romans 12:14—13:4 begins to apply only when one becomes insecure, vulnerable, and persecuted for Jesus' sake. After turning one's back on long-term security, beginning to speak and act prophetically, and receiving threats and persecution—then what? Paul's answer continues to look to Jesus and his faith. Jesus' way was never that of using the sword or any other dangerous weapon to seriously hurt someone.

Paul then adds that fear of the rulers' wrath against those using violence should not be the only reason to be subject (13:5). Since it is now clear that Christians are not God's appointed avengers, that inner knowledge (conscience) should also motivate them to be subject (see 2:15).

Because the authorities' function is to punish violent offenders, Paul's readers can continue to support them through paying taxes (13:6). Although Christians don't share the authorities' function, they do owe the authorities the required dues, taxes, and revenue (13:7; see Mark 12:17). Respect and honor are also due such rulers, but believers do not owe them the total obedience or the same honor one should give to God (see 1 Pet. 2:17).

Paul's word reflects the teaching of Jesus. Some Jewish leaders tried to trap Jesus with a question about paying taxes to the Roman Emperor, Caesar (Mark 12:13-15). They knew that Jesus had recently challenged Jewish rulers in Jerusalem (Mark 12:14). Yet when they wanted to arrest him, they were stopped by their fear of the crowd at the Passover festival (Mark 12:12). So they sent others to question him about paying taxes to Caesar, hoping that he would upset the Romans and the Roman rulers would arrest him. If he had strongly condemned the evil of the leaders of God's people, Israel, wouldn't he condemn even more strongly the evil of the hated Romans?

Jesus saw what they were up to and asked that they bring him a denarius, a Roman coin used to pay taxes (Mark 12:15). Then he asked whose picture and writing were on the coin (Mark 12:16). It was Caesar's picture, with the inscription "Tiberius Caesar, son of the deified Augustus."[14] Why would Jews want to keep such blasphemous coins? Jesus said to give it back to Caesar. Pay Caesar's taxes. But neither Tiberius Caesar nor his father, Augustus Caesar, were God! Jesus also said to give back to God the things that are God's (Mark 12:17). Caesar could be honored in certain ways (like paying taxes), but he was not divine.

An important question is whether honor is owed to government authorities who become ministers of offense more than ministers of defense. When one's government promotes militaristic expansion and the torture and killing of thousands of nonviolent people, what respect is due? Or what about third-world military leaders who use imprisonment, torture, or assassination of labor and political leaders who speak out for higher wages, active labor unions, and more governmental social services?

This is a different situation than that of 13:1-7, and it seems that nonviolent protest is more appropriate. Christians should not hesitate to speak, rally, or demonstrate against powerful governments whose actions are consistently offensive. When Paul was on trial before the Roman governor Felix, Paul spoke so boldly about righteousness, self-control, and the judgment to come that Felix became afraid and asked him to leave

(Acts 24:25). Jesus also knew about political intrigue and once referred to Herod Antipas as a lowly fox (Luke 13:32).

As far as taxes are concerned, my wife and I have chosen to earn less so we pay no income tax to the most militarized nation the world has ever known, the United States. A significant percentage (around 50 percent) of current U.S. income tax goes to military related spending, including interest on past military spending. We are trying not to be financial supporters of American military might with its long, cruel history.

In 13:8, Paul uses a strong negative statement to say that nothing should be owed anyone, except love. While 13:7 refers to paying taxes that are owed, the mention of love in 13:8 shows that Paul is now returning to the emphasis of 12:14, 17-21. Instead of owing hate or revenge to one's persecutors, the only thing owed is love.

The law of Moses and the law of every nation provides for punishment of violent offenders. But the faith of Jesus proclaims that the law (of Moses) is fulfilled in the way of love (13:8). One command sums up such commands as do not commit adultery, do not kill, do not steal, do not covet, and others. The one command is to love your neighbor as yourself (13:9; see Gal. 5:14). That was the way of Jesus (see Matt. 19:18-19; 22:39-40).[15] Whoever joins Jesus' mission of love will not do evil against a neighbor (13:10; see 12:14, 17-21; 13:3). Jesus' faith teaches consistent nonviolent love of all people by God's new chosen people, the worldwide network of small, persecuted churches (see Matt. 5:17, 38-48).

Paul reminds his readers of the importance of the present time (13:11). The time is now fulfilled with the beginning of God's kingly rule (Mark 1:15). The hour has already come for some to be raised by God's power from the dark sleep of this evil age (13:11; see 12:2; Eph. 5:14-16; 1 Thess. 5:5-7). God is at work in a new way, and the final goal is salvation (see 1 Thess. 5:8-9). One can be sure that the time is limited, that God's final salvation is nearer now than when one first believed (13:11). Yet only God knows how near.

The power of the night or of evil has now seen the breaking in of the morning light (13:12). Both the power of evil (darkness) and the power of God (light) are at work during the present time. Those who will share the faith of Jesus must stop the dark deeds of drunken partying, sexual immorality, and jealous fighting (13:12-13).

Even fighting because of zeal for God is not the way of Jesus (see 10:2; 12:14, 17-21; 13:10). Instead of those works of darkness, Paul's readers are to dress for the new day by putting on the weapons of light (13:12). Those weapons will not hurt or kill others but will enable them to love and do good. By putting on such weapons as salvation, righteousness (see 6:13; 2 Cor. 6:7), and faith, one can overcome evil with good (see 12:21; 1 Thess. 5:8; Eph. 6:14-17).

By sharing the faith or weapons of Jesus, one is also putting on the Lord Jesus Christ (13:14). Through the power of Jesus the divine Lord, one can overcome the old attitudes and desires (see 6:12; 7:7; 13:9) of the flesh (see 8:5-6). Some had favored the fleshly fun of sexual immorality and drunkenness (13:13; see 1:24-27; 2:22). Others, like Paul in an earlier day, had been jealous, even violently zealous, to uphold their fleshly inheritance and law. They were willing to fight others who challenged those privileges (13:13; see 2:17-20, 25; 3:1; 9:3-5; 10:2).

All such fleshly actions come to an end for those conformed to the image of Jesus through sharing Jesus' faith and submitting to Jesus' lordship (13:14; see 8:29). The faith of Jesus preaches and practices compassion (mercy), kindness, lowliness, meekness, patience, and peace; and now all believers can do the same (Col. 3:12, 15-17; see 2 Cor. 10:1; Gal. 5:22; Phil. 1:8; 2:3, 5, 8; Matt. 5:3, 5, 7, 9; 11:29).[16] That same Jesus will now empower them to continue his mission of love.

Romans 14:1-12

Cultural Conflicts Among the Lord's Servants

T HOSE who share the faith of Jesus differ on certain details concerning the will of God. Such differences lead Paul to describe some Christians as weak in the faith (of Jesus). Weak Christians are committed to Jesus' faith, but they insist that believers should keep certain former customs or cultures. There is a danger of arguing and fighting over one's understanding of God's will. (See 13:13 for that danger as a result of mission contact between Christians and non-Christians.)

In 14:1, Paul calls on his readers to welcome into their fellowship the one who is weak in the faith. As they continue Paul's mission, they should accept new Christians even if there are still minor differences in how others understand the faith. The minor differences should not lead to major debates which cause division. The main example Paul gives of such minor differences concerns what one eats. Most believe they may eat anything, but those who are weak eat only vegetables (14:2).

The faith of Jesus declares that all foods are acceptable (Mark 7:15-19; see 1 Cor. 8:8). Yet some new Christians consider it wrong to eat meat because their previous religious culture strongly condemns eating meat. Perhaps there are some Jewish Christians who, like Daniel (Dan. 1:8, 12, 16), consider Gentile meat as defiled. It has not been slaughtered according to Jewish standards or has been dedicated to idols and pagan gods (1 Cor. 8:7). As they join house churches that share food and fellowship together, they may be shocked by the eating practices of the others. Paul is concerned that his readers not despise or reject new Christians due to such weakness (14:3). Mission means being more flexible concerning such cultural differences. A world mission will come into contact with a wide variety of cultural traditions.

People usually feel more welcome with others who share their own culture. Some church-growth studies have suggested that a homogeneous church (limited to one cultural group) is better because others from the same culture join more easily. Regarding contacts between non-Christians and Christians, one can recognize the value of sharing the same language and general culture.[1] But to the extent that those holding the homogeneous principle prefer such groupings in the fellowship of Christians, they wear out their welcome; they do not warmly welcome Christians from other cultures. Especially in bigger cities with a rich variety of cultures, church growth which favors ethnic churches ignores both the unifying culture of urban life and God's power to bring unity among diversity.

Paul is dedicated to uniting different peoples and cultures under the lordship of Christ, not under the lordship of a common culture. What is easiest and most comfortable does not need God's power. But while division and distrust multiply due to differing cultures, acceptance of others who are quite different manifests God's power. A multicultural unity in diversity is a strong witness to a divided world.

Another danger is the weak in faith who reject the strong. Paul also does not want the weak Christian to condemn the others, mostly Gentiles and certain Jews like Paul, who have more freedom (14:3; see Col. 2:16). For God has already welcomed or received the strong. If God has graciously received the strong, who made up most of the fellowship, who is the weak one to condemn another servant of God (14:4)? By using the word *condemn* again (see 14:3), Paul addresses the weak Christian who is confusing Jesus' faith with an earlier (Jewish) religious culture. By condemning the one who shares Jesus' faith, the weak Christian is also presuming to be the lord who gives the final judgment (see James 4:11-12).

Nevertheless, the strong Christian knows who the true Lord is, and stands or falls before God alone, not before the weak Christian (14:4). Indeed, the strong Christian is made to stand by God's gracious power (see 5:2). For the Lord is able to make each one stand (14:4). Paul contrasts the power of God, which enables the strong Christian, with the weakness of one who condemns another Christian because of minor cultural differences. Weakness in the faith can lord it over or dominate other Christians.

The faith of Jesus warns against judging or condemning one's Christian brother or sister (Matt. 7:1-5). Whether one eats meat or not is a small speck and of little importance. On one hand, to demand that Christians not eat meat is disobedience to Christ's teaching that all foods are acceptable. Yet one can disobey one of the least of Christ's commands and still be part (among the least) of the kingdom of heaven (Matt. 5:19).[2] On the other hand, to condemn another Christian because of such specks is to have a large log in one's own eye. Only when one sees clearly who is lord and judge, and what God's will is according to Jesus, can one act rightly when faced with cultural differences (Matt. 7:1-5). Otherwise, the one who condemns will be in danger of God's judgment (Matt. 7:1; see Matt. 5:22).

Among the controversial cultural issues throughout the history of Christian mission have been clothing, marriage, and respect for dead ancestors. Supposedly strong missionaries required naked natives to wear Western clothes, even if sexual lust due to nakedness was the problem of the missionaries, not the natives.[3] Because the missionaries required such a cultural tradition, they showed themselves to be weak in faith on that particular issue. The larger issue at stake was the white missionary desire to "civilize barbarian savages." Not content to stick to the faith of Jesus, the white man's burden usually included attempts to acculturate nonwhite peoples to the white culture. If they refused to go along, they were condemned as enemies of Jesus. Those who did agree to wear Western clothing were welcomed as true converts to the white man's religion.

Similarly, weak white missionaries too often insisted that mixed marriages between different races were wrong. On the other hand, missionary insistence on monogamy had a basis in Jesus' faith. Jesus affirmed God's original intention of marriage between one man and one woman (Matt. 19:4-6). Some macho males try to defend polygamy (polygyny, more than one wife) as a valuable cultural tradition. They must not continue to dominate and manipulate women. The prestige of having the most wives or the most children might mean more wealth, more people to share the work load, and more protection from enemies. So the issue of polygamy must be discussed along with those issues of status, wealth, sacrifice, and suffering. Apart from God's power, men (and some women) will not want to lose their own privilege, power, and possessions.

Some have pointed to the difficulty of what to do with the various wives of an already existing polygamous marriage. Rejecting polygamy must not mean condemning those wives to a miserable existence. Sometimes when missionaries required polygamists to choose one favorite wife, many of the other wives were forced to become prostitutes.[4] In such cases, the family of God must be ready to welcome those in need and to show mercy in practical ways. Yet in Africa, clan society often welcomed discarded wives, so their difficulty was less than usually supposed.[5]

Remembering dead ancestors can also be confusing. Some missionaries denounced such remembrances as reverence or worship. While that may often have been true, others were careful to respect the dead through rituals that didn't involve worship. It may have looked like idolatry to missionaries from a different culture, but it was not necessarily wrong. Those who condemned all such rituals reflected weak faith.

In the late sixteenth century, Matteo Ricci, an Italian Jesuit, was allowed into China because of his scientific knowledge. He tried to be especially sensitive to Chinese culture. At first he shaved his head and wore the clothes of a Buddhist monk. Later he switched to the attire of a Confucian scholar. He wanted to let the Chinese know that he did not aim to bring Western learning or culture so much as a Christian belief that was compatible with Confucianism.

Ricci also allowed Chinese converts to join in rituals honoring dead ancestors. He thought they merely showed respect for dead family members. Perhaps the Confucian intellectuals he worked with could view the rites as more formal ceremonies, with no religious worship involved. At the same time, many other Chinese, with their animistic beliefs, probably worshiped the dead.[6]

While in the Philippines, we once joined some Chinese friends at the cemetery on Memorial Day. We saw the gifts of food they left at the graves of their departed loved ones. We also heard them joke about how Americans sometimes asked if they really thought the dead could eat or enjoy that food. Their reply was to ask those Americans if they really thought the dead could smell or enjoy the flowers they left at graves on Memorial Day.

Another Jesuit missionary, Robert de Nobili, wore the clothes and followed the laws of the Brahmin caste in India in order to reach that caste for Christ. Thus at a time of increasing European imperial expansion and mission, Ricci and de Nobili were among the few willing to adapt in depth to foreign cultures. While appreciated by those cultures, their missionary peers found them highly controversial and responded with both romantic praise and shocked repudiation.

Often missionaries did not make even simple cultural adjustments like using the language of the people they were trying to reach or living in similar conditions. David Brainerd, who became famous as an apostle to the American Indians, still thought native languages were defective and preferred to use English. Despite a reputation for heroism in going to the Indians, he greatly disliked living with them and called them filthy and lazy savages.[7]

Again, though, there were a few exceptions to the rule of missionary disrespect for most Indian culture. The Mayhews (over several generations) in New England and Samuel Kirkland in New York showed more sensitivity to Indian customs. In the Middle Colonies the Moravian leader David Zeisberger served well by living among different tribes and learning, teaching, and recording Indian languages.[8]

Many African churches have increasingly chosen to separate from churches started by missionaries. Missionaries introduced prayer books, hymn books, pews, choirs, white names and dress, mission compounds, and denominations. Independent African churches have rightly seen them as nonessential. They have replaced such customs with more appropriate ones like keeping African names and dress, adapting African songs and dances, and using their own language for worship.[9]

The missionaries had trouble thinking of a church without their honored cultural traditions, but those traditions were not central to the faith and mission of Jesus. Africans who became part of the missionaries' church and cultural traditions also became isolated from other Africans. That isolation and strong connection with white people, white culture, and white mission led to a weak connection with their own people and culture. Even when heard, their mission message was usually not good news to Africans weary of white domination.

Another cultural difference Paul mentions is the observance of special days. Some set aside special days, while others consider every day the same, equally dedicated to God's service (14:5). Again, such minor details should not become major problems. No one should insist that everyone observe certain days like the Sabbaths or festivals commanded in the law of Moses (Gal. 4:10-11, 21; 5:1; Col. 2:16). Thus even one of Moses' Ten Commandments is no longer commanded.[10]

The original purpose of the Sabbath was to minister to those who needed rest and to provide a time for Israel to celebrate God's creation and liberation (see Exod. 20:8-11; Deut. 5:12-15). Jesus claimed to be lord over the Sabbath and did not always interrupt his mission for the sake of Sabbath rest (Mark 2:27-28). Sometimes he would go away to be alone and pray, but not necessarily on the Sabbath. The Pharisees often accused

Jesus of working on the Sabbath (for example, see Mark 2:23-24; 3:1-2). Because Jesus disobeyed their civil and religious Sabbath laws, they condemned him and plotted to kill him (Mark 3:6). Yet Jesus' faith emphasizes loving those in need and doing good more than observing special days (Mark 2:25-26; 3:4).

Special times of rest, reflection, prayer, and celebration are important, but they do not need to be scheduled at any particular time. Many Christian cultures have strongly emphasized Sunday as the special day when no work should be done and when worship must always take place. Sometimes they did not allow recreation on Sunday. Anyone who broke such Sunday laws might be condemned. The makers of those laws presumed to be lords of the Sabbath instead of Jesus.

Each should be fully convinced in one's own mind that God accepts their practice (14:5). If so, then the one who observes special days will do so to the Lord (14:6). The same is true for those who don't set aside special days because of their understanding or preference in serving the Lord.

Jewish groups like Messianic Jews, which confess Jesus as the Jewish Messiah, still celebrate Jewish festivals and other Jewish rituals. They do not condemn Gentile Christians and they, in turn, should not be criticized or required to acculturate to Gentile rituals or special days. Moreover, they should not have to join standard Gentile churches to be acceptable. They receive enough accusations already from other Jews, even from the Hebrew Christian movement associated with and supported by Gentile fundamentalist Christians. Both conservative and liberal Protestants tend to think Messianic Jews are too Jewish.[11] But Gentile sisters and brothers in Christ should welcome them as they are. Actually, a mixture of different cultures within one fellowship or church should be preferred.

Paul then returns to his first example of eating or not eating meat. If one can give thanks to the Lord as one eats, that reflects a fully convinced faith (14:6; see 1 Cor. 10:30; 1 Tim. 4:3-5). If someone can give thanks to the Lord as they eat only vegetables, that also demonstrates faith (14:6). Faith here involves certainty that one's practice is acceptable to God (see 12:2). The truth is that in many areas of life, different ways of doing things are all acceptable to God. The key is knowing whether those differences are important or not. Above all, it is Jesus' faith that makes clear what is most important in God's new age.

Minor cultural differences are not to become serious life-and-death issues. In 14:7, Paul emphasizes what is most important. Just as the daily details of life are done out of a thankful faith (14:6), so all Christians live or die for the Lord, not for their own sake (14:7). Instead of living for themselves and their own interests, Christians live for the Lord and continue Jesus' servant mission. The life and death of all who belong to the Lord are in God's hands or power, not their own (14:7-8). Whether they live or die, all remain servants of God (14:8). Christ has shown the way by remaining a faithful servant even unto death on a shameful cross (Phil. 2:7-8). Moreover, one purpose of Christ's death and consequent resurrection life is that he might share divine lordship over the dead and the living (14:9).

Missionaries who continuously criticize foreign cultures come across as power-hungry lords. The issue becomes social control. Who is in control of a society? In many parts of the third world, the missions have tremendous social, religious, and political power. Missionaries who play God, however, are not acceptable.

Paul turns again to the judgmental Christians (see 14:3-4) and asks, Who are you to condemn your (strong) brother? Or, who are you to despise or reject your (weak) brother? For all of them will finally stand before the judgment seat of God (14:10). Then there will be no more of sitting in judgment on other Christians. God the Father and God the Son will be the final judges of one's brother or sister in Christ (see 2:16). Everyone should know who is Lord and who are only servants who live and die under God's powerful kingship.

In 14:11, Paul quotes from Isaiah 49:18 and 45:23 to prove his point. Isaiah 49:18 refers to the Lord as living (see 14:9). Isaiah 45:23 speaks of God as the judge before whom everyone from every culture will humbly bow and confess, for better or for worse. (See Phil. 2:10-11, also using Isa. 45:23 and applying it especially to Jesus as Lord.) Each of Paul's readers will in the end give an account of themselves before God (14:12).

✦ ✦ ✦

Protestants have used countless cultural details to cause divisions and multiply denominations. Most denominational distinctives have to do with religious traditions that have little basis in the faith of Jesus. Often those traditions or cultural details are mere excuses for divisions due to power, prestige, and social position.

During the nineteenth century, U.S. churches and denominations divided over slavery. On one hand, mostly northern churches and denominations were correct to denounce the repressive, racist treatment of slaves in the South. Religious revivals, especially in the Midwest of the United States, also called for the abolition or end of slavery. On the other hand, the "correct" stand against evil went on to support the Union or northern armies in the Civil War. To overcome the evil of slavery, they identified with national lords and leaders who had also chosen to stop slavery, for their own special reasons. Thus by desiring not only to denounce but to overpower the cultural evil of slavery, those churches, denominations, and evangelists actually promoted an American cultural religion. President Lincoln's new Republican Party came to dominate a conservative civil religion.[12]

In the 1896 and 1900 U.S. campaigns for president, Democrats nominated William Jennings Bryan. He stressed "national" issues like strict Sabbath laws and prohibition from making and selling alcoholic drinks. Yet the winner both times was William McKinley, a Republican. Just before the 1900 election, he received a hero's welcome at a missionary conference in New York. He had earlier decided, after winning the Spanish-American war, that the Philippines needed many American missionaries to civilize and Christianize Filipinos. Even the London Missionary Society applauded McKinley as the answer to prayers of missionaries around the world. McKinley also received the Catholic vote by promising that friars could keep their lands in the Philippines.[13]

Most recently, the "religious right" has applauded Republican presidents like Reagan and Bush and candidates like Pat Robertson. The right-wing evangelicals claimed to be the nation's moral majority but discovered they were merely a cultural minority. Ronald Reagan promised to outlaw abortion and put God back in the schools, but he lacked wider support and failed. Pat Robertson of TV's *700 Club* failed to be elected as Republican nominee for president. Yet he did continue the fight for "family values" under the banner of the Christian Coalition.

American religious conflict has recently centered not so much on denominational differences as on a struggle between religious conservatives and religious liberals. Both of those groups are now found in most denominations, and too often they condemn and despise each other, and try to lord it over the other side. Both have strongly supported political power structures and blessed social systems that adopted their particular positions on specific cultural issues.

During the 1960s, religious liberals in the United States united on a national scale to protest the Vietnam War and to support the civil-rights struggle. Many of them were condemned for their strong public stands on such national issues. Then, during the 1970s and 1980s, religious conservatives united on a national scale to protest Supreme Court decisions that banned prayer in public schools (in 1962) and legalized abortions (in 1973). Many of them were condemned for their strong public stands on such national issues. The gap between the two groups continues to grow. The national media and national lords continue to add more fuel to the fire.

Both groups need to remember who is Lord and who are but servants. Also, both need to stop condemning or despising one another over such political problems. Finally, both need to welcome each other on a low-key local level on the basis of Jesus' faith. Then they could gradually discover together how Jesus' faith might relate to such issues.

A key question on most of those issues is how to separate the morality expected of Christians and churches from the morality expected of societies or nations. Will solving those issues really save America for God? Will losing the power struggle destroy America for God's enemies? Jesus' mission did not build political power structures in order to create Christian societies. Jesus clearly called his followers to love their enemies, including national or ethnic enemies.

Can nations be expected to follow Jesus' faith? The evil of nations must be denounced, but nations themselves cannot become Christian. How can any nation consistently love its enemies (see 13:1-10)? If the nation remains secular, why should believers insist on prayer in public schools? As for abortion, Christians who respect unborn fetuses should not expect a society to show the same level of respect. While denouncing abortions as a form of birth control or abortion on demand, Christians should not condemn all abortions as murder or harbor hate against women who choose abortions.

Above all, Christians must not seek to control the larger society around them. Those seeking to reform societies, churches, families, or spouses usually depend more on their own power and manipulation. Religious zeal for Christian societies, cultures, or families often leads to becoming religious lords. But the phrase "Christian lords" is an oxymoron, a contradiction. Only Jesus is Lord. All faithful Christians are servants of that one Lord. Sometimes Christians just need to agree to disagree. Sometimes one group might clearly be weak in faith. And sometimes both groups might learn from each other and manifest a unity in Christ in the midst of all their diversity.[14] Christ can overcome cultural conflicts among genuine servants of the Lord.

Romans 14:13-23

Conflicting Cultures and the Danger of Destroying Weak Faith

I N 14:1-12, Paul introduces the subject of different customs and cultures which can cause conflict. He emphasizes the freedom that Jesus' faith allows concerning most minor cultural differences (14:1-5). Paul is especially concerned that Christians not condemn, despise, or reject other servants of the Lord because of such differences. He summarizes that concern in 14:13 by asking his readers never to judge or condemn one another.

Paul then adds that if they want to judge the affairs of other Christians, they should judge (decide) how to keep from putting a stumbling block in the way of another Christian (14:13). Jesus also warned against despising the "little ones" (new disciples) and causing them to stumble (Matt. 18:4-7, 10). Paul himself knows in the Lord Jesus that nothing is unclean by itself (14:14). He is certain that the faith of Jesus declared all foods as acceptable to eat (see 14:2; Mark 7:15-19). Paul's own faith is fully convinced that it is okay to eat any food (see 14:5; 1 Cor. 10:25-26; Acts 10:15).

But if someone thinks a food is unclean (probably going by food laws of the Old Testament or the Pharisees), it becomes unclean for that particular Christian (14:14). In such cases, it is the thought that counts and that defiles someone, not the food itself (compare Mark 7:20-23). Other Christians who disagree because of Jesus' faith must still be sensitive to the one with weaker faith. If their practice of eating meat causes serious injury to another brother or sister, they are no longer walking in love (14:15).

They should not allow their freedom to eat meat to destroy that one for whom Christ died (14:15). Because Jesus loves the "little ones" enough to give up his life for them, those who are strong in Jesus' faith should be able to give up food for the weak in faith. After all, the strong know that food should not be a life-and-death matter. Yet if their eating causes the weaker Christian to leave their group and to give up the faith, they will be guilty of destroying another Christian (see 1 Cor. 8:11, 13).

That was also the point of the Jerusalem Council's decision to ask Gentile Christians not to eat blood or strangled food (Acts 15:20, 29). They needed to show love to new Jewish Christians who joined their fellowship and might be shocked at such eating (Acts 15:21). As for Jewish Christians who did not want to eat with Gentiles at all, there was to be no compromise with such separation (see Gal. 2:11-14). So as they meet for food and fellowship in house churches, strong Christians should not let weak Christians condemn eating practices they consider good (14:16).

Minor details like what one eats or drinks are not to become important in the kingdom of God which started with Jesus (14:17). Jesus' message majors on the powerful kingship of God. Eating or not eating certain food makes no difference as far as pleasing the God of Jesus (see 1 Cor. 8:8). The salvation of God's rule means a life of righteousness, peace, and joy through the power of God's Holy Spirit (14:17; see 1:17; 5:1-2; 8:4, 6, 10).

Jesus welcomed and ate with supposed sinners, who didn't follow all the Pharisaic rules about foods (Luke 15:1-2). Jesus challenged Pharisees to accept outsiders to their feasts (Luke 14:1, 12-14). The great final feast in the kingdom of God would invite, welcome, and bring outcasts to join in the celebration (Luke 14:15, 21-23). For Jesus, the traditions of the Pharisees about clean and unclean foods and people were cultural rules in conflict with God's peacemaking kingdom.[1]

According to Paul, the Holy Spirit enables one to serve Christ and to share Jesus' faith so that one is acceptable to God and at peace with other followers of Jesus (14:18). Since the fruit of God's powerful Spirit includes peace and joy, Paul's readers are to pursue peace by joyfully welcoming and loving sisters and brothers whose backgrounds are different (14:19; Gal. 5:22). God's righteousness is manifested through the love created by the Holy Spirit (1:17; 5:5; 14:15, 17, 19; Gal. 5:22). That love doesn't destroy, but it builds up one another (14:19; see 14:15).

For the sake of food, no believer should destroy the weak faith of others for whom Christ died and in whom God's kingship has begun (14:20; see 14:3-4). If someone stumbles and falls out of fellowship, they should pursue a renewed relationship. Matthew gives Jesus' story about leaving the ninety-nine sheep to pursue the one lost sheep. This is in a context of not being a stumbling block (Matt. 18:6-7, 10-14).

Jesus taught that all foods are clean and can be eaten (14:20). Yet if someone eats while still thinking it is wrong, the evil result will be their turning away from what they believe to be the will of God (14:20). The freedom of the strong in faith to eat anything could lead the weak to eat anything, even if they are still not convinced it is right. Thus the example of others may cause the weak to stumble and act as if their own faith convictions don't matter (see 1 Cor. 8:9-11; 10:23-33). Because of such dangers, it is better not to eat meat or drink wine or consume anything else if it will cause the weak to stumble so as to fall from faith (14:21; 1 Cor. 8:13).

Hence, when such cultural conflicts arise, one should be careful that self-confidence about such details doesn't harm other Christians. Instead of forcing the issue, one should humbly hold on to one's own convictions quietly before God (14:22). Perhaps as time goes on they can tactfully convince weak Christians of the truth. Blessed or happy are those who don't condemn themselves because of what they approve and practice (14:22). If some eat while still doubting whether that is

God's will, they judge or condemn themselves. They have not acted out of a fully convinced faith (14:23; see 14:5).

Whenever someone does something while doubting if it is God's will, that becomes sin to that person (14:23). Such doubt supposes that what is done is actually sin. Whoever eats meat while doubting that it is God's will has sinned. If one doubts that a certain action is God's will, it is better not to do it even if other Christians are doing it. For those other Christians, it isn't sin if it is according to the faith of Jesus. Yet to the one who doubts, it is sin. If someone cannot give thanks to God while eating meat or drinking wine (see 14:6), that person is trying to please others instead of God (see 2:29).

During the past century, certain Christians have twisted Paul's teaching about drink and stumbling blocks to force their own religious culture on others. While rightly denouncing the sin of drunkenness (see 13:13), they wrongly denounced any drinking of wine or beer. Claiming to be on the side of temperance and moderation, they strongly preferred total abstinence. They considered themselves to be strong in the faith, while those who drank moderately were regarded as weak in the faith. But according to Paul's definitions, those who refused to drink were the weak in faith, while those who felt free to drink (temperately) were the strong in faith.

Since Christians who abstained completely from drinking could find no biblical command to support their stand, they used Paul's stumbling-block principle. Supposedly, those who drank would cause young Christians to stumble. Yet why would they stumble if drinking moderately was not a sin? Was it because young Christians might get drunk? If so, that sin would not have been due to having doubts about drinking moderately, the subject of Paul's discussion in Romans 14.

Others defined stumbling blocks as merely upsetting others who disliked certain actions like drinking. Then, those who wanted to impose their religious culture on others kept complaining when others would upset them by drinking. Thus missionaries could become upset if their converts did not go along with all their customs. They might then warn those converts not to become stumbling blocks to others. Thus they used Paul's principle to manipulate others to accept their own culture. But again, for Paul, stumbling was a much more serious matter and led to destroying one's faith and participation in Christian fellowship. Actually, those who imposed their culture, using Paul's stumbling-block principle, could be the real stumbling block themselves since they caused some to leave the fellowship because of that culture.

As missionaries from one culture traveled to other cultures, it was easy to impose their own religious culture on converts. That is why so many churches in the world are so similar to the mother churches in cultural details. Common examples are the use of church buildings, meeting on Sunday mornings, the use of Western worship rituals and songs, and the prohibition of drinking, smoking, going to movies, or dancing. Third-world churches thus became associated closely with Western nations. They became foreigners in their own land because they left their own culture for the sake of a foreign culture.

Yet one cultural adaptation by many missionaries has been crucial. Those who translated the Bible into local languages left a gift of great weight. When people heard or read the Bible in their own tongue, the truth could touch them deeply. Christian truth was no longer like the traditional religions where spiritual mediums guarded their powerful secrets. By possessing the Bible in their own tongue, they had a basis for evaluating the claims of others, including the missionaries. The cultural gift of mission translators could come back to haunt other mission attitudes of cultural superiority.

Thus an African tribe no longer needed to perform special rituals to gain access to spiritual truth. The unusual religious language of their own spiritual leaders could give way to the Bible being read in their everyday language. Because the Bible came to be translated in many different languages, no one culture can claim the Bible as its exclusive truth. Multiple translations show that no culture or language is absolute. There are no favorite cultures before God (see 2:11). Yet every culture has its distinct place as part of the pluralism of God's worldwide family. Such truths can lead to a new respect for cultures formerly despised by others around them.[2]

Many practices in each culture are acceptable to God while some practices in every culture are clearly evil. There is a more recent emphasis on indigenization or contextualization, which adapts more to a local culture, and this has helped some. But there still remains too much imposing of Western religious culture. When one culture is seen as supreme, it becomes absolutized, and the result is civil religion.

Cults like Mormons or the Unification Church have been especially bold in promoting a certain national culture. Both cults hoped their future national power would rule the world. They wanted to make their version of civil religion absolute. Mormon missionaries tried to follow the original U.S. model as much as possible. By joining the Mormons, converts had a connection with American power and prosperity. Thus many were willing to submit to Mormon cultural rules like forbidding coffee, tea, tobacco, and alcohol.[3]

The Unification Church combined Korean spirituality and U.S. influence. The founder, Sun Myung Moon, pointed to a Korean Messiah (probably himself). Yet he also had powerful connections with anticommunist right-wing groups in the United States.[4] He was preparing a power base to enforce his absolute rule over various cultures.

Jesus confronted the Pharisees and their many respected traditions. Respectable Jewish culture meant following the civil religion of the Pharisees. Jesus' faith, however, said all their traditions merely sidetracked people from doing God's will (see Mark 7:1-13). Similarly, Jesus' world mission calls for confronting Western Christian traditions which abandon his faith for nice, respectable, and easy-though-trivial pursuits. It is one thing to use much of one's own culture to live out the faith of Jesus. It is quite another thing to use one's religious culture as a substitute for the faith of Jesus. At that point, one has become faithless and gone beyond being weak in faith and confusing only a few aspects of culture with Jesus' faith.

When Hudson Taylor arrived in China in 1854, he first stayed at the London Missionary Society compound in Shanghai. He soon developed a dislike for the other missionaries there because they lived in traditional British comfort and luxury. They seldom traveled outside Shanghai, and they constantly criticized one another. Taylor began to travel into the interior of China and discovered that the people were more interested in his British clothes and manners than in his Christian message. So he decided to wear Chinese clothes and adopt Chinese culture, including dying his hair black and wearing a pigtail.

Taylor's burden for the millions of Chinese who had never heard the gospel led him to form the China Inland Mission. The task was too great to depend on traditional missionaries, so he looked for others like himself: uneducated, unordained, and unconnected with a denomination or mission society. Coming from the working classes, they served with dedication despite the dangers and difficulties. They bypassed much of the usual missionary culture to work on the level of those they sought to lead to Christ. Another departure from Western mission culture was the welcoming of many single women for mission service. They even expected missionary wives to be missionaries and not just wives.[5]

Paul was flexible as he lived in different cultures. He was willing to adjust to the customs and traditions of Jews or Gentiles in order to win them to God's saving power (see 1 Cor. 9:19-22). He could abandon his former Jewish customs for the sake of living the gospel among Gentiles. If he had insisted on his own previous culture, then Gentiles would have confused that culture with Paul's faith. By being flexible concerning the multitude of customs of different peoples, Paul could make clear what was absolute—the kingdom of God. Thus, one of the most important characteristics of those involved in cross-cultural mission is cultural flexibility and an understanding of what Jesus' faith requires and doesn't require.

Icthus Fellowship in East London is one model for reconciling vastly different cultures. It consists of a large network of small home groups made up mostly of West Indians, Pakistanis, working-class Brits, and Asians. The network is growing rapidly and thus contradicts the homogeneous principle of some church planters. Cultural groups with a long history of enmity are joining to worship, study Scripture, and help each other find work, housing, or meet other basic needs. They also emphasize evangelism and planting new home groups.

The small groups meet together as a region once a month. Since they use homes, schools, and existing churches for their various meetings, they are not using money for building programs. As a result, they can help other poor people in East London while manifesting their unity in diversity as sisters and brothers in Christ. Cultural obstacles have given way to the uniting faith of Jesus.[6]

Such a mixture of cultures in one fellowship helps new Christians see that no one culture is absolute. Former traditions still thought necessary by weak Christians can be welcomed while gently educating those new Christians about the freedom of Jesus' faith. Strong Christians do not insist on their own preferences if it might cause others to stumble and fall out of the fellowship. But they also do not just let weak Christians have their own way all the time. Some are bothered by the cultural preferences of others, but that doesn't mean they can impose their own culture. Strong Christians seek to lead them in the way of Jesus so that he becomes the only stumbling block—not minor cultural details.

Romans 15:1-13

Jesus' Servant Mission, the World's Cultural Diversity, and God's Unified People

WORLD mission means different peoples with diverse cultures coming to share the faith of Jesus. But to be united in Christ, they must value Jesus' emphasis on God's kingship more than national traditions or cultural treasures (14:17; see Matt. 6:33). Paul knows that most Jews cling to exclusive food laws despite Jesus declaring all foods to be clean (14:14; see Mark 7:19). So those who are strong in Jesus' faith should help weak disciples who treasure such traditions. The weak might even judge the freedom of the strong to be faithless.

When weak Christians condemn strong Christians, how should the strong respond? First, the strong should see the irony that strong words of condemnation against them reflect weakness, not strength. When that happens, the strong don't owe the weak similar words. The strong will not overcome weakness with weakness (compare 12:21). Yet the strong, including Paul, do owe a debt to the weak. They owe a love that will help them bear their weaknesses (15:1). Such love fulfills the law of Moses and, more importantly, the law of Christ (13:8, 10; Gal. 6:2).

The weak carry cultural burdens which the strong can help bear in order to make the weak feel welcome in the fellowship (see 14:1-2; Acts 15:28-29). For example, in Asia Minor some new Christians continue observing certain Jewish holy days (Gal. 4:10; Col. 2:16; compare Rom. 14:5). They think such traditions are unchangeable. Paul, however, connects such laws with the weak spirits or angels who gave the law of Moses (Gal. 3:19; 4:9; Col. 2:8, 15, 18). Other related regulations, including rules against tasting certain foods and drinks, are mere human commands (Col. 2:16, 20-22).

Such laws and their harsh enforcement can be a heavy burden. Jesus now offers release and rest (Matt. 11:28; 23:4). Jesus' yoke or burden is light. Jesus' kind of love is humble and gentle (Matt. 11:29-30; see 2 Cor. 10:1). Strong Christians are to bear humbly and patiently the burdensome traditions of the weak.

Rather than pleasing themselves, the strong are to please (serve) the weak neighbor for the sake of building up faith (15:1-2; 1 Cor. 10:24, 33). Earlier Paul wrote to the Corinthians about a mission of becoming weak in order to win the weak (1 Cor. 9:22). That means going along with some cultural bias so as not to drive others away. When in Rome, do as the Romans, as long as the issue is cultural details allowed by the faith of Jesus. When among Jews, do as the Jews; when among Gentiles, do as the Gentiles (1 Cor. 9:20). That does not mean doing away with all law. It does mean keeping the law of Christ, which calls for love and mutual respect instead of cultural conflict or domination (1 Cor. 9:21).

Humble love also doesn't mean pleasing every wish or demand of the weak. Here *pleasing* means serving them for their own good and building them up in the faith. The good work of loving neighbors by promoting peace and continuing fellowship will please both God and the weak (15:2; see 14:18-19).

The best example of such servanthood is Christ (see 1 Cor. 10:33; 11:1; Mark 10:45). Throughout his life, Jesus didn't please himself (15:3; see Mark 14:36; John 6:38; 8:29). He remained God's faithful and true servant. In the midst of an evil world, Jesus pleased God by seeking God's good purposes for the weak in faith (see Matt. 18:5-6, 10). God's will is that not one of the weak (the little ones) should perish (Matt. 18:14). Welcoming the weak in faith shows a willingness to be servant of all and to be last of all (Mark 9:35-37). Those who argue about greatness become stumbling blocks to the little ones (Mark 9:33-37, 42, 50). By wanting to be great, they exclude others from their group (Mark 9:38-40).

Jesus fulfilled the role of the righteous sufferer. The insults of those insulting God fell on him (15:3, quoting Ps. 69:9). Those who condemned (Jesus) the Servant of God were insulting the Servant's Master (see 14:4; John 15:23-24). Psalm 69:9 was written to help those who would join the servant mission of Christ (15:4). Such Scripture can inform and encourage the strong concerning Christlike endurance in the face of insults as well as hope for harmony (15:4; see 5:3-5).

Scribes and Pharisees criticized Jesus for eating with tax collectors and sinners who were beginning to follow him (Mark 2:14-16). Jewish crowds murmured when Jesus went to the house of Zacchaeus, a tax collector and a sinner (Luke 19:2, 7). Since Jesus suffered and even died for such outcasts, can't the strong now please the weak in faith instead of themselves (see 5:6; 14:7, 9, 15)? Serving the weak in faith will be acceptable worship to God and help unify the one body of Christ (12:1, 3-5).

More modern attempts to unify Christian denominations have sometimes been deceptive. The Interchurch World Movement (IWM) began in 1919 to unite struggling rural churches. However, the motives were more to ensure respectable benefits for full-time pastors than to restore broken relationships. The IWM also showed its weakness by imposing "superior" traditions. They claimed that all rural churches should have an organ (or a piano at least), a properly equipped kitchen, and a moving-picture projector. Thus small churches needed to unite and create larger community churches. Most rural churches were not fooled by such cultural arrogance. They did not bow before such burdens. They knew the Rockefeller-funded IWM leaders in New York City were not rural specialists.

The IWM also thought the established denominations

could unite while ignoring less-respectable churches. Those latter groups met in homes, vacant stores, or tents. They had uneducated leaders who were paid little or nothing. Since they attracted mostly poor people of mixed race and little schooling,
the IWM looked down on them. The call to unity was thus
mostly a call for some small churches to please a few higher officials. By adopting middle-class standards of respectability,
they would supposedly be strong. Wrong![1]

✦ ✦ ✦

Only the God of Jesus produces strong faith. That strength
of endurance along with mutual encouragement will unify
God's people (15:5). God endures and gives the same endurance and encouragement to those being recreated in God's or
Christ's image (15:5; see 8:29). The future result will be a united
mind or purpose among strong and weak which reflect Jesus'
way (15:5; see 1 Cor. 1:10; Phil. 2:2). Jesus emptied himself, taking the form of a humble servant. All who share that mission
will be of the same mind (Phil. 2:5-8). Now Paul calls on God to
grant such unity. Then with one voice the strong and weak can
glorify the God and Father of their Lord Jesus Christ (15:6;
compare Phil. 2:11).

How can Christians among the various peoples of the
world celebrate the glory of God unless they welcome all into
the house churches (15:7; see 14:1)? Welcoming the little ones
(or new disciples) is the same as welcoming Jesus (Matt. 18:5-
6). For the sake of God's glory, Christ accepted both Jews and
Gentiles, both the strong and the weak. So the Roman Christians should welcome one another into their home meetings
and meals (15:7).

Jesus was led to serve the (circumcised) Jews out of his
faithfulness to the promises God gave Israel's forefathers. Furthermore, he continues to serve them through his followers
(15:8). Gentile Christians should remember that Jesus became
a Jew in order to bring God's saving power to some other Jews.
Despite conflict, suffering, and even death, Jesus confirmed that
God's promises to the Jews are true and faithful (15:8). The
promised Christ (Messiah) of Israel has come (see 1:2-3; 9:4-5).

The coming of the Servant-Messiah should lead Jewish Christians especially to glorify God for such faithfulness.

Christ welcomed certain children of Abraham to share what is becoming a worldwide faith and fellowship. That faithful fellowship fulfills God's promises to Abraham (see 4:11-13, 16-18). Christ's faith is the foundation for a worldwide faith (see 1:16-17; 3:22, 26, 29-30). Through the Jewish Messiah, Abraham's descendant, blessing will spread out among all the earth's peoples. Jesus envisioned a world church of Jews and Gentiles who would glorify God with a united voice.

Paul and his audience know that Gentile Christians in Rome and in most other places now actually outnumber Jewish Christians. The strong in faith are mostly Gentile Christians. They know that Jesus the Jew set aside the national culture of Moses' law in order to be the cornerstone of a worldwide church (see Eph. 2:11-22). Christ came not only for the sake of other Jews, but also for Gentiles (15:9; Matt. 28:18-20). The Gentile Christians are now glorifying God because of the mercy and kindness shown in Christ's empowering them to be part of God's people (15:9).

So, will the strong in faith follow Jesus' example of sacrificial service? Will they reflect God's mercies shown them by sacrificially showing mercy to the weak in faith (see 12:1)? Can Jews and Gentiles, the weak and the strong, really unite in glorifying the God of Jesus?

Jewish Scripture prophesies a united worldwide worship of Gentiles as well as Jews. Paul quotes several Scriptures in 15:9-12 to encourage Jews and Gentiles to welcome one another and to join together in celebrating God's faithfulness and mercy (see 15:4-6). Such worship will begin with the risen Messiah, who confesses God's glory and expresses praise to God among the Gentiles through his Jewish apostles, including Paul (15:9; see 10:8-10). Then together with Jewish Christians, Gentile Christians will also celebrate God's unexpected, powerful mercy (15:10; see 11:30).

All God's children will cry out together to their divine dad. They can use Jesus' favorite Hebrew word (in Aramaic dialect) for his heavenly father, *Abba;* or the Greek word for father, *patēr;* or any other language, even if it sounds "barbarian" (see 8:15; compare 1:14; Col. 3:11). Thus all the peoples (Jews and Gentiles) will praise God with a united voice and spirit (15:11). The climax is a quote of Isaiah 11:10 in Romans 15:12. The root of Jesse will grow and produce a Messiah, a Son of David, who will rise to rule the Gentiles (see 1:3-5; Isa. 11:1-5). Jesus, the risen Messiah, will be king over all the peoples, not just the Jews. As peoples from all over the world come to a confident hope in Jesus the Jew, they can honor him by uniting with Jewish brothers and sisters who are weak in faith (15:7, 12).

The scope of that hope is worldwide. Paul is not focusing on problems in Rome. He is more concerned about future problems concerning cultural differences that might divide Christians. Paul has already experienced various divisions that developed mainly between Jew and Gentile in the body of Christ (for example, 1 Cor. 10:31-33; 12:13; Gal. 3:24-28). As Roman Christians extend Paul's mission elsewhere in the world, they will face similar challenges. They can carry the same hope of unity in Christ. In 14:1—15:13, Paul writes to encourage them and strengthen them for that mission.

As God's mission continues in the present, different races and cultures are still being united in Christ. Believers are welcoming new Christian friends from other races or cultures into their homes and fellowship. Yet in most churches, there is also a striking separation of races and cultures. In the United States, the Sunday morning worship service is the most segregated hour of the week. White church members have historically not welcomed other races into their church "clubs." While preaching love, their racism has blasphemed God's name (see 2:23-24).

Early in U.S. history, African-Americans left white or mixed churches because of racial discrimination. When they left white-controlled congregations and denominations, they formed their own. Mixed churches were still segregated, and white people would not give up their powerful positions. Black Christians then joined smaller, poorer Baptist churches. But as

Baptists became more concerned about respectability, racial integration was more and more rejected.[2]

In the past few decades, white churches have been more open to welcoming a few people from other races. Yet too many such additions are still seen as a threat. Paul proclaims a freedom in Christ to practice most of one's own cultural preferences. That does not include continuing cultural evils like racism and division. Civil religion comfortably falls in line with the good and evil of a dominant culture. Such religion might claim to be Christian. But it is not based on Jesus' servant mission and does not really unify or welcome diverse peoples. Such so-called Christians are only pleasing themselves and others like them.

Much of the cultural imperialism carried out by white missionaries assumed that the white race and civilization were superior. Many missionaries spread Western civilization and civil religion with an optimism that their race would rule others.

The most noted success of that enterprise during the nineteenth century was Hawaii (then called the Sandwich Islands). Popular portrayals like James Michener's *Hawaii* did not describe the realities of the Protestant mission there. The first American missionaries were young, enthusiastic, athletic, and attractive to the Hawaiians. Their mission "converted" the main chiefs and almost one-fifth of the population. Their influence was massive, and they came to dominate the society, including the government.

The white men won! That meant Hawaiians and their culture lost. As usual, white missionaries were reluctant to give up control. Even their own mission board kept reminding them to do that and finally forced them to do so. During the 1850s, the mission was finally turned over to Hawaiians. The problem, though, was that the missionaries had become Hawaiian citizens![3]

Kosuke Koyama, a Japanese Christian, has pointed out that most Christian mission workers in Asia have failed to listen. Mission leaders loved to speak and teach. Yet they mostly neglected any serious dialogue where they might learn from Asians. Missionaries did listen to their own bishops, theologians, and financial sponsors. Together they planned various mission campaigns or crusades. The one-way traffic of their strategies guarded their prestige and reflected their arrogance and racism. Koyama called for two-way communication traffic, where the self-denial of Jesus would welcome others who are different and build community with one another. The money, theologies, plans, and prestige of crusading minds needs to give way to the crucified mind of Christ.[4]

For Paul, Jesus' faith is a worldwide faith which welcomes and unifies diverse peoples and cultures. His hope is that God will be glorified through the united praise of that world faith. God is the one source of that hope. The God of patience and encouragement can fill them with peace and joy (15:13; see 15:5). As their faith remains focused on the God of Jesus, despair over division will decrease or disappear. God's power promotes peace and joy. Peace will prevail among those with whom the God of glory is pleased (Luke 2:14). A joyful, secure hope will abound only as it focuses on the power and glory of God (15:13).

Joyful united worship centering on God's power will finally replace domineering cultural expressions of joy. Respectable white churches have seldom allowed a show of emotion in their worship. Revivalistic or evangelistic churches of whatever race have usually required strong emotional worship. As a young pastor in a rural Baptist church in Kansas, I discovered that such requirements begin with the pastor. My preaching style was more low-keyed and conversational. Certain worshipers could not feel inspired unless the preacher became more animated and emotional. They tried to mold me according to their cultural style of worship. I tried to accommodate somewhat but didn't feel like putting on a show. I was not against them showing genuine emotion and tried to encourage their participation in different kinds of worship. But they expected the preacher to be the star of a religious drama.

Such cultural differences over emotion have also been used to excuse racial division. Since African-American churches prefer strong emotion, "respectable" white churches said it was better to remain separate. Yet can there not be united worship which includes both styles, and which focuses on God more than on pulpit stars? Can't each one please or serve others who are different by encouraging their participation? No one needs to require a certain worship style for everyone. No one needs to insist on a particular emotional level for true spiritual worship. The depth of faith does not depend on the degree of passion expressed. Joy can assume many cultural forms. God's people can unite in a diversity of joyful worship.

Issues of power use such diversity to divide. People who like to dominate insist on their personal preference. Others who don't fit in can leave. Excited ecstasy, happy friendliness, or quiet reverence—these become the test of whether a church has the right spirit.

The Holy Spirit rejects such divisive tests and power struggles. God's Spirit does not take sides on such cultural issues. God's power humbles all proud religious bullies and welcomes all humble faithful servants. The Spirit joins together joy, love, peace, and patience (Gal. 5:22; see 14:17). Paul has abundant hope in the power of God to call forth a united voice of Jew and Gentile glorifying God.

Romans 15:14-33

Paul's Vision for World Mission and the Purpose of Romans

PAUL'S earlier letters were mostly responses to particular problems in churches he helped start. But in Romans, Paul's vision is more broad. The worldwide scope of 15:7-13 shows that the general approach of 14:1-23 is not primarily addressing a Roman problem. Paul confirms this in 15:14 by expressing his confidence in the Roman house churches. Though he has not visited Rome, he is sure they are full of God's goodness and righteousness (15:14; see 1:17). That God-given goodness and knowledge has enabled them to teach one another (15:14; see 12:7). Roman Christians are strong in the faith of Jesus (see 1:8, 12; 15:1).

So why does Paul write such a long letter to them? Paul admits that he is bold to write such a letter, full of deep theology and direct exhortations. Nevertheless, he wants to remind them of important truths that will further his vision for world mission (15:15). God's powerful grace has enabled him to be a minister of Christ among the Gentiles (15:15-16; see 1:5; Eph. 3:7). His ministry glories in the gospel of God, in the good news from God and about God (see 1:1).

Paul is a priest with the purpose of presenting Gentile Christians as a holy and acceptable offering to God (15:16; see

Isa. 66:18, 20). Above all, the Holy Spirit has sanctified (made holy) that offering (15:16). By reminding his readers of God's power at work in world history, Paul prepares for God's further work in the Roman Christians. They too can participate in Paul's priestly mission. The power of the Holy Spirit will enable them to offer themselves as holy sacrifices and carry on Paul's world mission (see 12:1).

Thus Paul emphasizes his mission and magnifies what he has done for God in union with Christ (15:17; see 11:13). Paul quickly adds that his work is in fact what Christ has done in him (15:18). The powerful Son of God has given Paul a world mission and a vision for the obedience of faith (15:18; see 1:4-5). The righteousness of God will be manifested in everyone who unites with Christ and shares Jesus' faith (1:17).

God's righteousness is seen in Paul's words and deeds (15:18). Included among Paul's powerful deeds are miracles (15:19). This is Paul's first mention of miracles in Romans. Unlike 1 Corinthians 12:28, Paul does not include the grace-gift of physical healing in 12:6-8. People today who emphasize wonders should wonder why Paul hardly mentions them in Romans.

◆ ◆ ◆

Pentecostal churches and so-called charismatics in other churches often focus on "power encounters" like "power healing." For them, "power evangelism" works through miracles. Signs and wonders seem to be their favorite way to show God's power. God's new kingly power did perform many wonders in Jesus, climaxed by the resurrection. God did various miracles through the first apostles, including Paul. However, the world mission commanded by Jesus and carried out by Paul and his partners does not major in miracles. I believe God's power still works miracles, but not nearly as often as we would like.

In Romans, Paul has tried to prepare his readers to carry on his world mission. He has magnified God's power and Jesus' faith with hardly a word about miracles. Those who continually want "power encounters" are missing the main work of God's power. When excited crowds or critical Pharisees wanted still more signs or wonders, Jesus refused. He just went on to other places to fulfill his main mission of announcing God's kingdom and righteousness (see Mark 1:32-45; Matt. 12:38-39; John 2:23-24; 6:14-15). Jesus warned that on judgment day many who performed deeds of power in his name would be rejected. The reason is that their lives were still basically evil (Matt. 7:22-23).

Large crowds wanting to see miracles can lead to church growth. Yet a growth based on excitement over signs and wonders is fragile. It can still stumble on the rock of Jesus' faith. The fast growth of Pentecostals in Latin America the last several decades can be connected with earlier folk Catholicism. Both groups used popular traditions of holy intoxication or ecstasy and miraculous healing. The ecstasy of Pentecostal worship helped poor, oppressed people forget the harsh realities around them. Pentecostal faith healing also took the place of popular folk healers or of prayer to the virgin Mary.

In Mexico, some rural Pentecostal pastors were former folk healers who continued their art in churches. Was Christianity just another form of magic for them? If so, would they later trade Pentecostal religion for other miracle workers who came along? Indeed, the Umbanda religion from Africa has been growing even faster than Pentecostalism in Brazil. Umbanda is a form of spiritism that uses magical power to persuade certain spirits to perform miracles like healing.[1]

God's Holy Spirit empowers Paul to fully serve and to practice as well as preach the gospel from Christ and about Christ (15:19). Starting in Jerusalem (by not counting Damascus; see Acts 9:20-30; 22:15-21) and proceeding around the Mediterranean Sea as far as Illyricum (modern Albania), Paul has been an instrument of God's power (15:19). That power is effecting salvation in everyone who is believing, beginning with some Jews in Jerusalem (1:16).

After years of difficult travel and severe suffering, Paul still wants to enter new areas that have not heard or seen the gospel (15:20). In each place, Paul's pioneering mission will lay a foundation (Jesus). On that foundation, God can use others to build up the temple (people) of the Holy Spirit (see 1 Cor. 3:10-11, 16). When a community of faith is in place, including apostles who can spread faith in their local area, Paul pushes on to new territory (see 2 Cor. 10:15-16). By doing so, he helps fulfill the mission of the suffering servant of Isaiah (Isa. 52:15, quoted in 15:21). Now he wants to strengthen the Romans so they can share that same mission. That, above all, is his purpose in writing Romans.

◆ ◆ ◆

Paul does not need to remain a long time in a place before his task is done. So why have many missionaries settled down in a foreign place with a task that is never finished? The reason is that they were not sent for the temporary task of establishing a foundation of faith and mission. Instead, they were sent to administer, teach, or serve in expensive Western schools, hospitals, or churches. Those Western institutions required their permanent presence.

The nineteenth-century mission executive Rufus Anderson rediscovered Paul's vision at a time when "civilizing" other peoples was considered preparation for evangelism. Anderson replied that the missionary should only be a planter. After planting the seed, the missionary should leave. Some missions had worked for decades without allowing a single native pastor to take over their work. Anderson encouraged them to let the native leaders do it. Most of the schools should just be closed, and the mission should emphasize church planting. Yet part of the problem was that even the churches were developed according to Western traditions. Anderson argued that missionaries should not export debatable details of doctrine or church organization.[2]

The churches' response was to form their own denominational mission boards. Then their missionaries could organize churches and teach doctrine in line with their denomination. As American mission activity multiplied rapidly during the late nineteenth and early twentieth centuries, there was also much said about the priority of evangelism. Energetic, optimistic mission leaders often repeated the slogan: The evangelization of the world in this generation. But that evangelization included all the old "civilizing" projects. Both conservative and liberal church leaders agreed that mission schools and hospitals were all part of evangelization.[3]

Missions continued to affirm the conversion of non-Christians as their main goal. That goal pleased U.S. churches and potential donors. Many missionaries, however, were not as concerned about conversions as about being good school teachers, doctors, nurses, and administrators. Their specialized roles were more important to them than multiplying disciples of Jesus' faith.

During the late nineteenth century, John Nevius, a Presbyterian missionary in China, decided to return to Paul's way of planting and developing missionary churches. He disliked the usual method of starting churches: constructing a building with mission funds, and paying Chinese to preach there. Foreign funds paid men to leave their former work and preach, often in a different village. All the outside help made the church appear foreign. Such churches remained dependent on foreign funds and foreign "agents." Mission agencies hoped they could gradually reduce the funding. But the mostly small rural churches found it hard to give much support. As long as there were paid preachers, few would volunteer to preach for nothing.

Many saw the moneymaking motives of such preachers. Some became "rice Christians," hoping to receive some profit ("rice") themselves. Rice Christians thus resulted from "rice preachers." Both Chinese and Western "rice missionaries" were paid well for their efforts.

Nevius decided to have new Chinese Christians meet in homes. He asked volunteers who lived in the village to lead the meetings. No foreign funds were used in planting the new churches. Usually the leaders kept working at their former jobs. Nevius thought it was better to show how faith affected the normal work day than to set apart professional Christians. The informal meetings for worship emphasized reading and teaching the Bible. Later, he held annual Bible classes in a central location to help train the leaders.[4]

Vincent Donovan, a Catholic priest, faced similar decisions during the 1960s in Africa. He had joined an active mission in East Africa among the Masai people. There were four well-run schools, a nice hospital, and many friendships between the Masai and the priests. Yet when the priests visited different places, they seldom discussed religion. Amazingly, there was no adult Masai connected with the mission that practiced the Christian faith. When children left their schools, they abandoned Christianity.

Donovan decided that someone simply needed to go to the people and talk to them about the Christian message. He remembered how Paul planted churches by targeting specific areas. Paul was not just a wandering preacher seeking individual conversions. He had moved in a circular pattern around the rim of the Mediterranean Sea. Inspired by Paul's apostolic travels and methods, he divided a district of five thousand square miles into twenty-six sections. He could visit a different section each day, and would go to the same six sections every week for a year. It would take him about five years to evangelize all twenty-six sections.

Like Paul, he would go with nothing to offer but the gospel. Donovan planned no development projects, no schools, not even little gifts. He would stay no longer than necessary. After one year, there would either be a new Christian community in a certain section or a rejection of his message. Either way, he would go on to other sections after that year, with only occasional visits to the new Christian communities later.

Like Paul, yet unlike most missionaries, Donovan saw no need for buildings or institutions or experts. The new communities that sprang up also received no promises of financial aid or subsidies. What they did have was a community of Christian brothers and sisters who practiced the priesthood of all believers. They could begin to teach and encourage one another and help each other in practical ways. Some of them continued Donovan's apostolic mission to other places. As Paul prepared new apostles to complete his mission in various places, so Donovan trained others to continue his mission. They carried the same message in the same way to other Masai.[5]

Such missionary methods are still needed today. Even in North America and Europe, with church buildings everywhere, these methods are needed. Most people living near those churches seldom enter them. Sections of cities and towns and rural areas still need the foundation of an apostolic mission community. Instead of focusing on buildings and services, modern apostles could go out and form new groups in peoples' homes. After forming a group and bringing a foundation of faith and mission, those Christian pioneers would move on to other places. They would not settle down to enjoy a nice salary or oversee a building project. Even the leaders of the new communities would not do that. They would rather spend time building a community where all have a mission of serving one another and reaching out to others. Then the mission model of Jesus and Paul would again come to life.

If Paul is so interested in traveling to new places, why doesn't he continue his circle around the Mediterannean Sea and visit Rome (15:19-20)? If he is really concerned about strengthening the Roman Christians to share his mission, why not share a little time with them? Paul explains that his past work in regions circling from Jerusalem to Illyricum have hindered him from reaching Rome (15:22-23; see 1:13). Nevertheless, the way now is almost open to fulfill his dream of seeing the Roman Christians (15:23; see 1:10-12).

Yet since his vision is the world, Paul's eyes are also on the ends of the earth—Spain (15:24). He plans to visit Rome on his way to new regions, to the far end of the circle of the Mediterranean Sea. Consequently, his visit to Rome will result not only in sharing joyful fellowship with them. They can also speed him on as he journeys toward Spain (15:24; see 1 Cor. 16:6, 11; 2 Cor. 1:16). The Roman Christians can help provide money and supplies for the trip (see Titus 3:13; 3 John 5-8). They can also provide people to join Paul on that world mission. Paul is no lone ranger.

But first, Paul faces an even greater challenge. Instead of going directly to Rome and Spain, he plans to go back to the beginning of the circle, to Jerusalem (15:25; see 15:19). Like Jesus, he will become a servant to the circumcised (15:25; see 15:8). Paul's service includes another collection of money for the poor Jewish Christian saints in Jerusalem (see Acts 11:29-30; Gal. 2:10). Paul's most recent plan for a new mission of mercy (see 12:8) has been developing for many months. His previous mission in the Roman provinces of Macedonia and Achaia has collected an offering for the poor among the saints in Jerusalem (15:26; see 1 Cor. 16:1-4; 2 Cor. 8:1—9:15). The willing, sacrificial gifts of those provinces show their partnership with Paul and with Jerusalem in world mission (15:26; see 12:8, 13).

Yet this partnership involves not just a freewill offering. It recognizes the debt owed by Gentiles for the spiritual inheritance they now share with the Jews (15:27; see 9:4-5; 11:18, 24). Through Jesus, the Jewish Messiah, God's final, powerful kingship has broken into history. Through Jesus' Jewish apostles, including Paul, the good news of God has begun to circle the Mediterranean world, beginning from Jerusalem (see 15:19; Luke 24:47; Acts 1:8). Wouldn't it be appropriate for Gentile Christians to show gratitude for God's work among the Jews by serving them through material gifts for their poor (15:27)?

The Gentiles' participation in the collection for Jerusalem will climax Paul's mission thus far. They will offer both gifts and representatives of the Gentile givers, who will go with Paul to Jerusalem (see Acts 19:21; 20:1-4; 21:17-19). The gifts and the givers are the prized fruit of the Holy Spirit's power among them (15:28). While circumcision is the seal of Abraham's righteousness (4:11), Paul will offer the Gentiles themselves, and their gifts of love, as the seal of their righteousness (15:28; see 15:16). That righteousness will be a sign that the Gentile Christians share the same faith (of Jesus) as the Jewish Christians. God has circumcised the Gentiles' hearts, and the Holy Spirit has poured God's love into those hearts (2:29; 5:5). Thus the faithful mission of Jesus to the circumcised (Jews) will continue (15:8). As apostle to the Gentiles, Paul doesn't forget Jesus' mission to the Jews. Paul is also the apostle *of* the Gentiles—to the Jews (see 11:13-14).

Paul's return to Jerusalem with certain Gentile Christians

can result in a united voice of Jew and Gentile glorifying God (15:6, 8-12; see 2 Cor. 9:11-13). Christ's goal of mission to Jews is a worldwide fellowship of peace and faithful worship (15:8-9). That fellowship will fulfill Old Testament prophecies about Gentiles flocking to Jerusalem to give gifts and celebrate Israel's God (for example, Isa. 2:2-4; 61:5-9). The faithfulness of Gentile Christians to the God of Jesus and his apostles will be a witness to unbelieving Israel.

The Old Testament often connects God's righteousness with giving to the poor. As God's people gave generously, their righteousness would cause others to give thanks to God (see 2 Cor. 9:9-11, which includes a quote of Ps. 112:9). If Paul's plan is fulfilled, he can go to Rome overflowing with Christ's blessing and praise (15:29). It all depends on God's sovereign will (see 1:10; 15:32).

◆ ◆ ◆

Christians today who give money to help poor Christians in other parts of the world continue to manifest the righteousness of God and their unity in Christ. That help includes temporary relief as well as more long-term processes planned by the poor themselves. Sometimes a more wealthy church unites with a sister church or churches in the third world, creating new ties of Christian fellowship and practical help. Short-term help will not create the permanent dependence that so many mission projects have caused. For a Christian fellowship which honors the most humble and needy, helping with basic needs like food, medicine, or shelter from time to time is the best place to start—and to stop. Apostolic visitation among other churches or written correspondence with them can inform resourceful churches when help is needed.

Unfortunately, the need continues to worsen in the third world. Most Western churches share only a small percentage of their budgets with the poor. The need is also getting worse in the United States, especially among Native Americans, African-Americans, and Hispanics. Do white churches seek to work with nonwhite churches in order to show compassion? Many individuals or churches give less than 1 or 2 percent of their income to help the poor; do such really think they are faithful to Christ's servant mission?

As poverty increases in the world, due to imperial policies of the world's wealthy and powerful elite, Christian partners in giving and receiving must listen to the poor. The greatest needs are not the exporting of Western ways of healing (big hospitals) or educating (big universities) or worshiping (big churches). Large institutions will always require outside funding to continue. That funding can be put to better use. Most poor in the world cannot even afford to use hospitals or universities.

What is needed are more simple health strategies like primary health care. Community health workers can help prevent or treat the most common illnesses. With care like oral rehydration therapy and vaccines, the poor will be less likely to die from simple sicknesses like diarrhea or measles. Likewise, generic drugs and health education can stop more complex illnesses like respiratory infections or parasitic diseases, which cause millions of deaths every year. Many deaths are partly the result of malnutrition, which reduces the body's ability to overcome such sickness.

Poor nutrition, in turn, points to the need for processes that will help the poor feed themselves. Christians need to live with the neglected poor and listen to them. The slow process of analyzing complex causes of poverty must be done with the poor, not for them. Even a project that meets basic needs might not be their greatest need.

Jesus said to pray for daily bread. Only the poor who can't assume bread every day can really appreciate that prayer (Matt. 6:11). The poor don't need to go to college and become middle-class. They just need to have enough food, clothing, and shelter (see 1 Tim. 6:6-10).

Many so-called Christians have stored up treasures on earth at the expense of poor Christians around the world (see 2:21-24; Matt. 6:19-20, 24; 1 Tim. 6:17-19). When rich Christians became missionaries to the third world, they were much more wealthy than their new neighbors. They lived in the best houses, drove cars, and hired cooks, gardeners, babysitters, janitors, etc. Many of their neighbors became Christians because they believed their own wealth and power would increase. At the same time, they wondered why missionaries were not so willing to share with those in deep poverty. The poor could only conclude that the god or idol of the rich was money. Love of money was the root of all evil excuses not to help—such as blaming the poor for their own plight.

Paul's collection project for poor Jewish Christians will also not be easily fulfilled. It will involve a prophetic challenge to Jewish contempt for Gentiles. What if unbelieving Jews in Jerusalem become angry again (see Acts 9:26-30)? According to Acts (20:22-23; 21:4, 10-12), various people warn Paul not to go to Jerusalem at that time. Paul, however, answers that he is ready to be imprisoned or even to die in Jerusalem for Jesus' sake (Acts 21:13).

In 15:30, Paul asks the Romans to pray for him. He appeals to them to agonize with him over the dangers in Jerusalem. Paul doesn't want them feeling hesitance at his plan or hate for the Jews there. Instead, the grace of their Lord Jesus and the love of the Spirit (see 5:5) can help them sympathize with Paul's plan and plight (15:30). Jesus himself once set his face to go to Jerusalem, and to die (Luke 9:51; Mark 10:32-34).

Roman readers are to pray for two results: that Paul will be delivered from the disobedient (non-Christians) in Judea (see 10:21; 11:28, 30-31; Acts 9:29; 20:3, 23); and that his plans for ministry in Jerusalem will be acceptable to the saints (Christians) there (15:31). Paul has enemies among both groups. Some Jewish Christians in Jerusalem think Paul's mission among the Gentiles teaches Jews to give up the law of Moses and to forsake Jewish customs (Acts 21:20-21). They will reject the fruit of such a mission. Moreover, they will not join any gathering designed to show the unity of such Gentiles and Jews in Christ.

But non-Christian Jews are the greatest danger. Paul reflects the Lord's Prayer as he requests prayer that he might be delivered from them. Jesus taught his disciples to pray that their heavenly Father and powerful King would deliver them from the evil one (Matt. 6:13). The severe testing Paul receives from Jewish opponents is seen as the work of Satan (see 16:17-20; 2 Cor. 11:13-15, 22; Phil. 3:2-3, 18-19). Such instruments of Satan are the main hindrances of Paul's mission (see 1:13; 15:22; 1 Thess. 2:14-16, 18). Now they can hinder Paul's plan for Jerusalem. They can also cancel his plans for Spain and Rome. Or can they?

Now that Paul has informed the Roman house churches of his plans, they can fulfill them if necessary. That is the ultimate reason for Paul to write this letter. If Paul is not able to continue his world mission, he has enabled his Roman readers to carry on his concern for Spain and Jerusalem. His letter has tried to strengthen them for future mission among Jews and Gentiles.

Paul sees Jerusalem as the beginning of his own world mission. As that mission circles the Mediterranean world, its climax at each stage is celebrated back at the beginning point, at Jerusalem (see Acts 14:26—15:31; 18:22; 19:21; 20:16; 21:15-26). If Paul dies in Jerusalem, some Roman Christians can take up his cross and eventually set *their* face to go to Jerusalem.

If, by God's will, Paul is able to fulfill his plans for Jerusalem and Rome, he will joyfully join them for his journey to Spain (15:32). Until then, his readers will be anxious to know what happens in Jerusalem. Thus Paul ends with a benediction, asking that the God of peace be with them (15:33).

Romans 16:1-16

Paul's Co-Workers in World Mission

PAUL is the special apostle to the Gentiles. But he doesn't minister alone. He prefers to serve as part of a team. Throughout his wide travels, he receives help from many sisters and brothers in Christ. Several have now surfaced in Rome. Paul concludes his letter with some final exhortations and greetings for past co-workers now in Rome.

First, he commends a Christian sister, Phoebe, who will take his letter to Rome (16:1-2). She has been serving in a special ministry in the church at Cenchreae and has helped many, including Paul (16:1-2; see 12:7-8). Servant ministry is a calling for all Jesus' followers. Yet some are especially gifted for such leadership. Phoebe has that gift. She doesn't travel to Rome as just a pawn in Paul's postal service. Paul asks his readers to receive her in the Lord, in a way that is worthy of holy people (16:2). She is a valued co-worker, and they should warmly welcome her (see 14:1; 15:7). He further requests that they give her whatever she needs (16:2).

Many have criticized Paul for his supposed bias against women. But 16:1-2 portrays a Paul who chooses a female leader as his representative to Rome. As a helper of Paul in the past, Phoebe will help to prepare the Romans for future mission. If

Paul is successful in Jerusalem, he will find the Romans ready to participate in his world mission when he arrives. However, if Paul never reaches Rome, his letter and representative will encourage them to continue his mission without him. What a crucial ministry—and Paul picks a woman to fulfill it!

In 16:3, Paul begins to greet former co-workers, beginning with Prisca (Priscilla), another woman. She and her husband Aquila earlier served with Paul in Corinth and Ephesus (16:3; see Acts 18:1-3, 18-19, 24-26). They even risked their lives for Paul's sake, and Paul thanks them for that sacrificial service (16:4). Paul lifts them up as examples of those who follow in the footsteps of Jesus' faithful love (see 1 John 3:16). All the churches of the Gentiles give thanks for their courageous faith (16:4; see 1:8).

At that time, Prisca and Aquila were hosting a church in their house, to which Paul sends greetings (16:5; see 1 Cor. 16:19). During the first two centuries, homes were the main meeting places of the churches (see also Col. 4:15; Phile. 2). Instead of spending money on impressive buildings, they could give more for basic needs of the poor, like the needy in Jerusalem (see 15:26).

The world is still full of poor people, including many poor Christians. Yet now churches spend more money on buildings than they do on poor sisters and brothers in Christ. In just the United States, religious institutions use over 90 billion dollars worth of real estate. Churches construct new buildings at a cost of about one billion dollars each year. Various denominations arrange loans to finance new church structures.[1] This edifice complex has impoverished their mission.

Ministers take pride in new or improved buildings they have helped oversee. Most Western church staff expect a middle-class salary, like other professionals. The faith of Jesus that led to house churches and helping meet basic needs, including those of church leaders, is now seen as primitive. Jesus sent out the twelve, and later the seventy (or seventy-two), to gather new disciples in house groups in various towns (Mark

6:10; Luke 10:1, 5-8). If no house in a certain town welcomed them, they were to go into the streets and shake the dust off their feet as a sign against the town (Mark 6:11; Luke 10:10-11).

Modern church and mission institutions have built their own "homes." They shoveled tons of dirt to build "holy houses of God." They no longer need to shake the dust off their feet. They themselves are now the pillars of their towns. Churches and pastors have come to resemble corporations and executives more than countercultural groups of faithful servants and servant-leaders. American business has become more the basis of criteria for success in modern churches. The numbers game counts church attendance (the listening audience), church members, church offerings, and church missionaries. Bigger numbers supposedly equal better churches.[2]

Yet there is now a growing movement of house churches. Some are small-group fellowships that are part of a larger congregation. Others are individual house churches loosely associated with other house churches. Fellowship and personal sharing or study and prayer are important. Yet it is also essential that house churches have a sense of mission.[3] Where there is no building or middle-class staff salary, they can use most money to help others in need, near and far. Large homes are also not necessary. For many Americans, purchasing a newer, larger house means that both husband and wife must work full-time. That leaves little time or energy for mission service.

House churches are alternatives to houses of God. The first step of meeting in homes can lead to other steps along the narrow way of Jesus. In such settings, Christians can encourage and challenge each other to remain faithful to Jesus' way. As the body of Christ, they incarnate the faith of Jesus and sacrifice their bodies and possessions for others.[4]

Throughout E. Stanley Jones's mission in India, he stressed the difference between Christ and Western civilization, including the Western institutional church. He developed Christian ashrams as an alternative to the Western church. The ashrams were small fellowships that worked and discussed together throughout the day. They were more fitting for Indian social life than a church that only meets to worship a few hours each week. Their main purpose was spiritual growth. But the ashrams also helped break down caste and political barriers which previously separated Christians in their daily life.[5]

Sometimes missionaries built churches before there were any converts. Many frontier missions began their work by using interpreters to negotiate the purchase of land for the mission. Where villagers normally gathered under a large tree or by a river, missionaries said church meetings required buildings. It seemed that Western Christianity needed a church structure before it could be communicated. The Christian message was thus reserved for holy places and times. Yet a non-Christian entering a church building was often thought to be joining that new religion. For example, in a Meo Christian movement in Laos, meetings were first held in the chief's home. Many attended and showed great interest. However, after churches were built, there was much less interest and attendance.[6]

In Singapore, around three-fourths of the population live in high-rise apartments. Before 1980, churches had little to do with such urban networks. Then house (apartment) churches developed after identifying some Christian residents. Those Christians joined in the apartments for Bible study, worship, and evangelism. Other small groups were formed in the central business district, where a half-million people work. Christians now meet in many buildings there. Urban professionals form and lead their own groups.[7]

Similar is the urban mission of Steve De Bernardi in San Francisco. He reaches out to residents of several hotels where lower-income people live. In such residential hotels, people pay rent for one little room. De Bernardi has started Bible studies and shows his concern by visiting them in the hospital or health clinic, and by giving them rides to welfare or Social Security offices. He encourages other Christians to adopt a hotel and welcome its residents into a Christian fellowship.[8]

My wife and I have been part of house churches and neighborhood Bible studies. Meeting at various times of the week, usually during evenings, we studied, prayed, and worshiped together. Moreover, we encouraged individual and group missions among the poor. Most of the money contributed went into a helping fund for those in need. We decided as a group which needs or requests to give money to and how much. Sometimes those in our own group needed financial help. Unlike most social agencies, we even helped with utility bills and rent. We also tried to meet personally with those we helped so we could get to know them and their situation better.

My own hope is that God will multiply more and more house churches or Bible studies in our neighborhood and city. Such groups should not be temporary fads or evangelistic experiments. They should seek to become committed fellowships of faithful servants.

Small groups of disciples meeting in homes could also be more open to welcoming women servant-leaders. Among the many Chinese house churches, women have done most of the teaching. In small groups, there is no pulpit or altar or elevated platform where envious men might want to perform. In the early church, there were no such holy places. Old Testament culture has been changed so that now only Jesus' followers are holy. Furthermore, women are more likely to follow Jesus' humble servanthood than men (see Mark 14:3-9; 15:40-41; 16:1; Luke 8:2-3; 10:38-42; 21:1-4; John 12:2-8; 13:14). Jesus welcomed women among his followers. That new openness, in contrast to the Judaism of his day, continued in Paul's own faith and mission.

◆ ◆ ◆

After Paul greets Epaenetus, the first Christian convert in Asia (16:5), he notes another woman, Mary, as one who worked hard among them (16:6). So far, Paul has named five co-workers, and three are women. In 16:7, Paul greets another Jewish-Christian couple (like Prisca and Aquila), Andronicus and Junia. Earlier, that husband-and-wife team were prisoners for Jesus' sake (16:7). Above all, they are well known as apostles, and they became Christians before Paul (16:7). Thus they were probably part of the earliest church in Jerusalem. Junia is a woman apostle. Though not one of the twelve apostles, she is among a wider group of church representatives chosen and sent out on mission (see 1:5).[9]

A more recent example of a woman apostle who risked much and sacrificed greatly was Mary Slessor. At a time when most women served in established mission stations, Mary became a pioneer missionary. Leaving Britain for West Africa in 1875, she taught in a mission school for a few years and learned the local language. But she did not appreciate the luxurious lifestyle and social network of the other missionaries. So she moved inland and began the pioneering work that continued for almost forty years.

Mary lived simply, in a mud hut, eating local produce. She courageously challenged oppressive tribal customs like twin-murder. She adopted seven children from the many unwanted twins she helped rescue. Mary traveled to various places where no white man had survived. Due to the white man's past brutal treatment of Africans, she knew women would be less threatening. Janie, her oldest adopted daughter, later helped her in the work. At the age of sixty-six, Mary died in her mud hut.[10]

Paul has been misunderstood. By honoring a female apostle, a woman minister, and two women co-workers in 16:1-7, he clearly supported women in ministry. So 1 Corinthians 14:34-35 and 1 Timothy 2:11-12 must mean something else than a general put-down of women speaking in house churches.[11]

Women in mission have struggled against powerful men who misused Paul's call for some women to be silent. During much of the nineteenth century, women were strong supporters of new missionary societies. Nevertheless, they were not welcomed to serve as missionaries other than as wives with primary responsibility in the home.

An interesting later development was the case of Adele Fielde. Formerly a Universalist school teacher, she married a Baptist would-be missionary and became a Baptist herself. Her husband sailed first to Siam, and she followed several months later, only to discover he had died. Yet she decided to stay. When she discovered that her salary would be only half that of single males, she protested. As the only single woman missionary among the Baptists, she joined other groups such as the families of businessmen and diplomats. Their social gatherings included recreation like dancing and card playing. When the other Baptists confronted her about such "worldly" pleasures, she agreed to stop them for the sake of the mission. But some felt she was still not working out as a model missionary, and the Baptist mission board dismissed her.

After returning to the United States, her vision for women's work in China became strong. She begged her directors to let her train women in China. They agreed, and she began a plan which profoundly affected mission throughout the Far East. She organized, taught, and sent out Chinese "Bible women" to do pioneer evangelism. Her mission led many other female missionaries in Asia to serve in similar ways. Because of Fielde's efforts, numerous Asian women were sent out as apostles to fields that were often too difficult for men.[12]

During the late nineteenth century, many women's mission boards were formed in the United States. Traditional boards were still too dominated by male arrogance and power. Single women had not been acceptable as missionaries. So women started women's societies that supported single women. They became almost as numerous as the missionary wives of traditional boards.

In contrast to the well-paid male board members, most officers on the women's boards were unpaid volunteers. They expected female missionaries to serve sacrificially and live on much lower salaries. It cost much less to finance single women than the usual missionary families. Single women were more willing to live simply, closer to the lifestyles of those they served. They also made more personal contacts with women in U.S. churches than missionaries promoted by more official, centralized boards. Unfortunately, by 1930 most women's societies integrated with the general boards. The result was a rapid loss in the distinctive strengths of the women's societies.[13]

Currently, churches reflect the male domination of most cultures more than the male-and-female servanthood of Jesus' faith. The Roman Catholic church still refuses to ordain women, partly because they don't bear a natural resemblance to Christ. Yet resembling Jesus' male physical appearance has nothing to do with sharing Jesus' faith. Some Protestant churches use other reasons, including Eve's sin, to reject women's ordination. At stake is both male domination and clergy elitism. Even liberal Protestants who agree to ordain women are reluctant to hire them as senior pastors.

Jesus' faith would also not support feminist desires for power. He instead pursued servant leadership in humble settings. The real issue is not ordaining women (or men) into male power structures. It is inclusion of women into the servant mission of Jesus and Paul.

Throughout the world, home Bible studies and house churches are growing rapidly, and women are playing a key role. Especially in poor city neighborhoods, women are taking more active roles. They often receive little economic or emotional support from men. But they are mostly content to get by with a little help from their friends. House churches can provide such help.[14]

◆ ◆ ◆

In 16:8-15, Paul greets several other co-workers. The long list helps to link Paul with Roman churches he has never visited. In 16:12, Paul commends three women for their work "in the Lord." If there are house churches that have doubts about Paul and his mission, they can ask those named by Paul. From the lengthy list, it seems all roads do lead to Rome. Paul has met them elsewhere during his mission travels, but now they have found their way to Rome. Rome is the center and capital of the Mediterranean world. Paul's hope is that the Roman house churches will become the center of new mission outreach.

Paul finishes his greetings by asking them to greet one another with a holy kiss (16:16). He then adds that all the churches of Christ greet them. In the introduction of the letter, Paul states that the faith of the Romans is proclaimed in all the world (1:8). Now at the end, he writes that all those churches send greetings to them. The Roman churches stand out due to their past faithfulness and strategic location. By God's powerful grace, Paul's letter will help them proclaim Jesus' faith to the end of the world.

Romans 16:17-27

The Foundation and the Stumbling Blocks of World Mission

A s Paul travels around planting house churches, enemies of his mission will sneak in later to try to steal some of Paul's fruit. Those pests will plague the churches as long as their world mission continues to bear fruit. So Paul appeals to his readers to watch out for those who cause division and set up stumbling blocks (16:17). Earlier, in 14:13, Paul warns against Christians becoming stumbling blocks that trip other Christians, who then fall out of fellowship.

Paul's enemies especially use the law of Moses to draw converts away from Paul's teaching. The house churches have learned the true way of discipleship based on Jesus' teaching (16:17). But others stress a different foundation based on the written (Jewish) Scripture. Paul advises the Roman readers to avoid them.

The Old Testament is useful for teaching and training in righteousness (2 Tim. 3:16). Yet those Scriptures must now be interpreted by the faith that is in (union with) Christ Jesus (2 Tim. 3:15). Jesus and his faith are the foundation for God's final salvation and righteousness. Those who prefer the Old Testament to Jesus are stumbling blocks in the way of his world mission.

Weak Christians who emphasize certain Jewish customs are to be welcomed into the fellowship of those favoring the freedom of Jesus concerning such traditions (14:1, 14; 15:7). But non-Christians who try to persuade Christians to leave that fellowship and join them are not welcome (16:17).

Paul wrote Galatians earlier because of such unwelcome intruders (see Gal. 1:7; 3:1; 4:9-10; 5:1-4; 6:12-13). Then, just before writing Romans, Paul warned the Corinthians about such false apostles (see 2 Cor. 11:4-5, 12-13, 22). Even in previous parts of Romans, Paul exposes such misguided missionaries (see 2:17-24; 3:8, 13-18; 10:2).

Jewish opponents of Paul who follow him from city to city can even claim to be serving Christ (see 2 Cor. 11:13, 23). Yet their so-called gospel is not really the gospel of Christ (Gal. 1:6-9). The Jesus they preach is another Jesus, a different Jesus (2 Cor. 11:4). They are not serving Christ; they are serving their own stomachs (16:18).

Paul, like Isaiah 56:11 (see Ezek. 13:4), can describe certain Jewish leaders as dogs or wolves that have a large appetite (Phil. 3:2, 19; Acts 20:29). Instead of watching out for God's people (the sheep) like good shepherds, they only want to eat (the sheep) and sleep (see Ezek. 13:17, 19; 34:1-3, 7-10). Greed for personal gain and domination motivates their mission (see 2 Cor. 2:17; 11:20; Titus 1:11). Jesus' earlier conflict with various Jewish leaders led him to warn his disciples about false prophets. They wore sheep's clothing but were actually hungry wolves (Matt. 7:15; Luke 20:47). Those dogs were not to be welcomed into the holy fellowship of God's flock (Matt. 7:6). Paul warns that they will use kind words and flattery in order to deceive (16:18; see 2 Cor. 11:3, 13-15).

Paul quickly adds that he is sure his Roman readers know better. For their obedience is known by all the churches (16:19; see 1:8; 15:14; 16:16). They remain obedient to the type of teaching that is true to Jesus (6:17). So Paul is full of joy when he remembers them. However, he still wants to remind them of the importance of remaining wise about what is good and critical about what is evil (16:19; see 15:15).

Jesus sent his disciples out on mission as sheep among

wolves. He, therefore, said they should be wise as serpents and innocent as doves (Matt. 10:16). As that mission proceeds around the world, the same innocence and wisdom are needed. Otherwise, the sheep may turn into wolves.

Will the sheep always be dogged by such beasts? After describing the agony Jesus' sheep can expect, Paul adds a promise concerning God's future victory over such opposition. The God of peace will soon end that warfare (16:20). God's power will finally crush Satan under their feet. From the beginning, God promised that the ancient serpent would bite hard, but its head would finally be crushed (Gen. 3:14-15).

The faithful mission of Jesus and his disciples has walked all over Satan and his demons (Luke 10:17-20). Paul wrote that his Jewish opponents disguised themselves as angels of light, just like Satan (2 Cor. 11:14). Yet those angels of light could later reveal their dark purposes by persecuting those who shared the faith of Jesus (1 Thess. 2:14-16, 18).

Until the time of Satan's final defeat, Paul prays that the grace of their Lord Jesus be with them (16:20). As they face opposition to the teaching of Jesus, they can receive power from the risen Lord. Jesus has promised to remain with them until the very end (Matt. 28:20).

Christians still face persecution all over the world. In China, tens of thousands of house churches meet secretly because they are illegal. The only freedom of religion allowed is the limited freedom of state churches. All churches are required to register with the state. Those who meet in unregistered homes are sometimes imprisoned. Such persecution only attracts more people to the house churches. God is working in the midst of that opposition to bring about good (see 8:28).[1]

After Paul's warning about stumbling blocks, he returns to his list of greetings. Now he sends greetings from others with him as he writes. Timothy, one of Paul's closest co-workers, and several others greet the Roman readers (16:21). In 16:22, Tertius, who is penning Paul's words, sends his greetings. Then Gaius adds his greetings (16:23). Paul is staying with Gaius as he writes. Gaius's home has provided hospitality for others (probably in Corinth; see 1 Cor. 1:14), including perhaps traveling Christians who pass through Corinth.

Though Gaius has a house, he is not necessarily wealthy. Paul's words in 2 Corinthians 11:9 about not wanting to burden the Corinthians in any way could include Gaius. There might have been a burden on Gaius if Paul had not paid for food or rent. Unlike certain philosophers, Paul does not stay with urban elites who provide luxury and a large salary. By becoming a lowly manual laborer, Paul has chosen the least-favorite option among philosophers. Paul basically supports himself.[2]

Finally, Erastus, perhaps a more wealthy Christian since he is the city treasurer, and Quartus send greetings (16:23). Does Paul purposely include Erastus, who has some status, among the last? Remember that Paul first names Timothy, who teaches alongside Paul and will travel with Paul on the dangerous mission to Jerusalem. In God's upside-down kingdom, Jesus said the first would be last, and the last first (Matt. 19:30). Jesus promised greater rewards for those who left houses, family, and lands for his sake (Matt. 19:29). As for the rich, God enables a few to enter the kingdom (Matt. 19:24-26). God's powerful mercies upon them will produce generous acts of mercy on behalf of the needy (see 12:1, 8).

◆ ◆ ◆

In contrast, many churches prefer to be first—in the eyes of the world. In popular opinion, the most special Christians are the richest, smartest, and most powerful. They are the main donors, the chief officers, and the full-time ministers. Successful bankers, lawyers, and doctors lead church boards and manage prestigious organizations. Religious leaders have built monuments to themselves, structures where their influence and power might live on after they are gone. Yet their desire for immortality is an exercise in futility.[3]

On the other hand, some church leaders have chosen to be last in the eyes of the world. In the Philippines, three Catholic priests and six layworkers on the island of Negros were brought to trial for the murder of the mayor of Kabankalan. The court case of the Negros Nine was punishment for their work with peasant farmers. During the middle 1970s, two of these priests began organizing Basic Christian Communities. They were Brian Gore, an Australian missionary priest, and Niall O'Brien, an Irish missionary priest.

Earlier, Gore had served in the large Kabankalan Cathedral, dominated by rich hacienda owners. He eventually tired of what he called the numbers game: getting masses of people, especially children, into catechism classes and into the church. As Gore learned more about the unjust social order, he became critical of the oppressive leaders. Near the end of his time there, a municipal judge died and his family requested a funeral blessing and mass. After considering the judge's corrupt history of favoring the rich, Gore and the other priests denied the request. Only after pressure from the bishop did Gore preside at the funeral. But he still refused to say a mass. For too long, money had dominated the church. Especially the rich had received blessings through church rituals.

Similarly, Niall O'Brien spent his first several years serving on a hacienda near Kabankalan. He also decided that leading the cult (worship) of mass Christianity was not the best service priests could offer. Like Gore, he began a new mission in the neighboring mountains among the poorest of the poor. With the help of Filipino priests like Vicente Dangan (also one of the Negros Nine), O'Brien formed new Christian Communities. He reformed certain rituals and at baptism asked some pointed questions of parents or adult applicants: Do you reject land grabbing and usury? Will you stand up for your rights if oppressed? The age for confirmation was pushed back to age eighteen, and marriages were performed in groups on set days. No one could buy a large church wedding.

O'Brien also wrote a health manual to teach self-diagnosis and the use of herbal medicines. Most peasants could not afford costly doctors, hospitals, and imported medicines. The Christian Communities supported the training of forty paramedics. They promoted prevention more than cure, homes more than hospitals, herbs more than drugs. Gore's Christian Communities also helped farmers produce their own organic fertilizer by means of an earthworm ranch. The worm manure was much less expensive than chemical fertilizers that multinational corporations developed for the new "miracle" rice.

Both priests encouraged lay leadership. They did not allow any elite to lead since they would have dominated the communities. Religious power would then have been added to economic and political power. The priests tried to share power (though not always successfully) by being just one voice on the parish councils. In a culture marked by patrons and the patronized, by masters and workers, the priests stressed equality in Christ. Only by breaking out of the dominant social structures could real dialogue begin. They wanted all to participate. Injustice even among their own Christian Communities, like land grabbing or unfair interest, needed correcting. Only then would there be real reconciliation.

Their mission of justice and peace would also take sides with other poor and oppressed people. The Christian Communities formed nonviolent marches to protest land-grabbing, corrupt tax collectors, and abusive village officials. Sometimes they marched to other villages to join rallies against abusive military men who tortured and killed. They confronted the violence of the powerful, and paid for it dearly. Some were arrested numerous times. Others were tortured and killed. They were a threat to the evil power structures. So the Negros Nine landed in prison, charged with killing the abusive town mayor.

Actually, their imprisonment resulted from the mayor's family wanting revenge for their embarrassing marches. The highest military, political, and economic leaders in the Philippines wanted them silenced. The judge and the whole trial were manipulated by President Marcos, Roberto Benedicto (a Marcos crony given vast power over sugar production, the main crop of Negros), and Colonel Agudon (in command of the Negros Constabulary).

After almost two years of delays, bribed witnesses, and courtroom farce, the nine were released on a legal technicality. Marcos had seen enough and agreed to let them go, as long as Gore and O'Brien left the Philippines. They did go free and did leave the country. But the Christian Communities did not forget their sacrificial service. Those whom the world's lords considered last, God's servants honored as first.[4]

✦ ✦ ✦

Paul concludes his letter with a doxology of praise. He addresses it to the one who is able or powerful to make them strong (16:25). God's power is the highlight of Paul's gospel, just as it is of Jesus' good news. Paul, following Jesus, describes the new demonstration of God's power as a mystery that was formerly secret but is now being revealed (16:25; see Mark 4:11).

Paul's purpose in writing Romans is to manifest the marvelous mystery of God's power. Although hidden for many generations, the eternal God foretold its appearance through the prophetic writings (16:26). The good news of God's final kingly rule was promised through the prophets in the Scriptures (1:2). They wrote those promises for others who would later see God's power at work. Throughout Romans, Paul quotes Old Testament prophets as proof for his teaching and mission. The law and the prophets witness to the righteousness of God now manifested through the faith(fulness) of Jesus (3:21-22; 1:17).

The goal of God's revelation through the prophets, and Jesus, and Paul, is to spread the obedience of faith throughout the world (16:26; 1:5; 15:18). By writing Romans, Paul shares that goal with his readers. The churches' mission is to expand that obedience among all the peoples, both Jews and Gentiles (1:5). Jesus himself first preached and practiced such obedience to all peoples, to Gentiles (and Samaritans) as well as to Jews (16:25-26; see Matt. 4:12-17; 28:16-20; Mark 7:24—8:26; Luke 9:51-56; John 4:4-42).

Through the wise way of Jesus' faith, the only wise God has drawn near (16:27). To that God, the God of Jesus, be glory forever!

Notes

Abbreviations

Matt.   Matthew. Books of the Bible are abbreviated to their first letters.
NRSV   New Revised Standard Version
NT   New Testament
OT   Old Testament

Introduction

1. Gottlob Schrenk also emphasizes Paul's purpose to help Roman Christians share his world mission: "Der Römerbrief als Missionsdokument," in *Studien zu Paulus* (Zurich: Zwingli-Verlag, 1954), 82-87. Compare Lucien Legrand, *Unity and Plurality: Mission in the Bible,* trans. Robert Barr (Maryknoll: Orbis Books, 1990), 115-124.

2. F. F. Bruce, "The Romans Debate—Continued," *Bulletin of the John Rylands Library* 64 (1982): 358-359, says Paul wanted the Roman Christians—known for their faith and maturity (1:8; 15:14)—to associate with his vision for world mission. If one individual, namely Paul, ended up in prison or dead, a church could carry on. So his letter instructed, exhorted, and shared with them his own experiences, concerns, and hopes so his readers might see the vision and respond to it.

3. Stanley Kent Stowers, *The Diatribe and Paul's Letter to the Romans* (Chico, Calif.: Scholars Press, 1981), 76-78, 110-117, 148-153, 174-184, points out similarities between numerous passages in Romans and the use of diatribe in Greek philosophical schools.

4. David E. Aune, "Romans as a *Logos Protreptikos,"* in *The Romans Debate,* ed. Karl P. Donfried (Peabody, Mass.: Hendrickson Pubs., 1991), 278, 283, 290, 296, agrees with Stowers that the main setting of the diatribe style was the philosophical school, but argues that some Greek philosophers also used diatribe in mass propaganda. Thus diatribe could be used in situations like that of Acts 18:4 or 19:8, where Paul argues and pleads with opponents. The arguments in Romans were developed orally in such earlier mission dialogues. Daniel Fraikin, "The Rhetorical Function of the Jews in Romans," in *Anti-Judaism in Early Christianity,* vol. 1: *Paul and the Gospels,* eds. P. Richardson with D. Granskou (Waterloo: Wilfrid Laurier Univ. Press, 1986), 91-105, emphasizes that throughout Romans, Paul provides his Gentile-Christian readers with arguments making the gospel credible to Jews.

5. But note the statement of Paul Achtemeier, *Romans* (Atlanta: John Knox Press, 1985), 22, that the central theme is "the plan God is pursuing to extend his gracious lordship to all peoples by his act in Christ." He thus emphasizes God's lordship or power, especially in the historical action of Christ, and now being extended to all peoples.

6. Compare Robert Jewett, "Romans as an Ambassadorial Letter," *Interpretation* 36 (1982): 9-10, 15: "Paul presents himself in Romans as the ambassador of the *dynamis theou,* the 'power of God,' extending the sovereign's cosmic foreign policy through the preaching of the gospel." Earlier Jewett states that the purpose of Romans is "to advocate in behalf of the 'power of God' a cooperative mission to evangelize Spain so that

the theological argumentation reiterates the gospel to be therein proclaimed and the ethical admonitions show how that gospel is to be lived out in a manner that would ensure the success of this mission."

7. Michael Thompson, *Clothed with Christ: The Example and Teaching of Jesus in Romans 12:1—15:13* (Sheffield: JSOT Press, 1991), 37-76, 237-241. He suggests several criteria for deciding whether connections between Paul's writing and the teaching or example of Jesus are direct allusions to the Jesus tradition or merely echoes. In the many connections between Paul and Jesus which I will note, I have tried to mention only those of real consequence—in terms of related content and context—as opposed to minor links of simply words or phrases. Yet in pointing out various connections, I have not normally tried to decide whether Paul intended a direct allusion to Jesus or was simply (consciously or unconsciously) echoing Jesus' teaching or example. Yet even if one decided there were no allusions—only many echoes—the foundational importance of Jesus' faith would still be affirmed. See also David L. Dungan, *The Sayings of Jesus in the Churches of Paul* (Philadelphia: Fortress, 1971), 148-150. G. N. Stanton, *Jesus of Nazareth in New Testament Preaching* (Cambridge: Cambridge Univ. Press, 1974), continually emphasizes the strong interest in Jesus' life and character in the early church's missionary preaching, especially in Paul's letters and Acts. Likewise, James Stewart, *A Man in Christ* (New York: Harper and Brothers, n.d.), 273-293.

Romans 1:1-12: God's Power, God's Son, and World Mission

1. Paul emphasizes both the fulfillment of the promise about a descendant of David and the resurrection. These can be seen in 2 Tim. 2:8 and Acts 13:22-23, 30-37. Compare the transition from talk about Jesus as Messiah to Jesus' prediction of death and resurrection in Mark 8:29-31. In Mark 12:35-37, Jesus contrasted the expected Messiah (Son of David) with one whom David called Lord, who ruled with God (Ps. 110:1).

2. Paul also linked God's power and Jesus' resurrection in 1 Cor. 6:14; 2 Cor. 13:4; and Phil. 3:10.

3. The Greek word *ethnē* ordinarily means the Gentiles, all other peoples besides the Jews. Translations which use the word *nations* might confuse modern readers who would think of modern political nation-states. Paul's mission focused on all the world's peoples, not on national political structures. Later ideas about a mission of nation building, national liberation, or national transformation were and are a return to the church's domination of society. Both the early twentieth-century social gospel and the later twentieth-century liberation theology have emphasized the historical Jesus and the kingdom of God as the basis for their transformation of society. They have correctly exposed and denounced structural evils in different nations. But they have also often approved coercion, manipulation, and power politics to achieve their social goals. Thus they might be further examples of imperial mission, in contrast to a servant mission of small groups of weak and poor disciples.

4. J. Andrew Kirk, "Apostleship Since Rengstorf: Towards a Synthesis," *New Testament Studies* 21 (Jan. 1975): 249-264. Also, Rudolf Schnackenburg, "Apostles Before and During Paul's Time," in *Apostolic History and the Gospel*, eds. W. Ward Gasque and Ralph Martin (Grand Rapids: Eerdmans, 1970), 287-303. A few times Paul refers to certain church delegates sent to care for the physical needs of other Christians as "apostles" (in the Greek: 2 Cor. 8:23; Phil. 2:25). Martin Luther, *Lectures on Romans* (St. Louis: Concordia, 1972), 5, wrote that the phrase "we have received" in 1:5 refers to all believers because all ministry is for the benefit of all.

5. When *ethnē* (see note 3) is used with the word *all*, it could mean "all the peoples—both Jews and Gentiles." In Luke 24:47 Jesus says that preaching to all peoples is to begin in Jerusalem among Jews. Similar is Matt. 24:9, 14; 25:32; 28:19. John P. Meier, "Nations or Gentiles in Matthew 28:19?" *Catholic Biblical Quarterly* 39 (Jan. 1977): 101-102, concludes that Matt. 24:9, 14 and 25:32 clearly refer to Jews as well as Gentiles. Thus the only other use of "all nations"—or better, "all peoples"—in Matthew (28:19) should also include Jews (and Gentiles). In Romans, Paul often shows his concern for

non-Christian Jews. In 4:16-17, Paul describes Abraham as the father of all believers, of many peoples—both Jews and Gentiles. Elsewhere in Romans, Paul uses "all/everyone" to mean both "Jew(s) and Gentile(s)" (1:16; 2:9-10; 3:9; 10:12).

6. On Paul's ministry to Jews, compare 11:13 and Gal. 2:7, 9 with Acts 9:15, 20-22, 26-29; 13:5, 14, 46-48; 14:1; 17:1-2; 18:4, 19; 21:15, 17; 28:17; Chalmer E. Faw, *Acts*, Believers Church Bible Commentary (Scottdale, Pa.: Herald Press, 1993), 112.

7. José Gallardo, "Ethics and Mission," in *Anabaptism and Mission*, ed. Wilbert R. Shenk (Scottdale: Herald Press, 1984), 140-147.

8. John Howard Yoder, *The Fullness of Christ: Paul's Revolutionary Vision of Universal Ministry* (Elgin, Ill.: Brethren Press, 1987).

9. Robert Jewett, *Paul's Anthropological Terms: A Study of Their Use in Conflict Settings* (Leiden: E. J. Brill, 1971), 197-198.

10. Essays of J. Norberto Saracco, "Search for New Models of Theological Education," 25-35; and Jorge E. Maldonado, "Theological Education by Extension," 37-49, in *New Alternatives in Theological Education*, ed. C. René Padilla (Oxford: Regnum Books, 1988). F. Ross Kinsler, "Theological Education by Extension: Service or Subversion?" *Missiology: An International Review* 6 (Apr. 1978): 181-196, tells how TEE might be used to subvert or transform the traditional structures of academic theological education, ordination, ministry, salaries, and professional status.

11. J. Andrew Kirk, *Theology and the Third World Church* (Downers Grove, Ill.: Inter-Varsity Press, 1983), 44-47.

12. Giorgio Tourn, *The Waldensians: The First 800 Years (1174-1974)*, trans. Camillo Merlino (Torino, Italy: Claudiana Editrice, 1980), 3-67.

13. Wolfgang Schäufele, "The Missionary Vision and Activity of the Anabaptist Laity," in *Anabaptism and Mission*, 70-87.

14. For a good study of how later Anabaptists often sold their birthright for a mess of Protestant traditions, see Theron F. Schlabach, *Gospel Versus Gospel: Mission and the Mennonite Church, 1863-1944* (Scottdale: Herald Press, 1980).

15. Roger Finke and Rodney Stark, *The Churching of America, 1776-1990: Winners and Losers in Our Religious Economy* (New Brunswick, N.J.: Rutgers Univ. Press, 1992), 56-86; Robert Wuthnow, *The Restructuring of American Religion: Society and Faith Since World War II* (Princeton: Princeton Univ. Press, 1988), 21-23; Nathan Hatch, *The Democratization of American Christianity* (New Haven: Yale Univ. Press, 1989), 174-179.

16. Viv Grigg, *Companion to the Poor* (Monrovia, Calif.: MARC, 1990).

17. Del Birkey, *The House Church: A Model for Renewing the Church* (Scottdale: Herald Press, 1988), 71-76. For a good introduction to basic Christian communities and similar evangelical groups in Latin America, see Guillermo Cook, *The Expectation of the Poor: Latin American Base Ecclesial Communities in Protestant Perspective* (Maryknoll: Orbis Books, 1985). Paul G. Hiebert, "Popular Religions," in *Toward the Twenty-first Century in Christian Mission*, eds. James M. Phillips and Robert T. Coote (Grand Rapids: Eerdmans, 1993), 261-264, writes sympathetically about such new church structures. After connecting these present "folk churches" to earlier examples in church history—including NT churches—he concludes that these new forms might be what much of the twenty-first century church will look like. Since more and more of those future churches will be in the third world among the poor and persecuted, some will have to survive underground, and most will have to do without much money or institutional structures. Cecília Mariz, "Religion and Poverty in Brazil: A Comparison of Catholic and Pentecostal Communities," in *New Face of the Church in Latin America: Between Tradition and Change*, ed. Guillermo Cook (Maryknoll: Orbis Books, 1994), 75-81, points out many similarities in the actual experiences of Brazilian Basic Christian Communities and Pentecostal churches, despite large theoretical differences.

18. David Barrett, *Schism and Renewal in Africa* (London: Oxford Univ. Press, 1968), 162-173.

Romans 1:13-18: God's Saving Power Among All the Peoples

1. David J. Bosch, *Transforming Mission: Paradigm Shifts in Theology of Mission* (Maryknoll: Orbis Books, 1991), 356-358; John V. Taylor, *Enough Is Enough: A Biblical Call for Moderation in a Consumer-Oriented Society* (Minneapolis: Augsburg, 1977), 1-21.

2. Rom. 2:2 has a very similar Greek grammatical structure: the judgment of God is according to truth upon those doing such things (see also the Greek grammar of 1 Cor. 14:22). For similar content and structure outside Paul's letters, see 1 Pet. 1:5 or Ezra 8:22: "The hand (power) of our God is unto good upon all who are seeking him." Also, compare Ps. 118:14: "The Lord is my strength . . . he has become my salvation." C. E. B. Cranfield, *A Critical and Exegetical Commentary on the Epistle to the Romans*, 2 vols. (Edinburgh: T. & T. Clark, 1975-79), 1:88, notes the close parallel of 1:16 to a statement about the Greek god Asklepios: the saving power of god has gone out to every place.

3. That was a different emphasis than 1 Cor. 1:18, which contrasts the foolishness of the word of the cross (to those perishing) with the power of that word (to those being saved). Paul's gospel in 1 Cor. 1 emphasizes the power of the cross, or the word of the cross. Paul does not preach the gospel with words of human wisdom so the cross of Christ will not lose its power (1 Cor. 1:17). He proclaims Christ crucified because God's "foolishness" is wiser than human "wisdom" and God's "weakness" is stronger than human "strength." Corinthian groups, divided over "strong" leaders, needed to reunite under God's power in Christ crucified. But in Rom. 1, the emphasis of Paul's gospel is the power of God in raising Jesus and enabling a world mission that results in the obedience of faith (1:4-5). God's resurrection power is now the key element, not the word of the cross.

4. The last part of 1 Thess. 2:13 refers to the word of God which is working in those who believe. Leon Morris, *The First and Second Epistles to the Thessalonians* (Grand Rapids: Eerdmans, 1959), 88, points out that the Greek verb translated as "working" is almost always used in the NT for supernatural activity. The power of God is at work as they continue to believe. Thus it is God—not some magical power in the word itself—that is at work. A. C. Thiselton, "Language and Meaning in Religion," in *The New International Dictionary of New Testament Theology*, vol. 3, ed. Colin Brown (Grand Rapids: Regency Reference Library, 1978), 1125, criticizes those who emphasize the power of words by means of a dynamic view of language in the Bible. He says they use passages, especially in the OT, that speak about the power of words spoken by God. Such passages should not lead to conclusions about the nature of language; the words of God have power precisely because they are spoken by almighty God. There are also many passages in the Bible which stress the weakness of words (for example, that words are no substitute for action). Paul likes to contrast mere words or talk with the power of God at work in the words and lives of a transformed people (besides 1 Thess. 2:13, see 1 Thess. 1:5; 1 Cor. 2:4; 4:19-20).

5. Stanley Kent Stowers, "Social Status, Public Speaking and Private Teaching: The Circumstances of Paul's Preaching Activity," *Novum Testamentum* 26 (1984): 59-82.

6. Lesslie Newbigin, *The Household of God* (London: SCM Press, 1957), 50-59.

7. David Stoll, *Is Latin America Turning Protestant? The Politics of Evangelical Growth* (Berkeley: Univ. of California Press, 1990), 49-50, 59-60.

8. The Greek pronoun *autō* in 1:17 can be literally translated as either "in it" or "in him." Ulrich Wilckens, *Der Brief an die Römer*, vol. 1 (Zurich: Benziger Verlag, 1987), 86, n. 110, refers to Glombitza, Scham 79, who rejected the usual translation "in it" in 1:17, referring back to the gospel of 1:16. Instead, Glombitza connected the phrase in 1:17 with "for everyone who believes" in 1:16, which would lead to a translation of 1:17 such as "in him" or "in the believing one." Wilckens suggests that if Paul wanted to refer to a revelation in the believer, he would have begun 1:17 with a relative pronoun: "in whom is being revealed" (the righteousness of God). But if my translation of 1:16 is correct, Paul is keeping the parallelism with the power of God in 1:16 and the wrath of God in 1:18 by beginning with the righteousness of God in 1:17. In Greek, emphasized words come at the beginning of a phrase or sentence. Karl H. Schelkle, *Paulus: Lehrer der Väter*

(Düsseldorf: Patmos-Verlag, 1956), 44, lists three church fathers (Akazius, Photius, and Ambrosiaster) who understood 1:17 as "in the justified one" instead of "in the gospel."

Regarding the long debate over whether the righteousness of God refers to an attribute, activity, or gift of God, my translation would favor an attribute of God—which in 1:17 is described as being given to the believing one as part of God's saving activity (see 1:16). God is thus the standard and source of righteousness. While appreciating the connection of God's righteousness and God's power by Ernst Käsemann, *New Testament Questions of Today* (Philadelphia: Fortress Press, 1969), 168-182, I think 1:16-17 connects God's righteousness more with *salvation*—both of which result from God's power at work in the believing one(s).

9. The OT connected God's saving power above all with the deliverance from Egypt (Exod. 15:6; 32:11; Josh. 4:23-24). Thus Psalm 77:14-15 celebrates the display of God's might among the peoples when God's own people are redeemed by his strong arm. To believe in God means to trust God's saving power (Ps. 78:22) as manifested in the exodus (Ps. 78:11-16, 23-26). Yet the OT also pointed to the broader scope of God's power at work among all the peoples. For example, Psalm 67:2 asks that God's way (righteousness) and saving power be known among all the peoples of the earth.

Jesus' good news about God's coming in power especially fulfilled and reflected the emphasis of Isa. 40–66. Isa. 40:9-11 describes the good news about the Lord's coming with strength and ruling with his arm (power), gathering the lost flock. Those who wait for their powerful Lord will renew their strength so that they can walk and run without weariness as God gathers them (Isa. 40:31).

Because Israel is God's chosen servant, God will strengthen her with his righteous right hand (Isa. 41:9-10). Above all, Jesus is the chosen servant who, empowered by God's Spirit, brought forth righteousness to the peoples (compare Isa. 42:1-4 and Matt. 12:18-20). The almighty Creator of heaven and earth will call and enable the servant to be a light to blind peoples in darkness (Isa. 42:5-7). There is no other Savior able to deliver (Isa. 43:11-13). The mighty works shown in redeeming Israel from Egypt will be exceeded as God now does a new thing (Isa. 43:14-21). The Lord will pour out his Spirit and create a new people who will witness to their Lord and King (Isa. 44:2-8).

The Lord will strengthen his servant, not only to gather Israel, but also to be a light to the other peoples so that God's salvation will reach to the end of the earth (Isa. 49:5-6). When the arm of the Lord becomes strong, the ransomed of the Lord will return with joy to Zion (Isa. 51:9, 11). The arm of the Lord is not too short, as though unable to save (Isa. 59:1). Despite the weakness of human flesh, God's own arm will bring salvation (Isa. 59:16; 63:5). The ultimate victory of God's power will be the creation of new heavens and a new earth, which is to remain forever (Isa. 65:17; 66:22).

10. Eph. 1:19 uses four similar Greek words to magnify God's power. Faith (believing) is the means of receiving that strength (see also Eph. 3:16-17). Markus Barth, *Ephesians: Introduction, Translation, and Commentary on Chapters 1-3* (Garden City, N.Y.: Doubleday, 1974), 152, gives the following literal translation of those words in Eph. 1:19: "what is the exceeding greatness of his power . . . in accordance with the energy of the force of his strength." Similarly in Col. 1:11, Paul prays that the readers will be empowered (by God) with all power according to God's glorious might.

11. Especially John's Gospel connects believing and receiving. To believe in (literally: into) Jesus' name means to receive him and his power, which produces children of God (John 1:12). Whoever believes into Jesus or receives Jesus will also receive eternal life, the life of the new age (John 3:15-16, 36). On the other hand, those who don't receive him cannot believe because they receive glory from one another instead of from God (John 5:43-44).

12. Those who with me interpret 1:17 as out of the faith of Jesus unto the faith of others include Markus Barth, "The Faith of the Messiah," *The Heythrop Journal* 10 (1969): 369; Luke Timothy Johnson, *The Writings of the New Testament: An Interpretation* (Philadelphia: Fortress Press, 1986), 319; Morna D. Hooker, "Pistis Christou," *New Testament Studies* 35 (July 1989): 339-340; Glenn N. Davies, *Faith and Obedience in Romans: A Study*

in Romans 1–4 (Sheffield: JSOT Press, 1990), 112; and Douglas A. Campbell, *The Rhetoric of Righteousness in Romans 3.21-26* (Sheffield: JSOT Press, 1992), 67-68, 204-213.

13. For a good discussion of Paul's phrase "in Christ," see Morna D. Hooker, *A Preface to Paul* (New York: Oxford Univ. Press, 1980), 77-95.

14. Dennis Hamm, "Faith in the Epistle to the Hebrews: The Jesus Factor," *Catholic Biblical Quarterly* 52 (Apr. 1990): 280-291, discusses the faith of Jesus portrayed in Hebrews, and the relationship between Jesus' faith and the faith of Christians. The conclusion of the well-done study on mission in the NT in Donald Senior and Carroll Stuhlmueller, *The Biblical Foundations for Mission* (Maryknoll: Orbis Books, 1983), 322, states that the authors have repeatedly shown how Jesus' own mission—empowered by his experience of God as sovereignly powerful and graciously saving—was a fundamental cause of the church's later mission.

15. James D. G. Dunn, *Jesus and the Spirit* (Philadelphia: Westminster, 1975), 105-112.

16. For the classic description of cheap grace, see Dietrich Bonhoeffer, *The Cost of Discipleship* (New York: The Macmillan Co., 1959), 45-60.

Romans 1:19-32: God's Creative Power, an Ungodly World, and God's Wrath

1. For similar views of a Great Spirit Creator among various religions, see Don Richardson, *Eternity in Their Hearts* (Ventura, Calif.: Regal, 1981).

2. Samuel G. Kibicho, "The Continuity of the African Conception of God into and Through Christianity: A Kikuyu Case-Study," in *Christianity in Independent Africa*, eds. Edward Fasholé-Luke, Richard Gray, Adrian Hastings, and Godwin Tasie (Bloomington: Indiana Univ. Press, 1978), 370-388.

3. Eugene A. Nida, *Message and Mission: The Communication of the Christian Faith* (Pasadena, Calif.: William Carey Library, 1990), 67.

4. Stephen C. Knapp, "Mission and Modernization: A Preliminary Critical Analysis of Contemporary Understandings of Mission from a 'Radical Evangelical' Perspective," in *American Missions in Bicentennial Perspective*, ed. R. Pierce Beaver (Pasadena, Calif.: William Carey Library, 1977), 146-209; J. Stanley Glen, *Justification by Success: The Invisible Captivity of the Church* (Atlanta: John Knox Press, 1979).

5. David F. Wells, *No Place for Truth, or Whatever Happened to Evangelical Theology?* (Grand Rapids: Eerdmans, 1993), 68-92, 171-177.

6. Leon Morris, *The Epistle to the Romans* (Grand Rapids: Eerdmans, 1988), 93.

7. J. N. D. Kelly, *A Commentary on the Epistles of Peter and of Jude* (New York: Harper & Row, 1969), 261.

8. See David J. Atkinson, *Homosexuals in the Christian Fellowship* (Grand Rapids: Eerdmans, 1981), for a good critique of writers who favor Christian homosexual activity to some extent, a treatment of relevant biblical passages, and a call for friendship and ministry among Christians with homosexual inclinations. He also describes various causes of homosexual orientation. Ed Hurst (with Dave and Neta Jackson), *Overcoming Homosexuality* (Elgin, Ill.: David C. Cook, 1987), discusses roots of homosexuality, gives case studies, and offers practical guides for those who want to help homosexuals. Hurst has struggled with and overcome homosexual activity and lust.

Romans 2:1-16: God's Judgment of the World

1. E. P. Sanders has argued against Christians who view first-century Jews as being legalistic, self-righteous, and saved by works. But while many Jews were aware of their sin and appreciated God's mercy and grace, they also usually looked down on lawless Gentiles. Sanders, in *Paul, the Law, and the Jewish People* (Philadelphia: Fortress Press, 1983), 123-135, discusses Rom. 2 only in an appendix because he believes it is based on a Jewish sermon encouraging Jews to be better Jews and says nothing specifically Christian. Thus Sanders tries to escape Paul's Jewish-Christian criticism of self-righteous pride among Jews.

2. Most translators and interpreters of 2:14-15 think Paul describes those Gentiles

who naturally follow their conscience. But the reference to "by nature" is better connected with their not having the Jewish law. Thus the law in their hearts is not their natural conscience but the new covenant. Cranfield, 1:156-159.

3. Penny Lernoux, *People of God: The Struggle for World Catholicism* (New York: Viking Penguin, 1989), 41, 47-49, 67.

4. Orlando E. Costas, *Christ Outside the Gate: Mission Beyond Christendom* (Maryknoll: Orbis Books, 1982), 126-132. Also, Stoll, 310-314.

5. Bosch, *Transforming Mission*, 228.

6. Søren Kierkegaard, *Attack upon "Christendom,"* trans. Walter Lowrie (Princeton: Princeton Univ. Press, 1968). The Dane knew something was rotten in Denmark.

7. For a good discussion of the problem of wealthy missions, see Jonathan J. Bonk, *Missions and Money: Affluence as a Western Missionary Problem* (Maryknoll: Orbis Books, 1991). Bonk, 143, notes that most Western mission agencies have depended heavily on certain rich individuals.

An earlier missiologist, Roland Allen, was a voice crying in the wilderness against such traditions of Christendom: professionally trained, salaried, full-time ministers and missionaries instead of voluntary clergy and lay ministry selected and trained in local congregations while earning their own living; Western worship rituals and buildings instead of local worship in homes; Western schools and hospitals instead of local evangelism by churches. The Western Christendom model guaranteed dependence on the West to pay for educational and medical work and full-time pastors. Thus missionaries connected with the traditions and wealth of the West found it next to impossible to give up their mission leadership to local leaders. Charles H. Long and Anne Rowthorn, "The Legacy of Roland Allen," *International Bulletin of Missionary Research* 13 (Apr. 1989), 67.

An even earlier missiologist, Rufus Anderson, constantly used his leadership position with the American Board of Commissioners for Foreign Missions to argue against trying to civilize other nations as a preparation for Christianizing them. He found a sympathetic ear in Francis Wayland, a director of Baptist missions, who wrote that Jesus did not want an apostolic ministry that first civilized the heathen and then Christianized them. Jesus' gospel did not command his followers to teach schools in order to build up Christianity. During Anderson's leadership, many mission workers like farmers, mechanics, and teachers returned to the U.S. Especially in Hawaii (at that time called the Sandwich Islands), where missionaries had come to dominate the society and were praised for their success, Anderson called for native leadership since the Hawaiians had not so much been Christianized as missionized. William R. Hutchison, *Errand to the World: American Protestant Thought and Foreign Missions* (Chicago: Univ. of Chicago Press, 1987), 84-88.

8. James A. Scherer, *Missionary, Go Home! A Reappraisal of the Christian World Mission* (Englewood Cliffs, N.J.: Prentice-Hall, 1964), 158, 175-176, 184-185. A. E. Afigbo, "The Missions, the State and Education in South-Eastern Nigeria, 1956-71," in *Christianity in Independent Africa*, 176-192, notes that when the Nigerian government took over the mission schools in 1971, no section of Nigerian society defended the missionary leaders. Even former employees of the missions preferred the government's leadership, from whom they expected (and got) better working conditions. The missionaries had developed a reputation for hierarchical domination, selfishness, double-dealing, and corruption. Such problems led the All-African Conference of Churches Assembly in 1974 to call for a moratorium on funds and personnel from outside Africa. Western missionaries and churches reacted emotionally to the call—another demonstration of their need to be in control (as supposedly benevolent dictators).

9. Senior and Stuhlmueller, 24-25, 79.

Romans 2:17-29: Lawless Teachers of the Jewish Law

1. Jesus' criticism of the temple used the prophetic challenge of Jer. 7:11. In Jer. 7:8-9, the prophet also criticized other Jews for trusting in their words, while at the same time they stole, murdered, committed adultery, etc. Compare Isa. 56:7, 10-11.

2. F. F. Bruce, *The Epistle of Paul to the Romans* (Grand Rapids: Eerdmans, 1963), 93.

3. Matthew Black, *Romans* (Grand Rapids: Eerdmans, 1973), 60.

4. See Ronald F. Hock, *The Social Context of Paul's Ministry: Tentmaking and Apostleship* (Philadelphia: Fortress Press, 1980), for the significance of Paul's labor as a leatherworker (which included making tents) in relation to his mission.

5. David B. Barrett, "Annual Statistical Table on Global Mission: 1989," *International Bulletin of Missionary Research* 13 (Jan. 1989), 20-21. However, I wonder how Barrett calculated those amounts.

6. Kibicho, 374.

7. Barrett, *Schism and Renewal*, 124-125.

8. A. J. Temu, *British Protestant Missions* (London: Longman Group, 1972), 91-114.

9. Bonk, *Missions and Money*, 53.

10. Costas, *Christ Outside the Gate*, 59-60.

11. Stephen Charles Mott, *Biblical Ethics and Social Change* (New York: Oxford Univ. Press, 1982), 16.

12. Nicholas Wolterstorff, *Until Justice and Peace Embrace* (Grand Rapids: Eerdmans, 1983), 44, 74-75, 86-95. Also, Adam Daniel Finnerty, *No More Plastic Jesus: Global Justice and Christian Lifestyle* (Maryknoll: Orbis Books, 1977), 46-70.

13. Dorothy Friesen, *Critical Choices: A Journey with the Filipino People* (Grand Rapids: Eerdmans, 1988), 49-62.

14. E. Thomas Brewster and Elizabeth Brewster, *Bonding and the Missionary Task* (Pasadena, Calif.: Lingua House, 1982). Also, E. Thomas Brewster and Elizabeth Brewster, "Language Learning Midwifery," *Missiology: An International Review* 8 (Apr. 1980), 203-209, where they compare natural childbirth and the natural art of language learning—in contrast to being a hospital patient or language school student. The normal way of acquiring a language is in a supportive context of relationships. Such learning would help missionaries to bond with the new community.

15. Geoffrey Moorhouse, *The Missionaries* (London: Eyre Methuen, 1973), 325.

16. Penny Lernoux, *Cry of the People: The Struggle for Human Rights in Latin America—The Catholic Church in Conflict with U.S. Policy* (New York: Penguin Books, 1982), 10-11, 24.

17. Stoll, 85-87. See David Martin, *Tongues of Fire: The Explosion of Protestantism in Latin America* (Oxford: Basil Blackwell, 1990), 212-214, for related but not identical developments among other tribes in Chiapas due to the mission of Wycliffe Bible Translators.

18. While Paul thought especially of Gentile Christians, the same would be true for certain Gentiles before the time of Jesus. Jesus praised the Gentile people of Nineveh who repented, and the queen of the south who came to hear Solomon. He said they would condemn the evil generation of Jews who rejected him (Matt. 12:39-42).

19. Paul's contrast between detesting idols and robbing temples (2:22) was related to Jesus' contrast between what was detestable (idolatrous) in God's sight and the money and honor highly valued and served by the Pharisees (Luke 16:13-15). For a good analysis of Luke's contrast of Jesus and the Pharisees concerning money, see Halvor Moxnes, *The Economy of the Kingdom: Social Conflict and Economic Relations in Luke's Gospel* (Philadelphia: Fortress Press, 1988). Moxnes, 8, 147, notes that accusations against opponents as being "moneylovers" and as seeking praise from people were often used in Jewish and Greek polemics, especially against philosophical and religious teachers. Contrast Paul's self-description in Acts 20:33-35.

Romans 3:1-20: Jewish Faithlessness and God's Words of Judgment

1. The two questions asked in 3:1 are basically the same: What then is the advantage of the Jew? What is the gain of the circumcised? Note 2:26-27, where "their uncircumcision" means the uncircumcised Gentile who keeps or fulfills the righteous requirements of the law. For "the circumcision" (in Greek) used in a context meaning the circumcised (Jew), see 3:30; 4:9, 12; 15:8.

2. Sara Diamond, *Spiritual Warfare: The Politics of the Christian Right* (Boston: South End Press, 1989), 116; David Martin, 143-147.

3. Diamond, 16-17.

4. Lernoux, *People of God*, 365-405; Stoll, 218-265.

5. William R. Cannon, *History of Christianity in the Middle Ages* (New York: Abingdon Press, 1960), 222, 306-307; J. C. Wenger, "The Inerrancy Controversy Within Evangelicalism," in *Evangelicalism and Anabaptism*, ed. C. Norman Kraus (Scottdale: Herald Press, 1979), 107-108.

6. Leonard Verduin, *The Reformers and Their Stepchildren* (Grand Rapids: Eerdmans, 1964), 31-58.

7. J. Lawrence Burkholder, "Popular Evangelicalism: An Appraisal," in *Evangelicalism and Anabaptism*, 29-35.

8. Frederick Douglass, "Slaveholding Religion and the Christianity of Christ," in *Afro-American Religious History: A Documentary Witness*, ed. Milton C. Sernett (Durham: Duke Univ. Press, 1985), 104-106.

9. John F. Alexander, *Your Money or Your Life: A New Look at Jesus' View of Wealth and Power* (San Francisco: Harper & Row, 1986), 3-15.

Romans 3:21-31: God's Righteous Power, Jesus' Faith, and World Mission

1. The Greek genitive construction was most often used as a possessive (called a subjective genitive) though sometimes used in other ways. Paul's use of the word *faith* followed by a proper noun or pronoun (other than a reference to Jesus or Christ) in the genitive case is always a subjective genitive. Paul often refers to the faith of his readers ("your faith") and a few times to the faith of Abraham (see 4:16)—and even to the faith(fulness) of God (3:3). Thus when Paul writes about faith and Jesus, using the genitive case for Jesus, or Christ, or his, the genitive is probably subjective. Verses like Eph. 1:15, Col. 1:4, and 1 Tim. 1:14, which speak of faith in Christ, do not use the genitive case. See Richard B. Hays, *The Faith of Jesus Christ* (Chico, Calif.: Scholars Press, 1983), 163-164. Ancient Greek (including Hellenistic Jewish) literature up to the time of Paul consistently uses the subjective genitive with the word *faith*. Though most interpreters assume an objective genitive in 3:22 (faith in Jesus), the burden of proof lies on them to show why it shouldn't follow the usual subjective genitive construction. See Leander E. Keck, " 'Jesus' in Romans," *Journal of Biblical Literature* 108 (Fall 1989), 453.

2. Among those who now interpret 3:22, 26 in terms of Jesus' faith are the following: Richard Longenecker, *Paul: Apostle of Liberty* (New York: Harper & Row, 1964), 149-150; Barth, "The Faith of the Messiah," 367-370; Sam K. Williams, "The 'Righteousness of God' in Romans," *Journal of Biblical Literature* 99 (June 1980), 274-278; Luke Timothy Johnson, "Rom. 3:21-26 and the Faith of Jesus," *Catholic Biblical Quarterly* 44 (1982), 78-81; Hays, 170-174; Brendan Byrne, *Reckoning with Romans: A Contemporary Reading of Paul's Gospel* (Wilmington, Del.: Michael Glazier, 1986), 79-80, 84, 86; John Driver, *Understanding the Atonement for the Mission of the Church* (Scottdale: Herald Press, 1986), 127, 200; Keck, 453, 456-457; Charles B. Cousar, *A Theology of the Cross: The Death of Jesus in the Pauline Letters* (Minneapolis: Fortress Press, 1990), 39-40, 58-61; Glenn Davies, 106-112; Campbell, 58-64.

3. Alister E. McGrath, *Iustitia Dei: A History of the Christian Doctrine of Justification*, 2 vols. (Cambridge: Cambridge Univ. Press, 1986), 1:29-33. Schelkle, 432, concludes that most of the early Greek and Latin fathers understood justification as both juridicial (reckoned as righteous) and as making righteous. John Reumann, *"Righteousness" in the New Testament* (Philadelphia: Fortress Press, 1982), 208, agrees that the early Greek-speaking church fathers understood Paul's use of the Greek forms of *dikaioun* as "make righteous."

4. McGrath, 1:41, 46-49, 79-81, 90-94.

5. McGrath, 1:154, 182-186; also, 2:2-18. Reumann, 123, does point out that the Lutheran Augsburg Confession (1530) defines justification/righteousness in a broader sense—beyond the narrower definition of a preliminary juristic status, as found in the

Formula of Concord (1577). Thus Lutherans do have differing views on justification. But most Lutherans and most Protestants do not identify justification with regeneration or God's making righteous.

6. McGrath, 2:37-38, 51-52, 99-101. More recent scholars who interpret justification as making righteous include Wolfgang Trilling, *A Conversation with Paul* (London: SCM Press, 1986), 27, 75-76; Driver, 184-204; and Campbell, 170-176.

7. Orlando E. Costas, *The Integrity of Mission: The Inner Life and Outreach of the Church* (San Francisco: Harper & Row, 1979), 11-12, 17-19. Also, Costas, *Christ Outside the Gate*, 14,92-98.

8. Campbell, 64-65, argues from syntax that the two phrases after the word *atonement* in 3:25 are best translated "through the faithfulness in his death," that is, through the faithfulness of Jesus' death. Bruce W. Longenecker, "*Pistis* in Romans 3:25: Neglected Evidence for the 'Faithfulness of Christ'?" *New Testament Studies* 39 (1993): 478-480, argues that since the words surrounding *pistis* (faith) in 3:25 refer to Christ's death, so should *pistis*. See Johnson, "Rom 3:21-26," 79-80.

9. For a discussion of Jesus' faithfulness, God's saving righteousness, and justification as new creation in 3:24-26, see Campbell, 65-67, 158-176.

10. Robert Banks, *Jesus and the Law in the Synoptic Tradition* (Cambridge: Cambridge Univ. Press, 1975), 210, 217-223, 234, 242.

Romans 4:1-12: Father Abraham and Worldwide Faith

1. Temu, 117-128.

2. Franklin H. Littell, "The Anabaptist Theology of Mission," in *Anabaptism and Mission*, 15-18; Cornelius J. Dyck, "The Anabaptist Understanding of the Good News," in *Anabaptism and Mission*, 26-33.

3. Stoll, 118-119.

4. Ruth Tucker, *From Jerusalem to Irian Jaya: A Biographical History of Christian Missions* (Grand Rapids: Zondervan, 1983), 462-467.

5. Stoll, 120-121.

6. Costas, *The Integrity of Mission*, 1-47; also, Costas, *Christ Outside the Gate*, xii-xiv, 91-94.

7. Costas, *Christ Outside the Gate*, 48-54.

8. Stoll, 90-92, 162-163.

Romans 4:13-25: Abraham's Faith and Fatherhood

1. The Greek construction of 4:16 (to the one out of the faith of Abraham) is the same as that of 3:26 (the one out of the faith of Jesus). Both the faith of Abraham and the faith of Jesus are foundational for fulfilling God's promises.

2. The focus on God's power to keep the promise to Abraham is reflected in the Genesis account by the use of the Hebrew words *El Shaddai* (God Almighty) as a name for God (Gen. 17:1; 28:3-4; 35:11-12; 48:3-4; Exod. 6:3-4, 8).

3. Walter Künneth, *The Theology of the Resurrection* (St. Louis: Concordia, 1965), 158-159, asserts that if we see only a forensic judgment in justification, we have not taken seriously the presence of salvation created by the resurrection. God's act of raising Jesus means both declaring just and making just. The risen Jesus is both the forgiver and the renewer. Everything depends on basing justification on a theology of the resurrection. After a thorough study of Paul's resurrection theology, Pheme Perkins, *Resurrection: New Testament Witness and Contemporary Reflection* (Garden City, N.Y.: Doubleday, 1984), 316, 319, concludes that often in Paul's letters, the life-giving power of God shown in Jesus' resurrection is the basis for the salvation experienced by believers. God's resurrection power reorients behavior from a pre-Christian life of sin to a new life of righteousness with the risen Lord.

4. J. Christiaan Beker, *Paul the Apostle: The Triumph of God in Life and Thought* (Philadelphia: Fortress Press, 1980), emphasizes the future apocalyptic power of God in redeeming the whole created order. While he discusses the inauguration of God's tri-

umph in Jesus, he interprets Paul's thought as centering on the imminent cosmic triumph of God. Paul is an apocalyptic theologian with a theocentric outlook. For Beker, 98, Abraham's faith in God's promise (supposedly the main point in 4:20-25) is an example for all Christians and characterizes both the OT and the Christian hope.

Romans 5:1-11: God's Love, Jesus' Death, and Christians' Suffering

1. Eph. 3:12 also refers to access to God through Jesus, and adds that it is through his (Jesus') faith. While most have translated 3:12 as faith in him, see the footnote of the NRSV. Barth, *Ephesians 1—3*, 347, points out the connections between 3:12 and Eph. 2:18, where Christ alone (not our faith) is described as the mediator of our access to God. He thus says that "through his faithfulness" in 3:12 refers to the same reality as "in Christ's blood," "in his flesh," and "through the cross" in 2:13-18. Eph. 2:13-18, like Rom. 5:1, also emphasizes peace with God (and among Jews and Gentiles) which comes through Christ.

2. Kierkegaard, 7-8, 17-21, 27-28, 47, 121-123, 149-151, 168-169, 221.

3. Jonathan J. Bonk, "Mission and the Problem of Affluence," in *Toward the Twenty-first Century in Christian Mission*, 295-309.

4. Keck, 457-458, connects Jesus' faith(fulness) with God's love in 5:8.

5. Martin Lange and Reinhold Iblacker, eds., *Witnesses of Hope: The Persecution of Christians in Latin America* (Maryknoll: Orbis Books, 1981), 27-36; Lernoux, *Cry of the People*, 69-74.

6. Lernoux, *Cry of the People*, 61-62, 77-78.

Romans 5:12-21: From Jesus' Faith to Worldwide Righteousness

1. When 5:15 (and 5:17) contrasts two men, Adam and Jesus, note that the order of the name is Jesus Christ, not Christ Jesus, thus stressing grace through his earthly life. In 3:22 and 3:26 Paul similarly emphasizes the human name of Jesus to refer to Jesus' faith. (Of course, Paul sometimes uses the name Christ Jesus, or simply Christ—as in 5:6, 8—to describe actions of Jesus such as dying for sinners.) Both 5:15 and 3:22 likewise refer to the many who will benefit from God's grace as manifested first in the obedient faith of Jesus. Jesus himself said he came to give his life for many (Mark 10:45).

2. According to Peter Gorday, *Principles of Patristic Exegesis: Romans 9-11 in Origen, John Chrysostom, and Augustine* (New York: The Edwin Mellen Press, 1983), 105-106, the excellent early (fifth-century) Greek interpreter Theodore of Mopsuestia stressed that in Romans, salvation for the believer comes through identifying with Jesus in his earthly life of obedient faith, wherein one receives grace.

3. John Garrett, *Roger Williams: Witness Beyond Christendom, 1603- 1683* (London: The Macmillan Co., 1970).

4. Bosch, 342-343.

5. Scherer, 35-38, 83, 93-94, 99-100.

6. Stoll, 92-96.

Romans 6:1-14: From Death to Life Through Christ

1. Cook, *Expectation*, 188, 190-191.

2. In Col. 1:11, Paul also closely connects God's glory and power (see also Eph. 3:16; 2 Thess. 1:9). Jesus did the same when he raised Lazarus (John 11:40). For the Bible's frequent use of the word *glory* to mean God's power, see Cranfield, 1:304-305.

3. See Arthur G. Gish, *Living in Christian Community* (Scottdale: Herald Press, 1979), 190-203.

4. The "body of sin" is more than an individual's sinful body. Robert C. Tannehill, *Dying and Rising with Christ: A Study in Pauline Theology* (Berlin: Verlag Alfred Töpelmann, 1967), continually contrasts the world power of sin through the corporate person (body) of Adam with the new world power of God through the corporate person (body) of Christ. After Christians die with Christ to the inclusive person of Adam under

sin's deadly power, they gain life as part of the inclusive person of Christ under God's resurrection power.

5. Both Jesus and Paul use the example of a body and its members. And both sometimes use the illustration to refer to an individual person's body with its parts or members (Matt. 5:29-30; Rom. 7:23; 1 Cor. 6:13-15), and other times to a corporate body made up of many people or members (Matt. 18:6-9, 15-17; 1 Cor. 12:12-27). Note the emphasis of 6:1-11 on unity with Christ, and the use of Adam and Christ as corporate persons with a worldwide following in 5:12-21. Both suggest that the use of body (singular) in 6:12 and members in 6:13 portrays a corporate body of many people or members. Compare the interpretation of T. W. Manson, "Romans," in *Peake's Commentary on the Bible*, eds. Matthew Black and H. H. Rowley (London: Thomas Nelson and Sons, 1962), 945.

6. Morna Hooker, "Interchange in Christ and Ethics," *Journal for the Study of the New Testament* 25 (Oct. 1985): 3-17.

7. Vincent J. Donovan, *Christianity Rediscovered* (Maryknoll: Orbis Books, 1978), 89-90.

8. Jonathan Chao, interviewer, and Richard Van Houten, ed., *Wise as Serpents, Harmless as Doves* (Pasadena, Calif.: William Carey Library, 1988), vii-x.

9. Lange and Iblacker, 102-105. See Lernoux, *Cry of the People*, 3-6, for a similar account of a torture victim (an Irish priest in Argentina) who identified with Christ's cry on the cross.

Romans 6:15—7:6: Liberated by God for a Righteous, Servant Mission

1. See Johnson, "Rom 3:21-26," 85-87, for connections between righteousness, obedience, and faith (including Jesus' faith) in 6:16-17 and earlier in Romans.

2. For a challenging introduction to Christ's teaching against the violence of both military and economic power, see Ronald J. Sider, *Christ and Violence* (Scottdale: Herald Press, 1979).

3. David Martin, *Tongues of Fire*, 177-179.

4. Ronald J. Sider, *Rich Christians in an Age of Hunger*, 3d ed. (Dallas: Word Publishing, 1990), 146-147.

5. Jon Butler, *Awash in a Sea of Faith: Christianizing the American People* (Cambridge: Harvard Univ. Press, 1990), 129, 139-151. In other letters, Paul sometimes calls on slaves to be obedient to their masters (as in Eph. 6:5; Col. 3:22). But because masters are mere men, Paul also challenges them not to mistreat their slaves (Eph. 6:9; Col. 4:1). As with wives and husbands, as well as children and parents, there is ideally to be a mutual submission between slaves and masters in the sense of humbly serving one another in love (Eph. 5:21—6:9). Paul's letter to Philemon, master of the slave Onesimus, shows that such love can include forgiveness of sins done by slaves and freedom from slavery for greater service elsewhere (for Onesimus, returning to serve Paul in his imprisonment). Thus Paul's teaching on slavery transforms oppressive treatment of slaves.

6. Milton C. Sernett, *Black Religion and American Evangelicalism* (Metuchen, N.J.: The Scarecrow Press, 1975), 39, 59, 74, 81-82, 87, 163; Douglass, 104-106.

7. John D. Earnshaw, "Reconsidering Paul's Marriage Analogy in Romans 7.1-4," *New Testament Studies* 40 (1994): 68-88.

8. In Phil. 3:2-6, Paul connects the "flesh" with circumcision (of the flesh) and with being part of Israel. Thus Paul was born of Hebrew parents from the tribe of Benjamin and was a strict Pharisee, following the law blamelessly and (before his conversion) punishing the church because believers threatened Jewish life under the law.

Romans 7:7-25: The Deadly Power of Sin Manifested Through the Law

1. For a good discussion of Rom. 7 and Christ's victory over sin, see Beker, 215-221.

2. Byrne, 135, says 7:14-25 described the same encounter with the law as 7:7-13 (a quasi-historical narrative set in the past), but now from inside the person under the law.

He later adds (146) that the use of the present tense is probably a dramatic device since Paul is describing an inner experience instead of a history as in 7:7-13. So 7:14-25 portrays the moral struggle without the Holy Spirit (145).

While Gal. 5:17 describes a conflict between the Holy Spirit and the flesh of the Christian, Rom. 7:14-25 develops a more desperate conflict between the human mind and the flesh. Because of the power of God's Spirit, the Christian walks by the Spirit and overcomes the sinful desires (temptations) of the flesh (Gal. 5:16). The human mind has no such power.

3. In 8:2, Paul refers to the one under the law of sin and death (see 7:23) as "you" (singular). While many English translations use "me" in 8:2, *The Greek New Testament* of the United Bible Societies (3d ed.), as well as the Nestle 25th edition, use "you." Early Alexandrian and Western manuscripts had "you." If "you" is the correct reading, it helps to show that Paul was not giving an account of his own personal struggle in 7:14-25 by using "I."

4. W. G. B. Ream, "The Support of the Clergy in the First Five Centuries A.D.," *The International Review of Missions* 45 (Oct. 1956): 420-421.

5. Ream, 424-426.

6. Ream, 427-428.

7. Kinsler, 192-193,196.

8. Carolyn Holderread Heggen, *Sexual Abuse in Christian Homes and Churches* (Scottdale: Herald Press, 1993), 57-63, 70-97, 121-134, 144-148.

Romans 8:1-16: The Life-giving Power of God's Spirit

1. Harry R. Boer, *Pentecost and Missions* (Grand Rapids: Eerdmans, 1961), 15-27, 205-254.

2. Byrne, 158, emphasizes the obedience of Jesus' faith in 8:9-11.

3. David Martin, *Tongues of Fire*, 169-171.

4. For a fuller treatment of the significance of the Holy Spirit in the life and ministry of Jesus, see Gerald F. Hawthorne, *The Presence and the Power* (Dallas: Word, 1991).

5. Richard F. Lovelace, *Dynamics of Spiritual Life: An Evangelical Theology of Renewal* (Downers Grove, Ill.: InterVarsity Press, 1979), 234-235.

6. Hawthorne, 35, says Jesus' faith in God was so radical that he accepted the death of a condemned criminal as God's will for him. Jesus was confident God would raise him from the dead. Hawthorne connects that faith with Paul's phrase, the faith of Jesus, in 3:22, 26; Gal. 2:16; 3:22; Phil. 3:9.

7. Allen Mawhinney, "God as Father: Two Popular Theories Reconsidered," *Journal of the Evangelical Theological Society* 31 (June 1988): 181-189; James Barr, "ABBA Isn't 'Daddy,' " *The Journal of Theological Studies* 39 (Apr. 1988): 28-47.

Romans 8:17-30: Sharing Jesus' Faithful Suffering and Final Glory

1. Johannes Munck, *Christ and Israel: An Interpretation of Romans 9-11* (Philadelphia: Fortress Press, 1967), 49-55, connects the suffering of 8:17-39 (and of 5:3 and elsewhere in chapters 9-11 and 15) with Jewish persecution. He gives a good summary of that persecution against Paul and the church as described in Paul's letters and in Acts.

2. Barry Commoner, *Making Peace with the Planet* (New York: Pantheon Books, 1990), 4, 9, 14, 25-40.

3. Commoner, 41-102, 152-155, 169-243.

4. Vishal Mangalwadi, "Compassion and Social Reform: Jesus the Troublemaker," in *The Church in Response to Human Need*, eds. Vinay Samuel and Christopher Sugden (Grand Rapids: Eerdmans, 1987), 203-204.

Romans 8:31-39: Secure in God's Love Through God's Power

1. Bonk, *Missions and Money*, xvii-xix, 73.

2. Fernando Bermúdez, *Death and Resurrection in Guatemala* (Maryknoll: Orbis Books, 1986), 46, 51, 62-65. Also, Lernoux, *People of God*, 6.

3. Owen Chadwick, *The Reformation* (Baltimore: Penguin Books, 1964), 40-75.

4. Chadwick, 82-92.

5. Hendrik Berkhof, *Christ and the Powers* (Scottdale: Herald Press, 1977), 18-22, 30-39, 44-52.

6. Costas, *Christ Outside the Gate*, 170-171; Glen, 9-28; and Lernoux, *Cry of the People*, 204-205, 456-458.

7. Howard Zinn, *A People's History of the United States* (New York: HarperCollins, 1980), 554. On Carter's inconsistency, see also Lernoux, *Cry of the People*, 198-199, 208.

8. Costas, *Christ Outside the Gate*, 95, 106.

9. Phillip Berryman, *Liberation Theology: Essential Facts About the Revolutionary Movement in Latin America—and Beyond* (New York: Pantheon Books, 1987), 115-118, 122-124.

10. Lernoux, *Cry of the People*, 454-455.

11. Lernoux, *Cry of the People*, 198, 278, 455-456.

12. Richard J. Barnet and John Cavanagh, *Global Dreams: Imperial Corporations and the New World Order* (New York: Simon and Schuster, 1994), 223-224.

Romans 9:1-13: God's Mission of Election and Rejection Within Israel

1. It is also possible to punctuate and translate the end of 9:5 so that Paul praises God the Father instead of Christ as God the Son. For a thorough discussion of the debate on this verse, see Cranfield, 2:464-470.

2. Charles Y. Glock and Rodney Stark, *Christian Beliefs and Anti-Semitism* (New York: Harper & Row, 1969), 148, n. 2.

3. Ruth A. Tucker, "Women in Mission," in *Toward the Twenty-first Century in Christian Mission*, 284-294.

4. J. I. Packer, *Evangelism and the Sovereignty of God* (Downers Grove, Ill.: Inter-Varsity Press, 1961), 106-126.

5. Chadwick, 95-96.

6. Anthony A. Hoekema, *Jehovah's Witnesses* (Grand Rapids: Eerdmans, 1963), 9-13.

7. Robert Gottlieb and Peter Wiley, *America's Saints: The Rise of Mormon Power* (New York: G. P. Putnam's Sons, 1984), 11-13, 36-42, 188-190, 223, 254-257; John Heinerman and Anson Shupe, *The Mormon Corporate Empire* (Boston: Beacon Press, 1985), 8-9, 13-14, 84-87, 196-202.

8. Gottlieb and Wiley, 21-23, 44-45, 53, 64, 67-68; Heinerman and Shupe, 2-6, 19-31, 79-84, 128-129, 141-142, 176-178, 256-258.

9. Gottlieb and Wiley, 130-133, 140, 143, 152, 154-156, 252.

Romans 9:14-29: God's Absolute, Righteous Power

1. John Piper, *The Justification of God* (Grand Rapids: Baker, 1983), 67, 97, 100-101.

2. Piper, 142-149, shows how Exod. 4–14 tied together God's hardening from the beginning with Pharaoh's own self-hardening.

3. Packer, 18-25, describes the issue as one of antinomy, which he defines as a pair of principles that stand side by side, yet seem to be irreconcilable even though both are undeniable. William Sanday and Arthur C. Headlam, *A Critical and Exegetical Commentary on The Epistle to the Romans* (Edinburgh: T. & T. Clark, 1902), 348-350, also refer to antinomy and conclude that one can only state the two sides without solving the problem. They do add that because God is all-powerful and all-knowing, the two sides can be reconciled in God's mind.

Romans 9:30—10:10: God's Righteousness, Christ's Faith, and Mission

1. Robert Sloan, "Paul and the Law: Why the Law Cannot Save," *Novum Testamentum* 33 (1991): 56-58, says 9:30—10:4 shows that the zeal of Israel's seeking or working under the law (connected with the power of sin) blinds them to the faithfulness of

Christ's (Messiah's) righteousness. He thus interprets the phrase "out of faith" in 9:30, 32 as referring to the faithfulness of Christ.

2. The Greek words for believing and confessing in 10:10 are in the present tense, pointing to a continuous process of believing and confessing.

3. William Martin, *A Prophet with Honor: The Billy Graham Story* (New York: William Morrow and Co., 1991).

4. Friesen, 10-11.

5. William A. Dyrness, *Invitation to Cross-Cultural Theology: Case Studies in Vernacular Theologies* (Grand Rapids: Zondervan, 1992), 51-56.

Romans 10:11-21: World Mission and the Word of Christ

1. The Greek construction suggests Christ as the one speaking. Sanday and Headlam, 296; Cranfield, 2:534; Morris, *Romans*, 389-390.

2. Michel Philibert, *Christ's Preaching—and Ours* (Richmond: John Knox Press, 1964), 8-13, 38-41, describes Christ's mobile, itinerant preaching which moves forward to meet people and mobilizes disciples to do the same. He contrasts that with modern Sunday sermons where the same preacher stays in the same place repeating the same abstract and remote words.

3. Verduin, 263-269.

4. Nida, *Message and Mission*, 35-36.

5. James O'Halloran, *Living Cells: Developing Small Christian Community* (Maryknoll: Orbis Books, 1984), 99-100.

6. Bonk, *Missions and Money*, 70-72.

7. Saphir P. Athyal, "Southern Asia," in *Toward the Twenty-first Century in Christian Mission*, 62.

8. Dyrness, 170-179.

9. Lernoux, *Cry of the People*, 123-134.

Romans 11:1-12: God's Ongoing Mission of Election and Rejection

1. Finke and Stark, 40-46.

2. Cook, 204-205, 228-231, 240.

3. Cook, 205.

4. Cook, 206-207.

5. Colleen Evans and Virginia MacLaury, "National Presbyterian Church—Washington, D.C.," in *Living More Simply: Biblical Principles and Practical Models*, ed. Ronald J. Sider (Downers Grove, Ill.: InterVarsity Press, 1980), 120-124.

Romans 11:13-24: God's Family Tree of Faithful Jews and Gentiles

1 Eugene A. Nida, *Religion Across Cultures* (New York: Harper & Row, 1968), 73-74.

Romans 11:25-36: The Revealed Mystery of World History

1. Stoll, 82-83, 96-98.

2. Bonk, *Missions and Money*, 72-76, 120-121.

Romans 12:1-8: God's Powerful Mercies and a Faithful Mission

1. For a classic critique of the U.S. religious establishment, see Peter L. Berger, *The Noise of Solemn Assemblies: Christian Commitment and the Religious Establishment in America* (Garden City, N.Y.: Doubleday, 1961).

2. Cranfield, 2:615, favors translating the latter part of 12:3 as "a standard (by which to measure, estimate, himself), namely, his faith." The usual translation, a measure of faith, suggests that some have a greater measure than others. Cranfield, 2:614, sees that the context of 12:3 is trying to encourage unity in the one faith instead of measuring different amounts of faith. While Cranfield does not refer to the faith of Jesus, he does conclude, 2:616, that since the standard in 12:3 is basic Christian faith, that really

means the final standard is Christ himself "by whom alone one must measure oneself and also one's fellow-men."

3. Otto Michel, *Der Brief an die Römer* (Göttingen: Vandenhoeck und Ruprecht, 1966), 298-299.

4. Jonathan T'ien-en Chao, "Crucial Issues in Leadership Training: A Chinese Perspective," in *Mission Focus: Current Issues*, ed. Wilbert R. Shenk (Scottdale: Herald Press, 1980), 379-408, discusses the history of Protestant theological education in the third world. He describes the modern Western model of academic professional schools preparing students to become paid full-time professional ministers who keep institutional, denominational churches going. This model he contrasts with the NT model of Spirit-empowered small Christian communities, where Christ's own ministry is being extended through leaders who have helped the others grow corporately into the likeness of Christ and his mission.

5. Lernoux, *Cry of the People*, 387-388.

6. Jonathan Chao, "Education and Leadership," in *The New Face of Evangelicalism: An International Symposium on the Lausanne Covenant*, ed. René Padilla (Downers Grove: InterVarsity Press, 1976), 193-204.

7. Yoder, *The Fullness of Christ*, 14-20, 28-34, 37-43.

8. David Martin, *Tongues of Fire*, 252.

9. See Mott, *Biblical Ethics*, 27-34, on God's powerful grace which produces gracious actions like Paul's collection (2 Cor. 8-9).

10. David Hilton, "The Future of Medical Mission," *International Review of Mission* 76 (Jan. 1987): 78-81; J. Samuel Hofman, "Using Indigenous Principles in Medical Missions," *Missiology: An International Review* 10 (Jan. 1982): 49-55.

11. P. A. Kalilombe, "The African Local Churches and the Worldwide Roman Catholic Communion," in *Christianity in Independent Africa*, 89-95.

12. Stoll, 266-304.

13. Sider, *Rich Christians*, 167-178, emphasizes the possibilities of a faithful lifestyle and mission of mercy through a network of small house churches.

Romans 12:9-21: Jesus' Love for Persecutors and Persecuted

1. Dyrness, 59-60.

2. Robert Moffitt, "The Local Church and Development," in *The Church in Response to Human Need*, 234-253.

3. Jack A. Nelson, *Hunger for Justice: The Politics of Food and Faith* (Maryknoll: Orbis Books, 1980), vii.

4. Nelson, 158, 182-183, 206-208. The basis for those conclusions is the earlier main body of a well-researched book.

5. Friesen, 99.

6. W. D. Davies, *Paul and Rabbinic Judaism* (New York: Harper & Row, 1967), 136-150, uses especially Rom. 12-14 as an example of Jesus' teaching being carried on by Paul. Davies emphasizes that Jesus' words (and character) are Paul's primary source for ethical teaching.

7. David Daube, *The New Testament and Rabbinic Judaism* (New York: Arno Press, 1973), 342-348, prefers to interpret 12:14-16 as Paul's use of Jewish missionary methods. The rejoicing, weeping, and being of the same mind would then refer to the missionary's attitude of accommodation toward non-Christians.

8. J. R. Michaels, "Apostolic Hardship and Righteous Gentiles," *Journal of Biblical Literature* 84 (1965): 27-37; G. E. Ladd, *A Theology of the New Testament* (Grand Rapids: Eerdmans, 1974), 118-119.

9. Michaels, 36-37.

10. Dennis Byler, *Making War and Making Peace: Why Some Christians Fight and Some Don't* (Scottdale: Herald Press, 1989), contrasts Jesus' way of loving enemies with the history of Christendom since Constantine and Augustine. Christendom has justified and participated in wars and in the enforcement of civil laws. For a discussion of a few

passages often used to portray Jesus as using or willing to use violence, see William Klassen, *Love of Enemies: The Way to Peace* (Philadelphia: Fortress Press, 1984), 98-101. He notes that only John's Gospel mentions Jesus using a whip in cleansing the temple, and only John refers to cattle. Klassen, 98-99, a former farm boy, argues that Jesus used the whip on the animals, not the people; his interpretation is supported by some translations (e.g., the TEV and the NRSV). By making a whip from the cords which had bound the cattle, Jesus might also have been protecting people from the trampling of the cattle. Klassen also discusses Jesus' metaphors about bringing not peace but a sword (Matt. 10:34-36; Luke 12:51-53) and about buying a sword (Luke 22:35-38), misunderstood by the disciples and finally dismissed by Jesus saying, Enough (of such talk).

11. Lernoux, *People of God*, 258-279.

12. Lange and Iblacker, 97-102.

Romans 13:1-14: God's Ministers of Wrath and Jesus' Mission of Love

1. See Cranfield, 2:660-663, for translating "be subject" and not "obey" in 13:1. Titus 3:1 begins with a reminder to be subject to rulers and authorities. The next word after that phrase means "be obedient." But did that word go with the first phrase and thus mean to be obedient to rulers? Most commentators think so, but the other words which follow the first phrase do not relate to rulers.

The word meaning "be obedient" is followed by the phrase "be prepared for every good deed." Titus 1:16 ends with criticism of those who are disobedient (see Titus 3:3) and unfit for any good deed, thus combining the negative equivalents of the second and third exhortations of 3:1. Since there is no mention of rulers in 1:16, why should the same combination in 3:1 be separated so that obedience is connected with submission to rulers? Also, right before 3:1 there is another reference to those who are zealous for good deeds (2:14), followed by the call to teach those things with all authority, insisting that others take them seriously and thus obey (2:15).

Hence, it seems better to connect the word "be obedient" in 3:1 with obedience to those who teach them to do good deeds. (On teaching about good deeds, see also Titus 1:8-9; 2:3, 7; 3:8, 14). The word translated "be obedient" in Titus 3:1 is used only three other times in the NT (Acts 5:29, 32; 27:21). In Acts 5:29, 32, the emphasis is on obeying God instead of human authority (Jewish rulers).

2. Zinn, 3-7, 13-16. On 15, Zinn quotes the famous Puritan theologian, Cotton Mather, whose response to the massacre of an Indian village was that 600 Pequot souls went to hell that day. Zinn, 16-17, mentions Roger Williams as similar to Las Casas in sympathy for Indians. On Williams, see Garrett, 126-144.

3. Helen Rand Parish, ed., *Bartolomé de las Casas: The Only Way* (New York: Paulist Press, 1992), 20-54, 201-208.

4. Zinn, 139-140; Henry Warner Bowden, *American Indians and Christian Missions: Studies in Cultural Conflict* (Chicago: The Univ. of Chicago Press, 1981), 176-177.

5. Stoll, 42-43, 52-67.

6. Costas, *Christ Outside the Gate*, 179-181; Butler, 214-215, 219-220, 293-295.

7. See Kenton J. Clymer, *Protestant Missionaries in the Philippines, 1898-1916: An Inquiry into the American Colonial Mentality* (Urbana: Univ. of Illinois Press, 1986), 3, 153-157, 162, 173.

8. Costas, *Christ Outside the Gate*, 59-60.

9. Costas, *Christ Outside the Gate*, 189-190.

10. Costas, *Christ Outside the Gate*, 59-61. William Carey, *An Enquiry into the Obligations of Christians to Use Means for the Conversion of the Heathen* (1792), did see the need to argue against evil structures of colonialism, including the evil of slavery. Also, at that time Protestants still accepted the Reformers' position that the great commission of Matthew 28:18-20 was fulfilled by the original apostles. Yet Carey emphasized the continued need to obey the Lord's command to go and make disciples. Johannes Verkuyl, *Contemporary Missiology: An Introduction* (Grand Rapids: Eerdmans, 1978), 18-19, 23-24.

11. Moorhouse, 131-136, 298-299.

12. Robert D. Linder and Richard V. Pierard, *Twilight of the Saints: Biblical Christianity and Civil Religion in America* (Downers Grove, Ill.: InterVarsity Press, 1978), 78, 80, 95, 98, 105-106, 148; Commoner, 237-238.

13. Bowden, 164-169.

14. The U.S. uses God's name in vain with the words "In God We Trust" on bills and coins. On problems connected with tax exemptions for churches, see Alfred Balk, *The Religion Business* (Richmond: John Knox Press, 1968), 37-38.

15. Even the order of the commandments named reflects Jesus' teaching. Compare Luke 18:20 and James 2:11 in contrast to the order of Exod. 20:13-14 and Deut. 5:17-18. (A certain Greek translation of Deut. 5:17-18 also reversed the original order.)

16. Thompson, 154-155 (especially n. 4), points out numerous passages where the characteristics listed in Col. 3:12 are connected with Jesus—and with God. Thompson, 150-160, says putting on Christ means he will transform them into his image, which is the image of God, so that they reflect his mind, character, and conduct (compare Rom. 13:14; 12:2; 2 Cor. 3:18).

Romans 14:1-12: Cultural Conflicts Among the Lord's Servants

1. C. Wayne Zunkel, *Church Growth Under Fire* (Scottdale: Herald Press, 1987), 100-119, emphasizes that the homogeneous principle is only a beginning point for people who could become Christians.

2. Banks, 222-223.

3. Nida, *Message and Mission*, 24, says there is no correlation between lack of clothing in a certain society and immorality. Each society has its own rules for decency or indecency.

4. Barrett, *Schism and Renewal*, 116-118, 146-147.

5. John V. Taylor, *The Growth of the Church in Buganda: An Attempt at Understanding* (London: SCM Press, 1958), 184.

6. Tucker, *From Jerusalem*, 64-65; Jacques Gernet, *China and the Christian Impact: A Conflict of Cultures*, trans. J. Lloyd (Cambridge: Cambridge Univ. Press, 1985), 15-16, 40.

7. Hutchison, 27.

8. Hutchison, 29. Bowden, 112, notes that five generations of Mayhews worked patiently with Algonquian-speaking Indians, producing beneficial results, but still ministering with some patriarchal condescension. Bowden, 146-150, contrasts Samuel Kirkland's earlier sensitivity, in wanting no forced socioeconomic or cultural changes, with his later persuasion of converts to adopt white standards. Yet even later, he remained more patient and flexible than most other missionaries. Bowden, 158-162, describes Zeisberger as a Moravian missionary who stayed with his Indian converts even when they faced danger and hostility from other tribes, or prejudice and insults from white colonists. But Zeisberger also created new Indian villages that reflected "Christian civilization," supposed Christian culture.

9. Moorhouse, 308.

10. For a good discussion of the transition from the seventh to the first day of the week as a "holy day," see Harald Riesenfeld, *The Gospel Tradition* (Philadelphia: Fortress Press, 1970), 124-131.

11. David A. Rausch, *Messianic Judaism: Its History, Theology, and Polity* (New York: The Edwin Mellen Press, 1982), especially 32-43, 87-88, 230-232, 241-244.

12. Gish, 300-301; Zinn, 182-187.

13. Stuart Creighton Miller, *"Benevolent Assimilation": The American Conquest of the Philippines, 1899-1903* (New Haven: Yale Univ. Press, 1982), 24, 136, 139.

14. Robert Wuthnow, *The Struggle for America's Soul: Evangelicals, Liberals, and Secularism* (Grand Rapids: Eerdmans, 1989).

Romans 14:13-23: Conflicting Cultures and Danger of Destroying Faith

1. Thompson, 206-207.

2. Lamin Sanneh, "Africa," in *Toward the Twenty-first Century in Christian Mission*, 84-85, 89-92.

3. David Martin, 208-210.

4. David Martin, 141, 152.

5. Tucker, *From Jerusalem*, 175-180, 184-185.

6. Tom Sine, *Live It Up! How to Create a Life You Can Love* (Scottdale, Pa.: Herald Press, 1993), 173-174.

Romans 15:1-13: Jesus' Mission, the World's Diversity, and God's People

1. Finke and Stark, 211-216.

2. Hans A. Baer and Merrill Singer, *African-American Religion in the Twentieth Century: Varieties of Protest and Accommodation* (Knoxville: The Univ. of Tennessee Press, 1992), 16-20.

3. Hutchison, 69-77, 86-89.

4. Kosuke Koyama, *Three Mile an Hour God* (Maryknoll: Orbis Books, 1980), 52-54.

Romans 15:14-33: Paul's Vision for Mission and the Purpose of Romans

1. Stoll, 108-114; David Martin, 68-70, 261.

2. Hutchison, 80-89.

3. Hutchison, 91-124.

4. John L. Nevius, "Planting and Development of Missionary Churches," in *Classics of Christian Missions*, ed. Francis M. DuBose (Nashville: Broadman Press, 1979), 256-267. Also, Bonk, "Mission and the Problem of Affluence," 295-300.

5. Donovan, 14-16, 31-40, 99-106, 129-163, 175-181.

Romans 16:1-16: Paul's Co-Workers in World Mission

1. Wesley Granberg-Michaelson, *A Worldly Spirituality: The Call to Redeem Life on Earth* (San Francisco: Harper & Row, 1984), 165-166.

2. Burkholder, 28.

3. For an emphasis on mission in a U.S. house church, see Donald R. Allen, *Barefoot in the Church* (Richmond: John Knox Press, 1972), 68-125.

4. Sider, *Rich Christians*, 167-178.

5. Tucker, *From Jerusalem*, 282-286.

6. Nida, *Message and Mission*, 111-112.

7. Harvie M. Conn, *A Clarified Vision for Urban Mission: Dispelling the Urban Stereotypes* (Grand Rapids: Zondervan, 1987), 56.

8. Conn, 79-80.

9. Cranfield, 2:788-789, argues convincingly for a female name (Junia) in 16:7, not a male (Junias). The Greek form could be translated as either Junia or Junias, depending on what accent is used. (Accents were not part of the original manuscripts.) There is no evidence in any ancient manuscripts of a male named Junias, but Junia was a common female name. Richard S. Cervin, "A Note Regarding the Name 'Junia(s)' in Romans 16.7," *New Testament Studies* 40 (July 1994): 464-470, argues that Junia—or more correctly, Iunia—was a feminine Latin name. When adapted to Greek, its accusative case would be exactly the form used in 16:7. The masculine Latin name Iunius would however be a different form in the Greek accusative, and thus different from the name in 16:7.

10. Tucker, *From Jerusalem*, 158-163.

11. Concerning 1 Cor. 14:34-35, in the same letter (1 Cor. 11:5, 13), Paul says women who pray or prophesy must do so with heads covered. Hence, Paul is not trying to silence all women. Prisca is helping lead a house church in Corinth (see 1 Cor. 16:19; Acts 18:1-3, 18, 26). While 1 Cor. 14:33 refers to all the churches, the context is clearly concentrating on a specific problem of confusion and disorder (1 Cor. 14:27-33, 39-40).

In 1 Cor. 14:27-28, Paul tries to limit how many speak in tongues during a meeting. If there is no one to interpret the meaning, those wanting to speak in tongues should all keep silent. Then, in 1 Cor. 14:29-30, Paul tries to organize orderly prophesying. If someone receives a revelation to share with the group, the one who is already prophesying should be silent.

Thus 1 Cor. 14:34-35 is the third in a series of exhortations to silence. Also, 1 Cor. 14:35 provides the particular problem behind Paul's call for women to be silent. The women in mind are asking questions during the meeting. Paul advises them to wait and ask their husbands at home since there is a danger of disorder due to some women's desire to know as much as possible, as soon as possible.

The reference to submission in 1 Cor. 14:34 also reflects the other primary passage used to put down women, 1 Tim. 2:11-12. According to 1 Tim. 2:11, women are to be submissive by learning in silence. Then the next verse clarifies that teaching by adding that no woman is to have authority over men or to teach. Instead of presuming to teach, those women are to listen in silence.

However, the reason now given for silence is that the women, like Eve, are easily deceived (1 Tim. 2:14). In 1 Tim. 1:6-7, Paul describes certain persons who want to be teachers but lack understanding. In 1 Tim. 4:1 he describes those who are departing from the faith due to deceitful spirits and demonic doctrines. Some have been deceived by such false teaching and have strayed after Satan; these are younger widows (1 Tim. 5:15; see 2 Tim. 3:6-7, 13). Thus the particular problem behind 1 Tim. 2:11-12 is that some women are being deceived by false (demonic) teaching and are then wanting to pass on that teaching. Such women should learn in silence, instead of teaching, and remain submissive, instead of seeking authority over those who teach the truth.

In the background of both passages (1 Cor. 14:34-35; 1 Tim. 2:11-12) is the historical reality that women were refused the same education as men. Yet now women have received a new dignity through Jesus' faith (see 2 Tim. 1:5; 3:14-15). The problem is that some are trying to make up for lost time too quickly. By wanting to learn too fast, some are beginning to dominate meetings (1 Cor. 14:35). By wanting to teach too soon, some are being deceived and in danger of deceiving others (1 Tim. 2:11-12).

For further on those passages, see Letha Scanzoni and Nancy Hardesty, *All We're Meant to Be* (Waco: Word, 1974), 68-71; and Tucker, "Women in Mission," 288-290.

12. Ruth A. Tucker, "Women in Missions: Reaching Sisters in 'Heathen Darkness,'" in *Earthen Vessels: American Evangelicals and Foreign Missions, 1880-1980*, eds. Joel A. Carpenter and Wilbert R. Shenk (Grand Rapids: Eerdmans, 1990), 251-263.

13. R. Pierce Beaver, *American Protestant Women in World Mission: History of the First Feminist Movement in North America* (Grand Rapids: Eerdmans, 1980), 87-88, 104, 109, 179-184, 201-206, 218.

14. Stoll, 318-319.

Romans 16:17-27: The Foundation and Stumbling Blocks of Mission

1. Chao and Van Houten, 140-141.

2. Hock, 30-31, 37, 53-54.

3. Cheryl Forbes, *The Religion of Power* (Grand Rapids: Zondervan, 1983), 21, 43, 63-69.

4. For an insightful study of both the two priests and the Philippines, see Alfred W. McCoy, *Priests on Trial* (New York: Penguin Books, 1984).

Bibliography

Achtemeier, Paul. *Romans*. Atlanta: John Knox Press, 1985.

Afigbo, A. E. "The Missions, the State and Education in South-Eastern Nigeria, 1956-71." In *Christianity in Independent Africa*, eds. Edward Fasholé-Luke, Richard Gray, Adrian Hastings, and Godwin Tasie, 176-192. Bloomington, Ind.: Indiana Univ. Press, 1978.

Alexander, John F. *Your Money or Your Life: A New Look at Jesus' View of Wealth and Power*. San Francisco: Harper & Row, 1986.

Allen, Donald R. *Barefoot in the Church*. Richmond: John Knox Press, 1972.

Athyal, Saphir P. "Southern Asia." In *Toward the Twenty-first Century in Christian Mission*, eds. James M. Phillips and Robert T. Coote, 57-68. Grand Rapids: Eerdmans, 1993.

Atkinson, David J. *Homosexuals in the Christian Fellowship*. Grand Rapids: Eerdmans, 1981.

Aune, David E. "Romans as a *Logos Protreptikos*." In *The Romans Debate*, ed. Karl P. Donfried, 278-296. Peabody, Mass.: Hendrickson Publ., 1991.

Baer, Hans A., and Merrill Singer. *African-American Religion in the Twentieth Century: Varieties of Protest and Accommodation*. Knoxville: The Univ. of Tennessee Press, 1992.

Balk, Alfred. *The Religion Business*. Richmond: John Knox Press, 1968.

Banks, Robert. *Jesus and the Law in the Synoptic Tradition*. Cambridge:

Cambridge Univ. Press, 1975.

Barnet, Richard J., and John Cavanagh. *Global Dreams: Imperial Corporations and the New World Order.* New York: Simon and Schuster, 1994.

Barr, James. *"ABBA* Isn't 'Daddy.' " *The Journal of Theological Studies* 39 (Apr. 1988): 28-47.

Barrett, David B. "Annual Statistical Table on Global Mission: 1989." *International Bulletin of Missionary Research* 13 (Jan. 1989): 20-21.

_____. *Schism and Renewal in Africa.* London: Oxford Univ. Press, 1968.

Barth, Markus. *Ephesians: Introduction, Translation, and Commentary on Chapters 1-3.* Anchor Bible. Garden City, N.Y.: Doubleday, 1974.

_____. "The Faith of the Messiah." *The Heythrop Journal* 10 (1969): 363-370.

Beaver, R. Pierce. *American Protestant Women in World Mission: History of the First Feminist Movement in North America.* Grand Rapids: Eerdmans, 1980.

Beker, J. Christiaan. *Paul the Apostle: The Triumph of God in Life and Thought.* Philadelphia: Fortress Press, 1980.

Berger, Peter L. *The Noise of Solemn Assemblies: Christian Commitment and the Religious Establishment in America.* Garden City, N.Y.: Doubleday, 1961.

Berkhof, Hendrik. *Christ and the Powers.* Scottdale: Herald Press, 1977.

Bermúdez, Fernando. *Death and Resurrection in Guatemala.* Maryknoll: Orbis Books, 1986.

Berryman, Phillip. *Liberation Theology: Essential Facts About the Revolutionary Movement in Latin America—and Beyond.* New York: Pantheon Books, 1987.

Birkey, Del. *The House Church: A Model for Renewing the Church.* Scottdale: Herald Press, 1988.

Black, Matthew. *Romans.* Grand Rapids: Eerdmans, 1973.

Boer, Harry R. *Pentecost and Missions.* Grand Rapids: Eerdmans, 1961.

Bonhoeffer, Dietrich. *The Cost of Discipleship.* New York: The Macmillan Co., 1959.

Bonk, Jonathan J. "Mission and the Problem of Affluence." In *Toward the Twenty-first Century in Christian Mission,* eds. James M. Phillips and Robert T. Coote, 295-309. Grand Rapids: Eerdmans, 1993.

_____. *Missions and Money: Affluence as a Western Missionary Problem.* Maryknoll: Orbis Books, 1991.

Bosch, David J. *Transforming Mission: Paradigm Shifts in Theology of Mission.* Maryknoll: Orbis Books, 1991.

Bowden, Henry Warner. *American Indians and Christian Missions: Studies in Cultural Conflict.* Chicago: The Univ. of Chicago Press, 1981.

Brewster, E. Thomas, and Elizabeth Brewster. *Bonding and the Missionary Task.* Pasadena, Calif.: Lingua House, 1982.

_____. "Language Learning Midwifery." *Missiology: An International Review* 8 (Apr. 1980): 203-209.

Bruce, F. F. *The Epistle of Paul to the Romans.* Grand Rapids: Eerdmans, 1963.

_____. "The Romans Debate—Continued." *Bulletin of the John Rylands Library* 64 (1982): 334-359.

Burkholder, J. Lawrence. "Popular Evangelicalism: An Appraisal." In *Evangelicalism and Anabaptism,* ed. C. Norman Kraus, 29-35. Scottdale: Herald Press, 1979.

Butler, Jon. *Awash in a Sea of Faith: Christianizing the American People.* Cambridge: Harvard Univ. Press, 1990.

Byler, Dennis. *Making War and Making Peace: Why Some Christians Fight and Some Don't.* Scottdale: Herald Press, 1989.

Byrne, Brendan. *Reckoning with Romans: A Contemporary Reading of Paul's Gospel.* Wilmington, Del.: Michael Glazier, 1986.

Campbell, Douglas A. *The Rhetoric of Righteousness in Romans 3:21-26.* Sheffield: JSOT Press, 1992.

Cannon, William R. *History of Christianity in the Middle Ages.* New York: Abingdon Press, 1960.

Cervin, Richard S. "A Note Regarding the Name 'Junia(s)' in Romans 16.7." *New Testament Studies* 40 (July 1994): 464-470.

Chadwick, Owen. *The Reformation.* Baltimore: Penguin Books, 1964.

Chao, Jonathan. "Crucial Issues in Leadership Training: A Chinese Perspective." In *Mission Focus: Current Issues,* ed. Wilbert R. Shenk, 379-408. Scottdale: Herald Press, 1980.

_____. "Education and Leadership." In *The New Face of Evangelicalism: An International Symposium on the Lausanne Covenant,* ed. René Padilla, 193-204. Downers Grove, Ill.: InterVarsity Press, 1976.

Chao, Jonathan, interviewer, and Richard Van Houten, ed. *Wise as Serpents, Harmless as Doves.* Pasadena, Calif.: William Carey Library, 1988.

Clymer, Kenton J. *Protestant Missionaries in the Philippines, 1898-1916: An Inquiry into the American Colonial Mentality.* Urbana: Univ. of Illinois Press, 1986.

Commoner, Barry. *Making Peace with the Planet.* New York: Pantheon Books, 1990.

Conn, Harvie M. *A Clarified Vision for Urban Mission: Dispelling the Urban Stereotypes.* Grand Rapids: Zondervan, 1987.

Cook, Guillermo. *The Expectation of the Poor: Latin American Base Ecclesial Communities in Protestant Perspective.* Maryknoll: Orbis Books, 1985.

Costas, Orlando E. *Christ Outside the Gate: Mission Beyond Christendom.* Maryknoll: Orbis Books, 1982.

_____. *The Integrity of Mission: The Inner Life and Outreach of the Church.* San Francisco: Harper & Row, 1979.

Cousar, Charles B. *A Theology of the Cross: The Death of Jesus in the Pauline Letters.* Minneapolis: Fortress Press, 1990.

Cranfield, C. E. B. *A Critical and Exegetical Commentary on the Epistle to the Romans.* 2 vols. Edinburgh: T. & T. Clark, 1975-79.

Daube, David. *The New Testament and Rabbinic Judaism.* New York: Arno Press, 1973.

Davies, Glenn N. *Faith and Obedience in Romans: A Study in Romans 1–4.* Sheffield: JSOT Press, 1990.

Davies, W. D. *Paul and Rabbinic Judaism.* New York: Harper & Row, 1967.

Diamond, Sara. *Spiritual Warfare: The Politics of the Christian Right.* Boston: South End Press, 1989.

Donovan, Vincent J. *Christianity Rediscovered.* Maryknoll: Orbis Books, 1978.

Douglass, Frederick. "Slaveholding Religion and the Christianity of Christ." In *Afro-American Religious History: A Documentary Witness,* ed. Milton C. Sernett, 100-109. Durham: Duke Univ. Press, 1985.

Driver, John. *Understanding the Atonement for the Mission of the Church.* Scottdale: Herald Press, 1986.

Dungan, David L. *The Sayings of Jesus in the Churches of Paul.* Philadelphia: Fortress Press, 1971.

Dunn, James D. G. *Jesus and the Spirit.* Philadelphia: Westminster, 1975.

Dyck, Cornelius J. "The Anabaptist Understanding of the Good News." In *Anabaptism and Mission,* ed. Wilbert R. Shenk, 24-39. Scottdale: Herald Press, 1984.

Dyrness, William A. *Invitation to Cross-Cultural Theology: Case Studies in Vernacular Theologies.* Grand Rapids: Zondervan, 1992.

Earnshaw, John D. "Reconsidering Paul's Marriage Analogy in Romans 7.1-4." *New Testament Studies* 40 (1994): 68-88.

Evans, Colleen and Virginia MacLaury. "National Presbyterian Church—Washington, D.C." In *Living More Simply: Biblical Princi-*

ples and Practical Models, ed. Ronald J. Sider, 120-124. Downers Grove, Ill.: InterVarsity Press, 1980.

Faw, Chalmer E. *Acts*. Believers Church Bible Commentary. Scottdale, Pa.: Herald Press, 1993.

Finke, Roger, and Rodney Stark. *The Churching of America, 1776-1990: Winners and Losers in Our Religious Economy*. New Brunswick, N..J.: Rutgers Univ. Press, 1992.

Finnerty, Adam Daniel. *No More Plastic Jesus: Global Justice and Christian Lifestyle*. Maryknoll: Orbis Books, 1977.

Forbes, Cheryl. *The Religion of Power*. Grand Rapids: Zondervan, 1983.

Fraikin, Daniel. "The Rhetorical Function of the Jews in Romans." In *Anti-Judaism in Early Christianity*, vol. 1: *Paul and the Gospels*, eds. P. Richardson with D. Granskou, 91-105. Waterloo: Wilfrid Laurier Univ. Press, 1986.

Friesen, Dorothy. *Critical Choices: A Journey with the Filipino People*. Grand Rapids: Eerdmans, 1988.

Gallardo, José. "Ethics and Mission." In *Anabaptism and Mission*, ed. Wilbert R. Shenk, 137-157. Scottdale: Herald Press, 1984.

Garrett, John. *Roger Williams: Witness Beyond Christendom, 1603-1683*. London: The Macmillan Co., 1970.

Gernet, Jacques. *China and the Christian Impact: A Conflict of Cultures*. Trans. Janet Lloyd. Cambridge: Cambridge Univ. Press, 1985.

Gish, Arthur G. *Living in Christian Community*. Scottdale: Herald Press, 1979.

Glen, J. Stanley. *Justification by Success: The Invisible Captivity of the Church*. Atlanta: John Knox Press, 1979.

Glock, Charles Y., and Rodney Stark. *Christian Beliefs and Anti-Semitism*. New York: Harper & Row, 1969.

Gorday, Peter. *Principles of Patristic Exegesis: Romans 9-11 in Origen, John Chrysostom, and Augustine*. New York: The Edwin Mellen Press, 1983.

Gottlieb, Robert, and Peter Wiley. *America's Saints: The Rise of Mormon Power*. New York: G. P. Putnam's Sons, 1984.

Granberg-Michaelson, Wesley. *A Worldly Spirituality: The Call to Redeem Life on Earth*. San Francisco: Harper & Row, 1984.

Grigg, Viv. *Companion to the Poor*. Monrovia, Calif.: MARC, 1990.

Hamm, Dennis. "Faith in the Epistle to the Hebrews: The Jesus Factor." *Catholic Biblical Quarterly* 52 (Apr. 1990): 270-291.

Hatch, Nathan. *The Democratization of American Christianity*. New Haven: Yale Univ. Press, 1989.

Hawthorne, Gerald F. *The Presence and the Power*. Dallas: Word, 1991.

Hays, Richard B. *The Faith of Jesus Christ*. Chico, Calif.: Scholars Press, 1983.

Heggen, Carolyn Holderread. *Sexual Abuse in Christian Homes and Churches*. Scottdale: Herald Press, 1993.

Heinerman, John, and Anson Shupe. *The Mormon Corporate Empire*. Boston: Beacon Press, 1985.

Hiebert, Paul G. "Popular Religions." In *Toward the Twenty-first Century in Christian Mission*, eds. James M. Phillips and Robert T. Coote, 253-266. Grand Rapids: Eerdmans, 1993.

Hilton, David. "The Future of Medical Mission." *International Review of Mission* 76 (Jan. 1987): 78-81.

Hock, Ronald F. *The Social Context of Paul's Ministry: Tentmaking and Apostleship*. Philadelphia: Fortress Press, 1980.

Hoekema, Anthony A. *Jehovah's Witnesses*. Grand Rapids: Eerdmans, 1963.

Hofman, J. Samuel. "Using Indigenous Principles in Medical Missions." *Missiology: An International Review* 10 (Jan. 1982): 49-55.

Hooker, Morna D. *A Preface to Paul*. New York: Oxford Univ. Press, 1980.

_____. "Interchange in Christ and Ethics." *Journal for the Study of the New Testament* 25 (Oct. 1985): 3-17.

_____. "Pistis Christou." *New Testament Studies* 35 (July 1989): 321-342.

Hurst, Ed, with Dave and Neta Jackson. *Overcoming Homosexuality*. Elgin, Ill.: David C. Cook, 1987.

Hutchison, William R. *Errand to the World: American Protestant Thought and Foreign Missions*. Chicago: The Univ. of Chicago Press, 1987.

Jewett, Robert. *Paul's Anthropological Terms: A Study of Their Use in Conflict Settings*. Leiden: E. J. Brill, 1971.

_____. "Romans as an Ambassadorial Letter." *Interpretation* 36 (1982): 5-20.

Johnson, Luke Timothy. "Rom 3:21-26 and the Faith of Jesus." *Catholic Biblical Quarterly* 44 (1982): 77-90.

_____. *The Writings of the New Testament: An Interpretation*. Philadelphia: Fortress Press, 1986.

Kalilombe, P. A. "The African Local Churches and the Worldwide Roman Catholic Communion." In *Christianity in Independent Africa*, eds. Edward Fasholé-Luke, Richard Gray, Adrian Hastings, and Godwin Tasie, 79-95. Bloomington: Indiana Univ. Press, 1978.

Käsemann, Ernst. *New Testament Questions of Today*. Philadelphia: Fortress Press, 1969.

Keck, Leander E. " 'Jesus' in Romans." *Journal of Biblical Literature* 108 (Fall 1989): 443-460.

Kelly, J. N. D. *A Commentary on the Epistles of Peter and of Jude.* New York: Harper & Row, 1969.

Kibicho, Samuel G. "The Continuity of the African Conception of God into and Through Christianity: A Kikuyu Case-Study." In *Christianity in Independent Africa*, eds. Edward Fasholé-Luke, Richard Gray, Adrian Hastings, and Godwin Tasie, 370-388. Bloomington: Indiana Univ. Press, 1978.

Kierkegaard, Søren. *Attack upon "Christendom."* Translated by Walter Lowrie. Princeton: Princeton Univ. Press, 1968.

Kinsler, F. Ross. "Theological Education by Extension: Service or Subversion?" *Missiology: An International Review* 6 (Apr. 1978): 181-196.

Kirk, J. Andrew. "Apostleship Since Rengstorf: Towards a Synthesis." *New Testament Studies* 21 (Jan. 1975): 249-264.

_____. *Theology and the Third World Church.* Downers Grove, Ill.: InterVarsity Press, 1983.

Klassen, William. *Love of Enemies: The Way to Peace.* Philadelphia: Fortress Press, 1984.

Knapp, Stephen C. "Mission and Modernization: A Preliminary Critical Analysis of Contemporary Understandings of Mission from a 'Radical Evangelical' Perspective." In *American Missions in Bicentennial Perspective*, ed. R. Pierce Beaver, 146-209. Pasadena, Calif.: William Carey Library, 1977.

Koyama, Kosuke. *Three Mile an Hour God.* Maryknoll: Orbis Books, 1980.

Künneth, Walter. *The Theology of the Resurrection.* St. Louis: Concordia, 1965.

Ladd, G. E. *A Theology of the New Testament.* Grand Rapids: Eerdmans, 1974.

Lange, Martin and Reinhold Iblacker, eds. *Witnesses of Hope: The Persecution of Christians in Latin America.* Maryknoll: Orbis Books, 1981.

Legrand, Lucien. *Unity and Plurality: Mission in the Bible.* Trans. Robert Barr. Maryknoll: Orbis Books, 1990.

Lernoux, Penny. *Cry of the People: The Struggle for Human Rights in Latin America—The Catholic Church in Conflict with U.S. Policy.* New York: Penguin Books, 1982.

_____. *People of God: The Struggle for World Catholicism.* New York: Viking Penguin, 1989.

Linder, Robert D., and Richard V. Pierard. *Twilight of the Saints: Biblical*

Christianity and Civil Religion in America. Downers Grove, Ill.: InterVarsity Press, 1978.

Littell, Franklin H. "The Anabaptist Theology of Mission." In *Anabaptism and Mission*, ed. Wilbert R. Shenk, 13-23. Scottdale: Herald Press, 1984.

Long, Charles H., and Anne Rowthorn. "The Legacy of Roland Allen." *International Bulletin of Missionary Research* 13 (Apr. 1989): 65-70.

Longenecker, Bruce W. "*Pistis* in Romans 3:25: Neglected Evidence for the 'Faithfulness of Christ'?" *New Testament Studies* 39 (1993): 478-480.

Longenecker, Richard. *Paul: Apostle of Liberty*. New York: Harper & Row, 1964.

Lovelace, Richard F. *Dynamics of Spiritual Life: An Evangelical Theology of Renewal*. Downers Grove, Ill.: InterVarsity Press, 1979.

Luther, Martin. *Lectures on Romans*. St. Louis: Concordia, 1972.

Maldonado, Jorge E. "Theological Education by Extension." In *New Alternatives in Theological Education*, ed. C. René Padilla, 37-49. Oxford: Regnum Books, 1988.

Mangalwadi, Vishal. "Compassion and Social Reform: Jesus the Troublemaker." In *The Church in Response to Human Need*, eds. Vinay Samuel and Christopher Sugden, 203-204. Grand Rapids: Eerdmans, 1987.

Manson, T. W. "Romans." In *Peake's Commentary on the Bible*, eds. Matthew Black and H. H. Rowley, 940-953. London: Thomas Nelson and Sons, 1962.

Mariz, Cecília. "Religion and Poverty in Brazil: A Comparison of Catholic and Pentecostal Communities." In *New Face of the Church in Latin America: Between Tradition and Change*, ed. Guillermo Cook, 75-81. Maryknoll: Orbis Books, 1994.

Martin, David. *Tongues of Fire: The Explosion of Protestantism in Latin America*. Oxford: Basil Blackwell, 1990.

Martin, William. *A Prophet with Honor: The Billy Graham Story*. New York: William Morrow and Co., 1991.

Mawhinney, Allen. "God as Father: Two Popular Theories Reconsidered." *Journal of the Evangelical Theological Society* 31 (June 1988): 181-189.

McCoy, Alfred W. *Priests on Trial*. New York: Penguin Books, 1984.

McGrath, Alister E. *Iustitia Dei: A History of the Christian Doctrine of Justification*. 2 vols. Cambridge: Cambridge Univ. Press, 1986.

Meier, John P. "Nations or Gentiles in Matthew 28:19?" *Catholic Biblical Quarterly* 39 (Jan. 1977): 94-102.

Michaels, J. R. "Apostolic Hardship and Righteous Gentiles." *Journal of Biblical Literature* 84 (1965): 27-37.

Michel, Otto. *Der Brief an die Römer.* Göttingen: Vandenhoeck und Ruprecht, 1966.

Miller, Stuart Creighton. *"Benevolent Assimilation": The American Conquest of the Philippines, 1899-1903.* New Haven: Yale Univ. Press, 1982.

Moffitt, Robert. "The Local Church and Development." In *The Church in Response to Human Need,* eds. Vinay Samuel and Christopher Sugden, 234-253. Grand Rapids: Eerdmans, 1987.

Moorhouse, Geoffrey. *The Missionaries.* London: Eyre Methuen, 1973.

Morris, Leon. *The Epistle to the Romans.* Grand Rapids: Eerdmans, 1988.

_____. *The First and Second Epistles to the Thessalonians.* Grand Rapids: Eerdmans, 1959.

Mott, Stephen Charles. *Biblical Ethics and Social Change.* New York: Oxford Univ. Press, 1982.

Moxnes, Halvor. *The Economy of the Kingdom: Social Conflict and Economic Relations in Luke's Gospel.* Philadelphia: Fortress Press, 1988.

Munck, Johannes. *Christ and Israel: An Interpretation of Romans 9–11.* Philadelphia: Fortress Press, 1967.

Nelson, Jack A. *Hunger for Justice: The Politics of Food and Faith.* Maryknoll: Orbis Books, 1980.

Nevius, John L. "Planting and Development of Missionary Churches." In *Classics of Christian Missions,* ed. Francis M. DuBose, 256-267. Nashville: Broadman Press, 1979.

Newbigin, Lesslie. *The Household of God.* London: SCM Press, 1957.

Nida, Eugene A. *Message and Mission: The Communication of the Christian Faith.* Pasadena, Calif.: William Carey Library, 1990.

_____. *Religion Across Cultures.* New York: Harper & Row, 1968.

O'Halloran, James. *Living Cells: Developing Small Christian Community.* Maryknoll: Orbis Books, 1984.

Packer, J. I. *Evangelism and the Sovereignty of God.* Downers Grove, Ill.: InterVarsity Press, 1961.

Parish, Helen Rand, ed. *Bartolomé de las Casas: The Only Way.* New York: Paulist Press, 1992.

Perkins, Pheme. *Resurrection: New Testament Witness and Contemporary Reflection.* Garden City, N.Y.: Doubleday, 1984.

Philibert, Michel. *Christ's Preaching—and Ours.* Richmond: John Knox Press, 1964.

Piper, John. *The Justification of God.* Grand Rapids: Baker, 1983.

Rausch, David A. *Messianic Judaism: Its History, Theology, and Polity.* New York: The Edwin Mellen Press, 1982.

Ream, W. G. B. "The Support of the Clergy in the First Five Centuries A.D." *The International Review of Missions* 45 (Oct. 1956): 420-428.

Reumann, John. *"Righteousness" in the New Testament.* Philadelphia: Fortress Press, 1982.

Richardson, Don. *Eternity in Their Hearts.* Ventura, Calif.: Regal, 1981.

Riesenfeld, Harald. *The Gospel Tradition.* Philadelphia: Fortress Press, 1970.

Sanday, William, and Arthur C. Headlam. *A Critical and Exegetical Commentary on the Epistle to the Romans.* Edinburgh: T. & T. Clark, 1902.

Sanders, E. P. *Paul, the Law, and the Jewish People.* Philadelphia: Fortress Press, 1983.

Sanneh, Lamin. "Africa." In *Toward the Twenty-first Century in Christian Mission,* eds. James M. Phillips and Robert T. Coote, 84-92. Grand Rapids: Eerdmans, 1993.

Saracco, J. Norberto. "Search for New Models of Theological Education." In *New Alternatives in Theological Education,* ed. C. René Padilla, 25-35. Oxford: Regnum Books, 1988.

Scanzoni, Letha, and Nancy Hardesty. *All We're Meant to Be.* Waco: Word, 1974.

Schäufele, Wolfgang. "The Missionary Vision and Activity of the Anabaptist Laity." In *Anabaptism and Mission,* ed. Wilbert R. Shenk, 70-87. Scottdale: Herald Press, 1984.

Schelkle, Karl H. *Paulus: Lehrer der Väter.* Düsseldorf: Patmos-Verlag, 1956.

Scherer, James A. *Missionary, Go Home! A Reappraisal of the Christian World Mission.* Englewood Cliffs, N.J.: Prentice-Hall, 1964.

Schlabach, Theron F. *Gospel Versus Gospel: Mission and the Mennonite Church, 1863-1944.* Scottdale: Herald Press, 1980.

Schnackenburg, Rudolf. "Apostles Before and During Paul's Time." In *Apostolic History and the Gospel,* eds. W. Ward Gasque and Ralph Martin, 287-303. Grand Rapids: Eerdmans, 1970.

Schrenk, Gottlob. "Der Römerbrief als Missionsdokument." In *Studien zu Paulus.* Zurich: Zwingli-Verlag, 1954.

Senior, Donald, and Carroll Stuhlmueller. *The Biblical Foundations for Mission.* Maryknoll: Orbis Books, 1983.

Sernett, Milton C. *Black Religion and American Evangelicalism.* Metuchen, N.J.: The Scarecrow Press, 1975.

Sider, Ronald J. *Christ and Violence.* Scottdale: Herald Press, 1979.

_____. *Rich Christians in an Age of Hunger.* 3d ed. Dallas,

Word Publishing, 1990.

Sine, Tom. *Live It Up! How to Create a Life You Can Love*. Scottdale, Pa.: Herald Press, 1993.

Sloan, Robert. "Paul and the Law: Why the Law Cannot Save." *Novum Testamentum* 33 (1991): 35-60.

Stanton, G. N. *Jesus of Nazareth in New Testament Preaching*. Cambridge: Cambridge Univ. Press, 1974.

Stewart, James. *A Man in Christ*. New York: Harper & Brothers, n.d.

Stoll, David. *Is Latin America Turning Protestant? The Politics of Evangelical Growth*. Berkeley: Univ. of California Press, 1990.

Stowers, Stanley Kent. *The Diatribe and Paul's Letter to the Romans*. Chico, Calif.: Scholars Press, 1981.

_____. "Social Status, Public Speaking and Private Teaching: The Circumstances of Paul's Preaching Activity." *Novum Testamentum* 26 (1984): 59-82.

Tannehill, Robert C. *Dying and Rising With Christ: A Study in Pauline Theology*. Berlin: Verlag Alfred Töpelmann, 1967.

Taylor, John V. *Enough Is Enough: A Biblical Call for Moderation in a Consumer-oriented Society*. Minneapolis: Augsburg, 1977.

_____. *The Growth of the Church in Buganda: An Attempt at Understanding*. London: SCM Press, 1958.

Temu, A. J. *British Protestant Missions*. London: Longman Group, 1972.

Thiselton, A. C. "Language and Meaning in Religion." In *The New International Dictionary of New Testament Theology*. Vol. 3, ed. Colin Brown, 1123-1143. Grand Rapids: Regency Reference Library, 1978.

Thompson, Michael. *Clothed with Christ: The Example and Teaching of Jesus in Romans 12:1—15:13*. Sheffield: JSOT Press, 1991.

Tourn, Giorgio. *The Waldensians: The First 800 Years (1174-1974)*. Trans. Camillo Merlino. Torino, Italy: Claudiana Editrice, 1980.

Trilling, Wolfgang. *A Conversation with Paul*. London: SCM Press, 1986.

Tucker, Ruth. *From Jerusalem to Irian Jaya: A Biographical History of Christian Missions*. Grand Rapids: Zondervan, 1983.

_____. "Women in Mission." In *Toward the Twenty-first Century in Christian Mission*, eds. James M. Phillips and Robert T. Coote, 284-294. Grand Rapids: Eerdmans, 1993.

_____. "Women in Missions: Reaching Sisters in 'Heathen Darkness.' " In *Earthen Vessels: American Evangelicals and Foreign Missions, 1880-1980*, eds. Joel A. Carpenter and Wilbert R. Shenk, 251-280. Grand Rapids: Eerdmans, 1990.

Verduin, Leonard. *The Reformers and Their Stepchildren*. Grand Rapids: Eerdmans, 1964.

Verkuyl, Johannes. *Contemporary Missiology: An Introduction*. Grand Rapids: Eerdmans, 1978.

Wells, David F. *No Place for Truth, or Whatever Happened to Evangelical Theology?* Grand Rapids: Eerdmans, 1993.

Wenger, J. C. "The Inerrancy Controversy Within Evangelicalism." In *Evangelicalism and Anabaptism*, ed. C. Norman Kraus, 101-124. Scottdale: Herald Press, 1979.

Wilckens, Ulrich. *Der Brief an die Römer*. Vol. 1. Zürich: Benziger Verlag, 1987.

Williams, Sam K. "The 'Righteousness of God' in Romans." *Journal of Biblical Literature* 99 (June 1980): 241-290.

Wolterstorff, Nicholas. *Until Justice and Peace Embrace*. Grand Rapids: Eerdmans, 1983.

Wuthnow, Robert. *The Restructuring of American Religion: Society and Faith Since World War II*. Princeton: Princeton Univ. Press, 1988.

_____. *The Struggle for America's Soul: Evangelicals, Liberals, and Secularism*. Grand Rapids: Eerdmans, 1989.

Yoder, John Howard. *The Fullness of Christ: Paul's Revolutionary Vision of Universal Ministry*. Elgin, Ill.: Brethren Press, 1987.

Zinn, Howard. *A People's History of the United States*. New York: Harper-Collins, 1980.

Zunkel, C. Wayne. *Church Growth Under Fire*. Scottdale: Herald Press, 1987.

The Author

S TEVE Mosher, a native of Kansas, was born in Hutchinson and grew up in Alden. His family was active in the Alden Baptist Church, where Steve was the teenage organist. After graduating from Sterling (Kan.) College and marrying Sandy Jessup, he ministered with inner-city youth in Washington, D.C.

After Mosher received an M.Div. from Gordon-Conwell Theological Seminary in 1972, he pastored a rural Baptist parish in Kansas. While there, Steve and Sandy expanded their family with Philip (1974) and Leanna (1975).

In 1976, Steve began doctoral study in New Testament at Southern Baptist Theological Seminary (Louisville). F. F. Bruce gave strong approval to his dissertation on Romans. After finishing his Ph.D. in 1979, the Mosher couple was commissioned by the American Baptist Churches as missionaries to the College of Theology, Central Philippine University, in Iloilo City, Philippines. Steve taught New Testament courses and traveled to churches and islands in a Theological Education by Extension program.

During a home assignment in 1983-84, the Moshers were missionaries-in-residence at Central Baptist Theological Seminary in Kansas City, Kansas. Steve taught courses on missions and Romans and often spoke in area churches. During their second four-year term in the Philippines, Steve continued his earlier duties, directed the seminary field education program for several years, and taught some Old Testament courses.

In 1988 the Moshers moved to Wichita, Kansas, to be near

Steve's mother. Steve and Sandy joined a neighborhood house church connected with the Mennonite Church of the Servant and also are members of the First Baptist Church. Steve became the volunteer staff person for twelve local Churches United for Peacemaking. He has organized multicultural Bible studies in his neighborhood.

In addition to his research and writing, Steve has worked part-time at jobs such as driving a van for handicapped people and in the YMCA outreach program. Since the end of 1994, Steve has devoted full-time to writing and is now researching for a book on Revelation. Late in 1995, the Moshers relocated to San Antonio, Texas, to carry on their ministries.